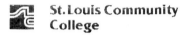
St. Louis Community College

```
TIME        : Tue Nov 11 2008 09:44PM
TERMINAL    : 500
TITLE       : Sugar is made with blood :
 the conspiracy of La Escalera and the c
CALL NUMBER : 972.91 P219s  lpsta
BARCODE     : 300080001401091
STATUS      : IN TRANSIT
PICKUP AT   : STLCC-M Circulation Desk
Received. Item has hold to be picked up
at STLCC-M Circulation Desk.
 When it arrives at STLCC-M Circulation
Desk, please check-in item to activate h
```

Sugar
Is Made
with Blood

Robert L. Paquette

Sugar Is Made with Blood

The Conspiracy of La Escalera
and the Conflict between Empires
over Slavery in Cuba

Wesleyan University Press
Middletown, Connecticut

"Africanization or Annexation to the United States?" originally appeared, in somewhat different form, in "The Everett-Del Monte Connection: A Study in the International Politics of Slavery," *Diplomatic History* (Winter 1987). Certain passages in "Cuban Whites and the Problem of Slavery" originally appeared, in somewhat different form, in "The Political Economy of Slavery and Freedom in Cuba," *Slavery and Abolition* (September 1987).

All inquiries and permissions requests should be addressed to the Publisher, Wesleyan University Press, 110 Mt. Vernon Street, Middletown, Connecticut 06457

LIBRARY OF CONGRESS CATALOGING-IN-PUBLICATION DATA

Paquette, Robert L., 1951–
Sugar is made with blood.

Bibliography: p.
Includes index.
1. Cuba—History—Negro Conspiracy, 1844. 2. Slavery—Cuba—History. 3. Cuba—Race relations. I. Title.
F1783.P25 1988   972.91'05   87–34503
ISBN 0–8195–5192–9

Manufactured in the United States of America

FIRST EDITION

For my parents,
Arthur C. and Dorothy L. Paquette

Preface

My interest in the Conspiracy of La Escalera stems from a long-standing interest in the comparative history of slavery in the Americas. The more I studied Cuba, the more absorbed I became by this episode about which the historians so sharply disagreed. In the early stages of my research a hunch paid off. In the Massachusetts Historical Society I uncovered pieces of the puzzle long sought by Cuban scholars: the letters of Domingo Del Monte, a white Cuban intellectual implicated in the Conspiracy, to Alexander Everett, a United States statesman. I became convinced that a complex revolutionary conspiracy of the people of color had existed in Cuba in 1844. I also became convinced that a full understanding of the events required a trans-Atlantic perspective.

Cuban scholars have tended to see the events of 1844 as the culmination of a lengthy process, which, in a sense, entered a climactic stage with the coming to Havana in 1840 of the abolitionist David Turnbull. I agree and have followed their lead. In certain places I have started well before 1840 to see with the eyes of the participants from the time of the development of Cuba's plantation system. I have not written a social history about the world the Cuban slaves made, although I discuss their world. Rather, I have used the process of La Escalera as an entry point into a larger exploration of trans-Atlantic politics and diplomacy as well as of Cuban society. I eschewed a strictly chronological approach because, as my perspective widened and the full interplay of external and internal factors were revealed, the process of La Escalera appeared to me less as one raging current than as many streams running inexorably to a violent confluence. The result is preeminently a political history in a socio-economic context. I argue that the Conspiracy of La Escalera existed not as one conspiracy but as several distinct yet overlapping conspiracies, central elements of which were revolutionary in their aspirations.

My initial study appeared in a 1982 doctoral dissertation. Since then I have had the opportunity to visit many more archives and pore over voluminous additional documentation. I traveled to Cuba in 1982 with the hope of gaining access to Cuban archives. But I was denied and so was forced to rely on materials in repositories outside of Cuba. Some of what I write about Cuban slavery is synthetic, and my debt to Fernando Ortiz, Pedro Deschamps Chapeaux, José Luciano Franco, Verena Martínez-Alier, and Franklin Knight will be apparent to specialists. To my great fortune, while pursuing information about the José Escoto Collection at the Houghton Library of Harvard University, I came in touch with Enildo García of St. Francis College, a native of Cuba and an authority on Plácido, the mulatto poet executed in 1844 as a leader of the Conspiracy. Professor García had preceded me to the rediscovery of the Escoto Collection, which turned out to be one of the richest sources for colonial Cuban history in the United States and an invaluable source of information on La Escalera. Professor García's research, the recent writings of Jorge Castellanos and Daisy Cué Fernández, to which he led me, and documents in the Archivo Histórico Nacional of Madrid together forced me to revise my original estimation of Plácido. In other respects, subsequent research strengthened my earlier arguments.

I also benefited greatly from the work, criticism, and warm encouragement of David R. Murray, who was completing his excellent study on the abolition of the Cuban slave trade while I was finishing my dissertation. His chapters on David Turnbull and the Conspiracy of La Escalera focus on the British connection. I agree with him on certain points; on others, I disagree and have attempted to extend the discussion.

In the process of researching and writing about La Escalera I have accumulated many other debts. I must first thank the staffs of all the libraries and archives listed in the notes. I am also indebted to Wendy Kramer and Olga Joya for special help in locating documents in Spanish archives. Peter Dalleo, in an act of uncommon generosity among academics, sought me out at a conference to apprise me of the Cuban materials in the Rodney Collection at the Historical Society of Delaware. William DeMarigny Hyland introduced me to relevant archival material in New Orleans.

I have exchanged ideas and information about slavery with David Eltis since our graduate school days at the University of Rochester. We have not always agreed, but I am truly grateful for the time he took away from his important book on the trans-Atlantic slave trade to give an early draft of my manuscript his careful attention. David Brion Davis, Kenneth F. Kiple, and David Barry Gaspar read the manuscript in its entirety and offered me indispensable advice and criticism. Edgar Paiewonsky-Conde regularly served as a resource on Caribbean culture and literature. Few studies of slavery appear these days without having profited from a careful reading by Stanley Engerman. This book is no exception. Jeannette Hopkins provided me with an education in editing. Her criticism did not always make easy reading; it did make for a better book. I would also like to thank her staff at Wesleyan University Press, particularly Eliza Childs and Peter Potter.

C. Duncan Rice as dean of Hamilton College not only provided financial support but read the manuscript in its entirety. I continued to receive generous support from his successor, Melvin B. Endy, Jr. For a special contribution I am grateful to Walter Beinecke, Jr. My colleagues in the department of history, Eugene Tobin, Alfred Kelly, and David Millar, provided friendship and encouragement. Joan Wolek of the inter-library loan department deserves a medal for filling my hundreds of requests. Laurie Moses, Sharon Gormley, Theresa George, and Jan Pieroni extended themselves for me on too many occasions typing various drafts of the manuscript.

Thanks prove embarrassingly inadequate to express what I owe Elizabeth Fox-Genovese. Without her criticism, generosity, and encouragement I would not have finished a dissertation on La Escalera, much less a book. She sets high standards inside and outside the classroom, and for that I am extremely grateful. Eugene D. Genovese directed my dissertation and has not ceased to show interest in my work. As I have said before, my debt to him I can neither repay nor articulate.

Zoya, my wife, has sacrificed much and endured much while I was completing this book. That she remains my wife may speak well for her love but not her good sense. As she knows, I am still trying to make it up to her.

Contents

Tables

Illustrations

It is right that what is just should be obeyed; it is necessary that what is strongest should be obeyed. Justice without might is helpless; might without justice is tyrannical. Justice without might is gainsaid, because there are always offenders; might without justice is condemned. We must then combine justice and might and, for this end, make what is just strong, or what is strong just.

PASCAL, *Pensées*

La Escalera and the Historians

Introduction: La Escalera and the Historians

———◦•◦———

The "Conspiracy of La Escalera" is, in short, the most illusive and contemptible page of our history.

> JOSÉ ANTONIO RAMOS,
> "Una muerte que no debe olvidarse,"
> *Gaceta del Caribe* 1 (July 1944): 6

The society built on slavery and colonialism appeared to be undergoing dissolution in Cuba in 1843. Slave revolts had broken out in March and November of that year. Separatist sentiment had increased among Cuba's whites in response to Spain's unwillingness to liberalize its imperial rule and its seeming incapacity to secure life and property. Rumors abounded that British abolitionists and United States annexationists were advancing their own designs by competing for the support of the dissidents. Cuba's sizable free colored population was restive. When, near Christmas, a planter in Matanzas province claimed to have uncovered a conspiracy to raise the slaves of the sugar district of Sabanilla, government agents under the orders of Captain-General Leopoldo O'Donnell, Cuba's new chief executive, moved in. They tortured suspects, then executed the "confessed" ringleaders.

O'Donnell, doubting that the proceedings in Sabanilla had located the root of the conspiracy, widened the circle of investigation. Persecution and torture spread throughout much of western Cuba in 1844. Government officials said they had exposed an even wider conspiracy, one that included slaves, free people of color, Cuban-born whites, and foreigners. They implicated two of Cuba's preeminent liberal intellectuals and proto-nationalist writers, Domingo Del Monte and José de la Luz y Caballero; they convicted *in absentia* David Turnbull, the former British consul in Havana, of being the "prime mover" behind the conspiracy; they executed

3

Gabriel de la Concepción Valdés, alias Plácido, a free mulatto and one of Cuba's most renowned poets, as head of a conspiratorial faction of people of color. By the year's end, thousands of people of color, free and slave, had been executed, banished, or imprisoned, or had simply disappeared. The so-called conspiracy acquired the name La Escalera—The Ladder—in remembrance of the principal implement to which slave suspects were bound before interrogation by the lash. The year 1844 itself has gone down in Cuban history as el Año del Cuero—the Year of the Lash.

The Conspiracy of La Escalera has received uncommon attention in Cuba. Generations of leading Cuban scholars have studied the events. Periodicals have devoted special issues to La Escalera and Plácido. Children's literature discusses them. Audiences have watched reenactments on stage. On the centenary of Plácido's death, in 1944, the Auténtico regime of Ramón Grau San Martín issued a two-centavo stamp with Plácido's picture and the inscription "Gloria de la Poesía Cubana, Mártir de la Libertad."[1] Fidel Castro's 1974 speech in honor of the twenty-first anniversary of the attack on the Moncada Barracks, his first blow against the regime of Fulgencio Batista, honored the slave rebels of 1843 as "precursors of our social revolution" and deserving of a monument for their heroic efforts on behalf of liberty and justice.[2] And before Fidel, it seems, the number 44 was popular in the casinos.

La Escalera remains one of the most controversial episodes in Cuba's colonial history. Some interpreters have called it a preempted revolution that threatened the foundation of Cuba's slave society. Others have doubted its existence, arguing that the government manufactured it to justify a Machiavellian policy of colonial repression. Some who are convinced that there was a sort of conspiracy, purposefully exaggerated by the government, have trouble separating the innocent from the guilty. Among the makers of Cuba's colonial history, probably only José Martí, the great nationalist thinker and revolutionary leader, who was martyred in 1895 during Cuba's War of Independence, has received more attention than Plácido. And debate has raged from the time of Plácido's death over whether he should be celebrated as a martyr for liberty or mourned as a docile victim.

In 1894, at a time when Cuba's people of color were calling for a statue in Plácido's honor, an article appeared using the official record to substantiate the existence of the Conspiracy of La Escalera as a revolutionary movement of the people of color, inspired by the example of Haiti, to overthrow Spanish rule and establish a nonwhite nation. Its author was José de Jesús Márquez, a prolific writer with a well-earned reputation for defending the interests of Cuba's working class. His prose and verse had appeared in periodicals throughout Cuba, most notably *La Aurora,* the anarcho-syndicalist Havana newspaper whose founding in 1865 coincided with the organization of Cuba's first tobacco union by Márquez and several other young socialists.[3] Márquez called Plácido a leader of the Conspiracy, a martyred hero who struggled against the oppressors of his race.[4]

In making his case for the Conspiracy as abortive revolution, Márquez in effect allied himself with such earlier conservative Spanish writers as José Ferrer de Couto, José de Ahumada y Centurión, and Justo Zaragoza, and against an influential circle of white Cuban intellectuals, liberal, propertied, and proudly nationalist.[5] Among this latter group was Manuel Sanguily, a rebel officer during the Ten Years' War (1868–1878) and a formidable orator. He replied to Márquez. Sanguily had studied under José de la Luz y Caballero, one of the intellectuals implicated in the 1844 events. It was Plácido, so it was said, who had contributed to Luz y Caballero's arrest and interrogation by naming him to the authorities as a conspirator. Sanguily's reply to Márquez was sharpened by his affection, even unapologetic reverence, for his mentor and by his anti-Spanish nationalism. In earlier essays, Sanguily had denied that Plácido had any poetic talent; even Plácido's famous "Plegaria a Dios" [Prayer to God], said to be composed in prison just before his execution, was, Sanguily contended, apocryphal.[6] In his response to Márquez, Sanguily declared that the truth about La Escalera would probably never be known, that the government's records could not be trusted, and that Plácido "as a Cuban and as a man merits only pity or oblivion."[7]

Although Sanguily's blunt dismissal of Plácido elicited criticism inside and outside Cuba at the time, after independence from Spain and well into the twentieth century denial of a conspiracy and acceptance of the innocence and docility of Plácido became the predominant view in Cuba.[8]

In 1901 Vidal Morales y Morales's tribute to Cuba's long struggle against Spanish rule, *Iniciadores y primeros mártires de la revolución cubana* [Initiators and first martyrs of the Cuban revolution], contained two chapters on the Conspiracy, "Sultanato de O'Donnell" [O'Donnell's sultanate] and "La Llamada Conspiración de los Negros" [The so-called conspiracy of the blacks]. Morales acknowledged that no one had yet established whether a conspiracy of the people of color had existed in 1844, although few could deny the bloodbath of reprisal. Although he offered little explicit analysis of his own, quoting extensively from his sources, his interpretation is easy to infer. La Escalera was largely an invention of rapacious Spanish officials, who manufactured it to sow mistrust and fear among the races, to repress dissidents, and to plunder well-to-do free people of color.[9] Plácido appears as an innocent victim of a politically calculated terror. Morales conceded the serious outbreaks of slave revolt in March and November of 1843, but his sources attributed them to local causes. The outbreaks were, typically, partial and isolated; they were put down quickly in a wave of torture. Morales concluded that "the supposed conspiracy marked in Cuba the zenith of the sufferings inflicted on the African race."[10]

Morales relied on information supplied by select members of Cuba's white intelligentsia. Some had studied La Escalera after the fact; many had lived through it and several wrote to Morales at his request to relate their experiences. He himself had family connections to the grim history of 1844. A distant relation and celebrated man-of-letters, Antonio Bachiller y Morales, was associated with Luz y Caballero and Domingo Del Monte; he had referred, if inconsistently, to the Conspiracy in several of his writings.[11] Morales's father-in-law, a Spanish-born military man named Ramón Flores de Apodaca, had actually participated in the investigations as one of the government's chief agents.[12]

Morales quoted his good friend Francisco Jimeno more than any other source. Future students of the Conspiracy would follow Morales in citing Jimeno as an authority. Jimeno had been consulted by Manuel Sanguily before he wrote his reply to Márquez.[13] Jimeno, a member of one of the leading families of the city of Matanzas, had been a nineteen-year-old student at a college in Havana in 1844. He acknowledged that he had witnessed the brutalization of people of color by government agents. He knew Plácido, although apparently not well, but from what he knew and heard, he rejected the government's charges against him on the grounds that, since he was almost white himself and seemingly meek and deferential, especially in his dealings with whites, he could not possibly have participated in a racist revolution, much less led one. Much of what Francisco Jimeno conveyed about the Conspiracy of La Escalera in letters to Morales and Sanguily came from his father. Jimeno's father, Simón Jimeno, had close ties to a priest named Nicolás González de Chávez, who had fathered a number of children by a free woman of color. A son, Santiago Pimienta, was executed with Plácido. A daughter, Gabriela Pimienta, had married a free colored dentist named Andrés José Dodge, also executed with Plácido. Simón Jimeno tried to save Dodge from danger in 1844 by counseling him to leave Cuba. According to his son Francisco, he strongly believed in the innocence of Dodge, Pimienta, Plácido, and other prominent free people of color and regarded the government agents as little more than assassins.[14]

Morales made no mention of his father-in-law's role as a government agent in investigating the Conspiracy. Private correspondence suggests that Morales, mortified by his father-in-law's participation, sought to play it down.[15] Indeed, except for the published judgments of the trial proceedings, Morales ignored the government's record of the Conspiracy altogether, a particularly noteworthy omission since in 1900, after the United States's intervention in Cuba's war for liberation from Spain, the provisional government of the United States had appointed Morales to direct its National Archive.[16] Whether he rejected the government's record out of hand because of its use of torture in extracting confessions or whether he had insufficient time before publishing his book to examine the voluminous trial documentation remains unclear. He died in 1904 while at work on a monumental study of the life and times of the liberal intellectual Domingo Del Monte, who had been implicated in the Conspiracy.[17] Had it been completed, it might have answered many questions.

Over the next several decades the Morales interpretation received no serious challenges. Because he had written the most widely used school text in Cuban history, his basic views on the Conspiracy would reach a wide audience.[18] A special edition on Plácido in the Matanzas periodical *El Álbum,* published sixty years to the day after his execution, assembled a variety of experts whose views largely conformed to those of Morales, although one acquaintance of Plácido did suggest a much more complex personality than the humble, apolitical, and obsequious bard described by others.[19] Assorted journals and newspapers featured stories on Plácido in 1909, the centenary of his birth, but these and many subsequent articles tended to engage more narrow questions about Plácido's character, his appearance, and the quality of certain of his poems than the facts about La Escalera.[20]

Still, here and there, new and potentially damaging information surfaced. Students of the Conspiracy benefited from the organization of the National Archive, carried on most skillfully by Joaquín Llaverías after Morales's directorship.[21] Fernando Ortiz, in his classic study of Cuban slavery, *Hampa afro-cubana: los negros esclavos* [Afro-Cuban life: the black slaves] (1916), found the Archive's voluminous holdings on the Conspiracy a "source of very curious data that could not be fitted into this work."[22] Nevertheless, while agreeing with Morales that Captain-

General O'Donnell exploited the idea of conspiracy, Ortiz did assert without qualification that a plot had developed in 1844 to raise the slaves of the plantation districts around Matanzas and Cárdenas.

The *Boletín* of the National Archive, which began publication under Morales's direction in 1902, issued a few important documents about the Conspiracy and its causes. In the year of Morales's death, it published a confession by Francis Ross Cocking, aide to David Turnbull, the British consul, that he had conspired with Cuban whites and people of color to end slavery and overthrow Spanish rule. Cocking had offered to sell his confession to the Spanish government seven years after 1844 and five years after trying to sell it to the British.[23] The Matanzas newspaper *Yucayo* [*Native Voice*], in 1909–1910, the centenary year of Plácido's birth, presented a series of documents on the Conspiracy, mostly reports on what was happening in Cuba in 1844 written by a Cuban correspondent of an obscure Paris-based newspaper. José Escoto, the compiler and editor of these documents, introduced them with an admission of their limitations and of the great "difficulties in giving a certain interpretation" to the Conspiracy.[24] They nonetheless delivered a clear message that in 1844 certain prominent whites in Cuba strongly believed that people of color were plotting in league with the British abolitionist David Turnbull.

Escoto's interest in the Conspiracy continued throughout his life. He published little himself but, from his position as head of the Matanzas public library, he relentlessly accumulated a treasure of manuscript material on the history and literature of Cuba.[25] In 1922 Carlos M. Trelles, the great Cuban bibliographer, listed as among Escoto's holdings eighty letters from Captain-General O'Donnell to Antonio García Oña, governor of Matanzas province, in which "the secret of the conspiracy is found."[26] These letters probably formed part of the Escoto Collection purchased by Harvard University in 1929, where they lay uncatalogued and largely ignored until recently.[27]

José Escoto married Dolores María de Ximeno y Cruz, the granddaughter of Simón Jimeno and the niece of Francisco Jimeno. Her memoirs, published in installments beginning in 1924, recall her conversations with her maternal grandmother about the Conspiracy and Plácido. Her grandmother knew Plácido, described his appearance before his death, and when asked about his innocence said noncommittally, "the innocence or guilt of Plácido was much discussed then." When asked if the Conspiracy really existed, she replied, "Of course the conspiracy existed; only it is not known with certainty who were innocent or guilty among those said to be its principal chiefs."[28]

Not until Francisco González del Valle presented his discourse, "José de la Luz y Caballero en la Conspiración de 1844," to the Cuban Academy of History in 1925 did a more detailed and far more analytical study than Morales's appear. González del Valle, like Morales, came from one of Havana's old patrician families and had matured into a major figure in Cuban intellectual and cultural life. On a previous occasion before the Academy, he had countered Manuel Sanguily on the question of the authenticity of Plácido's poem "Plegaria a Dios."[29] He intended his new discourse to be the first of a trilogy of works on La Escalera, concentrating first on Luz y Caballero, then on Domingo Del Monte, and last on Plácido.[30] He completed only the first, a painstaking attempt based on considerable original research. In the National Archive he had examined records of the military tribunal that had tried the alleged conspirators. He also had access to the unpublished epistolary of Domingo Del Monte, in the possession of Domingo Figarola-Caneda, another well-known Cuban scholar and specialist on Plácido.[31] He also used documents in the archive of Vidal Morales.

González del Valle's discourse began with a brief description of the antecedents of La Escalera. Census figures for 1841 told Cuban whites for the first time that they had become outnumbered by slaves. In the early 1840s a small band of white Cuban intellectuals, in response to the continuation of a massive illegal slave trade, was battling elements of the slave-trading interest to prevent what they saw as the Africanization of Cuba. David Turnbull had arrived in Havana in 1840 to fill the post of British consul. He brought with him the real possibility that Britain, through Spain, might impose on Cuba an agreement that would rapidly abolish slavery. The powerful slave-trading interest, fearing an abrupt end to a profitable business, began to stir up the populace by a slanderous campaign against Great Britain and Turnbull. After Turnbull was compelled to leave Cuba in 1842, Cuban authorities imprisoned several of his colored acquaintances for plotting an insurrection.

González del Valle's story turned next to the relationship between Domingo Del Monte and Alexander Everett, a United States intellectual and statesman. González del Valle learned from Everett's letters in Del Monte's epistolary that Del Monte, in a letter to Everett of 20 November 1842, had disclosed the existence of a revolutionary conspiracy inspired by British abolitionists. Precisely what Del Monte had written in this letter, González del Valle could not say. He had no knowledge of the whereabouts or even existence of Del Monte's letters to Everett. He did know that word of the conspiracy had passed from Everett to highly placed officials in the United States government and from them to Spanish officials. González del Valle concluded that Captain-General Valdés, O'Donnell's predecessor, had at least some intelligence about the abolitionist conspiracy and had taken precautionary measures, but Valdés seems to have thought the threat much exaggerated. He was quick to assert that Del Monte's 1842 denunciation of a plotted revolt, in the letter to Everett, bore no direct responsibility for the vengeful actions of O'Donnell. González del Valle wondered how Del Monte had learned about the abolitionist conspiracy. The most likely source seemed to be either Turnbull or Francis Ross Cocking. Why would either man or both confide in Del Monte? Del Monte claimed—and González del Valle agreed without investigation—that information about the abolitionist conspiracy had come to him unsolicited.

González del Valle found the primary cause of the events of 1844 in the Draconian personality of Leopoldo O'Donnell himself. O'Donnell had come to Cuba in October 1843. In November came slave revolts in the western sugar plantation regions. In December a female slave on a sugar plantation owned by Esteban Santa Cruz de Oviedo disclosed an extensive plot for a slave uprising in Cuba's sugar heartland. González del Valle blamed Santa Cruz de Oviedo for seeding in O'Donnell's head the idea that this plot and earlier unrest in the countryside had originated outside the plantations themselves and that they constituted a conspiracy. The ensuing investigations led to the torture and persecutions of 1844 and the discovery of "the Conspiracy of La Escalera." Once government agents had called a terror into existence to deal with the Conspiracy, González del Valle maintained, it took on a life of its own.

Was it fear, wickedness, or the belief there really existed the general conspiracy, of which so much had been said for so long, that motivated the use of such measures as the only means to know what was wanted to be known? All of these did but principally fear and unrestrained cruelty.[32]

To further substantiate his argument, González del Valle pointed to the irrational and contradictory testimony in the court records. Predictions had differed on when the Conspiracy was to break out. Of the caches of munitions and weapons, said to be in different places by different witnesses, none were ever found. And who really led the Conspiracy? Turnbull, after all, had left the island in 1842. Did the free people of color? The slaves? "In these proceedings," wrote González del Valle, "all is confusion and irregularity; all is contrary to reason and logic; all is arbitrary and unjust; all is false; all is crime and pain."[33]

A declaration of José Erice, a free colored militiaman, who committed suicide one day after giving it, had led to the initiation of proceedings in Havana and the arrest of Luz y Caballero and other prominent Cuban whites. González del Valle believed that a particularly corrupt government official named Pedro Salazar had advanced the idea of white involvement in the Conspiracy, possibly because of his own connections to the slave-trading interest. With Erice's suicide, Salazar needed more testimony to build a case and so tried to manipulate Plácido with a hollow promise of freedom into implicating those whom Salazar wanted to implicate. But the consequent cases against the white Cuban intellectuals never held up in court. Indeed, as González del Valle pointed out, Salazar himself was eventually tried and imprisoned for misconduct during the proceedings. Thus, beneath all the lies and distortion, the perversity and bloodletting, González del Valle had discerned in the Conspiracy only a fragment of truth, one that could be easily accommodated to the Morales interpretation. "For me," he concluded, "what existed [in 1844] was a projected [slave] uprising, fixed for a specific date which should have begun, certainly, on the estate of Esteban Santa Cruz de Oviedo, and which other [estates] would have followed later; neither more nor less than had already occurred so many times."[34]

González del Valle's study would exert considerable influence on the thinking in Cuba about La Escalera. He had proven to the satisfaction of most readers the innocence of Luz y Caballero and of other accused Cuban whites; he had substantially reinforced the belief that the Conspiracy did not exist or, rather, that it existed largely as the creation of a corrupt and ruthless Spanish government. When talking about the history of 1844, scholars began to replace the term "La Conspiración de la Escalera" [The Conspiracy of the Ladder] with "La Causa de la Escalera" [The Cause of the Ladder] or "El Proceso de la Escalera" [The Process of the Ladder].[35] But in concentrating on the exculpation of Luz y Caballero, González del Valle had left ample room for further research and debate.

At a time when Cuban historians, before their counterparts in the United States, were beginning to challenge the notion that Africans had passively accepted their enslavement, some students of the Conspiracy of La Escalera could not pass so lightly over the great unrest on the plantations in the early 1840s or the confession of Francis Ross Cocking and what it implied. Herminio Portell Vilá and Ramiro Guerra y Sánchez, for example, while agreeing with González del Valle that the Conspiracy of La Escalera did not exist as the government had depicted it, suggested that the abolitionist plotting by Turnbull and his minions had somehow encouraged plantation slaves, already prone to rebellion, to further excitation and rebellion.[36]

In 1941 Roberto P. De Acevedo and Benito Alonso y Artigas stimulated some reconsideration of Plácido and the Conspiracy with the publication of documents on an earlier arrest of Plácido, in 1843, in the town of Villa Clara. The authorities found in Plácido's possession a brief letter of introduction, written for Plácido to someone named Martínez, into which could be read references to a conspiracy. For example, Martínez was thanked for his interest "in the little affair" [*en el asuntico*] and was told that "better days are soon coming" [*días más serenos prontos por venir*], thus also suggesting that Plácido had been serving as a kind of courier.[37] Skeptics, however, could point to the comments of the editors themselves that the letter and the other documents could not prove Plácido's involvement or whether the Conspiracy existed at all.[38]

One year later, at a national congress of Cuban scholars, a member of the Ximeno family entered the debate with a stunning revisionist interpretation. In a twenty-seven-page paper, José Manuel de Ximeno, the nephew of Dolores María de Ximeno and José Escoto, argued that Cuban slaves and free people of color, with the help of Turnbull, Haitian agents, and a few Cuban whites, most certainly had plotted a sophisticated, island-wide revolutionary conspiracy to end both slavery and Spanish rule. Unlike González del Valle, Ximeno saw no disjunction between the abolitionist conspiracy, as revealed in Cocking's confession and as told by Domingo Del Monte to Alexander Everett in 1842, and what O'Donnell's agents had uncovered after they extended their investigations in the countryside in December of 1843. The so-called Conspiracy of La Escalera, according to Ximeno, actually originated in 1841 and underwent several transmutations in response to the loss of external support from Britain and Haiti and the growing distance between whites and people of color and between mulattoes and blacks. Toward the end, according to Ximeno, the conspirators had actually split into two distinctive movements, one of mulattoes and one of blacks. Plácido had joined the Conspiracy at the beginning and for years had traveled about Cuba to forward it. To many Cuban whites, Plácido had seemed weak and servile; to Ximeno, he was a talented actor. Imprisoned by the authorities, Plácido had demonstrated great dignity and courage in refusing to divulge information about the Conspiracy, long after some of his fellow conspirators had talked.[39]

Ximeno's original paper was abridged for publication in 1943 to condense his most original material into seven pages and it provided no identification of sources. He, like González del Valle, had entered the National Archive to examine the colonial records. He had paid particular attention to what the people of color had said under interrogation and had pieced together, much as the authorities had done in 1844, the broad outlines of a vast revolutionary conspiracy, one that, in Ximeno's words, was "the first great Cuban separatist conspiracy with ramifications throughout the entire island."[40] Yet, without references, further detail, or a critical look at his sources, his broad strokes looked far too impressionistic.

To some extent, reaction to Ximeno's interpretation reflected a larger struggle within the historical profession in Cuba between members of the older, more conservative, and more exclusive Academy of History and those of the revisionist Cuban Society of Historical and International Studies. The Society had taken shape in 1940 under the leadership of Emilio Roig de Leuchsenring, a well-known lawyer and historian, after Roig had resigned from the Academy. From his official position as Historian of the City of Havana he gathered around him a group of talented young minds, many of whom were influenced by Marxism and frustrated by the failure of revolution after the fall of the dictatorial regime of President Gerardo Machado in 1933.[41] Members of the Society focused more on the lower classes, on historical process, Yankee imperialism, and the centrality of conflict in Cuban history. Members of the Academy tended to practice a more traditional history with an emphasis on elitist politics and individual personalities.

The First National Congress of History, organized by the Society in 1942, provided the forum for the presentation of Ximeno's paper. It was an association that undoubtedly made him vulnerable to the charge of attempting to impose on the past a false continuity, of finding revolutionary precursors to comport with the political sensibility of the Society's members.

The coming of the centenary of La Escalera and Plácido's execution in 1944 generated a related burst of scholarly activity. Ana María Arissó added impressively to the list of *Placidiana* or of bibliographies of works by and about Plácido.[42] Jorge Casals compiled an anthology of his poetry.[43] Jesús Saíz de la Mora reexamined his poetry for insight into his politics and personality.[44] The *Gaceta del Caribe* featured critical essays on Plácido by several of Cuba's most distinguished scholars.[45] Leopoldo Horrego Estuch completed the best biography yet written.[46] José Manuel Pérez Cabrera, in response to a general directive of the Havana Athenaeum, surveyed the major interpretations of "Plácido y la Conspiración de 1844."[47] José Manuel de Ximeno presided over a section at the Third National Congress of History dedicated solely to the study of La Escalera.[48]

The results of these labors made distressingly slight progress in resolving long-standing disputes. Out of the individual presentations and group discussions of Ximeno's section of the Third National Congress came a series of resolutions which actually confirmed how little was known with any certainty about La Escalera after a hundred years of study. In listing factors that contributed to the events of 1844 and setting out an agenda for further research, the participants did dramatically enlarge the scope of study, showing admirable sensitivity to "factors of an international character" and the need to make more precise links between those factors and events and individuals in Cuba.[49] Ximeno's interpretation of the Conspiracy understandably found favor with many members of the Society. Roig himself carefully recapitulated it in his two essays in commemoration of the centenary.[50] Pérez Cabrera, in his review essay of 1944, clearly preferred the Ximeno interpretation to that of Morales and González del Valle. Others ignored it or more openly disagreed.[51]

Even within the Society not everyone concurred with Ximeno's depiction of Plácido. Ángel Augier, a close associate of Roig's, drew a "Silueta de Plácido" which showed him to be insufficiently revolutionary, an accommodationist who prostituted his talents for handouts from upper-class whites. Plácido did not die as a protomartyr for Cuban independence. "Far from it." He declared his innocence and informed on others when he should have denounced the unspeakable crime perpetrated against his fellow people of color.[52] When Augier's essay was reprinted in the popular Cuban magazine *Bohemia* a few years later, Leopoldo Horrego Estuch, a member of the Academy of History, rebuked Augier, an avowed Marxist, for reading the present into the past and being woefully ignorant of what had actually happened in 1844. For Horrego, Plácido, although not a member of a "formal organization with warlike ends," had condemned oppression and consistently promoted the idea of liberty in his verse. He had every right to proclaim his innocence since the government did not accuse him of being a liberator and an abolitionist but the instigator of a race war. As for the charge of informer, Horrego pointed out, the revelation attributed to Plácido was never signed by him and was most probably spurious.[53]

Scholarly production on the issues noticeably slowed from the end of World War II to the Cuban Revolution. Historians from both the Academy of History and the Cuban Society for Historical and International Studies worked together to publish the ten-volume *Historia de la nación cubana* (1952) in commemoration of the fiftieth anniversary of the Republic.[54] The references to the Conspiracy in volume 4, which covered the years 1837 to 1868, simply described the principal differences of interpretation and the continuing difficulties in separating fact from speculation.[55] The most significant work on the subject during this period came from Mario Hernández y Sánchez-Barba, a Spanish historian who, with the help of Cuban research assistants, examined documents in the Archivo Histórico Nacional in Madrid for clues to the activities of David Turnbull and the problem of slavery in Cuba. He concluded that Turnbull had persisted in conspiring against Spanish rule after his expulsion from Cuba in 1842. Turnbull's plan, which he promoted from his new post in Jamaica, "simply consisted of promoting an uprising of the blacks in the region of Matanzas . . . promising them English help and the creation of a black republic after the style of Haiti."[56] Hernández y Sánchez-Barba pointed out that once England learned of the formal charges made against Turnbull in Cuba in 1844, it challenged Spain to produce evidence. It did, in bundles, and Hernández y Sánchez-Barba read copies in the Spanish National Archives of at least some of what was sent, although he supplied meager details of them in his article. In support of his generalization about Turnbull's conspiratorial activities he found most revealing the very absence in the diplomatic correspondence of any response by England to the evidence that it had received. The British government, as will be shown, certainly had suspicions about Turnbull and may have thought silence was the best response.

The triumph of the Cuban Revolution in 1959 dramatically affected the study of history in Cuba. A new order had to be consolidated, a new sense of solidarity had to be created, and earlier sacrifices and struggles had to be justified. More than ever before, the media turned space and time over to the study of history from which the Cuban people could find revolutionary values. "Indeed," as Louis Pérez, Jr., has written, "the national past has served as a major source of moral subsidy, conferring on the process of revolution both continuity and, out of that continuity, legitimacy."[57]

That the Conspiracy of La Escalera still commanded great interest and feeling in socialist Cuba became obvious when Nicolás Guillén in his regular column for the newspaper *Hoy* ["Today"] (later *Granma*) suggested that the lighthouse in the Morro Castle overlooking Havana harbor be renamed from "El Faro O'Donnell" to "El Faro Plácido." An extraordinary outpouring of mail followed from scholars and lay people on why Plácido's name should or should not be used, and Guillén featured some of it in his later columns.[58] Was Plácido a courageous precursor of the Cuban Revolution or the sacrificial lamb of a ruthless imperialist regime? Was the Conspiracy of La Escalera Spain's desperate bid to suppress a legitimate movement of the oppressed? Or was it one of the most conspicuous examples of the collective sufferings of the exploited masses under a bestial Spanish regime? Any of these choices could easily accord with an emphasis of revolutionary historiography on continuity and struggle. Revisionist historians, who had provided help before, did not here, for socialist Cuba largely distanced itself from the interpretation of José Manuel de Ximeno to deny the existence of the Conspiracy and to endorse the victimization of Plácido. An author of a history book for adolescents has nicely summed up the predominant view.

Through the tenacious and profound historical studies that were carried out among us after the triumph of our socialist revolution, it becomes clearer each time that there never was a conspiracy of blacks and mulattoes [in 1844]. It is also clear that the colonial authorities vented themselves especially on the class of wealthy people of color and that to each group they attributed as the responsible chiefs those who enjoyed renown and respect gained by their conspicuous status.[59]

The historians of socialist Cuba have produced few works on the Conspiracy more original or detailed than those of Morales, González del Valle, or Ximeno. Leonardo Griñan Peralta, in an essay published posthumously, without citations, in 1964, essentially followed González del Valle in calling La Escalera a fabrication by Spanish authorities to persecute dissident elements within Cuba, "a judicial process, not a conspiracy."[60] Although the confession of Francis Ross Cocking persuaded Griñan Peralta of the existence of a plot hatched by Turnbull in 1841 and including whites and people of color, for Griñan Peralta, as for González del Valle, the Turnbull conspiracy had broken down several years before 1844 under the influence of annexationist agents from the United States. He saw no convincing evidence of any connection between a Turnbull conspiracy and the revolts of plantation slaves in 1843, much less the events of 1844.

Also in 1964, an article by Humberto Castañeda on Turnbull returned to a familiar theme in Spanish historiography, that British interference in Cuba in the early 1840s was designed to protect the interests of British capitalism and thwart the southward expansion of the United States. Turnbull, according to Castañeda, came to Cuba to forward this policy with abolitionism as the means; he defended the "ideas of independence among the whites and doctrines of liberty among the blacks and breathed into the island an insurrectional spirit." When seen in this light, Castañeda asserted, Turnbull "was not an enemy of Cuba, nor did he preach a crusade of any kind. He was an honest, energetic, diligent functionary of his government."[61] Thus, the Conspiracy of La Escalera never happened, and for obvious reasons, the slave-trading interest peddled the idea of Turnbull's involvement.

Pedro Deschamps Chapeaux pursued the theme of La Escalera in his truly ground-breaking writings on the social and economic position of Cuba's free people of color during the first half of the nineteenth century. Whether the Conspiracy existed or not, Deschamps Chapeaux declared, the persecutions and terror unleashed by government agents did, and they served three fundamental objectives:

1. To protect and perpetuate the security of the beneficiary classes of the slavist regime through the use of methods of terror, which tended to neutralize and extirpate the traditional rebelliousness of the black slaves and the results of England's secret abolitionist work.
2. To smash the nascent black petty bourgeoisie and the nascent black intelligentsia, as a budding economic rival in the first instance and as possible ideologues and agitators of the antislavery cause in the present and in the future in the second instance.
3. To avoid all possibility of resonance of the antislavery cause in the popular masses of white pigmentation who felt sincere indignation against slavery.[62]

The silence in socialist Cuba on the Ximeno interpretation might be at least partially explained by the stature of José Luciano Franco among both the earlier revisionists and the current crop of intellectuals. In 1962 both Franco and Ximeno responded to Guillén's column on the renaming of the O'Donnell lighthouse with letters that pointed to differences of historical judgment.[63] Franco, a mulatto and former tobacco worker, had matured within the Cuban Society of Historical and International Studies to become an internationally recognized authority on the African experi-

ence in the Americas, an authority, incidentally, generally ignored in the
United States. In 1944 Franco had shared the podium with Ximeno in
the section on the Conspiracy of La Escalera at the Third National Congress of History. There he helped to frame the final resolutions and presented a paper singled out for praise by Emilio Roig de Leuchsenring for
delineating the antecedents of the Conspiracy. "In the colonial history of
Cuba," Franco maintained, "La Escalera has been an episode of continuous struggle, silent or open, that has liberated the classes of which our society is comprised from the first days of the conquest."[64] During his career he would publish repeatedly on this theme.

Franco's view of the Conspiracy shares much with González del Valle's
and emerges fairly consistently from scattered writings. The Conspiracy
of La Escalera was a sham, a fabrication by Captain-General O'Donnell
in conjunction with the slave-trading interest "to assassinate, to martyr or
deport, and subject to the most cruel oppression all those men who could
have filled the ranks of the Cuban Revolution. The cruelty of La Escalera
deferred for a quarter of a century the possibility of forging the unity of
the Cuban people, the formation of the necessary climate that might give
them liberty."[65] That whites and people of color, including Plácido, had
been increasingly dissatisfied with colonial rule, Franco had no doubts.
The rising chorus of dissent exacerbated the fears of the slaveholders and
helped to propel the terror. But Franco produced some evidence from the
National Archive to argue that the dissent of the early 1840s hardly qualified as an organized revolutionary conspiracy of the people of color against
the whites. That line served as only the most insidious invention of O'Donnell so he could divide and rule. Franco, like González del Valle, believed
that the revolts of the plantation slaves in 1843 stemmed from local
causes. Thus, Franco preferred not to talk about the Conspiracy but the
Process of La Escalera. In an introduction to a collection of documents
gathered to shed light on this process, he named ten Cuban "historians and
investigators" who had done important work on the Conspiracy. Ximeno
was not included. Franco went on to dismiss the contents of the oft-cited
confession of Cocking, written seven years after the fact, as the product of
a rogue, badly in need of money, who had been expelled from the British
foreign service.[66]

Several voices from within Cuba in recent years have taken issue with
the prevailing view. Daisy Cué Fernández, for her study of "Plácido y la
Conspiración de la Escalera," had access to copies of documents once in
the private archive of Manuel Sanguily. She also reexamined much of the

relevant secondary literature produced in Cuba. Unlike Franco, she took Cocking's confession at face value and insisted on two points: "1) the real existence of a conspiratorial plan in the Island directed by the English; 2) the presence of two committees, one formed by whites and the other composed of mulattoes and blacks, of which the second seems to have been the most active."[67] While she admitted that Cuba witnessed numerous outbreaks of slave revolts before 1844, she argued that the number and timing of what occurred in 1843 raises serious questions about how isolated from this conspiratorial plan they could have been. She did not dispute the outrages committed on the people of color but legitimately asked if they were not the consequence rather than the cause of the Conspiracy. Her most important contribution centered on Plácido. She did not reject out of hand the copies she had seen of testimony given by the people of color in 1844 but stressed that they must be weighed carefully. She noted that Plácido had thirty-two accusations against him, more than any of those executed with him. She searched his life and poetry for clues to his personality and found a complex political figure, whose "imprisonment and punishment [in 1844] . . . was not an isolated act but the culmination of a stage of his life in which there were truly reasons to be suspicious of him."[68]

Dissatisfaction with the incompleteness of the Spanish translation of Francis Ross Cocking's confession led Rodolfo Sarracino, in 1985, to the British Public Record Office, where he located the original in the records of the Foreign Office. Largely on the basis of the original confession and a limited examination of related consular correspondence, he concluded that Turnbull had promoted a revolutionary conspiracy in Cuba and that "the insurrectional apparatus of the Committee of Free Blacks and Mulattoes," referred to by Cocking, "and that of La Escalera are one and the same."[69] Sarracino went on to charge the British government with bearing "direct responsibility" for the subsequent repression, although he was apparently unaware of studies of La Escalera by non-Cuban scholars a few years earlier that were based on more extensive research into the Foreign Office records that would have challenged his conclusions about the British connection.[70] The British government had directly supported Turnbull in his conspiratorial activities, Sarracino claimed, then, with a shift in administration from the Whigs to the Tories, had "sold out" black and mulatto conspirators by providing details of the conspiracy to Spain.

Walterio Carbonell, in a short interpretative essay on Plácido based on research in Cuba's National Archive, agreed wth Sarracino that Turnbull had promoted a revolutionary conspiracy in Cuba. But he rejected the notion that free mulattoes had any leadership role in it. He pointed to the growing separation during the sugar boom between mulattoes and blacks in Cuban society. Mulattoes owned property, practiced skilled trades, and had moved closer to white culture; they held their social gatherings apart from blacks. "The mulattoes, in general, were not a revolutionary stratum. As colonized people, they could not have been either mass or leaders in the antislavery conspiracy."[71] Carbonell saw the plantation slaves as the true purveyors of revolution. Captain-General O'Donnell savagely repressed the free colored class because he believed—mistakenly, according to Carbonell—that it would effectively link up with the plantation slaves. With this twist, Carbonell had, in effect, returned the interpretation of La Escalera to near where Francisco González de Valle had left it more than sixty years before.

Outside Cuba, the great historiographical debate about Plácido and the Conspiracy of La Escalera and the weighty historical issue of Cuban slavery related to them have not readily engaged scholars in this century. Robert Freeman Smith's observation in 1964 that "the historians of Cuba have produced a body of literature which is indeed worthy of respect, and which merits considerably more serious attention than it has generally received" still rings true with regard to the study of Plácido and the Conspiracy, despite a slight surge of interest during the last several decades.[72] The quiet in the English-speaking world during the first half of this century is particularly disappointing given a far better international climate in which to pursue study in Cuba and the esteem for Plácido by British and North American abolitionists of the previous century who translated his poetry, wrote about his life, and elevated him to their pantheon of martyrs.[73] What was produced tended to come from black scholars and students of Hispanic literature. Arthur Alfonso Schomburg tracked down relevant printed materials on Plácido for his now famous archive and published a brief article on his life.[74] The best studies in English of Plácido's life and work are Benjamin Frederick Carruther's dissertation and Frederick Stimson's short biography.[75] The serious work on the Conspiracy by historians during this time amounted to the publication by Duvon C. Corbitt of several documents with informed commentary on the support O'Donnell's actions elicited from whites in Cuba.[76]

The surge of interest in the Conspiracy in the last twenty years may be explained by two mutually reinforcing factors. First, the very success of Cuba's socialist revolution spurred academic interest in Latin America generally and Cuba specifically. Although much of the interest in Cuba has concentrated on the national period or, even more narrowly, on the years of Castro's rise and consolidation of power, some scholars began searching in the colonial period for the roots of revolution and Cuban nationalism. Second, the last several decades have witnessed the production of a truly remarkable literature on slavery, remarkable not only in quantity but in the standards of scholarship set by the best of that literature. Much of it, for historical and historiographical reasons that should by now be familiar, has originated in the United States. No longer do serious students approach slavery in the United States as a primarily national problem; no longer does the Old South's "peculiar institution" look peculiar in the sense of being uncommon. Frank Tannenbaum's *Slave & Citizen* and Stanley Elkins's *Slavery* greatly stimulated the use of the comparative method and the production of more specific studies about slavery in Latin America.[77] As the study of slavery in Cuba benefited, the study of La Escalera could no longer be ignored. Of those writers who have contributed, some have accurately recounted events and added fresh information and insights; others have not.

Philip Foner wrote his two-volume *A History of Cuba and Its Relations with the United States* (1962–1963) to enhance the understanding of the Cuban Revolution by providing a historical context. He closed volume 1 with a chapter on the Conspiracy of La Escalera, which he considered "a turning point" in the history of both countries for the stimulus it gave to annexationism. Foner carefully digested the major secondary works produced by the Cubans and contributed important information from diplomatic sources in the National Archives of the United States. On the basis of what he found, Foner could not firmly commit himself on whether "the conspiracy of 1844 had actually been organized or . . . was invented by O'Donnell and the slave interests to rid the island of those who might lead a movement against slavery."[78] He clearly leaned toward the Ximeno interpretation, for which, on a future trip to Cuba, he would be chided by José Luciano Franco. But of greater importance to Foner, as he looked at the physical treatment of Cuban slaves, at the ideas and attitudes of Cuban whites about the slave trade and slavery itself, at the promotion of emigrant free white labor to Cuba, and at the Cuban policy of the United States, the Conspiracy of La Escalera had a significant and, in some cases, decisive impact.[79]

Explaining the Cuban Revolution also led Hugh Thomas, a British historian, into a discussion of "the most famous of all Negro and slave conspiracies" in Cuba. Thomas had intended to write a short book only on the Revolution itself but soon found himself looking well back in the colonial period to "the absorbing question of slavery and how that decisively affected the character of Cuba."[80] After consulting Vidal Morales, Mario Hernández y Sánchez Barba, and several other secondary sources, he concluded that Turnbull had organized a conspiracy to end slavery and Spanish rule and that the authorities had used the Conspiracy to silence dissidents and destroy the free colored bourgeoisie. Thomas outlined how British abolitionism stimulated the Conspiracy and how its suppression affected the lives of slaves and planters and the growth of an annexationist movement. On certain details he erred. He has the place of Turnbull's arrest wrong; he has a female slave disclosing the plot to O'Donnell instead of to Esteban Santa Cruz de Oviedo; he has O'Donnell being warned by a mulatto sergeant "the year before the plot" when, in fact, O'Donnell had only arrived in Cuba in October of 1843; he has Domingo Del Monte being forced out of Cuba because he did not back O'Donnell's policy of suppression when, in fact, Del Monte had left Cuba before O'Donnell had ever arrived.[81] But his overview was perceptive.

Around the time of Thomas's book a succession of books in English on Cuban slavery appeared. All mention the Conspiracy of La Escalera. Herbert Klein, in a comparative study of slavery in Virginia and Cuba, relied heavily on Vidal Morales and thus came to doubt the existence of the Conspiracy. Curiously, in a chapter entitled, benignly, "The Freedman as an Indicator of Assimilation" and subtitled "An Integrated Community: The Free Colored in Cuba," Klein correctly pointed out that in 1844 the Cuban government "almost succeeded in totally destroying [the free colored community]."[82] His larger argument focused on the relative benignity of the Cuban slave system. In discussing the events of 1844 he jumped well beyond what Morales would have allowed by saying that the confession of José Erice "could not be collaborated [sic] and no evidence of unrest or sedition could be discovered." And further:

Before very long, however, the peninsular authorities recognized the utter stupidity and groundless fear behind this action, and even came to question the existence of the so-called Placido conspiracy, based as it was largely on perjured testimony and nonexistent documentary evidence.[83]

In a more recent work, influenced by a book by David Murray, Klein seems to revise his opinion: "Though more famous as a frustrated conspiracy than an actual rebellion, the Escaler [sic] or Placido slave revolt of 1844 . . . occurred in a period of increasing government repression within Cuba and during growing unrest of the free population over issues of self-government and even independence."[84]

Arthur Corwin, in a major study of *Spain and the Abolition of Slavery in Cuba* (1967), said that the Conspiracy of La Escalera probably did exist and that it was promoted by David Turnbull. In adding, "This charge has been sustained by Cuban historians," Corwin refers paradoxically to the same source that Klein cites in support of his first contention that "the very existence of the whole plot has been challenged not only by Morales y Morales, but by several more recent scholars."[85] The source in question, in fact, reviews the interpretations of Morales, González del Valle, and Ximeno. Corwin also has certain details wrong. He has the March 1843 slave revolt in the province of Cárdenas occurring after O'Donnell's arrival, not before. Of this revolt, which resulted in several deaths of whites and much destruction of property by hundreds of slaves, Corwin says, "It is true that the insurrection never got much beyond the stage of some emancipated Negroes vociferously asking other slaves to join them in a bid for freedom."[86]

In his well-known study of *Slave Society in Cuba during the Nineteenth Century* (1970) Franklin Knight noted the "supposed slave 'revolt' of 1844" warranted special mention; he has gone further than any previous historian in passing definitive judgment: It "had absolutely no foundation in fact"; it was "wholly fictitious."[87] To support these pronouncements he first refers to the bundle of documents in the Archivo Histórico Nacional in Madrid, the contents of which, in fact, were used by the Spanish government to substantiate their case against David Turnbull.[88] Later he translates a reference to the Conspiracy by José Gutiérrez de la Concha, a successor to O'Donnell as Captain-General of Cuba. Cuban students of the Conspiracy have frequently quoted this reference, which Gutiérrez de la Concha made in 1850 in the context of a self-serving argument about his own ability to rule Cuba and to control the free people of color, who are "always lying in ambush for a favorable occasion in order to throw off the yoke." Morales quoted the reference after Francisco Jimeno had brought it to his attention.[89] Because of the weight attached to Gutiérrez de la Concha's words, the original Spanish should be quoted:

Los fallos de la Comision militar produjeron el fusilamiento, la confiscacion y la expulsion de la Isla de muchos indivíduos de la raza de color; pero sin habérseles encontrado armas, municiones, papeles, ni otro objeto ó cuerpo de delito que comprobase semejante conspiracion, ni aún que la hiciese presumible, á lo ménos en la grande escala que abrazaron las investigaciones judiciales.[90]

Knight's translation, for which he cites the incorrect source, is this:

The findings of the military commission produced the execution, confiscation of property, and expulsion [*sic*] from the island of a great many persons of color, but it did not find arms, munitions, documents, or any other incriminating object which proved that there was such a conspiracy, much less on such a vast scale.[91]

A more exact translation seriously modifies the conclusion:

The judgments of the Military Commission produced the execution, confiscation of property, and the expulsion from the island of many persons of color, but without their having been found with arms, munitions, papers, or other incriminating evidence that confirmed the conspiracy, or to even make it presumable, at least on the large scale embraced by the judicial investigations.

Gwendolyn Midlo Hall has provided a more flexible assessment in her 1971 comparative study of slavery in Saint Domingue and Cuba. Hall had looked at evidence in Spain's National Archive and at the writings of a few of the leading authorities in Cuba for a special subsection of her book on the Conspiracy. She describes some of the findings of the Military Commission in the published summaries of their proceedings. She notes the complicated nature of the problem and limitations of her evidence. "While the conspiracy might have been exaggerated for the purposes of repression," she argues, "it seems very unlikely that the charges were a pure fabrication."[92] Indeed, from what Hall could determine about the widespread instability within the slave system of the time, she boldly diverged from many Cuban writers who saw in O'Donnell merely a crude and sadistic butcher and called his methods probably "the only means of holding the colony for Spain."[93]

Few, if any, published works, inside or outside Cuba, have made a greater contribution to the understanding of the British connection to the Conspiracy of La Escalera than David Murray's *Odious Commerce* (1980), a splendid study on the abolition of the Cuban slave trade. Murray, a Canadian historian, mined archives in Spain and Great Britain. His research into the Foreign Office records turned up new information about David Turnbull, his aide, Francis Ross Cocking, and their activities in Cuba. Turnbull and Cocking had promoted a revolutionary movement within Cuba, Murray said, which "was confined to the free blacks by the time Cocking left [Cuba in 1843]." Although, as Murray conclusively demonstrated, neither the British government nor the British & Foreign Anti-Slavery Society was involved in Turnbull's and Cocking's efforts, "The Escalera conspiracy marked the end of a decade in which a few British abolitionists had posed the most serious challenge to Cuba's plantocracy since the independence of Spain's mainland colonies."[94] Because Murray was concentrating on the British role, he did not delve into possible connections between the revolutionary movement promoted by Turnbull and the Conspiracy. He did say, "Whether the Military Commission really discovered the existence of a revolutionary plan [in 1844] or whether Captain-General O'Donnell decided to order an island-wide investigation because of suspicion of a conspiracy may never be known."[95]

Murray's evidence of free colored involvement in a revolutionary movement at the time of Turnbull's consulship raises old questions about Plácido's involvement, which the excellent essays of two Cuban scholars living in the United States have sought to address recently. The comprehensive reading and acute analysis of Plácido's poetry by Jorge Castellanos and Enildo García will persuade many that Plácido's character was highly political. Castellanos's examination of the documents in the Madrid archives has also led him to argue for Plácido's involvement in the Conspiracy of La Escalera and, in effect, for the validity of the Ximeno interpretation.[96] Enildo García agrees and offers supporting evidence from the Escoto Collection, although Franklin Knight, in the introduction to García's work, is "less convinced than Dr. García that Plácido was personally involved in the conspiracy which led to his untimely death."[97] With the work of Murray, Castellanos, and García, the historiography of La Escalera arrives at the present.

The story of what actually happened in Cuba in 1844 holds great fascination. The lengthy and complicated historiographical debate about the reality of the Conspiracy and the connection, if any, of Plácido to it, attests to that and provides, of itself, sufficient justification for further investigations. Did the Conspiracy of La Escalera exist? Was it independent of or connected to the conspiratorial activities of the British consul David Turnbull? If it existed, what groups and individuals participated and what were their relations with each other? Can Plácido and other conspicuous free people of color be linked to conspiratorial activities? If so, what were their objectives? What caused any or all of the groups to conspire? How important were external factors? Did the government have ulterior motives for initiating the terror?

As important as these and other questions are, the study of the Conspiracy of La Escalera affords even larger opportunities. If it really did exist, it could be considered to be one of the largest movements of its

kind in the history of slavery in the Americas. If it did exist, it might reveal crucial information about patterns of resistance among slaves and
among other groups within the slave system. Recent studies, for example,
have engaged the question of the influence of trans-Atlantic ideological
currents on the character of the Afro-American slave revolts. Eugene
Genovese has argued that the 1791 slave revolution in Saint Domingue
marked the integration of slave revolts into the Age of Democratic Revolution, a decisive shift away from restorationist revolts directed at with-
drawal from the prevailing social arrangements, to revolts directed at a
fundamental liberal-democratic restructuring of society. Michael Craton
and David Geggus have taken issue with this view, and numerous review-
ers of both Genovese's and Craton's work have called for more detailed
examinations of specific slave revolts in specific countries.[98] David Barry
Gaspar, in a superb study of slavery in eighteenth-century Antigua, has
shown how a slave conspiracy can be used as a "window" into the "relations between masters and slaves, the superstructure of control, the origins
and size of the slave population, the expansionary tendencies of slave labor utilization, the development of slave community and culture, and the
physical environment itself."[99] Some may argue that stability and acquiescence form the core of a society, but it is, however, precisely during outbreaks of collective resistance that the tensions and contradictions that always lie beneath the surface appear for all those willing to see. Thus,
looking at La Escalera, with all its contending forces, affords a promising
opportunity to observe the related workings of the trans-Atlantic political
economy and Cuba's slave society in an age when, in the words of Eric
Hobsbawm, the world was being transformed by "the 'dual revolution'—
the French Revolution of 1789 and the contemporaneous (British) Industrial Revolution."[100]

I

Sugar and Society
in 1840

I

Land, Color, and Class

———◆·◆———

Color establishes even a certain equality among men who, as is universally the case where civilization is either little advanced or in a retrograde state, take a particular pleasure in dwelling on the prerogatives of race and origin. When a common man disputes with one of the titled lords of the country, he is frequently heard to say, "Do you think me not so white as yourself?"

ALEXANDER VON HUMBOLDT, 1803
in *Political Essay on the Kingdom of New Spain* (New York, 1972), 87–88

Sugar cane trailed Columbus across the Atlantic, and to get what could be processed from it for Western Europe's seemingly insatiable sweet tooth, a world market developed that not merely changed areas of the Americas but transformed them. The sugar plantation emerged as an economic enterprise of the first order. It required a grand scale of operations, a sophisticated integration of production and processing, and an intensive use of the factors of production. It could generate riches. Boom times hit northeastern Brazil in the late sixteenth century, and when decline set in, as it invariably did where sugar monocultures developed, first one Caribbean country and then another moved to the fore of world sugar production.

In 1840 Cuba was the world's leading producer of sugar and the gilded remnant of Spain's once-mighty American empire. It was going through an extended period of unprecedented economic growth. Herman Merivale, a leading British political economist, in an 1840 lecture on colonization at Oxford University, pronounced Cuba "beyond contradiction, the wealthiest and most flourishing colony possessed by any European power."[1] Sugar production in 1840 had reached the record high of more than 160,000 metric tons, almost six times the tonnage at the turn of the century and a dramatic increase from the 5,000 metric tons of 1760. Merchant ships in record numbers and from every part of the trans-Atlantic world entered

Havana harbor and such rising ports as Matanzas, Cárdenas, and Trinidad. They carried handmade linens and mining equipment from the German states; jerked beef from Argentina and Uruguay; dyestuffs and chocolate from Middle America; flour, lumber, rice, and saltfish from the United States; cotton goods, metals, and earthenware from Britain; wine, sugar machinery, and elite vestments from France; liquor, fruits, oil, wine, and soap from Spain. They carried away sugar as well as coffee, tobacco, copper, hides, and mahogany. By 1840 the value of Cuban commerce had actually come to surpass the value of Spanish commerce. Imports had gone from $1,292,000 in 1770 to $25,217,000 in 1840; exports from $759,000 to $21,481,000.[2]

Markets in land and labor kept pace with the port traffic. From 1827 to 1846 total land in cultivation appears to have increased by more than 70 percent. Slave traders plied the Atlantic to respond to the planters' demand for labor, shipping hundreds of thousands of slaves during the first half of the nineteenth century. In response, Cuba's population swelled and darkened. What appears to be Cuba's first official census in 1774 enumerated 171,620 inhabitants, 56 percent of whom were white. By 1846 the total population had reached almost 900,000, 53 percent of whom were either slaves or free people of color.[3] The burgeoning foreign demand for tropical staples had transformed Cuba, as it had Barbados, Jamaica, and Saint Domingue before, from a sluggish, undersettled, largely self-sufficient outpost to a booming plantation society of masters and slaves.

The setting for this transformation could look as seductive as it was advantageous. Cuba, a short hundred miles from the Florida Keys, is by far the largest island in the Caribbean; it is roughly the size of England, with an area in excess of 44,000 square miles. It extends narrowly for some 800 miles as it weaves in breadth from extremes of 160 miles in the east to a bare 25 miles near the meridian of Havana. Rolling plains and shallow lowlands dominate the relief. What mountains there are prove less disruptive than elsewhere in the Caribbean, although throughout much of the nineteenth century even the modest ranges of central Cuba effectively secluded the southern port of Trinidad from the interior, helping to keep it conservative and Catholic well into the twentieth century. To the west the limestone slopes of the Sierra de los Órganos and several lesser ranges concentrate before running out on their way to Havana. To the east the Sierra Maestra, laden with minerals and legend, rises to the island's highest elevations of about 5,000 feet. Rivers and streams rarely flow long or deep in Cuba; there are no lakes; and the rainy season from May to October washed out the mud tracks that passed for roads in other months. But, thin and elongated as Cuba is, most cultivable land has access to the sea.

For navigators, Cuba answered a prayer. Hundreds of deep-water inlets indent the coast, and except for Matanzas and Cárdenas, principal harbors have pocketlike shapes to shelter vessels from the elements. Because of secure anchorages and the Caribbean currents and prevailing trade winds that drove ships to them, Cuba became an island bulwark and staging area throughout its early colonial period. Oliver Cromwell and a succession of other empire builders would covet Cuba as the most strategic area in the Caribbean. Havana was the principal prize, for its location at the exit from the Gulf of Mexico served as an ideal point of rendezvous for Spain's biannual convoys on their way home with Mexican or Peruvian treasure.

At the time of the conquest of Cuba, Bartolomé de las Casas claimed that it could be traversed from end to end under a covering of trees. But timber that Spanish settlers, miners, and shipbuilders had taken incrementally after 1511, sugar planters devoured during the nineteenth-century sugar boom: to open up new expanses for cultivation, to fuel the boiling process, and to build wooden containers to ship the molasses and sugar. In Cuba's western department, beyond the limits of Havana, Matanzas, and Cárdenas, a rich soil of friable red and black clay runs to depths of twenty feet.[4] It resists erosion, can be cheerfully plowed even after a downpour, and does wonders for cane shoots and coffee shrubs. Cuba's sugar and coffee plantations were clustered in the western department, and, according to the census of 1846, produced 80 percent of Cuba's sugar and 70 percent of its coffee.

Impressive woodland did survive the onrush of the sugar plantation. Palm trees: royal, bottlenecked, coconut, and about thirty other species grew east and west. Precious cabinet woods forested stretches of the interior, although they receded markedly in the west. Savannas of less fertile clay populated by wire grass, scrub bushes, and occasional palm or pine trees pierced and deranged the forests. Mangroves and peat bogs covered low-lying southern coastal areas and formed a near impenetrable jungle in the Peninsula de Zapata. In the higher elevations, vegetation varied from rocky plots of shrubs and dwarf trees to thick mixes of hardwoods and pines.

Away from the mosquito-infested swamps and lowlands of the coast, Cuba could have resembled Eden, and visitors often made the comparison. Heeding the latest medical wisdom, North American victims of dropsy, consumption, and a host of other debilitating complaints journeyed there for recuperation. A stroll on a clear day on a well-kept coffee plantation with bushes in bloom, embraced by groves of orange and lime, or a climb up the Cumbre north of Matanzas to overlook the beautiful Yumurí valley might prove to be curative. Invalids from the southern United States found the coffee estate Buena Esperanza, about thirty-five miles southwest of Havana, specially prepared to their tastes by Edward Finlay, a Scottish doctor whose son would become Cuba's greatest epidemiologist. In other spots, waterfalls, subsurface caverns, bizarre rock formations, and wild flowers charmed visitors. Mineral baths in Madruga and San Diego soothed their bodies. Medicinal plants abounded along with the *curanderos*—quacks—of every color who used them in an Africanized folk medicine. The temperature seldom ranges outside of seventy to eighty degrees, and the prevailing northeastern breezes moderate the humidity. In one respect Cuba surpasses Eden: It has no harmful snakes.[5]

Notwithstanding the centrality of the plantation to the economy, Cuban social life revolved around the municipality. For Cubans of standing, as for the Spanish language, *urbano* meant urbane and urban: to be civilized meant to live in a city, to enjoy the theater and philharmonic societies, the poetry contests and literary *tertulias,* not to mention the masquerades. Municipalities in Cuba, like those throughout Spanish America, took a characteristic gridiron form.[6] They had a main plaza, often but not always centrally located, around which were constructed a church, executive residence, town hall, and other public buildings. Streets extended from the main plaza in all directions and crisscrossed at right angles so that the surrounding land was broken into square or rectangular blocks. The layout of Matanzas probably came closest to the deeply rooted Spanish ideal of rational urban planning. Havana, as a coastal fortress city, deviated from the norm not only in having walls and more irregular streets but in the location of its main square, the Plaza de Armas, near the water on the western side of Havana harbor. Outside the walls, wild growth caused by the sugar boom had wiped out most signs of rational planning.

With more than 130,000 inhabitants and "one of the safest, most picturesque, and best frequented" ports in the world, Havana overshadowed all other Cuban cities in size and importance.[7] Travelers to Cuba in the first half of the nineteenth century compared it favorably in refinements and general tenor of life with European cities. Its salons, churches, university, lyceum, and societies for the stimulation of agriculture and commerce certainly attracted an island-wide clientele. So did its cockpits, illegal monte tables, and women of ill repute. The magnificent Tacón theater, completed in 1838, could accommodate six thousand people and uncurtained first-rank Italian operas. In 1841 no less a ballerina than the "Divine Fanny" Elssler would pirouette on stage, much to the delight of Havana's slaveholding patricians who ogled her silk stockings to their hearts' content and, perhaps, as one visitor observed, to hers.[8]

Visitors to Havana landed to clanging church bells—rung, more often than not, by colored bell ringers who imposed their own sense of rhythm— and the more sobered cadence of slave dockworkers. They ran a gauntlet of jostling soldiers, vendors, carters, animals, carriages, washerwomen, and street urchins to get to their place of stay. Within the walls of Havana, house after house of thick stone overlooked traffic like some foregone expression of Spanish resolve and sense of permanence. Streets had no sidewalks and were usually dark and narrow. The traffic from the sugar boom intensified the odors, congestion, and perhaps the excitement. Mud and ruts along with the pedestrians challenged the reflexes of the best postilion, thus Cuban chaises, called *quitrines* and *volantes,* with their outsized, broadly rimmed wheels as much as five and six feet in diameter, higher in many cases than the chaise itself. Not until the 1830s did sugar prosperity begin to bring the first macadam to the townhouses of the planter elite within the walled section of Havana.

Inside or outside Havana's walls, streets had their distinctive flavors.[9] The Calle de Mercaderes and Calle de los Oficios speak for themselves. The Calle de Muralla carried heavy traffic to shops of every description. The long Calle de O'Reilly, named after Field Marshal Alejandro O'Reilly, the man most responsible for Spain's reorganization of the Cuban military after the Seven Years' War, had the best tailors, bookstores, and cafés as well as the best confectionary adjacent to the Captain-General's palace. Walking down Calle de Obispo was like walking through a Middle Eastern bazaar. Every major street had a plethora of lawyers' offices. Like Spain, Cuba was a litigious society, so litigious that most Creole planters took the precaution of educating a son or two in the profession. Other streets were known by the ethnicity of their inhabitants. Asturians, Catalans, Frenchmen, North Americans all had their neighborhoods. Free people of color found themselves increasingly pressed into shabby dwellings outside the walls; color prejudice may have helped to bid up the price of property within. By contrast, the planter elite generally located itself near the main plaza, at the social center, in magnificent townhouses. Typically they had two stories and entresol, frugally baroque, with arcaded galleries, built around a spacious square or a rectangular inner patio and with a coat of arms chiseled in stone above a main entranceway large enough to accommodate the family chaise. The family of the Conde de Santovenia, for example, resided on one side of the Plaza de Armas in a townhouse next to the Captain-General's palace. A block away, the noble families of Lombillo, Peñalver, Chacón, and Ponce de León occupied all but the northern side of Cathedral Plaza. Even their final resting place reflected the status consciousness that seemed everywhere in Havana. Cemeteries were subdivided into plots by rank. Titled nobles had plots separate from wealthy citizens, who in turn had plots separate from those of poor whites and people of color.

People of all shades and descriptions could be seen intermingling on Havana's streets: white noblemen in fine broadcloth, colored shopkeepers in striped gingham, slave porters in loincloths of coffee sacking. But not ladies, for they would lose social face if they traipsed about.[10] The prevailing mores restricted upper-class women to the family townhouse like some precious bird in a cage of masonry and wrought iron. Aversion to sunlight and faces chalked with *cascarilla,* a powdered eggshell makeup, did not distinguish them from sister aristocrats in Europe, but the proportions, adjudged as excessive by aristocratic European travelers, did, and they suggest the influence of racial slavery on the prevailing mores. On those occasions when a lady did decide to step out, say to church or to hear the evening military bands at the Plaza de Armas as a cover for a moonlight rendezvous, she rode in the family *quitrín,* its leather top richly ornamented to allow street people to readily identify their betters, and driven by a colored postilion properly attired in waistcoat, top hat, and jackboots. Should she want to buy something on the way, vendors walked the merchandise to the *quitrín* for her inspection.

To outsiders, Havana and the other major Cuban cities tended to seem festive, as well they should in a country where Sundays and festival days accounted for one day in four. The planter elite sponsored much of the festivity and participated in it. Even on a normal day, cockfights and other gaming would have looked strange without the elite wagering and debauching in proximity to lower-class whites and people of color. To some Anglo-Saxon onlookers, however, all the color and hustle appeared surreal if not libertine. As Fanny Calderón de la Barca, the decorous Scottish wife of a Spanish diplomat, mused after successive stays in New York City and Havana in 1839, "The sudden change from Yankee land to this military, monkish, Spanish negroland is dreamy."[11]

Santiago, Puerto Príncipe, Matanzas, and Trinidad were the other Cuban cities worthy of the name. Each had populations of 10,000 or more, and each had lesser versions of Havana's social life, although Matanzas was recognized as the "Athens of Cuba" for having given birth to a disproportionate number of Cuba's intellectuals. All of the cities except Puerto Príncipe, which had developed as an inland ranching and bureaucratic center, were thriving in 1840 as ports closely tied to the plantation hinterland.

Social relations during the sugar boom projected a nervous as well as an exotic countenance. The tale of the sugar plantation in Cuba, like that of Dickens's two cities, recalls the best and worst of times. With plantation slavery had come intensified land agglomeration, reduction of smallholding whites, and the brutal use of African labor on an unprecedented scale. In becoming an economy based on racial slavery, Cuba developed a mutually reinforcing social hierarchy broadly divided into whites, free people of color, and slaves. Life reflected a much more complex reality, for each of the three major social divisions had numerous subdivisions in which often confusing combinations of color, wealth, and privilege sorted out superior from inferior.

Only a pathetic handful of Indians lived in Cuba in 1840, scattered about the village of Holguín in the east, where they attracted the curious. If not truly the descendants of Cuba's pre-Columbian inhabitants, they could have been castaways from Florida or some other circum-Caribbean area or perhaps mestizos in whom Spanish blood ran thin. In any case, virtually all the indigenes had long since succumbed to epidemic disease, coerced labor, and miscegenation. Thus, to get labor in required numbers, planters had turned to the trade in African slaves.

At the bottom of Cuba's social hierarchy were the recent arrivals from Africa, the *bozales* or *negros de naciones,* who usually ended up doing fieldwork on the plantations of Cuba's western countryside. Their numbers were small in the beginning. From the time of the settlement expedition of Diego Velázquez in 1511 to the capture of Havana by the British in 1762 during the Seven Years' War, only a few thousand African slaves had entered Cuba. By the end of the century the numbers had jumped to thousands per year and would continue to climb to tens of thousands per year in the 1830s as the demand for sugar propelled economic takeoff.[12] Precisely when in the second half of the eighteenth century takeoff began may be disputed, but the capture of Havana in 1762 shook Spain into a major restructuring of its colonial defenses and, as a necessary consequence, of the colonial polity and economy as well. Britain's liberalization of the Havana market during its ten-month occupation may also have served as an object lesson for Charles III (1759–1788), the most able of the Bourbon reformers, on his way to the elimination of the privileged system of contracts (*asientos*), which had for centuries stipulated the number of slaves that could be imported into specific regions of the Spanish empire, and his approval of unlimited introduction of slaves into designated ports. The slave revolution in Saint Domingue followed in 1791, and the devastation of the world's leading producer of sugar and coffee more than doubled sugar prices overnight. Cuban whites moved quickly to take advantage; to satisfy their labor requirements they relied on Spanish merchants resident in Havana who, by 1820, had taken over the Cuban slave trade.

Imports of *bozales* peaked in the winter and spring less to coincide with the sugar harvest as some scholars have speculated than to avoid the hurricane season. Most slave-trading emporia ranged along the West African coast, north of the equator, although sizable cargoes were smuggled in from Angola and Mozambique as well. Africa's internal politics and fluctuations in Anglo-Spanish relations rerouted traffic, and in the decade or so before 1840, imports appear to have declined from the Bight of Biafra and the Gold Coast, risen from Mozambique, and maintained a steady flow from the Bight of Benin.[13]

Captains of slave-trading vessels had explicit instructions to treat their cargoes with great care, not to overcrowd them on ship, to feed them well, and to land them without delay. Pedro Martínez of Cádiz, who was probably running the largest slave-trading operation to Cuba by 1840, told one of his captains to use "extreme vigilance with the slaves for fear of an insurrection, of which there have been instances."[14] The 80 to 90 percent of the slaves who survived the Middle Passage landed in select anchorages usually along the northern coast to the windward of Havana, where they were deposited in barracoons, inspected by doctors, and either auctioned oiled and loinclothed on the block or transported for sale to other insular locations. Many slavers dumped their *"bultos"* ("bundles") or *"sacos de carbon"* ("bags of charcoal") on the docks of the infamous

Havana suburb of Casa Blanca to be delivered into La Misericordia (the House of Mercy) barracoon. They filed through a solitary iron gate into whitewashed, one-story buildings arranged like barracks about a spacious square court. Even Joseph John Gurney, the Quaker abolitionist, after inspecting one of the six in greater Havana in 1840, had to concede that these barracoons were "commodious and airy": "for these places, for filthy lucre's sake, are intended to be curative of the effects of the middle passage."[15]

The keepers of the barracoons, mindful of the slaves' value, superintended recuperation. Each cargo could vary dramatically in health, and each new arrival had to undergo "seasoning," a deadly process of biological adaptation and forced acculturation to a new environment. The time spent on the Middle Passage, the availability of rest and nutritious food on arrival, advances in medical knowledge, and many other factors affected the rate of seasoning deaths. Estimates ranged widely across the slave societies of the Caribbean, from less than 10 percent for one year to more than 25 percent for several years. If Alexander von Humboldt was right, seasoning deaths in Cuba numbered at the lower range at between 7 and 12 percent for one year. The effect of seasoning explains why a prime male *bozal* might bring $250 to $300 in 1840, and a prime seasoned male would bring $350 to $400 or more.[16]

The more common names of Mandinga, Gangá, Mina, Lucumí, Carabalí, Congo, and Macuá, used by Cuban whites to differentiate among the imported slaves, roughly identified ethnicities and were retained by many slaves and former slaves as ethnonyms. The Mandingas and Gangás corresponded to the Malinkes of the Sierra Leone region; the Minas to the Akans of the Gold Coast; the Lucumís to the Yoruban-speaking peoples of the Bight of Benin; the Carabalís to the Ibos and Efiks of the Bight of Biafra; the Congos to the Congos of Angola; and the Macuás to the Makwas of Mozambique. Slaves made finer distinctions, as evidenced by their oral history and the varieties of Afro-Cuban fraternal societies known as *cabildos*.[17]

Whites labeled each ethnicity with certain temperaments, at times inconsistently. The prevailing prejudices around 1840 seemed to be that the Mandingas and Gangás were the "most tractable and trustworthy"; the Lucumís were "quick-tempered, warlike, cunning," but "hard-working"; the Minas and Carabalís resembled the Lucumís; the Congos were "stupid, great drunkards, and sensualists"; and the Macuás were "brutal as the Congos."[18] Whatever the prejudices, planters purposely bought mixed ethnic groups to encourage division within the slave quarters. The strength of Yoruban culture in Cuba in 1840 and a century later derived from the constancy of imports of Lucumís from the Bight of Benin during the sugar boom.[19]

Bozales graduated to *ladinos* when they could communicate in Spanish or an Afro-Spanish patois but seldom to work beyond the field. *Criollo* slaves, born and reared in Cuba, with a better understanding of the language and the system fared better. Although thousands of Cuban-born slaves labored in the fields side by side with *bozales* and *ladinos,* some obtained more advantaged positions as artisans, drivers, urban slaves for hire, or house slaves. As the former slave Juan Francisco Manzano related in his autobiography, masters or mistresses would go to their rural properties to make selections of the "best" creole slave children to take them to the city for training in domestic service.[20] With white as virtue in a society finely stratified by skin color, the light-skinned creole slave and particularly a light-skinned creole female had the best chance to obtain a margin of physical comfort and narrow access to freedom.

Since foreign observers rarely ventured outside the city, they saw only the small, best part of Cuban slavery. Perhaps 20 to 30 percent of Cuba's slaves worked in the municipalities; they tended to be *criollo* (American-born), female, and members of the master's household, specializing in personal services: the men as body servants, butlers, porters, gardeners, postilions, and liverymen; the women as cooks, washerwomen, wet nurses, maids, and concubines. Urban slaves generally dressed better, ate better, worked fewer hours at a more leisurely pace than plantation field hands. They had the spare time and the space to enjoy city diversions such as taverns, dances, nonwhite social clubs, and cockfights. Money changed hands in the city, and so with more time and opportunity for self-employment and for contacts with moneyed people, a slave might scrape together, here and there, the sum to purchase his freedom. Although penetration by the world market had weakened the ties of paternalism throughout Cuba, the city continued to prove more hospitable to master-slave intimacy since Cuba's planters lived there more than in the country. And because of the greater distance of Cuban-born slaves from the values and social patterns of their African past, masters relied more on the force of colonial acculturation in directing slave behavior and less on the whip. Should physical treatment become grossly abusive, the urban slave could turn more readily to a sympathetic priest, government official, or white patron.

Urban slaves worked under a wide range of conditions. Cuba's many slaves-for-hire might well have enjoyed more space, more freedom of movement away from the master's eye, than slave butlers. Slave dock-workers could have imagined and might have had rosier work life on certain coffee plantations. Still, from what the testimony of former slaves and Afro-Cuban oral tradition says, urban slaves had reached a consensus about the hardships of life on the sugar plantation, and whatever advantages they enjoyed away from there, they lived with the uncertainty that a slight trespass beyond the circumference of permitted spheres could bring down on them the master's correction by removal *al campo,* to labor in a canefield.

A sizable and internally stratified population of free people of color occupied the middle of Cuba's social hierarchy. During the sugar boom their numbers had quintupled from about 30,000 in 1774 to about 153,000 in 1841 while their proportion in the total population hovered fairly consistently at between 15 and 20 percent. They tended to live in urban areas where economic opportunities and social space permitted modest relief from white oppression. Every Cuban city and town had its predominantly colored sections. In Havana during the sugar boom, the districts of Belén, Jesus María, and Chávez had developed into colored barrios. Pueblo Nuevo had done so in Matanzas. One out of five free persons of color lived in Havana in 1840; one out of three lived in Cuba's four largest cities, Havana, Santiago, Puerto Príncipe, and Matanzas.[21]

Out of all proportion to their numbers free people of color had entered Cuba's skilled trades. In the cities and towns they worked in a wide variety of skilled jobs, from butchers, bakers, and yes, even candlestick-makers to bloodletters and hairdressers. They literally served whites from the womb to the grave: free colored midwives brought them into the world; free colored undertakers ushered them out. Despite laws designed to assure whites that their employment in trades or crafts would not deprive them of high status, traditional attitudes continued strong. Those professions remained *degradante,* without honor, leaving people of color to seize the abandoned economic opportunity.

After a vacation in Santiago in 1837, F. W. P. Greenwood, the editor of the Boston-based *Christian Examiner,* observed that "the blacks or mulattos who become free on the plantations, commonly repair to the cities and villages, and become mechanics and small shopkeepers."[22] Hiram Hastings, the United States consul in Trinidad in 1842, in discussing local business conditions, described the "mechanical industry, carried on by free labour, mostly by blacks and mulattoes."[23] Former Captain-General Vives responded to a question about the state of the mechanical trades in Cuba by saying that "the people of color are the ones who occupy this branch of industry, and from its abandonment to these hands comes that which has been communicated to them [the mechanical trades], the stain of the castes."[24]

In the countryside free people of color were a less conspicuous presence but significant nonetheless. Cuba had thousands of smallholding free colored farmers, considerably more in eastern Cuba than in the plantation districts of the west. While they did not live in "perfect fellowship" with whites, as one traveler observed, in the backwoods away from the plantation districts, examples of white and black camaraderie could be found. Hundreds of free colored merchants and peddlers helped to elaborate a limited internal market in addition to arousing the suspicions of whites during periods of slave unrest. Few western sugar plantations could do without the seasonal employment of rural-based free colored artisans. Any ranch of note had free colored drovers or herdsmen. Hundreds of landholders hired free people of color as administrators and, contrary to law, as plantation overseers. Two years after the repression of La Escalera, when thousands of free people of color left Cuba or were exiled, about 7 percent of the overseers and 12 percent of estate administrators still were free people of color.[25]

The examination of records of contested marriages by Verena Martínez-Alier has revealed just how finely stratified Cuban society generally and the free colored class specifically were. As a general rule, a free *pardo,* or person of partial African ancestry, enjoyed greater status than a free *moreno,* or pure-blooded African. But wealth produced exceptions. A wealthy free *pardo* artist or tradesman would likely top his class in prestige and influence because of his closeness to the white ideal and his assumed distance from the stain of slavery. A poor free *pardo,* however, could be surpassed in rank by a wealthy *moreno.* Prosperous free *pardos* and free *morenos,* like prosperous whites, could enhance their status by purchasing positions. The rank of officer in the government-sponsored free *pardo* and free *moreno* militias could be purchased and afforded the bearer certain prerogatives in white society. Free people of color also looked to whitening to enhance their status. Those of a darker color tended to prefer marriage to a lighter member of their class. The lighter skin of one spouse gave immediate social benefits to the other and eventual benefits to the offspring. Marriage between two parties of unequal color might well engender dissent from parents of the lighter side, but not the reverse, although wealth might preempt it. A rich free *moreno* would have a better chance of marrying a poor free *parda,* just as a free *parda* from a prosperous family would have a better chance of marrying a poor white.[26]

For its white population, Cuba replicated the general experience of the Spanish colonies during the first century of colonization by drawing heavily from the southern half of Spain. Andalusia and the great inland port city of Seville contributed more than any other region. The Andalusian influence lingered on in 1840 in the city cathedrals and in some of the most powerful planting families.[27] Other white emigrant groups had a more recent history. During the sugar boom, Asturians had firmly established themselves as urban retailers of dry goods. Catalans practiced ignoble commerce, for which they were branded "Spanish Jews" or "Spanish Yankees." The more fortunate operated merchant houses and made money by exporting sugar and shipping slaves. The less fortunate found their way to the sugar plantations to work as wage-earning substitutes for slaves.[28]

The Canary Islands furnished more white immigrants to Cuba than any other region except peninsular Spain. Of the more than 55,000 foreign-born inhabitants of Cuba listed in the census of 1846, 19,759, or 36 percent, came from the Canary Islands and 27,251, or 49 percent, came from Spain. The stream of *isleños* had run from virtually the time of Spanish settlement and had widened during the sugar boom. The progenitors of the Betancourt family, the leading family in the city of Puerto Príncipe in 1840, had participated in the conquest and administration of the Canary Islands prior to the family's settlement in Cuba in the mid-seventeenth century. In 1840 the Frías family owned much of what is now the Vedado section of Havana. The accumulation of property started with the arrival of Antonio Sánchez de Frías from the Canary Islands at the end of the eighteenth century. Francisco de Frías, one of Antonio's three sons, became a celebrated sugar agronomist, political activist, and the fourth Conde de Pozos Dulces. The rich and powerful Alfonso family of Havana also came from the Canary Islands at the end of the eighteenth century. It made a fortune in sugar cultivation and came to possess several titles of nobility. Most Canary Islanders, however, had much less success. They landed as poor whites, and as poor whites they died. Lead-

ing planters recruited them for the rural peasantry to act as a restraint
on the slaves. Some Canary Islanders joined some of the Catalans as
wage-laborers on the plantations.[29]

France, Great Britain, the United States, and the German states contributed small but significant numbers. Thousands of French refugees
from the slave revolution in Saint Domingue put their luggage of capital
and plantation expertise into the building of Cuba's sugar and coffee in-
dustries. British emigrants owned plantations near the Indians of Holguín.
A small but influential group of businessmen established themselves in
Havana and in Santiago near the mines of the Sierra Maestra.[30] Emigrants
from the United States shared in Havana's business and commercial
activity, helped to develop the port town of Cárdenas, and worked on the
railroad and in the copper mines between Nuevitas and Puerto Príncipe.
A number of families planted staples on the red lands of Matanzas and
Cárdenas provinces.[31] Of the several hundred Germans or Cubans of
German origin in 1840, few engaged in agriculture, although *cafetal*
Angerona, one of the largest coffee estates in Cuba, was founded by a
native of Lübeck. Not until 1844 would smokers begin to savor the
tobacco rolled by the workers of H. Upmann. Most of Cuba's resident
Germans came from Hamburg and Bremen, lived in Havana or one of
the larger ports, and worked as merchants or artisans.[32]

Lesser whites, like the people of color, lived in the shadow of Cuba's
planting elite of several hundred families. *Monteros* or *guajiros,* a class
of rural poor whites, ranked at the bottom of the white stratum. They
herded cattle on a hacienda, carted plantation crops to port, or crudely
farmed small plots of land precariously surrounded by the big planters
and their slaves. Their hovels resembled those of the slaves, constructed
Indian-style with walls of wooden poles and mud plaster or, less often,
of stones, an earthen floor, and roof of palm thatch. They had few possessions, a hammock or two, a table, stools, a few plates, a core diet of
pork and plantains, and a jug, which, according to many reporters, was
chronically empty. They could be fiercely provincial, using their machetes
not only on bandits and runaway slaves but on intruders from other
districts. Yet, once convinced of a legitimate purpose, they could be leg-
endary hosts, ready to offer travelers a cup of coffee and to guide them
through the wilds to a desired location. Some travelers stressed their
roughness and barbarity, others their independence and verve, pairs of
attributes by no means exclusive. No one accused them of overwork, for,
like poor whites in every American slave society, they had developed a

work ethic distinguishable from the Protestant. Planters or administrators continued to hire them as overseers and slave hunters only to curse them for their unreliability and independence. Also by reputation, they excelled as horsemen and horse thieves as well as gamblers and philanderers. If a *montero* had "a fine horse, a pair of silver spurs, a silver-mounted Toledo blade, a pair of linen trousers, a cambric shirt, and yellow cowskin shoes" he considered himself lucky.[33] *Monteros* held dear the freedom that elevated them above the slaves and often served as vigilante cavalrymen during slave uprisings, during which they could display a viciousness that exposed the intensity of their racism. Alexander von Humboldt could have had a Cuban *montero* in mind when he wrote, "In Spain it is almost a title of nobility to descend neither from Jews nor Moors. In [Spanish] America the greater or less degree of whiteness of skin decides the rank which man occupies in society. A white who rides barefooted on horseback thinks he belongs to the nobility of the country."[34]

Urban whites matched or surmounted the status of the *monteros* as grocers, traders, cigarmakers, carpenters, and public employees. Thousands attached themselves to the white elite in domestic service. Some of the most talented artisans and tradesmen worked out of rented space on the ground floor of the elite townhouses. In domestic service and other urban jobs, whites competed with free people of color, who were, however, legally excluded from such technical and prestigious professions as pharmacy, medicine, law, higher education, and government. The traditional Spanish stigma attached to manual labor was reinforced by the Cuban association of manual labor with slavery and people of inferior status, and unsuccessful competition with free people of color made white vagrancy a major problem. Urban whites by the thousands chose to roam city streets picaro-fashion rather than seek steady work.[35]

Cuba had a nobility, recognized as such by its titles, landed wealth, bloodlines, and history of military and administrative services to the Spanish Crown. In 1840 Cuba's high nobility, the so-called *títulos de Castilla,* comprised twenty-six marquis and thirty counts. A ladder of titled whites extended down from them, through several *grandes cruces,* through the dozens of *caballeros* of Isabel the Catholic and Charles III, through numerous other grades of status to, in a sense, the crudest *montero,* for in Cuba the mere fact of whiteness prefixed Don or Doña to a person's name. Wealth generated by the plantation economy appears to have speeded the process of elevation to the high nobility. Of the fifty-six marquis and counts, thirty-one had obtained their titles since the turn of the century.[36]

Planters of any standing absented themselves from their plantations for much of the year. Sugar planters ordinarily visited with their families on or near Christmas and remained for part of the January-through-May harvest. Their presence helped to control the slaves and reduce the number of runaways during the most grueling period of labor. Since the leading planters usually had more than one plantation, the winter months meant running circuit. As soon as possible, they would hand over the management of their estates to hired subordinates so they could return to the culture and local politics of their patron cities. Preference for city life came to Cuban planters honestly. Their lack of enthusiasm for estate management derived at least in part from the attitude of the old peninsular elite, which "felt neither the economic advantages nor the social obligations of landholding."[37] The survival of the so-called *privilegio de ingenios* ("privilege of the sugarmills"), a sixteenth-century concession made by the Spanish Crown, allowed sugar planters to abdicate their responsibilities more easily since no matter how indebted they became, creditors could not confiscate their plantations.[38]

Wealth and connections might make a nobleman but not a gentleman, and in a society so preoccupied with status, the origins of comelatelies with high titles competed with the private lives of the clergy as the leading subject of polite gossips. Claudio Martínez de Pinillos, the second Conde de Villanueva, despite many years of service in the interests of Cuba's planting class as *intendente,* Cuba's highest ranking fiscal officer, when he was also the highest-ranking Cuban-born official, could not shed the whispered reproach that his peninsular-born father had once been a shopkeeper. José Buenaventura Esteva, a native of Galicia and, as of 1833, the first Marqués de Esteva de las Delicias, was stained by having allegedly started his career as a doorkeeper. A few years before Esteva's ennobling, Santiago de la Cuesta Manzanal became the first Conde de la Reunión de Cuba with the help of a fortuitous marriage. His father-in-law had made and left behind a fortune, said to have come from the peddling of "needles and other trifles."[39] Julián de Zulueta, a well-known middleman in the slave trade, whose "cousin" Pedro was tried by the British on slave-trading charges in a famous case of 1842, came to Cuba about a decade earlier in poverty. By 1845, through the inheritance left by an affluent uncle and slave-trading profits, he built the vast Alava sugar plantation southeast of the port of Cárdenas. He married three times, the last two to nieces. Before his death in 1878 he obtained the titles of Marqués de Álava and Vizconde de Casa-Blanca.[40]

After mingling with members of the elite during his visit to Cuba in 1839, José Jacinto de Salas y Quiroga, a Spanish writer and publisher, named Cárdenas, Herrera, Peñalver, Calvo de la Puerta, Chacón, O'Farrill, O'Reilly, Montalvo, Núñez del Castillo, and Pedroso as the ten most distinguished families in Cuba. All were long established in Cuba. The oldest, the Calvo, Cárdenas, and Pedroso families, dated from the sixteenth century; the youngest, the O'Reilly and the Montalvo families, from the middle of the eighteenth century. Only the O'Farrills lacked a title of marquis or count from Spain in 1840, but they did descend from an Irish earl and the first factor of the British South Sea Company in Cuba. Members of the other nine families held twenty-one titles of marquis and count, more than one-third of the total in 1840. And the land and slaves of these ten families may well have produced between one-quarter and one-third of all the sugar in Cuba's western department.[41]

That the plantation system owed its development to new men and new money no longer seems likely, for families like the Calvos and Pedrosos had distinct advantages in responding to the price incentives of the world market. Cuba's *cabildos* or *ayuntamientos* (municipal councils) had exercised the right to distribute land until they were taken over by the Crown in 1729. Since the established families controlled the municipal councils and had court connections due to military or bureaucratic service to the Crown, they were able to acquire large grants of quality land; some of these grants remained large over the generations because of the families' ability to obtain entailment. Control of the town councils and court connections had also translated into more liquid capital through the control of local prices, the vending of local offices, and the participation as owners and investors in various, royally sanctioned trading monopolies during the mercantilist era. With the best land to grow sugar on and with access to the credit and hard currency needed to buy slaves and equipment, the established families seem to have led Cuba's agricultural transformation.[42]

Inbreeding kept elite boundaries stiff, although hardly impenetrable, and over generations had intertwined noble families into clans. Genealogies resemble that "tangle of fishhooks" found by Bertram Wyatt-Brown for landed families of the Old South. Cousins married cousins; less often, uncles married nieces, and nephews married aunts. Family names of the ten highest families when they did not end as Herrera y Cárdenas, O'Reilly y Calvo, or O'Farrill y Montalvo ended as Herrera y Herrera, Cárdenas y Cárdenas, and so forth. Of the eighteen members of the ten highest families who together held twenty-one titles of count or marquis in 1840, five apparently died unmarried; six married kin; six married other members of Cuba's noble families; and one married a member of an elite Spanish family.[43] The sugar boom may well have reinforced traditional intraclass marriage patterns and preexisting habits of land agglomeration, since economies of scale in sugar production would have given planters, who were under pressure from Spanish laws of partible inheritance, an incentive to consolidate their properties.

Feuds between Havana's elite planting families were common. The families were able to call forth impressive forces in support of their disputes not only because of blood and marital ties but because clientage relations extended through all classes and colors of society, as might be expected where wealth is narrowly concentrated. Roving gangs of people of color committed theft and mayhem in Havana in service to the white elite, as well as for their own purposes. Public order had improved by 1840 but it still required courage to walk on a Havana side street after 10 P.M. Captain-General Francisco Dionisio Vives complained in 1832 that "the influential white families flaunt the protection and patronage that they dispense to them [the people of color], either because their mothers suckled the children in those white families, or because of fear, or, lastly, because of relations even less pardonable. Hence the result is that they persist in mocking the Government, that they redeem their clients from punishment, and by abetting impunity, they increase the audacity of the delinquent."[44]

Parvenus and their offspring penetrated elite families noticeably during the sugar boom, even if profits from the slave trade had helped them to "purify their blood" with the purchase of titles and genealogies. Elite indebtedness, which had always caused problems for the established families, seems to have worsened under the twin pressures of conspicuous consumption and interest charges, elevated to perhaps fourteen or fifteen points above the European norm to as much as 20 percent by the *privilegio de ingenios*. One Spanish legal official pointed out in 1845 that what was intended to encourage the costly business of sugar production by sheltering the planters actually encouraged contraction of debt, "not so much for the development of their estates but for the sustenance of their vices."[45] A wealthy merchant who wanted to break into the highest rank took the proper first steps by setting up a plantation and a baronial

Mid-nineteenth century Havana: (*Top*) Plaza de Armas, the city's main square and social center for elite white families, the Captain-General's townhouse to the left, a noble's townhouse to the right. (*Bottom*) Havana harbor as soon from the town of Casa Blanca, notorious site of illegal slave trading activity.

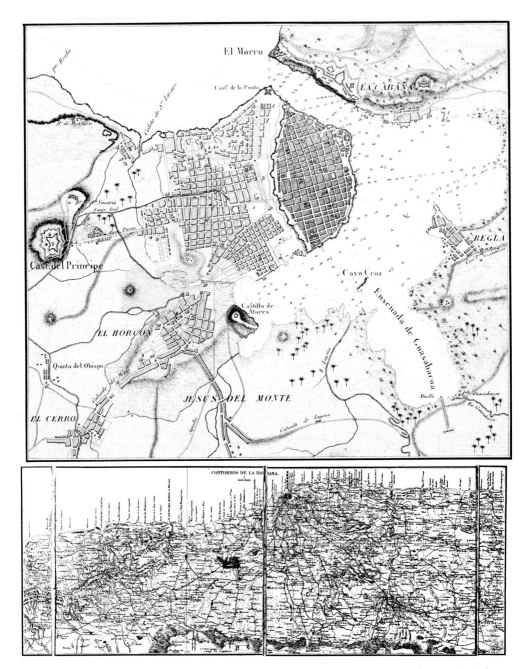

(*Top*) Havana, *c.* 1840. (*Bottom*) Map of Havana and neighboring plantation districts in Cuba's Western Department, where scattered slave uprisings broke out in the 1830s and early 40s.

Ácana sugar plantation, site of slave unrest in 1843. *Courtesy, Library of Congress.*

(Top) Slaves serving whites and working in the boiling house, Cuban sugar plantation. *(Bottom)* Cuban tobacco farm.

Upper and lower class whites: (*Top*) Black postilion drawing a *quitrín,* a Cuban chaise with women of planter or merchant class. (*Bottom*) *Monteros,* class of poor rural whites.

Watercolors of street scenes with slaves and free people of color. There were more free blacks in Cuba than in most slave societies in the Americas. The man in livery is a postilion, a more privileged urban slave.

Free and slave: (*Top*) Free *parda*, a woman of partial African ancestry. (*Bottom*) Free colored midwife in attendance. Free people of color dominated many skilled trades.

Festivities: (*Top*) *Ñáñigo,* prankster, member of an Afro-Cuban secret society. (*Bottom*) An annual street celebration on *Día de los Reyes,* the Day of Kings, held on January 6. *Cabildos,* Afro-Cuban brotherhoods, marched in streets in vivid costumes under tribal banners.

townhouse. Another step was a useful marriage. James Drake emigrated from England to Cuba in the 1790s, established himself as a merchant and planter of consequence, and married into the Núñez del Castillo family; his son Carlos secured the title of Conde de Vegamar in 1847. The wealth of Pedro Forcade, one of the most notorious slave traders in Cuba during the first half of the nineteenth century, appears to have eased his son into marriage with a member of the Cárdenas family. One of the three sons of Pedro Diago, an immigrant from the Basque country and another success story as a slave trader and planter, married the daughter of the Marqués de la Cañada Tirry. Gabriel Lombillo y Herce, who came to Cuba at the turn of the century from a small village in Old Castile, struck riches in the slave trade and after 1820, became one of the leading slave traders of the contraband era. He was a notorious skinflint and probably a borderline lunatic. When he died in 1830, his business partner was accused of poisoning him with the help of Lombillo's own wife, who subsequently married the partner. Despite the family scandal, one of Lombillo's sons married into the respected Montalvo family, a second into the Pedroso family.[46]

Not all of Cuba's planting families had the money or the penchant for titles. Certain planters in successful Cuban families, old and new, and the progeny of planters, an educated vanguard, had assimilated liberal-democratic ideas. Creole lawyers, doctors, and educators, in some cases schooled outside Cuba, with a knowledge of political life in Western Europe and the United States and a recollection of the separatist revolutions in former Spanish colonies, began to speak of restraining privilege, an end to court politics, and the inseparability of representative government and human progress. They longed for changes in the Spanish imperial system that would give them a louder voice in their own affairs.

Cubans had experienced representative government during two peninsular upheavals, the first following Napoleon's invasion of Spain in 1808 and the second following an uprising against the restored monarchy of Ferdinand VII in 1820. After Ferdinand recovered his throne, the experiment in representative government ended. Peninsular political turmoil would continue into the 1840s, but none of the shifts in regimes, whether to the right or to the left, relieved political repression in Cuba.

Cuba's nobility or other prosperous whites had certain political influence, but decisive power rested outside their grasp with a Spanish bureaucracy of military men that had superimposed itself on the society and the economy. Cuban whites rarely held any political office of extralocal importance; those posts Spain reserved for its own. The peninsular-born who ventured to Cuba to fill these posts brought with them a condescending attitude toward the Creoles (American-born whites), whom they regarded as effeminate, dissipated, and culturally backward. Resentment surfaced in everything from dress—Creole women preferred blue, peninsular women red—to the seating arrangements at the Tacón theater.[47]

What peninsular bureaucrats encountered in Cuba during the sugar boom once they arrived must have aroused their greed and envy to the further detriment of colonial relations. Cuba seemed to flaunt its prosperity: in Havana's new macadamized roads, water system, and sculpted fountains; in the Havana-to-Bejucal railroad completed in 1837, eleven years before Spain's first railroad; in the imports of European high technology, from steam engines to flush toilets. The plantation economy had given birth to what Cuban historians have called the First Dance of the Millions as Cuba's elite strutted and displayed in excess of their Spanish counterparts. In the frescoed palace of one of Cuba's big planters or merchants, a Spanish military officer with a new political position might easily be envious of the colonial and his wife, adorned in ensembles of precious stones and waited upon by French cook, Italian decorator, and African servants.[48] Spain exploited Cuba's prosperity with burdensome taxes, and individual officials frequently took their personal share by abusing the power of their office.

Spain had concentrated power to facilitate the imposition of the imperial will in Cuba by a bewildering system of political checks and balances, no Montesquieuian division into legislative, judicial, and executive branches but by a distribution of overlapping power among persons or institutions. No clear-cut jurisdictional boundaries existed. Overlapping military, civil, and ecclesiastical jurisdictions recognized privilege in a society of privilege. They also ensured the king a powerful check on the overweening ambition of individuals, and continually reaffirmed his own role as patriarch and ultimate authority.[49]

Captains-General overcame jurisdictional disputes during the sugar boom by a steady accretion of power. When the *audiencia,* the highest colonial court, was moved from Santo Domingo to Puerto Príncipe in 1800, the Captain-General assumed a presiding role over it. A second *audiencia* established in Havana in 1839 also came under his control. The Captain-General and the judges of the *audiencia* had confronted each other many times in the early colonial period, far less so by 1840, for by then the *audiencia* intervened in executive affairs only upon the Captain-General's request.[50] The desperate situation caused by separatist revolutions in Spain's mainland colonies justified further concentration, and after restoration to the Spanish throne, Ferdinand VII placed virtually unlimited power in the hands of the Captain-General, and in 1824 Ferdinand authorized the creation of a special military tribunal in Cuba, the Comisión Militar Executiva y Permanente (Permanent Executive Military Commission). Similar tribunals in Spain had served Ferdinand well in dismantling liberal political opposition, and in Cuba the Military Commission enabled the Captain-General to dispense summary justice by cutting through the ponderous bulk of Spanish seigneurial privilege and law. The Military Commission quickly evolved into the principal tribunal for adjudication for those individuals, whatever their color, who could be said to have committed crimes against the social order. It had the power "to hear and judge crimes of those who by arms, papers, or pasquinades, or by actions of any kind are enemies of the legitimate rights of the throne . . . and those who promote disturbances that alter the public tranquility."[51] Proceedings started when the Captain-General ordered an indictment and ended with his approval or disapproval of the verdict. Two months after the birth of the Military Commission, Ferdinand went further by granting to the Captain-General "the plenitude of powers that by the Royal Ordinances are conceded to the Governors of besieged cities." Henceforth he could expel a civil servant regardless of his "office, rank, class, or condition" who acted against the interest of the Spanish Crown and could replace him with someone of his own choosing. He could also "suspend the execution of any orders or general dispositions issued in any branch of the administration to the degree that Your Excellency [the Captain-General] thinks convenient to the royal service."[52]

Ferdinand's death in 1833 and the liberal reascendancy after the First Carlist War changed little; Cuba kept the Military Commission, and the Captain-General retained his extraordinary powers. By 1840, with special courts, legal advisers, governors, lieutenant-governors, district magistrates, and thousands of regular troops, nearly all from Spain and nearly all military men, the Captain-General, if he so chose, could rule Cuba as a military dictatorship.

Cuba's complex and multilayered social hierarchy reflected values appropriate to a booming plantation economy based on African slavery. The Captain-General, as the chief military and executive authority, was required to protect colonial prosperity and, thus, the attendant social relations, from domestic and foreign enemies. But, by 1840, the Captain-General confronted the paradox of slavery in the modern world. As Cuban sugar production reached dizzying heights the process of abolition had already begun. Outside of Cuba, precisely in those countries in which capitalism had created mass markets for slave-grown staples, people were increasingly finding slavery an unacceptable form of labor. Great Britain had given birth to a radical new ideology that championed the sacred natural right of individuals to have property in their own persons. This ideology was radiating outward to mainland Europe and across the Atlantic. It won adherents and throughout the Americas it would decisively condition the struggles that brought slavery to an end.

The Conspiracy of La Escalera was a particularly bloody and violent part of these interconnected yet discrete struggles. Its analysis should begin with the slaves themselves.

2

Of Blood and Sugar

—•—

Por lo que dices, Fabio,
un arcángel tu abuelo fue con sus esclavos.
Mi abuelo, en cambio,
fue un diablo con sus amos
El tuyo murió de un garrotazo.
Al mío, lo colgaron.

From what you say, Fabio,
your grandpa was an archangel with his slaves.
My grandpa, on the other hand,
was a demon with his masters.
Yours died cudgeled
Mine they hanged.

NICOLÁS GUILLÉN, "Ancestros," in
Selected Poems of Nicolás Guillén
(Amherst, Mass., 1972), 64–65

Between one-quarter and one-third of Cuba's slaves in 1840 worked on sugar plantations. In the early 1840s coffee plantations still outnumbered sugar plantations (1,838 to 1,238 in 1841, and 1,670 to 1,442 in 1846), but sugar had been gaining since the 1820s. Factors causing the shift in production included competition from Brazil in the coffee market; a drop by about half in world coffee prices, from more than twenty cents per pound in 1822 to less than ten cents per pound in 1840; an unfavorable U.S. tariff policy on coffee in retaliation for a restrictive Cuban tariff on U.S. flour; and, probably most important, the rising cost of slave labor bid up by Cuba's sugar boom.[1] Planters had to produce large amounts of sugar to make a profit, which meant planting an extensive acreage and securing gangs of laborers. Coffee could be grown by a family on a few acres of hillside, but sugar required heavy investments in buildings and equipment to process the cane.

A statistical record compiled in 1826 for seventy-nine districts in Havana province that make up much of the western department shows 437 sugar plantations with an average of 105 slaves and 35.7 *caballerías* (about 1,189 acres) per plantation and 1,180 coffee plantations with an average of 43 slaves and 2.9 *caballerías* (about 97 acres) per plantation.[2] At first glance these figures might suggest greater labor intensiveness on coffee plantations, but how much of the land on either coffee or sugar plantations qualified as improved cannot be determined readily, although an educated guess for the coffee plantation would be more than half and for the sugar plantation much less than half. The figures for the sugar plantation support the argument for a steady process of land concentration during the sugar boom since other calculations place the average size of Havana-area sugar plantations in 1762 at 10 to 12 *caballerías* (333 to 400 acres); in 1792 at 22 *caballerías* (733 acres), and for the entire western department in 1860 at 43 *caballerías* (1,432 acres).[3] Thus, Cuban slaves would have worked on sugar plantations that were on average among the largest plantations in the history of slavery in the Americas.

Sugar far exceeded coffee, tobacco, and cotton in the rigors of cultivation. Large tracts of land had to be cleared and grubbed out; ditches had to be dug and cleaned to ensure proper drainage; wood had to be chopped and fetched to fuel the train of boilings; and, above all, the cane had to be cut with backbreaking and arm-dulling monotony, then rushed to the mill before its precious contents were dissipated. "Breathless haste" and "brute strength" rule on the sugar plantation, Fernando Ortiz, Cuba's greatest anthropologist, observed. "The operations of cutting, hauling, grinding, clarification, filtration, evaporation, and crystallization, must theoretically be carried out one after the other, but without interruption; nearly all of them are going on at the same time in the mill. While one field of cane is being cut, others are being converted into sacks of sugar. And all at top speed."[4]

Because delay could drastically affect the amount and quality of the sugar, the laborers had to be constantly disciplined. As Manuel Moreno Fraginals has described so well, harvest on the sugar plantation resembled a factory in its rhythms. During the grinding season, time and the machine condemned the slaves to an arduous and dreary routine, as slaveholders and their surrogates attempted to induce them or break them into greater efficiency. Precolonial Africans practiced agriculture, some of it large-scale, which in no small way explains their desirability as slaves, and Africa's agricultural past influenced the work habits of American slaves, strongly in some regions, weakly in others. Africans practiced a tradi-tional agriculture, instituted not by a capitalist-driven world market but by a society that conceived of time as flexible and that placed a high value on rest and leisure. In the Old South, slaves fashioned a distinctive black work ethic out of both the slave resistance to economic exploitation and an "autonomous assertion of values generally associated with preindus-trial peoples."[5] Among Southern slaves, many generations gone from Africa, African notions of work lived on in the slave's preference for hard work over regular work. Among Cuban slaves, more than half of whom were African-born, African patterns of work and leisure must have car-ried ponderous force and clashed mightily with the alien schedules of the most factorylike of plantations. The ferocity of the struggle between African-influenced slave work habits and the sugar-plantation regimen may help to explain the relative prevalence of Cuban slave runaways and rebels.

Cutting cane in Cuba spanned about five months, from December/January through May/June, compared to little more than sixty days in Louisiana, with daily labor at least as intense. Up before dawn, field hands toiled under the shadow of the lash fourteen to sixteen hours a day, six days a week during *tiempo muerto,* the "dead season," sixteen to twenty hours a day, seven days a week during the harvest. The task system pre-ferred by the slaves, with daily work allotted in fixed amounts, seems to have made far less headway on the sugar plantations of Cuba than it did on the sugar plantations of the British Caribbean or the rice plantations of South Carolina, or even the cotton plantations of the southern United States, where it was far from a majority practice.[6]

Technological developments, far from easing workloads, added to them and promoted instability within Cuban society as a whole. In 1817 the steam engine began to replace oxen to drive the mills' grinding cylinders. Although it gave no clear advantage in the amount of fluid extracted from each cane, the amount of cane that could be processed per unit of time increased. Plantations and slave gangs expanded and the pace of work escalated to satisfy the ravenous hunger of a mechanized mill.[7] Dr. J. G. F. Wurdemann, a visiting physician from South Carolina, commented on the rhythms. Slaves in Cuba "worked more constantly" than the slaves of his native South Carolina. "The chief object in Cuba seems to be never to let them remain idle; and I have excited the astonishment of many a Creole, by stating the quantity of leisure our slaves enjoy after their daily tasks are over."[8] In 1830 a French nobleman witnessed a day of harvest on a sugar plantation to the west of Havana owned by a member of the Montalvo clan. "The women, the children, all work," he recorded in his travel diary; "it is continuous movement."[9] The Reverend Abiel Abbot, after spending a good deal of time watching slaves in both South Carolina and Cuba, did "not think the opinion extravagant, that the slaves in Cuba accomplish one third more labor than the tasked slaves of Carolina."[10] Now, the Reverend Abbot hardly had the skills to measure precisely the relative productivity of labor in the cultivation of South Carolinian rice and Cuban sugar, two quite dissimilar crops, but his observation surely does point to the regularity and intensity of labor needed to get the sugar out. Cirilo Villaverde, the son of a doctor on a Cuban sugar plantation, raised with slave companions, an acquaintance of the British consul and abolitionist David Turnbull, and the author of the great Cuban antislavery novel *Cecilia Valdés,* drew on his memory of slave life to write a scene at the Big House of a sugar plantation with a new steam-driven mill. The planter, his administrator, a local magistrate, and a priest have just adjourned from dinner and stroll out to the veranda for cigars and man-talk. When the planter and the administrator puzzle over the cause of the late rash of runaway slaves, the priest intones:

It is . . . a curious coincidence that so many negroes should have run away at the same time and precisely from those plantations where the method of grinding cane has been recently changed. Is it not possible that those stupid creatures may have imagined that they would have to work more because the cane is ground by means of a steam engine instead of oxen and mules?[11]

About 20 percent of Cuba's sugarmills (286 of 1,442) used steam power in 1846. This percentage proved deceptive. In the western department, where Cuba had its most dynamic plantations, on those plantations of the greatest size and with the greatest number of slaves, 34 percent (251 of 735) of the mills used it. That sugar cultivation took a terrible toll on slave life everyone agreed. Long hours of intense work caused accidents. Arms and legs were slashed, crushed, and dismembered along with the cane. Cuts and punctures from work in and around the fields easily led to serious infections like tetanus. Conscientious overseers tried to prepare themselves by bringing primitive first aid into the field— rags, thread, and oil of turpentine. Moreno Fraginals has concluded after studying many Cuban sugar plantation records that "it was normal for 15–20 percent of the slaves of a gang to be in the sick bay. By the end of the sugar harvest, this figure might well have reached 40 percent."[12] The sugar plantations of the British Caribbean appear to have approached these percentages.[13] Crude demographic rates calculated from census data and estimates of slave imports show that in Cuba, unlike in the United States, slave-population deaths exceeded births; that is, Cuban slaves did not reproduce themselves naturally. David Eltis has calculated a rate of natural decrease for the Cuban slave population at about 2.2 percent per year from 1817 to 1846, and it may well have been higher.[14]

Among Cuban planters a perception prevailed, true or not, that it was cheaper to work field slaves to death in five years or so and replace them by purchase than to see to their long-term maintenance and reproduction. Francisco Arango's attempt to counter a charge of slavebreeding in Cuba brought by a particularly uninformed antislavery delegate to the Spanish Cortes of 1810 unintentionally indicted his fellow planters on another count:

The slave who is pregnant or has lately delivered a child is useless for many months, and during this long period of inaction, her food ought to be greater in quantity and quality. This loss of work, this increase in the cost of the mother comes out of the pocket of the master. From him also comes the large and the frequently barren costs of the recently born child, and to him are attached the risks that are run in the lives of the mother and the child. And all form an expenditure of so much account for the master, that the black that is born at home has cost more, even when he is able to work than the one who is purchased at public auction.[15]

In a similar vein decades later David Turnbull asserted, as though he knew what he was talking about for the South, "The planters in Louisiana, and along the banks of the Mississippi are pretty much on a par with those of Cuba and the Brazils; with this difference, that as the prime cost is greater compared with the food and maintenance of the slave, they cannot afford to work him to death in so short a time."[16]

The specific contribution of sugar cultivation to slave mortality in Cuba has yet to be quantified adequately. Contrary to what many scholars believe, crude rates of natural increase or decrease can be misleading measures of the comparative physical well-being of slaves since areas like the antebellum United States with a stable slave population, i.e., a slave population with no significant in- or out-migration, would possess a different age and sex composition than a slave population such as Cuba's with its continued mass infusions from Africa. Slaves entered or left the United States in negligible numbers after the legal end of the African slave trade in 1808; almost 290,000 slaves, the majority of whom were more than fifteen years of age and males, entered Cuba from the legal end of its

African slave trade in 1820 to 1840. Thus Cuba came to have an older slave population than the U.S. with more slaves clustered in the upper-age brackets and exposed to greater risks of dying. Elaborate computations and demographic models of problematic applicability may be used to factor out migration to derive stable populations and more meaningful rates. Had the contraband slave trade come to an end, a stable Cuban slave population might well have shown a slight excess of births over deaths, although high mortality from sugar cultivation would have presented problems. Jack Ericson Eblen's computations have shown a naturally in-creasing slave population in colonial Cuba but one with an increasing mortality rate from 1820 to 1850.[17] If true, white slave traders were pro-curing record numbers of Africans precisely when the physical conditions of slave life on the plantation would appear to have been worsening.

Studies of slave demography in the British Caribbean have shown a highly positive correlation between sugar cultivation and slave mortality, with slave mortality rising with the size of the slaveholding. The same almost certainly held true in Cuba. One Cuban insurance company in 1855 drew up a table of indemnities in which the age-specific values for slaves who worked on coffee and tobacco plantations were lower than those for the average urban slave, and the values for slaves who worked on the docks or on sugar plantations were the lowest of all.[18] Domingo Del Monte asserted that deaths exceeded births on sugar but not coffee plantations. He estimated the overall slave mortality rate at 5 percent per year, the rate on the sugar plantation at 8 percent, and the rate "in the towns, on coffee properties, and other farms . . . much less."[19] Most ob-servers reckoned the slave mortality rate on the sugar plantation at be-tween 5 and 10 percent annually, and it may well have risen after the steam engine's introduction. Little wonder that planters of the antebellum South used the threat of deportation to Cuba as an instrument for disci-plining their slaves. Cuba's planters themselves had a saying, which says enough: *"Con sangre se hace azúcar"*—"Sugar is made with blood."[20]

A bell from the mill tower sounded the end of a long day's work. After a perfunctory prayer recital in the field, the slaves filed back, often in song, to secured quarters, on the newer estates to barracks of white stone and red tile, on most others to *bohíos:* crude, pest-ridden palm-thatched huts. Once there, they could look forward to a meager repast. Fresh meat was the exception; the rule was an allotment of three to eight ounces of jerked beef and a handful of plantains, supplemented or replaced by saltfish and cornmeal or rice, or some other grain or tuber. Flitches of the worst of the imported jerked beef, so-called "planter's beef," went to the slaves, often spoiled and swollen juicy red by exposure to air and salt water. Some masters allowed their slaves to raise pigs and chickens and to cultivate small provision grounds known as *conucos,* but this time-honored privilege receded during the sugar boom. Where the *conuco* did survive, the slaves of sugar plantations found they had less time to work it. Sundays and festival days could blur on the sugar plantation, for as the mill kept going, so too did the slaves. Sundays started when the mill stopped, although administrators and overseers knew well that days off denied to the slaves during the harvest could lead to violence. Manuals advised the giving of some weekday off, if not a Sunday, but warned administrators of neighboring plantations to get together to ensure that each of them gave a different day so as to prevent slave gatherings.[21]

During the grinding season, wise slave owners or, more correctly, wise plantation administrators enlarged food portions if they could, and permitted slaves to quaff cane juice. Yet the nutrients in slave food whether doled out, self-grown, or filched, did not prevent such "black" deficiency diseases as beriberi and doubtless made slaves who were working and living in miserable conditions more vulnerable to cholera, lockjaw, dysentery, tuberculosis, and other infectious diseases. Since Cuba had developed sugar plantations of the largest average size yet seen in the hemisphere, the resulting concentration of slave laborers inevitably facilitated contagion.

Ángel José Cowley's pioneering study of mortality in Havana in 1843 identified consumption and dropsy as the two primary afflictions of people of color. Consumption, another name for tuberculosis, has a well-established preference for the malnourished and impoverished. What Cowley identified as dropsy, based no doubt on the observed accumulation of fluid in body cavities, may have been rather, as recent research has suggested, beriberi. Beriberi did reach epidemic proportions on slave plantations in Cuba, where a regular diet of saltfish, jerked beef, and polished rice precluded thiamine sufficiency. Moreover, as Kenneth Kiple has pointed out in explanation of the notoriously high rates of slave infant mortality in Cuba and elsewhere in the Caribbean: "For all the major nutritional diseases, only beriberi is a killer of otherwise normal infants receiving an adequate supply of breast milk."[22]

One study of height data in the Caribbean has shown that native-born slaves who came from countries dominated by a sugar-plantation economy were shorter than native-born slaves who did not. This finding suggests that the factorylike regimentation of slaves on sugar plantations left relatively little time or space for the supplementation of protein into the diet by hunting, fishing, or gardening. In yearly totals of calories and protein, the Cuban slave diet probably improved on what was available in West Africa, to judge by the comparative data on African-born and Cuban-born slave stature. But the relations between human growth, environment, genetics, and nutrition are not well enough understood to permit an interpretive leap to conclusions about relative well-being, material or other. Human populations can show growth over time while still being seriously malnourished. Changes in diet can lead to growth while leaving slaves more vulnerable to certain deficiency diseases.[23] For Cuban-born slaves, serious nutritional imbalances and hungers persisted. Even had they consumed, on annual average, more calories and protein, under the plantation regimen they would consume, on annual average, more calories and protein. Annual averages homogenize a life that was anything but homogeneous. Seasonal shortages, abrupt shifts in work pace from dead time to harvest, periodic administrative austerity, and enforced deprivation eventually affected most slaves. The comparative susceptibility of Cuba's colored population to cholera in 1833, the repeated ravages of beriberi on slave plantations, and the smaller stature of Cuba's native-born slaves compared to the native-born slaves of the British Caribbean suggest a negative response to the more appropriate question of whether Cuban-born slaves were physically better off compared to a life they could have fashioned for themselves in a Cuba not shaped by slavery and racism.

Cholera, like tuberculosis, tends to prey on the underside of society. Its deadly bacteria spread secretively through squalor and poverty to kill horribly. To survive a cholera epidemic is not to escape the memory of it, as Plácido learned after one hit Cuba in 1833—like a "comet launched from Hell."[24] It took Fela, his beloved *morena* (black woman), and thousands of other people of color. In and around the ports, sugar carts heaped with cadavers rumbled through back streets to makeshift *campos santos,* or cemeteries. The epidemic cut down 26,920 Cubans in one seven-month period, according to government documents. Of this number, people of color numbered 22,705 or 84 percent in a total population that, according to the nearest census (1827), was 44 percent white and 56 percent colored. In the country, sick or diseased slaves of crack plantations may have had an infirmary irregularly attended by a physician, but to those familiar with the quackery of nineteenth-century *médicos,* whose cures often did more damage than the disease, an ailing slave's preference for a good cigar and a liberal prescription of *aguardiente,* the native liquor, will come as no surprise.[25]

The physical demands of sugar cultivation and the continuation of the external slave trade clearly discouraged slave family formation. Planters placed a premium on male slaves over female, and slave traders obliged by providing them two to one.[26] The sex ratio of the typical slave cargo around 1790 had more than three males for every female; by 1820 it had probably dropped to fewer than two males per female; and from 1820 to 1840 it seems to have risen to between two and three males per female.[27] Sales of female slaves to Cuba during the early decades of the sugar boom proved slow despite the efforts of the more liberal and educated Cuban planters. Their attempts to stimulate slave reproduction by proposing a head tax on male imports or a penalty on those planters with slave gangs less than one-third female met stonewalling by the majority of planters. A confidential royal order of 1804 instructed Cuban officials to promote slave marriages and the number of females on rural estates but only by appealing to—*mirabile dictu*—the planters' conscience and sense of justice, even forbidding publication of the order so as to "avoid the difficulties that would result if the blacks know about it."[28]

Francisco Arango y Parreño, one of the most prominent of those liberal and educated Cuban planters during the early decades of the sugar boom, set an example the majority of his fellow planters failed to follow. In 1829 his La Ninfa sugar plantation had 180 males and 160 females. Yet for all his interest in slave reproduction, Arango, like most other Cuban planters, had few reservations about putting females in the fields to cut cane, perhaps because, as some overseers contended then as they would also after emancipation, females worked with greater constancy. So acute an observer as Anselmo Suárez y Romero thought Cuban slave women were "made of iron" in handling their double responsibilities in the field and in the quarters.[29] They seemed tireless, and when all their loved ones had been cared for, they could be seen in and around their quarters, attempting as best they could to groom away the tedium, for their own self-respect and in preparation for another long day. A few Cuban sugar plantations, perhaps more, resembled the typical sugar plantation in the British West Indies, with females as the majority of cane cutters and males as the carters and processors. On Arango's La Ninfa, admittedly an atypical plantation because of its sex ratio, all but two of the seventy-one cane cutters were female.[30]

Plantation manuals advised masters to give slave mothers a forty- to fifty-day exemption from fieldwork after giving birth. It seems doubtful that Cuban planters adhered to this at a time when the most generous cotton planters in the southern United States, who produced a far less physical crop to be sure but under a far less commanding set of productive pressures, were allowing only a month. One old black woman who had spent her early years as a slave on a Cuban sugar plantation recalled for a white chronicler with perhaps a touch of boasting that "when slave women gave birth, in two days they went back to work."[31] When they did return to the fields, their infants appear not to have usually accompanied them, leading certain Cuban doctors to see in the resultant deprivation of regular feedings of breast milk at least a partial explanation for the high rates of slave infant mortality.[32]

The ratio of male to female slaves generally and in the countryside specifically probably declined despite fluctuations over the first half of the nineteenth century, as far as can be judged from the crude Cuban census data, but not by much, and never did it approach the experience of the antebellum Southern United States where the ending of the external slave trade in 1808 and a high rate of natural increase in some areas well before that year resulted in a rough equality of the sexes. By 1846 the leading sugar provinces of Matanzas, Cárdenas, and Mariel had sex ratios (males per 100 females) in the 16–40 age group of 173, 201, and 158 respectively. The sex ratio for the 16–40 age group in all of Cuba that year was 173 males to 100 females. According to Domingo Del Monte, Cuba's sugar plantations had an average three males for every female. Foreign travelers and Spanish officials who had been in the countryside commented that scarcely any women lived on certain plantations that had hundreds of male field hands. Male slaves rebelled in 1838 in Trinidad province on a sugar plantation that had no women. The southern United States in 1840, by comparison, possessed nearly equal proportions of male and female slaves. In the sugar state of Louisiana, the sex ratio was 106 and in the 24–54 age group, 118, high for the South but not for Cuba.[33]

Archives in Spain or Cuba may never yield the data necessary to compute reliably the rate of infant mortality for slaves, but a rate of 300 to 500 deaths per year per 1,000 live births during the year seems probable, in the light of what is known about slave demography on the sugar plantations of the British Caribbean. The death of slave infants in Cuba happened with such frequency that slave mothers were punished regularly and severely to break them of what was called their "habit" of losing them.[34] The traumas of forced migration, plantation regimentation, the imbalance of the sexes, disease and poor diet, breast-feeding practices, and deliberate sexual abstinence all combined in various ways to limit Cuban slave reproduction and, by extension, the slave family. Peoples with enduring traditions based on reverence for family and community must have found these hardships particularly galling.

Oratories and resident priests, common on the self-sufficient estates of an earlier age, were burdens to the more materialistic planters of the vastly more secular Cuban society of the sugar era. For one government official in the 1840s, the decaying oratories on the sugar estates evidenced "the faith of our fathers as well as . . . our fall and our neglect."[35] The government's conversion of city churches into customhouses in the early 1840s suggests the same. Planters could not lead where they themselves did not go. The apparent minority who went to Sunday Mass went early in order not to miss the Sunday cockfights. A priest questioned by David Turnbull in the western province of Bejucal in 1839 could only bewail the present religious languor and the passing of the good old days. "In general he [the priest] said a field negro was never in church in the whole course of his life, except at the time of his baptism."[36]

The "little difference paid to the sabbath in Cuba, that this should be the day of pleasure, cockfighting, for bulls, theatre instead of a day of devotion" disturbed numerous visitors during the sugar boom, not Anglo-Saxon Protestants alone.[37] Eulalia Bretton des Chapelles, a pious Catholic whose French kinfolk had set themselves up on several Cuban plantations, traveled up the San Juan River from Matanzas in 1839 to the former property of a titled family to take in the landscape. What moved her most was the condition of the estate chapel. "Said to be one of the oldest in the island," it lay "in ruin."[38] What she found inside suggests a dramatic revision in chapel services, for in place of a priest someone had put the stocks.

Matanzas planter Pedro Hernández Morejón recalled the meager result from laws of the early 1840s that restated the planters' religious obligations to their slaves. Cuban priests, as creatures of flesh and blood, many of them members of elite planting families, had the planter's distaste for the isolation and dreariness of rural life. Some planters did have priests on their estates during the 1840s, according to Hernández Morejón, but in Cuba's booming society it proved next to impossible to find priests with the necessary training, patience, and dedication—not to mention virtue— to bridge effectively the cultural chasm and to impart the desired social discipline.[39]

The Church fought and lost the struggle for orthodoxy in the countryside at the turn of the century when the Crown agreed with the planters' demand to liberate the plantation from religious burdens such as meatless Fridays, work-free Sundays and holidays, and the all-important tithe. Later, official attitudes toward the Roman Catholic church in Cuba, at least by the time of Miguel Tacón's rule (1834–1838), increasingly reflected the outcome of the Carlist struggles in Spain. The church's capacity to resist the secularizing power of the world market surely diminished as its property in Cuba, as in Spain, was being seized and alienated by liberal politicians to raise money. In 1840 those voices within the church not silenced or drowned out by the sugar boom largely chimed in with those of the planters.[40] José del Castillo heard one troubled curate's confession—or justification—about slavery in 1843. "The good curate with a mind candid and sincere, as his profession requires, told me he did not approve at all of slavery, as a system, that although he might have many slaves, he would never have more *than two*—one to drive his carriage, and the other, to cook, whom he did treat as children."[41]

The sheer number of slave imports must also have attenuated church efforts to attend effectively to the slave's spiritual and physical needs. Cuba had more slaves per priest in 1841 than later. The census of 1846 enumerates 481 priests to save 323,759 slave souls, a ratio of 1:673. The ratio in 1861 was 1:476. The leading sugar provinces of Matanzas, Cárdenas, and Mariel had priest/slave ratios in 1846 of 1:2,707, 1:4,786, and 1:2,355 respectively. Priests preferred to shepherd flocks in Havana: 131 of the 481 resided there. Planters could send for a priest to perform church services, but services cost money and took slaves away from their tasks. With the price of burials at about seven dollars each, minimum religious expenses on a large sugar plantation could run into hundreds of dollars annually.[42] Hearing the tingling bell of the itinerant priest no doubt pained more than one plantation administrator.

Domingo Del Monte, in response to the questions of Richard Robert Madden, a British abolitionist and friend of David Turnbull, blistered the Catholic church for its performance in the countryside. Asked if priests regularly visited plantations, Del Monte replied: "They go there only when they are sent for to baptize or marry slaves." Asked if slaves were permitted to attend church services, he replied: "On the sugar estates it is not, on the coffee estates in a very few, on the smaller farms which are situated near a church, the slaves are permitted to go to church on Sundays." Asked if the slaves were instructed in Christian doctrine, he replied:

"When the time of making sugar is over during the crop time, it is customary to repeat the rosary on the estates, *this is the only religious practice;* as to instruction in the morals or in the dogma of religion, the masters themselves are not conversant with them."[43] Del Monte might have wondered how much an African-born slave could have benefited from a sermon in an unfamiliar tongue after a sixteen-hour work day. The new administrator of the Perseverancia coffee estate in Matanzas province wrote in his diary: "The first Negro I struck was this evening for laughing at Prayers."[44]

Manumission afforded slaves a flicker of hope for self-betterment, although the prospects appeared much brighter in theory than in practice. Spanish law sanctioned an unusual process of monetary redemption known as *coartación,* in which a slave could have his value fixed by a third party, then purchase his freedom in installments. Once a slave was *coartado,* his master's dominion was supposedly limited. The law specified that in each district a special "royal defender of the slaves," the *procurador síndico,* would uphold slave rights.[45]

The British abolitionist R. R. Madden challenged this rosy view by pointing out that the *síndico* was chosen by *regidores* (town aldermen), most of whom were slaveholders themselves, and that among his duties was the conflicting responsibility of defending planter interests before district tribunals. The royal defender of the slaves, as it turned out, was also the defender of the masters. Madden, Turnbull, and other antislavery critics, while conceding that urban domestic slaves had a greater opportunity to avail themselves of Spanish law, rightly questioned the benefits of the law to illiterate field hands who were impounded on a plantation and miles distant from the nearest *síndico.* They also suspected that Cuban masters were manumitting favored female slaves or old or infirm males. Turnbull recorded the opinion of Charles Tolmé, his consular predecessor and no friend of abolitionism, that the *coartados* were "in the aggregate so numerically insignificant, as not sensibly to affect the total amount of the black and coloured population, which was previously free."[46] Recent scholarship has largely sustained these views.

Less well known but certainly as revealing is that during the sugar boom, confusion existed in Spanish law; substantial differences of opinion arose within Cuba as to precisely what *coartación* meant, whether a "slave *coartado* continues being as much a slave as the one who is fully so."[47] Many Cuban slaveholders believed that *coartación* was a privilege to be bestowed on a slave by the master, not a right to be initiated by the slave. One legal expert who strongly disagreed with this position still had to acknowledge that *"coartación* is almost unavailing on the estates. In fact almost never is it practiced. Very few are the estates that have any slave *coartado* among all those who comprise their holdings."[48]

Of the 954 slaves who gained their liberty in Havana in 1810 and 1811, 755, or about 79 percent, had gained it by purchase either on their own or with help from the Afro-Cuban *cabildos.* The Spanish government estimated manumissions in 1846 at only 500 per year, a rate of 1.5 per 1,000 slaves. If that is true, manumission in the years preceding La Escalera may have been proportionately less frequent in Cuba than in most of the supposedly more restrictive and more prejudiced British West Indian slave colonies during the first decades of the nineteenth century. Of the twelve British colonies for which there are data in 1808, eight had higher annual manumission rates than Cuba in 1846. Of the sixteen colonies for which there are data in 1820, nine had higher annual manumission rates.[49] Rare figures compiled by Spanish officials for the less repressive period of 1858–1862 (see Table I) show an annual average of 1,892 manumissions. For the census year of 1861 the manumission rate would be 4.4 per 1,000 slaves, higher than all but a few of the British colonies in 1808 and 1820 and substantially higher than the 0.45 per 1,000 slaves in 1850 for the antebellum South where access to freedom was notoriously limited.[50]

Slave family life did not fare well on Cuban sugar plantations. Thus planters lost a means of social control that might have ameliorated the slave's lot, for the family serves to replicate social patterns in individuals, to instruct them in prevailing norms and values. In the Americas, wherever African slavery was the central labor system, whites and nonwhites

TABLE I. *Manumissions, 1858–1862*

Year	Men	Women	Total
1858	895	1161	2056
1859	845	1147	1992
1860	761	1158	1919
1861	694	935	1629
1862	822	1044	1866
TOTAL	4017	5445	9462

SOURCE: Cuba. Centro de estadística, *Noticias estadísticas de la isla de Cuba en 1862* . . . (Havana, 1864).

to varying extents shaped and shared a common culture. The experience of the slave family in the southern United States indicates that a stable, native-born slave family would more greatly facilitate the internalization of elements from the white-dominated culture and social order, no matter how much a slave family might reshape those elements to fit its particular needs. A stable family more firmly attached the slave to the plantation and infinitely raised the stakes should he want to rebel. In Cuban slave society there was much less attachment. The stakes were lower.

Because Cuba has no equivalent to the slave narratives systematically collected in the United States in the 1930s under the Work Projects Administration (WPA), any attempt to construct the slave's view of slavery in Cuba around 1840 necessarily requires considerable extrapolation from a slender body of evidence. The autobiography of Juan Francisco Manzano, one of the first of few slave narratives from Spanish America, tells a poignant and insightful story for the period immediately before Turnbull's appointment. Manzano was not a typical Cuban slave; he spent most of his youth as a house slave in noble families; he learned to read and write; he received his freedom.[51] Still, precisely because his situation relative to the mass of field hands can be seen to have been in some ways favored, his voice does provide a standard against which to measure the probable conditions under which other slaves lived.

Manzano's treatment as a slave under a succession of masters and mistresses oscillated wildly between paternalistic benignity and capricious brutalization. Some, he said, he grew to love; others filled him with terror. He suffered most under María de la Concepción del Manzano y Jústiz, the Marquesa de Prado-Ameno. He became her "lap-dog," with little space of his own, tailing her almost everywhere "like an automaton with my arms crossed." Punishment happened frequently and varied in severity according to his misstep or the whim of his mistress.

As a young boy:

It was the custom to shut me up in a place for charcoal, for four-and-twenty hours at a time. . . . Here after being flogged I was placed, with orders to the slaves, under threats of the greatest punishment, to abstain from giving me a drop of water. What I suffered from hunger and thirst, tormented with fear, in a place so dismal and distant from the house, and almost suffocated with the vapours arising from the common sink, that was close to my dungeon, and constantly terrified by the rats that passed over me and about me, may be easily imagined.[52]

As a teen-ager:

My ordinary crimes were—not to hear the first time I was called; or if at the time of getting a buffet I uttered a word of complaint; and I led a life of so much misery, daily receiving blows on the face, that often made the blood spout from both my nostrils; no sooner would I hear myself called than I would begin to shiver, so that I could hardly keep on my legs, but supposing this to be only shamming on my part, frequently would I receive from a stout negro lashes in abundance.[53]

Manzano came to know the hard life on the sugar plantation, for several times he was sentenced there for correction and, as he recalled, the very name of the family *ingenio* and that of a particular overseer would fill him "with horror." What slavery had done to him, that sense of natal alienation in slavery, which Orlando Patterson has discussed with great erudition in *Slavery and Social Death,* Manzano tried to express in a letter to Domingo Del Monte about the writing of his autobiography:

A sketch of so many calamities does not seem but a massive record of impostures and even from such a tender age the cruel lashings made me aware of my humble condition. I feel mortified in telling it and I do not know how to really show the facts, leaving the most terrible part in the inkwell. I wish I had other facts with which to fill the history of my life without having to remember the excessive rigor with which my former mistress [the Marquesa de Prado-Ameno] treated me, obliging me or placing me out of dire necessity to appeal to perilous flight in order to relieve my poor body of the constant mortification which I could not suffer any more. Thus being prepared to see a debilitated creature, wallowing in the most grave sufferings, delivered to various overseers, being without the least exaggeration the target of misfortune, I fear to be totally undeserving in your eyes. But remember, sir, when you read this that I am a slave and that a slave is a dead being before his master.[54]

Slaves regarded as recalcitrant could expect severe punishment. In the countryside the overseer silenced most slave complaints with application of the lash. Planters old and new never doubted that force ultimately kept the mill rollers turning. A dying breed like the sugar noble José Montalvo y Castillo, who lectured on the value of paternalism and religion, and on the importance of planter residence on the site to the smoother operation of the sugar plantation, called for the humane management of slaves on the grounds that their nature demanded it, yet in the same breath acknowledged that to instill a required level of work discipline meant first to instill fear.[55] Cuban slaveholders were accustomed to say, *"Es preciso tiranizar ó correr el riesgo de ser tiranizado"* ("One must tyrannize or run the risk of being tyrannized").[56]

Bocabajo ("mouth downwards") was a plantation technique in which slaves were bound or held face down and given a number of stripes with a platted, raw bullhide whip. The law said no more than twenty-five, but that limit was transgressed with frequency and seeming impunity. Whipping canes, something like the *sjamboks* currently being wielded by South African policemen, appeared to be more popular in eastern Cuba. Some overseers swore by whips of manatee skin rather than of bullhide. *Boca-bajo "llevando cuentas"* or "keeping count" called for the slave to count his own lashes out loud as they were being applied. Should pain short-circuit either his voice or memory, the count would return to zero. *Boca-bajo "a dos manos,"* "two-handed," meant the alternative application of the whip to the slave's back by two whippers. By 1840 a plantation "novena" had come to mean not a Catholic devotion but nine stripes laid on a slave's back for nine consecutive days.[57]

Overseers also resorted to stocks, chains, shackles, and other paraphernalia to inculcate discipline or gratify their own urges. Upon the return of two runaways, both prime field hands, the administrator of the Perseverancia coffee plantation ordered punishments of four consecutive days in the stocks with heavy irons and twenty-four lashes each "on the naked bottom," after which their wounds were to be lanced and rubbed down with rum and salt.[58] A young doctor from the northern United States on a Cuban plantation in 1830 described what commonly happened to runaways. "The poor wretches fettered and hoppled as they were from the waist to the feet with long heavy links & rings of iron [were] scarcely able with the burdens on their heads to drag the ponderous weight over the ground or place one leg before the other. For to prevent any further attempts to escape beside the links which pass down outside of each leg from the waist there is a ring around each ankle & a cross piece connecting these two together in the manner precisely that cattle are hoppled."[59] The doctor thought such treatment cruel and unusual punishment, but, as he recorded in his diary, the Señora who owned the estate, a good woman in other respects, could not understand his complaint about what, to her, was normal.

If not the overseer, a slave driver (*contramayoral*) applied the punishment. Like their counterparts in the United States, Jamaica, and indeed throughout most of the slaveholding regions of the New World, the Cuban drivers had a reputation for brutality. There was much contradictory evidence. Overseers had some sense of the dangers of their work; they often served as the first targets during plantation uprisings. To put a slave in a position of authority, to get the work out, to dispense punishment, gave useful distance to the overseer. Where the African slave trade fluctuated in numbers and direction but continued effectually as in Cuba during the first half of the nineteenth century, elevation of a field slave to the position of driver promoted ethnic animosities and thereby enhanced white efforts to divide and rule the slave population. Lydia Cabrera, the well-known Cuban ethnologist, has documented, through conversations with former slaves, one Lucumí driver who singled out Carabalí or Congo field hands for punishment.[60]

But a blanket condemnation of the slave driver is too easy. Some Cuban slave drivers were brutes, to be sure. But a careful reading of evidence indicates that the behavior of drivers reflected the ambivalence of their position. They might lead those of their color in rebellion as well as punish them. They had, for example, led revolts on the Peñas Altas sugar plantation in 1812, the Esperanza coffee plantation in 1817, and the Salvador coffee plantation in 1833.[61] No doubt Cuban slaves, whether Lucumí or Carabalí, linked together by a common oppression, might have contributed to the drivers' very existence by their recognition that if whipping must occur, as on every New World slave plantation it inevitably must—and on the Cuban sugar plantations of the 1840s frequently so—much better to have one of their own doing it. As practitioners of the sadomasochistic arts know well enough, a lash can be laid on creatively. Former slaves from plantations on which slave drivers did the whippings might not have reflected on the depth and number of stripes if the white overseer had applied them. Situations must also have occurred when a driver had to be tough on some hothead to protect the slave community as a whole. Young slaves who witnessed black whipping black would not always have known whether the stripes were well laid on or not, but the distressing image would remain to be conveyed to chroniclers.

As a means of promoting order among multiethnic, African-born slaves, paternalism would have acted to bind individual slaves to the master instead of to other slaves and, in general, to allow moral authority to push brute force into the background. Yet paternalism never sank deep roots in the countryside the way it had in the towns because the majority of Cuban planters spurned the rural residency required to instill it. Their exemplars in the town were the absentee nobles, the Peñalvers and the Chacóns, not the parvenu Forcades or Diagos. Francisco Diago, whose father Pedro, a Basque immigrant, had made a fortune as a merchant-planter, had not acquired the habits of an absentee landlord, at least not by 1841. "I am scarcely ever in the city." But he was learning. "The desire to increase our crops obliges me to spend the greater part of the year in the country: sometimes contrary to my liking."[62]

Machiavelli counseled the ruler of a newly acquired state to reside there, because a resident ruler can confront problems as they happen, can more readily prevent despoliation by surrogates, and can form bonds of personal attachment with his subjects. "Consequently, they have more reason to love him if they choose to be good, and more reason to fear him if they choose to behave otherwise."[63] Without those bonds of personal attachment, Cuba's planters could not generate that "moral force" about whose loss they complained so often in the early 1840s. When the planter Andrés Zayas, in an essay published posthumously by the Havana Economic Society in 1836, offered as his first rule to improve order on the *ingenios* that the administrator treat the slaves as a "proper paterfamilias," he offered no rule at all, for hired surrogates had little incentive to act that way, and the slaves knew better.[64] The tendency of the Cuban slaveholder, by his chronic absenteeism, to give his overseer a free rein on the slaves elicited comment from Southern slaveholders, as in this self-serving yet insightful observation from George Fitzhugh of Virginia, perhaps the most interesting of Southern ideologues:

It is remarkable at first view that in Cuba, where the law attempts to secure mild treatment to the slave, he is inhumanly treated. . . . In Cuba, many of the slaves are savages, and do not elicit the domestic affection of the master, who sees in them little more than brutes. The master is, besides, often an absentee, and tho' overseers be far more humane than Irish rent-collectors, they have neither the interests nor feelings of resident masters.[65]

David Turnbull noticed one Cuban overseer dressed for work "armed to the teeth" with pistols, whip, and sword.[66] More than occasionally slaves repaid brutality in kind. Some slave gangs even acquired a dangerous reputation for indiscipline; one anonymous report of March 1839 manifested great concern about the unruly slaves of *ingenio* Viejo, owned by Juan de Dios Gómez. They had rebelled earlier when an overseer had attempted to punish one of their number. They placed the overseer in the stocks, and then whipped him almost to death. They were still restive.[67] Slave behavior, collectively and individually, in whatever country it existed, ranged across a spectrum from rebelliousness to docility: sabotage, arson, hamstringing of stock, poisoning, theft, shirking, feigned sickness and stupidity, flight, assassination, insurrection, as well as suicide and self-induced abortion.

Although all protest, passive and violent, asserted the slaves' basic hu-

agency

manity in opposition to the logic of slavery, not all protest was effective
political resistance or an aid to liberation. The suicide of an able slave
leader, or an individual outburst of blind rage, for example, may well
have impaired the possibilities for the whole. Collective slave resistance
need not be system challenging. Like the jacqueries of medieval Europe,
they could aim to redress purely immediate grievances or to respond to
local violations of the unwritten ground rules between master and slave
within the general framework of accommodation. Certain slaves showed
loyalty to their masters by betraying their fellows, or by fawning, cring-
ing, or indulging in self-hate. Yet the absence or infrequency of resistance
does not prove acquiescence. In nearly every major slave revolt in the
Americas, skilled or privileged slaves were among its leaders; hence, docility coexisted with militancy within many individuals. The slave revolution
in Saint Domingue occurred in a slave society where acts of collective
slave violence seem to have been relatively infrequent. As Sidney Mintz
has argued:

Considerable resistance involved as its precondition some processes of culture
change, of adaptation, on the part of the slaves. . . . The house slave who
poisoned her master's family by putting ground glass in the food had first to
become the family cook. The runaway slaves who created viable communities
in the hinterlands of so many slave societies needed to learn techniques of
cultivation in an alien environment. And the slaves who plotted armed revolts
in the marketplaces had first to produce for market and to gain permission to
carry their produce there.[68]

The Cuban Countess Merlin de las Mercedes Santa Cruz tells a story
that expresses the range of possibilities. In 1839 on the estate of her
cousin Rafael Montalvo, a "sugar noble," slaves turned their machetes on
the overseer, then paraded to the Big House to pass the corpse from man
to man before the horrified eyes of Montalvo's wife. Several whites suffered wounds, but only the one overseer was killed. Dr. Pedro Bauduy attended the casualties, and his mother-in-law recorded his story. According
to Bauduy, some twenty-five to thirty Lucumís had risen up in revenge
against a cruel sugarmaster. Montalvo had gone to Matanzas, and, as the
rebels approached the Big House, the house servants "continued faithful
& shut themselves up with their mistress and her children." The local
magistrate with eight poorly armed irregulars confronted those who were
outside. "They fired but their opponents well trained formed in a line &
each provided with a shield of hide . . . the ball glanced and they [the
slaves] remained unhurt & would immediately close upon their adversaries

with their *machettes*." The irregulars withdrew. The Marqués de Cardenas, Montalvo's neighbor and brother-in-law, rode onto the scene a short time later in response to the general alarm. His command to the rebels to retire led to a new attack instead, and he barely escaped, thanks to the selfless defense of his slave body servant, who absorbed "15 wounds in the head, had one arm broke in two places & the other broke & so lacerated as to render amputation of it necessary."[69] The return of Montalvo and the arrival of regular troops reestablished order. Many of the rebels fled into the cane fields. Some escaped reenslavement by suicide, hanging themselves. One defiant rebel, allegedly a tribal leader, who was captured despite mortal wounds, only regretted his inability to kill "all the white men."

Slave suicides were frequent in Cuba around 1840, the more so where the African slave trade continued, since West African theology generally approved of suicide for prisoners of war. Rare is the Cuban plantation diary or account book that has no mention of them. Plantations of several hundred or more slaves recorded at least two or three suicides each year. Joseph Goodwin, overseer on a large coffee estate in Matanzas in 1821, entered in his diary for September 28: "Found the two Bosals [*bozales*] this morning, suspended by a rope in the woods, not far distant from the House, they were the two best Bosals on the Plantation. I have not yet learned the cause of the unfortunate circumstance, for the present suffice it to say they are no more."[70] An island-wide study of suicides initiated by the Real Audienca Pretorial of Havana in 1847 showed that of the documented cases from 1839 to 1846, about 88 percent were slaves. The numbers jumped dramatically from 1843 to 1845 because of, as one report argued, "the rigor and severity used to repress the conspiracies of the blacks."[71]

Individual and collective slave outbursts occurred with regularity in the decade or so before Turnbull's consulship. Franklin Knight's observation that "large organized slave revolts . . . were rather rare in Cuba" can be sustained only if *large* is defined as meaning hundreds of slaves from more than a single plantation and if the standard of comparison is not the other slave societies in the Americas.[72] In June and August of 1825 hundreds of slaves on more than twenty estates in Matanzas looted houses, burned fields, and killed whites. Scattered plantation uprisings broke out in western Cuba in 1826, 1828, 1830, and 1831. In August 1833 more than 300 slaves revolted on the great Salvador coffee plantation then moved on to attack the town of Banes and several neighboring plantations in the western district of Guanajay. In June 1835 slaves rebelled on *in-*

genios Carolina and Magdalena and *cafetal* Burato in Matanzas province. The same year, about fifty people of color, primarily of the *cabildo* Lucumí Eyó, rose up outside the walls of Havana at the Chávez Bridge. In 1838 slaves celebrated the Day of Kings in the Trinidad Valley by erupting on the sugar plantation of Juan Batista Armenteros. In that same province that same year, frustrated slaves rebelled on the estate of a former Philadelphian, John Baker—a slaveholder who held no female slaves. Numerous estates in Matanzas province suffered uprisings in 1839. Slaves rebelled on estates in the provinces of Havana, Cienfuegos, and Trinidad one year later.[73] Saúl Vento, the director of the Archivo Histórico of Matanzas, has turned up no fewer than 399 reported cases of slave violence from 1825 to 1850 in Matanzas province alone.[74]

"Revolution in Cuba," Carlos Franqui, once a member of Fidel Castro's 26th of July movement, has written, "means burning sugar cane—it did in 1868, 1895, and 1930–33, and it did for us."[75] But it did before 1868 too, with such frequency in the province of Cárdenas around 1840 that planters conducted an inquiry. It concluded that they could best prevent fires by ugrading the slave diet and by ringing the trash shed (the arsonists' prime kindling—the remains of processed cane were stored for fuel) with a pen in which slaves would keep their own pigs.[76]

Short-term absenteeism was epidemic in Cuba as it was in every American slave society despite punishment by chains and lashes. Gross sexual imbalances on Cuban sugar plantations alone gave male slaves necessary reason to prowl away from the compound. Fewer runaways escaped to anonymity in the city or to an arduous life in the wilderness. Sometimes all the slaves on a particular plantation, women and men alike, would run off together, as they did on *ingenio* Pan in 1830.[77] Maroon enclaves, the larger ones known as *palenques* and the smaller ones as *rancherías,* appeared as early as the sixteenth century and reached full prominence in the first half of the nineteenth. These enclaves continued to disrupt the slave system down through the wars for Cuban independence.

In 1796 the planter-dominated Economic and Governing Committee of the Havana *consulado* (a planter-merchant organization to promote economic development) compiled a comprehensive program on the registration, capture, detention, and return of runaways, pending proper identification and payment of costs by owners. In essence this program continued in force in the early 1840s. It defined a *palenque* as a gathering of seven or more maroons or runaways and enjoined slaveholders to provide detailed, monthly reports on the number and description of the maroons from their respective plantations. *Capitanes de partidos* (district magistrates) had to furnish monthly reports on the *palenques* and *rancherías* in their districts. Most *palenques* had fewer than fifty members; a few had hundreds; at least one confederation of maroon villages in eastern Cuba in the early eighteenth century seems to have had more than a thousand members. The number of maroons in Cuba east and west in the 1840s could have sustained concentrations of more than a thousand, but maroon leaders had more sense than to make the government's job of search and destroy easier. The number of *palenques,* based on the denunciations to be found in the Junta de Fomento, rose sharply in the decade of the 1830s and reached a high point in the early 1840s. The Havana *consulado* itself set aside funds for expeditions against them and maintained a prison for the recaptured in Havana. On almost any sunny day in and around Havana, recaptured runaways, women as well as men, could be spotted in a chain gang with distinctive tin dog tags and "a scantiness of clothing deserving of censure" breaking stone and doing road work.[78]

In 1840 Captain-General Pedro Téllez de Girón was concerned about maroons, for estimates of their number in the eastern end of the island exceeded one thousand. He was worried about securing the countryside: "Besides the excessive number of blacks in *palenques* in various parts of this Island, we have as neighbors Jamaica and St. Domingue where the greater part of their inhabitants are freed persons of color, very disposed to contact with the maroons and inclined toward rebellion for the idea of liberty, which they have always tried to impress on slavery [here]."[79]

Sophisticated maroon communities grew up in the Sierra de los Órganos in the west and the Sierra Maestra to the east, but any forbidding location—a belt of mangroves, a veiled cavern, the crater of a mute volcano—might lodge a maroon band. On the cays of the giant Ciénaga de Zapata ("Shoe Swamp"), just north of the Bay of Pigs, scores of maroons struggled for space with the crocodiles, mosquitoes, and black flies. The sugar plantation was no heaven, so prospective maroons, unlike Satan, usually had to choose between rule in one hell or servitude in another. The Matanzas black belt lacked the most favorable terrain for maroons, but in the 1840s it did have a notorious patch called El Espinal, near the source of the Puerto Escondido River.[80] The first meaning of *espinal*—a place of thickets and brambles—explains why maroons located there. Slave hunters would have appreciated the second meaning—a hard and perilous undertaking.

The state and individual planters hired professional slave hunters (*rancheadores*) with their packs of trained bloodhounds—by reputation the best in the Caribbean—to track down and subdue maroons. The survival of the remarkable diary of Francisco Estévez permits a rare close-up of this hard-bitten job around 1840. Estévez, like most slave hunters, was a *montero,* from the Vuelta Abajo region, who hunted slaves in addition to scratching out a little coffee with a few slaves on a meager plot along the lowlands and foothills of the Sierra de los Órganos. From 1837 to 1842 he led slave-hunting parties against the region's maroons. The highland cracks and crevices sheltered hundreds of them: men, women, and children. Estévez knew them as formidable adversaries who played the hostile surroundings to advantage, whether to cover a strategic escape or to fend off a frontal attack. Days of tracking through wilderness, downpours, and a merciless sun often led to deserted encampments. In one Estévez found

spears . . . many powderhorns with good quality powder, sharp knives, much shot of the type that is sold in taverns, seven or 8 bundles of coarse cloth for wadding in different dwellings. From what I can reckon, they had 6 or 7 firearms. We also found 14 or 15 crates of plantains, pork and beef, 40 old blankets, much men's and women's clothing, an assortment of pots and kettles, all of which we heaped together and burned along with the encampment.[81]

Estévez's typical confrontation with maroons ended indecisively with dead dogs but few maroon casualties or prisoners. Unless the government was willing to commit much larger money and forces, he doubted whether the maroons could ever be eliminated. He would have understood the ten-to-one ratio laid down by modern military experts as essential to wiping out guerrillas. On one occasion he encountered a stronghold of about fifty of them.

We were not able to surprise them because they had lookouts everywhere, and we were only able to capture 6 alive and one dead. Besides it was midday and excessively hot. The dogs were weakened by fatigue and thirst. [The maroons] left behind 14 spears, some sharp knives, and machetes. We also found some 25 arrobas of pork and beef and three places where they had their slaughterhouses. In one of them we found a great many skeletons and more than 50 head of cattle.[82]

The very existence of maroon communities inspired many slaves to desert their masters. And in carrying out their own depredations, maroons frequently liberated slaves and ravaged plantations. But at the margin of Cuba's slave society maroons did not necessarily pose a revolutionary or protorevolutionary threat. As David Barry Gaspar has indicated for Antigua prior to 1700, maroon activity might well have acted as a safety valve against the complete overthrow of the planter regime.[83] For most of their history in Cuba, including the early 1840s, maroons possessed neither the overall unity nor the inclination to end slavery per se, however much they struggled against their own enslavement. They largely aspired to restore a traditional and hierarchical African or modified-African society in an American setting, to live relatively isolated from and untrammeled by the slave system. Maroons in Cuba, like maroons elsewhere in the Caribbean, did not always have good relations with plantation slaves and could act in alliance with whites as an instrument of repression. At times, maroons took property and loved ones from plantation slaves as well as from their masters.

Maroon activity in the nineteenth century would, nevertheless, have a particularly debilitating, if not structurally destructive, impact on the Cuban regime. First, revolutionary contagion had swept over neighboring Saint Domingue in 1791. Thousands of slaves under the masterful leadership of Toussaint L'Ouverture had thrown out their white oppressors and in 1804 forged the second independent nation in the New World. In the wake of the Saint Domingue Revolution, conspiracies with revolutionary potential had surfaced in Cuba, with the Conspiracy of Morales in 1796 and the Conspiracy of Aponte in 1812 the two most conspicuous examples. Haunted by Saint Domingue and its legacy, Cuban slaveholders could never be sure whether a maroon foray was business as usual or the beginning of the end.

Second, if the estimates of Manuel Moreno Fraginals are correct, the proportion of creole slaves in the plantation slave population was increasing from about 4 percent in the period from 1791 to 1822 to about 20 percent in the period from 1823 to 1844.[84] As maroons, some creole slaves would develop new patterns of resistance, some of which indicate pollenization from the "Age of Democratic Revolution," which extended well beyond 1815. To be sure, the restorationist outlook would continue to have force among them, but a few would reformulate strategy, eschewing collaboration, accommodation, or desertion for an implacable hostility to slavery and the planters who sustained it.

Verification of the influence of liberal-democratic ideology on the patterns of slave resistance in the Americas cannot and should not be measured by the mere counting of overt acts of resistance in immediate response to events in Saint Domingue. Liberal-democratic ideology did not directly teach slaves to revolt for a society of their own with a government of their own. These ideological currents emanated from a variety of sources over a long period of time, and how slaves and free people of color in the Americas received and used them in combination with their own traditions of resistance to enslavement varied from place to place according to a complex of local conditions and constraints.[85] In the Americas, well before the Saint Domingue Revolution, movements led by African-born slaves, native-born slaves, or some combination in several regions threatened to overthrow their masters and construct new social and political institutions. The slave conspiracy of 1736 in Antigua and Cuffee's rebellion of 1763 in Berbice are two examples from the British Caribbean.

But, as slave and free colored resistance to slavery increased in the nineteenth century in Cuba and elsewhere, signs of change can be identified in the language of resistance and objectives of leaders, their attitudes toward property, and the willingness of rebels to engage the political and economic realities of a wider world. Liberal-democratic ideology increasingly taught leaders to challenge the system of slavery itself—even though tactical considerations might present short-term difficulties—and to seek to survive in a web of nations by becoming one.[86]

How Cuba's slaves and free coloreds came into contact with foreign ideological currents remains somewhat obscure. Physical and cultural barriers certainly militated against the transmission of liberal-democratic ideas and their assimilation by the majority of Afro-Cubans, especially those African-born slaves on remote plantations. But oppressed people have their own intelligence and communication networks. Slaves and free coloreds walked the docks of Cuba's port towns; they hawked news and goods with peddlers and foreign smugglers; they picked up white table-talk and passed it to more worldly comrades on Sundays, festival days, and in the Afro-Cuban *cabildos;* they overheard conversations among whites; they mixed with the thousands of slaves who had emigrated with their French masters from Saint Domingue; and they heard the messages from the drums. The mass of Cuba's slaves may not have had a firm understanding of liberal dogma and the Age of Democratic Revolution, but they did know the difference between "them" and "us," between life in the cane field and the promise of something better from a colored leadership that clearly had some such understanding, a leadership that took from liberal dogma to fashion a political language adequate to express and fundamentally challenge the day-in, day-out experience of oppression in a slave society. Slaves in Saint Domingue had rallied around Toussaint L'Ouverture's restatement of French Revolutionary ideology, becoming, in C. L. R. James's words, black Jacobins, when the majority could not even speak French.[87] Spanish authorities were quick to point the finger at British abolitionists for spreading antislavery sedition. But Cuba's colored classes were performing well on their own.

In 1842 Captain-General Gerónimo Valdés attempted to address the specific problem of slave unrest by attaching a code of forty-eight slave regulations to his *Bando de Gobernación y Policía* or edict of police regulations. (See Appendix I.) Even though this code was tougher than the more celebrated but disregarded one of 1789, Valdés had actually put it forth in an attempt to tread a middle line, to keep peace, and to encourage reproduction on the plantation by striking a balance between fair treatment and discipline, for he understood how far practice had diverged from previous law with respect to the planters' physical treatment of their slaves. To Cuban slaveholders, the 1842 slave code did not represent, as Franklin Knight has asserted it did, "increased repression" or a "severe hardening" of their attitudes toward their slaves.[88] The slaveholders, in fact, complained that the code, as an attempt to rein them in, treated them too harshly and the slaves not harshly enough, particularly articles 6 and 12.[89]

A look at the regulations reveals why slaveholders were so upset. Articles 1 through 5 deal with the master's religious obligations to his slaves. Articles 6 through 15 establish guidelines for the proper physical treatment of slaves. Articles 16 through 33 lay down rules for plantation management and social control. Articles 34 through 40 fix the legal means by which slaves can obtain their freedom. And Articles 41 through 48 establish rules for punishments and fines. Articles 6 and 12 say this:

Masters shall necessarily give their slaves in the country two or three meals a day as they may think best, provided that they may be sufficient to maintain them and restore them from their fatigues, keeping in mind that six or eight plantains or its equivalent in sweet potatoes, yams, yuccas, and other edible roots, eight ounces of meat or codfish, four ounces of rice or other pottage or meal is standardized as daily food and of absolute necessity for each individual.

In ordinary times slaves shall work nine or ten hours daily, the master arranging these hours as best he can. On sugar plantations during harvest time, the hours shall be sixteen, arranged in such a way that the slave shall have two hours in the day to rest and six at night to sleep.

In light of the chronic unrest of the 1830s and early 1840s, Valdés may have reasoned that planter attempts to rationalize production were businesslike but politically foolish. While trimming expenses and expanding production, planters had been wiping out traditional obligations and institutions that promoted order on the plantation. Overworked slaves without religious indoctrination, without provision grounds, without a family life were becoming intractable. The planters themselves confessed that "the edifice of their authority [was] crumbling down by its very foundation."[90] Their moral force had vanished. What discipline was left only physical force could maintain.

Francisco Arango had contended in 1791 that Cuba would never suffer the same fate as Saint Domingue because, for one, "The French have looked at them [the slaves] as beasts, the Spanish as men."[91] Had Spanish slave laws defined substance rather than form, he might have had a point. And perhaps the memory of slave life in Cuba before the intensification of the plantation system had colored his vision of the future. But by 1840 Arango's words sounded like only gross promotion for himself and his class. Then what Prospero said to Caliban might have more accurately described the mood of Cuban planters: "Thou most lying slave whom stripes may move, not kindness."

The slaves themselves were also changing. "Some people have begun to see that the refractory spirit now prevailing among slaves is not one of a kind to be tamed again into a passive conformity to their unnatural condition, as it was with slaves in ancient times, when slavery was understood to be what Aristotle defined it to be [i.e., as a natural condition]." The slaves, according to planter José del Castillo, were starting to comprehend that slavery was as Las Siete Partidas, the famous Spanish law code of the thirteenth century, had defined it—"un estado contra natura."[92] However isolated or individual the acts of slave resistance had been before 1840, their cumulative effect had unsettled the slave system and the whites who dominated it. The bonds of control had weakened in the countryside, never to the extent of making mass insurrections commonplace but certainly to enhance among members of more organized elites their sense of the possibility of uprisings and to make white planters more conscious of their own insecurity.

To counteract the slaves' refractory spirit, a few planters in the early 1840s returned to older, more paternalistic, and less businesslike methods. Castillo had looked around him in 1843 and saw religion as a "coin out of currency." Rapid change, rampant materialism, an out-of-control slave trade, and an uncontrolled market were dissolving the old bonds in which adherence to the Catholic faith had reinforced a stable hierarchy of reciprocal obligations between master and slave. More slaves were entering Cuban households but fewer as members of them. The paternalistic family was not extending, not even in the towns. Former slaves remembered the days when slave children were baptized on the plantation as a favorite time, a day to serve the interests of slaves and their master, when a master might even demonstrate that he really possessed the superior trait of generosity by implementing the process of *coartación* for the slave parents of the baptized child. If the testimony of the 1840s is to be believed, fewer masters were feeling duty bound to cultivate those institutionalized intimacies that were the hallmark of patriarchal rule, whether to witness slave baptisms or to call Masses for the salvation of a dearly departed slave soul. Castillo recalled those bygone days in the household of his eighty-year-old aunt and the personal, playful atmosphere between her and one young slave, who expected and got a regular ration of fruit and sweetmeats. But "Our new fangled, heathenish civilization has banished those habits of life out of our present society."[93]

But now a few planters sought to return to earlier patterns of paternalism. They reintroduced religious instruction, recruited more female slaves, and restored slave privileges like the *conuco*.[94] But belated concessions from a minority of planters could not undo the damage already done: deteriorating slave working conditions; planter absenteeism; a burgeoning number of unacculturated African slaves concentrated on larger plantations; a growing numerical imbalance between whites and people of color; persistent maroon activity; serious rifts among the whites; sufficient social maneuverability, especially in urban areas, to permit slave and free colored leaders to organize their people; and the penetration of a liberal-democratic ideology that was turning rebels into revolutionaries. These factors overmatched both the slave code of 1842 and Valdés's edict of police regulations of which the slave code was a part.

Any benefits slaves might have obtained from the implementation of the slave code of 1842, they hardly received. Subaltern officials charged with enforcement under article 48 reported back to Valdés that hostile planters had obstructed their efforts. Slave violence had fostered a general feeling of insecurity among the planters, and insecurity had fed their intolerance. They refused to abide by a set of rules that would raise costs, regulate production, and undercut their authority on the plantation. At a time when planters were projecting blame for slave unrest on the lax discipline on someone else's estate, a call for moderation in the physical treatment of slaves went largely unheeded. Planters who were checking their flanks for abolitionists regarded such benignity inappropriate. "Now," Gaspar Betancourt despaired, "it is a crime, even to have or show compassion to the slaves: humanity, good treatment, none of this can be recommended today because they are synonymous with abolitionism."[95]

Valdés was compelled to retreat. The status quo required the peninsular government to maintain its alliance with Creole planters. Shortly after the publication of the slave code, Valdés issued a circular that relieved his subordinates of their duties to enforce it. They could not "introduce themselves into the estates of the country, nor in the domestic management of the slaves, nor in any kind of search direct or indirect."[96] The code would remain on the books as the legal standard of slave treatment, as an ideal. But Cuban slaveholders, to greater and lesser degrees, would continue to ignore it in reality.

What V. S. Naipaul has observed for Spanish slave laws in general could be said for the slave code of 1842. It was relatively humane. "Doubtless for this reason it was seldom followed."[97]

3

Cuban Whites and the
Problem of Slavery

Terrible is the slavery one suffers, but even more terrible is the slavery one imposes. You say, "Ah, if only Cubans were not slaves." I say, "Ah, if only Cubans did not own slaves."

ANTONIO ZAMBRANA, *El negro Francisco*, 1875, in *El negro Francisco; Novela de costumbres* (Havana, 1953), 158.

Spanish officials baldly confessed to the use of slavery to secure their "most precious jewel" to the imperial crown. In 1836 the Spanish minister Calatrava, in a meeting with United States Minister to Spain Cornelius Van Ness, looked incredulous when asked how Spain could continue to milk Cuba of revenue, deny political reforms, and still hope to maintain control. According to Van Ness, Calatrava "believes that the fear of the negroes is worth an army of 100,000 men, and that it will prevent the whites from making any revolutionary attempts."[1] "In Cuba," Lorenzo Allo, a Cuban lawyer and separatist, would say in 1854, "there is no wild beast other than the Spanish Government—a wild beast which has engendered a two-headed monster, domestic slavery and political slavery."[2] Allo agonized over the common chain of dependency that bound masters and slaves in Cuba. By denying personal freedom to hundreds of thousands of Africans, Cuban planters were denying political freedom to themselves. When they spoke to each other about servility they spoke with all the insight supplied by life under a fitful imperial authoritarianism.

Cuba had plunged into the world market during a portentous historical moment. While in some regions of the Americas slaveholding planters were thriving on the abrogation of human rights, people in Europe and the Americas were following the example of the French and taking up the sword to extend them. Cuba's sister colonies in Mexico and South America fought wars of liberation from 1808 to 1825. Cuba did not.

Masonic conspiracies in 1810, 1823 and 1826, a potentially revolutionary conspiracy of the people of color in 1812, and a constitutional *pronunciamiento* in eastern Cuba in 1836 indicate the receptivity of Cuba to liberal propositions and the wishful thinking embodied in the label "ever-faithful island."[3] Jacobin writings were in demand among young Creoles in the several decades before 1840. One vacationer in the 1840s who heard their songs wrote, "the air . . . sounded very much like the Marseillaise, and . . . the word *libertad* occurred oftener than would have been agreeable to the ears of the Captain-General."[4] But what resistance there was the authorities scattered. It never assumed the dimensions that it did on the mainland, where a disaffected Creole elite stepped forward, however gingerly, to preempt social revolution.[5]

Well before 1840 during the formative years of Cuba's plantation system, from the end of the Seven Years' War in 1763 to the outbreak of the Spanish-American revolutions, Cuba's planters had benefited from Spanish economic and political concessions, which had prepared them to take advantage of Saint Domingue's demise to become major world sugar producers.[6] Planters in Cuba had profited at the expense of sugar-planters-made-victims by Saint Domingue's slave revolution and so continued to import thousands of Africans annually to work their plantations. As a result, they dared not risk participation in a violent political movement of which they could lose control to the detriment of their newfound prosperity and their lives.

But the events of the early 1840s presented threats that tested the limits of the relationship between metropolis and colony. Acquiescence could turn to desperation if Spain could not properly manage the slave trade and safeguard the lives of whites and their property from slave revolt and the rising tide of abolitionism. Relying on African slave labor was one thing; allowing Cuba to become Africanized quite another.

Understanding what Cuban whites thought about slavery in 1840 proves difficult because there was no single, undivided mind. José del Castillo, an antislavery slaveholder, had a point when he said in 1843 that "the great mass of the whites do not even suspect the existence of other motives or reasons [besides self-preservation] why the trade should stop, or slavery cease among us! It is a habit, a custom, and they see nothing wrong in it."[7] But thinking Creoles, influenced by liberal-democratic currents, knew what the slave trade and slavery were doing to them and their political ambitions. They complained. Some of what they said would appeal to abolitionists like the British consul David Turnbull. But, in the end, Turnbull judged these enlightened Creoles to be far more radical than they were.

Studying the problem of slavery in Cuba might well begin with Francisco Arango y Parreño, the reputed Jovellanos of Cuba and the father of Cuba's plantation system. Although Allan Kuethe has argued that Arango by the first decade of the nineteenth century did not "stand at the head of the planter aristocracy," Arango was a prolific writer, important thinker, and, as Kuethe himself admits, a "capable spokesman for the Cuban elite."[8]

Arango was born in 1765; as a student, he quickly outstripped his Cuban teachers in learning. He was furthering his education in Spain, a young man of twenty-two, when the Havana *ayuntamiento,* or town council, a planter stronghold, called upon him to act as its Court agent. In that role he achieved stunning success, or so it seemed at the time. His lobbying efforts before and after the outbreak of the Saint Domingue slave revolution won Cuban planters greater freedom to import slaves. He scored his most significant triumph by fashioning the Havana *consulado* into an economic-development corporation under planter control. He initiated a plan for a junta of planters with the promotion of agriculture as its primary objective and with funds to be provided from fines levied by the *consulado* and from a tax of ½ of 1 percent on all Cuban imports and exports. The Crown consented to Arango's proposal in 1794, but insisted on the incorporation of the junta as a joint body of planters and merchants within the framework of the *consulado.* Additional politicking by Arango to structure the voting arrangements ensured planter dominance over merchants in the resulting Junta Económica y de Gobierno (Economic and Governing Committee).[9]

La Sociedad Económica de Amigos del País de la Habana (the Havana Economic Society) formed in 1791 by twenty-seven Havana planters complemented the work of the *consulado,* and although Arango did not respect its informality or its political weakness, he did contribute to its development. The Economic Society patterned itself after the various economic societies that had flowered in Spain during the Spanish Enlightenment. It "expressed in words what the Consulado expressed in figures."[10] Cuba's planters used it as a forum to trade ideas and to promote schemes for their material advancement. Efficiency, industry, and prosperity became its watchwords. It organized projects for technological modernization, scientific development, public education, and expanding trade; it published its own newspaper, the *Papel Periódico,* and other literature

of interest to progressive planters; it sponsored prizes for agricultural innovation and essays on economic subjects, and opened Cuba's first public
library. The members of the Economic Society saw themselves as mod-
erns, an enlightened vanguard who would advance their own material
interests to the general happiness of society by cultivating Reason and
applying it to the environment.[11]

Cuba's planter elite, by and large, pointed themselves toward economic
liberalization, their call for freedom sounding principally like a call for
free trade. The *consulado* and the Eonomic Society existed to advance
them in that objective. The problems still to be overcome under Spanish
reformed mercantilism Arango elaborated in step-by-step fashion in 1792
in his well-known *Discurso sobre la agricultura de la Habana y medios de
fomentarla* [Discourse on the agriculture of Havana and the means to promote it]. Cuban agriculture needed two essential ingredients to compete
with other plantation colonies in the world market: a cheap, steady supply
of labor and free trade.[12]

Arango's successful lobbying to open up the African slave trade answered the labor question, and unprecedented prosperity followed. Not
until the 1830s, the last years of his life, did he try to put an end to
what he had fostered. The Saint Domingue slave revolution of 1791 had
prompted some Cubans to demand an immediate end to slave imports.
Arango took issue with them, and his views held sway. Cuba remained
safe from slave revolution, he argued in 1794, because of its demographic structure. In Saint Domingue the slave masses had overwhelmed
a few thousand whites, whereas in Cuba whites held a comfortable numerical advantage. Planters could continue to import slaves, although
cautiously "with the census figures in hand, in order that the number of
Negroes may not only be prevented from exceeding that of the whites,
but that it may not be permitted to equal that number."[13] Arango again
defended the slave trade in 1810, when the Cortes of Cádiz, formed in
response to Napoleon's invasion and the flight of Charles IV, began its
sessions, for the first time with colonial representatives. Mexican delegates, unencumbered by a burgeoning slave system, spoke up against
slavery and proposed the abolition of the slave trade throughout the empire. Arango riposted with a defense that decried the existence of slavery
in the abstract but justified its maintenance on practical grounds.[14]

Arango did draw a line, and Cubans became devoted census watchers
in acknowledgment of it: When the number of slaves exceeded the number of whites, the slave trade should cease. In 1794 and 1810 Arango

probably never dreamed that Cuba's slave population would exceed its white population. Or, better, as José Antonio Saco, a Cuban liberal of the generation after Arango's, exclaimed, "The prosperity of the moment blinded them [Cuban planters] to the dangers of the future."[15] That a civilized people would rid itself of slavery, Arango could agree. But from his perspective and, indeed, from the perspective of most of the world at the beginning of the nineteenth century, "slavery has always existed and always will exist."[16] He looked upon slavery much as the Southern slaveholders who came of age during the American Revolution did, as a temporary expedient until adequate supplies of free white labor became available. Both his racial prejudice—he disdained people of color—and his liberalism disposed him more toward free white labor than black slaves.

The Spanish-American revolutions confronted Arango and the rest of Cuba's planter class with hard choices. Instead of political separation, they advocated reform within the imperial system, the fear of social disorder and economic ruin dissuading them from fulfillment of their liberal economic program. Although Arango never fully renounced liberal-democratic principles he did say that Cuba's masses could not yet appreciate those principles—unprepared, without education, without virtue, they had not yet learned how to be citizens of a nation: "He who does not have informed understanding does not know how to be free, and he who does not have virtue is not worthy of being free." To sustain liberty Cuba must educate its people first. "How may we know it [a constitution]," he reasoned. "How will we love it, living in ignorance and with the political vices to which three centuries of despotism have committed us?"[17] At the same time, the restored Bourbon monarchy, in the person of Ferdinand VII, passed out rewards. Absolute free trade and private property became legal realities for Cuba in 1818 and 1819 respectively; Arango accepted an appointment as intendant. Twenty-six sugar planters obtained the noble titles of either marquis or count, three fewer than the entire number of such titles handed out in Cuba's previous three hundred years.[18]

A general crisis of identity was readily visible within Cuba's planter class during the years immediately before La Escalera, an internal struggle to reconcile bourgeois aspirations with slavery and colonialism. Education, on which Arango hinged his argument against immediate national liberation, illustrates the contradictions. A capitalist system develops human capital by guaranteeing a secular education to all its people so they might better freely pursue their individual material interests and thereby contribute to the general progress of society and nation. In Cuba, planters appealed for programs of public education. They stressed the need to cultivate an open, critical mind as an integral part of individual development within a general climate of technological development. They attacked scholasticism and the rote memorization of catechism in church schools as unproductive and unprogressive. They sparred among themselves on the relative merits of the philosophies of education of John Locke and Victor Cousin in the Economic Society and at the Havana lyceum. Yet the reports of the Economic Society on primary education tell of dreadful privation within the schools and among the teachers. Voluntary contributions supported the schools, and "all suffered from local poverty."[19] For all the talk, neither the *consulado* nor the Economic Society collected adequate funds to support a system of primary education. The Spanish government reinvested tax money in colonial education spottily or not at all. It granted a yearly token equivalent to little more than $30,000 for public education in 1816, and several years later withdrew it because of the hardening attitude of Ferdinand VII toward liberalism. A modern system of primary education in a colonial slave society could encourage instability among the masses by weakening the principles of dependency upon which Spanish imperialism and slavery were based. The Spanish government feared the Creoles, and the Creoles feared the slaves. Private tutors, exclusive echools, and terms abroad would meet the educational requirements for Cuba's advantaged young, that is, when the government was not putting hurdles in the way, as it did with the royal orders of 1828 and 1832 that restricted young Creoles from getting an education in the United States.[20]

In 1836 Domingo Del Monte, one of Cuba's outstanding liberal spokesmen of Saco's generation, undertook a systematic inquiry for the Economic Society on the state of primary education in Cuba. Dismaying answers returned to his questions. No area approximated the educational needs of the young. Most districts had no teachers with proper training, many had no teachers or schools. Rural areas lacked more than urban areas, and the central and western departments, the major plantation regions, lacked more than the eastern department. Of the fifty-five western districts that responded to Del Monte's questions, twenty had no schools. The correspondent from the district of Managua said that it used to have a school; the district of Alacranes, with some of Cuba's largest and most technologically advanced sugar plantations, never had a school; the district of Vereda Nueva had one but could not afford a teacher; the district of Guava's local magistrate suppressed its lone teacher; and the districts of Bauta and San Antonio Chiquita, among others, blamed their total lack of schools on the generally "deprived and miserable condition" of its population, which they attributed to the irresponsibility of absentee planters.[21]

Del Monte put the total number of Cuba's eligible white and free colored children at more than 100,000, less than 10 percent of whom received anything close to a primary education. "A wise government," he remarked, "will see in this enormous mass of 100,000 ignorant people, 100,000 restless proletarians, enemies of the tranquility of the country, and if it is sincerely interested in the fortune of this country, it will adopt measures to guarantee social order by diffusing and paying for primary schools."[22] The government answered by preventing publication of Del Monte's report.[23]

Cuba's intellectuals waged constant battle with the censor both on what could be published in Cuba and on what publications could come in from outside. In 1830 the government turned down Del Monte's request for the establishment of a public chair in the humanities. Three years later, José de la Luz y Caballero, the best metaphysician among the liberal thinkers in the generation of Del Monte and Saco, one who would be attacked in La Escalera, attempted to convert the abandoned Havana facilities of the old tobacco monopoly into a progressive school, similar to one established by Jovellanos in Spain, for the study of technology, mathematics, and science. Despite the multitude of unemployed whites, Cuba was compelled to import foreign technicians and engineers to operate the sugarmill complex; the big merchant houses imported foreign bookkeepers. Ten years after making his proposal, Luz y Caballero was still seeking to overcome government objections.[24] Manuel Moreno Fraginals, the Cuban historian, has observed that Cuba's "first physics, chemistry, and botany schools failed. . . . The chairs of Political Law and Political Economy had hardly been founded when they vanished."[25] The chair of political economy, which the Economic Society had supported in Havana in 1818, was eliminated because the Spanish government preferred that year to make room for the return of scholasticism.

Each setback, every obstacle to Creole education, disgusted men like Del Monte. In the face of every slave he and other Creoles could see a mirror image of their own colonial servility. In a letter of 1830 to his exiled friend Tomás Gener, Del Monte told of the "tremendous blow" delivered by the government to the petition of the Library Section of the Economic Society to establish a professorship in the humanities. His next sentence dropped the proper metaphor: " 'Blacks do not dance' as Cienfuegos [José Cienfuegos, Captain-General from 1816 to 1819] put it to a memorial presented to him by some blacks who wanted to dance."[26] When the time came to add up the abuses of Spain's colonial system, dissidents appraised education—the lack of it—dearly. The "Address of the Young Creoles to the London Anti-Slavery Society" of October 1841, a virtual separatist manifesto, said this:

Even thought is fettered by the censorship of the press, and our youth are denied the means of instruction. They ask for lessons in literature, and it is refused; they propose a lyceum, where they might have an opportunity of exercising their talents, and it is forbidden; Sunday-schools are opened for the instruction of the poor, but the doors are immediately closed; a chair of civil history is founded, but the lectures are prohibited; a school of declamation is proposed, and they prescribe the presidency for some Spanish authority.[27]

Within a confidential report of 1843, Captain-General Valdés summed up his policy toward education in Cuba as an attempt to redress a previous history of excessive freedom with "unity and concentration [of power]," for "your excellency knows how much education influences social fortunes and how the interests of the Government are served by having over it the vigilance and influence necessary so that it not degenerate and turn prejudicial and dangerous."[28] Metropolitan officials during and after Valdés agreed; they sought to offset the corrupting effect of education in the United States and elsewhere by establishing alternative schools for Cuban youths in Spain where the desired habits of "loyalty and subordination" would be taught.[29] Both the censuses of 1846 and 1861 have occupational distributions with listings for *"estudiantes,"* whose meaning can be inferred as students concerned with higher education. The census of 1846 enumerated 1,472 students, none of them free colored; the census of 1861 2,694 students, 2,248 white and 446 free colored. Despite a rate of economic growth that was among the highest in the trans-Atlantic world, the ratio of white students to the total white population appears to have worsened from 1:289 to 1:353.[30]

The fate of education in Cuba exposes the speciousness of Arango's argument. Education depended on national liberation, not the reverse. And neither popular education nor national liberation could easily prosper within the confines of the slave society. The sugar boom had surely generated economic growth in Cuba, but how effectively its benefits were distributed, given the cultural conditioning and the structures of power, is another matter. Del Monte's report and Luz y Caballero's frustrations do not deny the dismal showing of public education in stratified societies without slaves, such as in Cuba prior to its development into a slave society. But they do indicate how the wealth of the sugar boom could not be readily translated into investment in human capital because of slavery's influence on political choices.

In early modern Spain, the tenacious retention of the values of a seigneurial past impeded economic development. While wealth continued to be concentrated and opportunity limited, traditional values resisted calculation, money-dealing, and regular labor. Spain's seigneurial past had crossed the Atlantic to be reinforced in Cuba by the slave system. Captain-General Vives in 1832 answered Spain's query about the state of the mechanical professions in Cuba in this manner: In Cuba, he said, they projected low status, and when not filled by foreigners, they were filled to a disproportionate degree by people of color, to their further degradation. "Even the most lowbred and miserable classes [of white Cubans] disdain to apply themselves to any [mechanical profession], preferring vagrancy and idleness."[31] That Vives would have considered vagrancy and idleness among whites in Cuba to be particularly troublesome is revealing because these problems were notorious in Madrid where he had spent much of his life.

When Charles Augustus Murray visited Cuba a few years later, he thought Havana had more idlers than any other city of comparable size he had seen. "There seem to be hundreds of respectably dressed persons who have nothing else to do than to smoke cigars, and play at dominoes or billiards." Within the households of the elite families, he was struck by the "immense and apparently useless number of house servants."[32] Robert Francis Jameson, a British resident in Cuba in 1820, commented on the crying lack of entrepreneurial spirit. Contrary to what he saw in the United States, "No one [in Cuba] is disposed to *strike out*. The stream of industry and trade struggles through the obstructions of habits and manners with difficulty."[33] Jameson observed what he called the worst sloth among the poor whites. The situation improved as he observed the higher ranks of society, but even there, "You find men of intelligence and education *awake* to the interests of their country, but they sit in their studies with their *night-caps* on."[34] The sons of the planter elite displayed more interest in privileges and status than in maximizing profits on the *ingenio*. What the leading authority on the Cuban militia concluded for the end of the eighteenth century may have applied with less force in 1840 but nonetheless applied. "For Havana's hierarchy, which still looked to the past for its sense of identity, military offices evoked images of nobility and reinforced pretense of social excellence. Throughout its history, the Havana militia would never lack an abundance of elite aspirants to volunteeer office."[35]

An occupational distribution for the free working population in Cuba's census of 1846 shows that if housewives and farmers are excluded from the total, the four categories of seamstresses, washerwomen, day-laborers-servants, and persons without a fixed occupation accounted for 22 percent of the working white population and 48 percent of the working free colored population—and slaves made up another 36 percent of the total population.[36] Despite the munificence of the world market, Cuba in 1840 remained a markedly hierarchical, underdeveloped country where every Saturday poor whites queued up to noble townhouses for charity of bread and vegetables, where a tradesman or a merchant had to acquire a noble *padrino* if he was to have a chance at a local office or in getting a fair hearing in court. "Anything that appertains to a monarchy or aristocracy I dislike," wrote Joseph Loring, a Maine sea captain after anchoring in Havana in 1844, "and here it can been seen in its glory."[37]

A system of production is a system of relations among human beings. Colonial Cuba answered the world demand for agricultural staples by erecting a productive system based on masters and slaves. While production for a world market stimulated spectacular economic growth, in addition to planter profit-consciousness and market-responsiveness, slavery as an extraeconomic or nonmarket means of labor control militated against the type of internal qualitative growth, of what neoclassical economists call social and human capitals, normally associated with a productive free-labor system. Had Cuba's planters won separation from the metropolis and held formal political power before the full-fledged integration of the slave system, as the planters of the southern United States had, their political course might have seemed clearer. Cuba's Catholic, seigneurial antecedents, with their emphasis on status and hierarchy, would have aptly prepared Cuban planters to command a slave society without a fundamental crisis of conscience or religious and social consciousness. But in their colonial position, without formal political power, Cuban planters could not construct a coherent world view that embraced slavery, the foundation of their economic life, as the foundation of a proper social life. Unlike the slaveholders of the southern United States, they could not elaborate a philosophy of slavery as a positive good, that is, as the proper relationship between capital and labor. To do so would have been to sanction positively the superordination-subordination relation of metropolis to colony and the attendant political repression and social condescension that weighed uneasily on even the most affluent and titled among them.

No Calhouns, Hammonds, or Fitzhughs emerged in Cuba, nor for that matter in any slave society in the Americas except in the Old South, not because, as Gordon Lewis has suggested for the Caribbean, the "plantocracy constituted the most crudely philistine of all dominant classes in the history of Western slavery."[38] Cuba's planters did display dissipation, frippery, and gluttony in abundance. Peninsular-born Spaniards frequently charged the Creoles with effeminacy. But in Cuba there were impressive minds, like Arango, Del Monte, Andrés Zayas, Antonio Bachiller y Morales, Francisco de Frías, and others. Yet though Cuban planters functioned in a social sense as a dominant class, they were not a ruling class, a class for-itself, and that made the necessary, if not sufficient, difference. No sane planter could, as a scorned colonial embedded in a slave system, seek state power, either by national liberation or democratic reform on the basis of a positive good ideology, for the arguments could easily be turned to justify metropolitan imperialism and colonial subordination.

Without formal political power, Cuba's planters seemed incapable of stopping what Arango had labored to release. Instead of a temporary means to progress, the African slave trade by 1840 looked more like an instrument of national destruction. The numbers of slaves seemed to be exceeding Arango's stipulated limits. Whites would soon become a minority, if they were not already. Dissidents looked back at 1823, when Captain-General Vives suppressed the liberal Constitution of 1812 in Cuba, as the start of a conscious Spanish policy of encouraging imports of blacks to scare whites into political acquiescence. Shiploads of contraband slaves were being used as shiploads of troops to quiet revolutionary aspirations. The policy of Spain, David Turnbull asserted in his *Travels in the West,* is "to keep the island of Cuba in her dependence; and this, it is supposed, can only be done effectually by the salutary terror inspired by the presence of a numerous, half-savage negro-population."[39] The abiding terror of a race war led Luz y Caballero to call the slave trade "our real original sin, so much more so since the just were paying for the sinners."[40]

In the aftermath of the Spanish-American revolutions, Spain combined tacit connivance in the slave trade in defiance of anti-slave trade treaty-agreements with Great Britain of 1817 and 1835 with stepped-up political repression, browbeating, censorship, surveillance, banishment, and imprisonment, to keep Cuba within the fold. The bared knuckles of Captain-General Miguel Tacón (1834–1838) should have rid Cuba's planters of any delusions. Service in the Spanish-American revolutions had given Tacón a predilection for imperial order. He commanded the substitution of the word loyalty for liberty in the Cuban performance of an Italian opera and banished supporters of Spain's suppressed Constitution of 1812. He coerced liberal intellectual and *grand seigneur* alike. He expelled José Antonio Saco in 1834 for an accumulation of wrongs, from speaking out against the slave trade to offending the peninsular intellectual Ramón de la Sagra and his patron, the Conde de Villanueva. He expelled the popular and politically defiant Marqués de Casa Calvo shortly thereafter on the pretext of his running a gaming den in his Havana palace.[41]

Tradition dictated that the Captain-General recruit important Creole planters for his kitchen cabinet. Tacón relied instead on big peninsular merchants. He expelled scores of well-known Creoles, in putting down a constitutional *pronunciamiento* of 1836. He built a prison and a theater the likes of which Cubans had never seen, made Havana's streets both cleaner and safer, sweeping up the colored gangs attached to the white elite along with the common criminals, all the while enriching himself by contriving in the contraband slave trade. Fanny Calderón de la Barca, the Scottish wife of a Spanish diplomat, jotted down in her diary in 1839 that "the hatred of all these Spanish officers to the Habana is almost equal to that of the Habaneros for General Tacón—at least the grands seigneurs. . . . His contempt of the nobles seems to have been unbounded and his disgust openly shown. In return, they speak of him as 'the wild beast,' the 'infirm old brute,' and 'General Tacón of unlucky memory,' etc. They hate the theatre he built, the walk he planted, the fountain he constructed."[42]

The suspect Cuban census of 1841 shocked the Creoles with numbers that indicated, for the first time, numbers of slaves in excess of whites.[43] Angry young liberals, like the Colombian-born, Cuban-raised Félix Tanco, began to locate the source of Cuba's predicament where it belonged. "All the Spanish that live on the island fully believe that they are *morally* better than us and that our corruption proceeds from ourselves and not from them. Now you see the error cannot be more absurd."[44] By 1840 classical liberal political economy had inoculated Cuba's educated circles against the long-term acceptance of slave labor. Turnbull's contact, Pedro José Morillas, spoke for a majority of his fellow members of the Economic Society when he drew upon the variant Adam Smithianism of Spaniard Alvaro Flórez Estrada, the most influential political economist in Cuba in the first half of the nineteenth century, to elucidate the "Means to Promote and Generalize Industry." To Morillas the promotion of industry meant the promotion of *"oficios y artes,"* that is, crafts and skilled trades, as an adjunct of the sugar plantation. He said little that anyone with a nodding acquaintance of the Manchester School did not already know: Man must be guaranteed the fruits of his own labor; government should free up the engine of self-interest by patterning its intervention to that of "oil in a machine"; education must be extended, although Morillas would have apparently excluded people of color; lines of communication and transportation must expand to develop internal markets; large unimproved landholdings must be broken up and redistributed. He envisioned a nation geared to the production and export of sugar but with sufficient incentives to stimulate the power of self-interest and to do away with white idleness, vagrancy, and underemployment. That Cuba had not yet developed in this way, according to Morillas, remained quite simply because of "the use of slave labor." Had the political climate in Cuba been other than what it was, Morillas would have gladly elaborated, but his essay was shortened, the editor noting, "We would have wanted to see his ideas on this point expressed in another way so that we would not have had to suppress them."[45]

Most Cuban planters could accept the wisdom of the abolition of the slave trade for self-preservation alone even as recurrent labor shortages at harvest time and the anticipation of future sugar profits continued to drive them to Cuba's slave-trading merchants. When free white laborers refused to work in the cane fields, whether because of low wages, the nature and degraded status of the work, or for the opportunity to farm their own plot of land, sugar planters, antislavery in the abstract, would have had little recourse but to purchase more slaves. And while the thinking planter might admit that if Britain succeeded in strangling Cuba's slave trade, Cuba would ultimately benefit socially and politically, the rising planter with major investments in sugar's expansion or at least with the hope of making them, could imagine that such success might raise the price of a $400 slave to $1,000.[46] But, even so, purchasing a slave implied no necessary long-term commitment to slavery in a country where a sugar bonanza could pay off the price in a few years. A short operating horizon for planters, as Stanley Engerman has noted, might well be reflected in the material conditions of life for field slaves, which in Cuba were, indeed, notoriously bad.[47] The aggregate of individual decisions made by planters with large investments and under short-run productive and competitive pressures could generate strong demand and bid up slave prices. High slave prices by themselves—*pace* economic historians—does not necessarily mean long-term optimism in the slave system.

To perhaps a majority of Cuban whites, planters and nonplanters, however, in whom anti-slave-trade principles were weak or nonexistent, British policy actually served to affront honor to the point of demanding audacious continuation of slave imports. Francisco de Armas recalled that in the early 1840s Cubans "were accustomed to celebrate with great praise the exploits of one or two slave-trading captains who had brought in a great number of uninjured cargoes, frustrating the pursuit and persecution of English vessels."[48] White folk of middle rank in Cuba's western port cities—shopkeepers, rentiers, and such—were accustomed to celebrate the success of slaving ventures; such celebrations represented both cupidity and affirmation of honor. By 1840, much of the capital for illegal slaving ventures was raised locally, and there were many such small investors.[49]

Poor whites grumbled against the slave trade on occasion. Domingo Del Monte reported a dinner remark by a friend in June 1834, shortly after a great cholera epidemic had consumed tens of thousands of Cuban slaves, that "only the poor speak badly of the slave trade." Could that reflect an incipient consciousness of free laborers about what the continuation of the slave trade could do to wages and opportunity?[50] Cuban authorities kept their eyes on what they called the restless and turbulent element of the cities, for the most part young, middle- to lower-class Creoles, denizens of the municipal coffeehouses, where men drank, smoked, and played billiards but also talked politics and read newspapers, in English and French as well as Spanish. Some of their anti-Spanish denunciations would on occasion mix in the language of abolitionism. In 1844, for example, seven whites who had created a public disturbance by refusing to leave the Café Escauriza in Havana were arrested and eventually expelled from Cuba. One of them, Andrés López Consuegra, a young lawyer from Havana, was described to Spanish authorities as "bold and of very bad conduct. He lives in concubinage with a woman of bad repute. He boasts of being an abolitionist and, as such, propagates false news and ideas in order to cause alarm and unease among the landholders. He assiduously attends the cafes, where, in bad circles, he promotes conversations criticizing the dispositions of the authorities and of the Government."[51] Another lawyer, Francisco Sánchez del Pardo, was called, "a man dissipated, immoral, and without fondness for work. He does not occupy himself at his desk or at any honest business. He is a decided and very strong defender of the liberty of slaves and proclaims it with grave danger to the tranquility of this Island."[52]

To counteract the slave trade and prepare for a future free-labor system, Arango and his ideological descendants promoted white immigration from Spain, but planters had trouble attracting whites in sufficient numbers, and considered those who came too costly and too frail for hard work in a tropical climate; they found them rebellious and disinclined to work with slaves, and, bringing with them notions of liberty, they could contaminate the slaves. The much-talked-about experiment of Miguel Estorch in 1840–41 to use none but imported Catalan labor to harvest the sugar on his plantation failed miserably. Catalans already in Cuba nearly rioted, one observer said, because "they did not want any black Catalans here . . . the sons of Catalans were no longer Catalans but Cubans."[53] By 1845 Vincente Vázquez Queipo, a government legal official, said of the experiment:

Of the 90 young Catalans, robust and hardened to field work in their own country, brought at great cost and established by don Miguel Estorch in his sugarmill situated in one of the most salubrious sectors of the Island, many have succumbed to the rigors of climate and the rest have taken refuge in the municipalities to seek work in domestic service or in trade, which are quicker and more secure ways to seek their fortune.[54]

The complaint of Domingo Del Monte's brother-in-law during the 1845 sugar harvest other planters would paraphrase at other times. Although he had hopes that an expected group of Biscayans would work out as field workers, he reluctantly went ahead and rented fifty slaves, for the Spanish-born whites already available to him " 'were disposed to kill blacks' and it would cause a dreadful harm to put this class of people on the estates."[55]

On the correlate questions of slavery and independence, the Creole elite fragmented. Intellectuals like Saco, Del Monte, and Luz y Caballero, the doctors, lawyers, educators, and writers who were working to cultivate a national consciousness, envisioned the end of slavery by moral suasion in some misty future. During the first half of the nineteenth century, no Cuban-born white, or at least no Cuban-born white of standing, held anything near to the uncompromising, immediatist abolitionism of a David Turnbull or a William Lloyd Garrison. The liberationist ideology that emanated from the dual revolution, the British Industrial Revolution and the French Revolution, had penetrated but after refraction in the Cuban air.

Although Francisco Arango in his maturity and his followers had come to accept that a system based on free labor was the best guarantor of material progress and had come to see the holding of slaves, or, rather, the not-holding of them, as the acid test of being civilized, virtually no big planter advocated the immediate end of slavery. Yet neither did they, as noted earlier, consider it a positive good. Santiago Drake, one of Cuba's wealthiest sugar merchants and planters, wrote after Turnbull's arrival, the slave trade is "pernicious." But "we are very far from considering with those who wish not only the abolition of the trade, but that of slavery in the island. . . . In one point we are unanimous and that is in declaring ourselves independent, the instant any attempts [are] to be made in Spain to destroy our rights as owners of the slaves we hold."[56] For Cuban slaveholders, the question of slavery's abolition never required a death struggle but a gradualism that would respect property rights, cut losses to a minimum, keep order, and allow time to substitute alternative sources of cheap labor.[57]

Cuban notables and corporations had to define their position on slavery explicitly in 1841 in response to the request of Captain-General Valdés for opinions on Britain's official presentation to Spain of an anti-slave-trade proposal by David Turnbull. (Much more will be said about the specifics of this proposal in a later chapter.) Turnbull had traveled to Cuba in 1839, before his appointment as British consul. As a result of his examination of the contraband slave trade, he intended to invest British officials with the power to investigate whether slaves already existing in Cuba had landed after 1820 in violation of a previous Anglo-Spanish agreement. Franklin Knight has pointed out that neither the church nor a single Cuban cleric figured among the "illustrious" consultants called on by Valdés, but, contrary to what David Murray has stated, the responses were not confined to the European population.[58]

The Turnbull proposal distressed the Junta de Fomento (Committee on Cuban Development), a direct descendant of Arango's Economic and Governing Committee of the Havana *consulado,* dominated by noble Creole planters and peninsular merchants. In a report on the Turnbull proposal they denounced as an outrage the idea of giving British officials the right to investigate lawful ownership of slaves: "Masters and slaves are to appear in a kind of tribunal of the last resort, in which England is to appear at once as the accuser of the one and the advocate and defender of the others—as arbiter, judge, and administrator of the law." Such a proceeding would endanger "the right of property that arises from possession . . . that fundamental basis of all property and of all social order." Turnbull's proposal would precipitate a deadly sequence of events. "Fresh instances of the declaration of freedom would soon engender insubordination [among all the slaves]; insubordination would promote mutiny; and mutiny would degenerate into open rebellion." Is Britain "ignorant of the magical effect which the word liberty produces?" The report ended with the admission that the abolition of the slave trade was "important and even necessary," and slavery too must come to an end in order to "strengthen our internal organization . . . and provide against the dangers with which we are threatened."[59] The junta of planters and merchants included an addendum on the means to effect the eventual abolition of both slavery and the slave trade but Captain-General Valdés suppressed it.

José María Martínez de Campos, the Conde de Santovenia, in a similar report, rejected Turnbull's proposal as a threat to life and property although he called British efforts to suppress the slave trade "highly laudable" and condemned slavery as the "odious system" in which "the slave groans and the master trembles." Britain and Spain had wisely decided in 1817 to adopt a gradual course to the abolition of the slave trade, but the "odious system" was preferable to the risks of freedom.

A state of freedom would be attended with greater evils than slavery itself; because all the foundations of our civil existence would speedily be overturned; because our agriculture would be destroyed in its very roots; while our trade and our capital would take their departure in quest of more promising channels for their application; and also because our disbanded slaves, when left without discipline or restraint, ignorant, vicious, and revengeful, would exterminate the remnant of our white population who had not been able to fly from danger. So that our beautiful Cuba would return to its primitive condition, uncultivated and filled with barbarians, lost at once to us and the rest of the world.[60]

To save Cuba, Martínez de Campos recommended severe punishments for slave traders and the energetic promotion of white colonization.

Plutocrat Wenceslao de Villaurrutia, a Spaniard by birth, a merchant-planter by occupation, and a member of the exalted Montalvo clan by marriage, framed the lengthiest rebuttal to Turnbull's anti-slave-trade proposal. He saw it for what it was, an indirect attempt to abolish slavery. Villa-Urrutia, in effect, admitted the abolitionist claims on the proportion of the contraband trade, but British philanthropy, he declared, masked British *realpolitik*. Immediate abolition would ruin Cuba's economy to the benefit of British West Indian plantations and probably lead, as well, to the overthrow of Cuba's white race. Another Africanized state would join the "Negro Archipelago" to thwart United States expansionism to the south. He advised Britain to reserve its concern for its own working class or the natives of Ireland or India. He argued for slavery neither as a temporary expedient, nor as a positive good—he called it "a plague"—as an inherited evil that was the best of available alternatives.

All the reason in the world founded in history, physiology or morals have proved that the Negro is not a man like the white man, that when left to himself he is incapable of civilization, if from no other cause than his invincible aversion to labour. . . . It is conferring on him a benefit to accustom him to labor, because it gives him and lets him hope for enjoyments, which he never knew, and never could know, in the state of barbarism in which he was vegetating in his own country. . . . Negro slavery as it exists among us does not deserve the exaggerated execration by means of which the English religionists, and the French philosophers have connected it throughout Europe into a theme of opprobrium, without knowing anything of the matter.[61]

His argument, in essence, approached what might be called the "necessary evil" argument of the Southern slaveholders during the early stage of their ideological development.

Havana's Economic Society divided over the appropriate response to Turnbull's proposal. A special committee of the Society under the influence of José María Calvo and Francisco Chacón, members of two of Cuba's interrelated, pro-French *grandes familias* (Calvo's father was the uncle of Chacón's mother), prepared a report exceptional only in its rancor toward Turnbull and Great Britain. A general meeting of the

Society rejected the report and had a new one drawn up under the auspices of Manuel Martínez Serrano, a liberal lawyer and friend of Domingo Del Monte and Luz y Caballero. This second report contained a more solemn discussion of slavery and the slave trade. It also condemned Turnbull's proposal as politically unjust and economically ruinous. But it affirmed the necessity for the extinction of both the slave trade and slavery in order to develop a free-labor system and to spare Cuba's white population from impending disaster. Slavery, it said, injures the master more than the slave. It corrupts human beings, promotes unnatural distinctions among men, and leads to idleness among Cuba's white youth.

The people of Cuba, endowed with sensibility, and naturally philanthropic, are imbued with the most favorable dispositions for the extinction of slavery, because they believe it to be prejudicial even to their own interest. . . . Slavery must always be odious, that the service it furnishes is imperfect and forced; and its products can never be so advantageous as those arising from free labor, stimulated by the desire of earning wages, and the fear of not being employed again, if the task is not properly performed.[62]

Cubans were submitting to "the calamity" of slavery because they had no choice. Although the report never quite revealed how, it foresaw a safe, gradual end to slavery with the immediate end to the slave trade. Such optimism may have derived from a common perception among whites that the severe mortality among Cuban slaves represented an inability to reproduce themselves naturally.

A curious incident in the Economic Society in 1842, with Turnbull again in the middle, opened certain of his liberal contacts to government persecution. When Turnbull first visited Cuba in 1838, unofficially and before publication of his anti-slave-trade polemic, *Travels in the West,* he had received a special corresponding membership from the Society for being an "illustrious British traveler." The Society habitually handed out these memberships to distinguished foreign visitors to enhance its image and to foster interaction with the wider world. In a poorly attended session of the Society in May 1842, near the end of Turnbull's tumultuous term as consul, the Calvo-Chacón faction called Turnbull an "enemy of the country" and purveyor of "perverse doctrines," and expunged his name from the membership rolls.[63]

The hasty action violated the ground rules of the Society, and José de la Luz y Caballero, director of the Society, who was sick in bed, was moved to compose a denunciation, to be read before a more representative membership in the next session. He addressed himself only to the violated procedures of the Society. In a vote of reconsideration, the Society membership, twenty-six to twelve, overturned the ouster. Domingo Del Monte was prominent among the majority. Despite Luz y Caballero's meticulous attempt to steer away from a personal defense of Turnbull and his ideas, the mere fact of Turnbull's reinstatement sufficed to draw government suspicion and innuendo down upon him and his fellow liberals. In accordance with his guiding principle of "unity and concentration," Valdés used the incident to initiate a process of reform within the Economic Society itself, designed to bring it under greater control by the Captain-General.[64]

Valdés, writing to Madrid of the incident, explained Luz y Caballero's behavior: "although born in the Island, [he] does not hold in it properties that give the roots so necessary in this question [of slavery]." "Sickly and ill," he seems not to have had the strength "to resist the extravagances and insinuations of a small number of young men who are lost in theory and not in a position to understand the true interests of the country in which they were born."[65]

Like Luz y Caballero, Del Monte was one of those young men "lost in theory." A Venezuelan by birth, he had come to Cuba at an early age and adopted it as his native land. He married into the Aldama family, one of the wealthiest planting families in all of Cuba, and, like many of the liberal Creoles, owned slaves himself, even though he longed for Cuba's deliverance from them. His house became the gathering spot for Cuba's young literary talent, and his guidance helped produce three powerful, protonationalist, antislavery novels: Félix Tanco's *Petrona y Rosalía,* Cirilo Villaverde's *Cecilia Valdés,* and Anselmo Suárez y Romero's *Francisco.* These novels, as Ivan Schulman has observed, "were commissioned by him, owed their inspiration to his leadership, and, more often than not, were modified in response to his criticism."[66] Along with Gertrudis Gómez de Avallaneda's *Sab,* written in Spain because of her family's concern with slave revolution, these books express a generation's frustration with slavery and a romantic search for national identity. The authors had learned to love Cuba, and in between their intense but one-sided portrayals of the evils of slavery, there exists rich and enthusiastic description of the land and the society.

The novels appeared in close succession, *Petrona y Rosalía* first, in 1838, *Cecilia Valdés* and *Francisco* in 1839, and *Sab* last, in 1841. Suárez y Romero handed over *Francisco* to R. R. Madden departing for

Britain as ammunition in the abolitionist campaign. Except for Gómez de Avallaneda, the novelists intended to examine intimately and scrupulously Cuba's people, institutions, manners, and customs for the purpose of moral regeneration. Previous Cuban writers had ignored people of color. These writers put them on center stage, but to a great extent to show how the system was corrupting whites. Félix Tanco wrote Del Monte upon the completion of *Petrona y Rosalía* that he had striven to present "the blacks and the whites working on each other, corrupting each other even in the least important aspects of life, in such a way that in the white man we see the black and in the black man the white."[67]

Del Monte and his circle comported with international liberalism in seeing slavery as a malignancy, a source of moral turpitude, and the antithesis of that autonomy essential to the moral and material progress of humankind. They did from time to time extend a helping hand to a tragic victim of the slave system; they obtained the freedom of Juan Francisco Manzano, the talented poet whom Del Monte commended as "docile and humble," like the *Francisco* portrayed by Suárez y Romero. But precisely because Del Monte considered Manzano's character exceptional he singled out for criticism Suárez y Romero's portrayal of *Francisco* as a slave with "angelic virtues."[68] Slavery typically produced harmful and degraded beings, Del Monte maintained, and for Cuban whites who needed to be alerted by the *costumbrista* literature to the dangers and corruption of the system in which they lived so that they would eventually move to abolish slavery, that typical slave had to be centrally represented.

However much Tanco and the other members of the Del Monte circle contributed, their particularist vision of *cubanidad* would have emptied Cuba of its blacks, not only its slaves. Rarely did they confound sympathy for the slave with sympathy for the Negro. Their passion to end the slave trade was the necessary first step in the whitening of Cuba in which the miserable demographic performance of the slaves, white colonization, gradual slave emancipation, emigration of freedmen, and assimilation would all play parts. In the liberal vision, a Cuba based on free labor would also mean a Cuba increasingly segregated by color. "To plead that there be no slaves in a country," maintained Lorenzo Allo, one of these Creoles, "is not to plead for the mixture of two different races."[69] Although racial mixing could not be totally eradicated, borrowing from the Western world's ranks of scientific racists, such as Georges Louis Leclerc Buffon, the French naturalist, and Georges Cuvier, the Swiss anatomist, Arango and his descendants took comfort that in miscegenation "the black color defers to the white" to the long-term benefit of Cuba.[70] Unlike the Southern ideologues, they counted on the leopard to change its spots, should it remain in Cuba. The gradual emancipation program of those "Young Creoles" who wrote to the British and Foreign Anti-Slavery Society in 1841 contains provisions to return all African-born free people of color, to remove from Cuba the children of all slaves born after 1842 once they turned fifteen years of age, and to establish various funds and societies to promote white immigration. In this, they shared the solution offered by many to the north who would become members of the mainstream of the party of Lincoln.[71]

Progress to Cuba's liberals meant extension of individual freedom to whites, republican government, and retention of much of the culture Spain and Western Europe had bequeathed to them. African slavery prepared them for none of these. As Francisco de Frías, the noted agronomist and political activist, remarked, "Black slavery corrupts and demoralizes the white man; it disposes and conditions him to receive the political yoke with all of its consequences."[72] Justo Reyes, the Lancasterian educator, who like most of his fellow liberals staked so much of the future on the moral rehabilitation of Cuba's youth through education, had to wonder aloud if they could be taught properly in a slave society. "All those who for whatever reasons come in contact with children serve as their moral instructors, and in a country such as ours in which they are constantly surrounded by slaves what morality are they to learn from beings so degraded and debased?"[73]

The infiltrations from Africa into music, language, and customs appalled Cuba's liberals. Tomás Gener, another of Del Monte's associates, whose career included a stint as Cuban deputy to the Spanish Cortes of 1820 and political exile after its dissolution, repeatedly despaired at the narrowmindedness of Cuba's planters to whom " 'more blacks means more sugar and coffee,' without seeing what is more obvious that more blacks means more risks, more corruption, and more misfortune for the whites."[74] In 1837, after watching young Creoles dance, Félix Tanco relieved himself to Del Monte: "Everything is African, and the poor, simple blacks, without asking for it and without any other force than that born of the relation that they are in with us, are returning our cruel treatment by infecting us with simple customs and manners proper to the savages from Africa."[75] The famous aphorism of José de la Luz y Caballero, "Lo más negro de la esclavitud no es el negro" (The blackest thing in slavery is not the black man), expresses a concern similar to that of Gener and Tanco that slavery's effect on the politics and culture of white society was a worse evil than the conditions of the slaves themselves.

To get their ideas across, Del Monte and his protégés resorted to the passing of manuscripts and word of mouth, for insular publication proved unhealthy under the government's baleful eye. Some of them must have wondered how they could end slavery by moral suasion when the government choked their message in their throats, interpreting any attack on slavery as an attack on Spanish rule in Cuba. Even their proposals for white colonization, the "great object of the Creole patriots," attracted government obstruction. The writings on white colonization and the comparative efficiency of slave and free labor by Gaspar Betancourt Cisneros, a self-professed disciple of Thomas Jefferson from the leading family in Puerto Príncipe, a friend of Domingo Del Monte, and a tireless advocate of a free-labor system, were censored by the authorities. "What does this mean? It is clear! That it [the government] does not want to hear the truth; that it wants only blacks in the country; that we will be carried to the devil unless the force of public opinion and public morality makes modern people stop buying blacks and bring in whites.[76]

Spanish imperialism and British abolitionism were perceived to be driving Cuba toward Africanization. For Betancourt and other thinking Creoles, annexation to the United States loomed larger as a political alternative, although what it would mean for the future of slavery in Cuba was a matter of dispute among its advocates. Some, like Betancourt, thought it would hasten the end of slavery. Others saw annexation as a means of more securely maintaining slavery for posterity. But both sides agreed that annexation would end the slave trade and spare slavery for the moment, providing Cuba's planters with the political forms to enable them to control the matter better. When asked to explain himself, Betancourt replied: "Annexation is not a sentiment, it is a calculation, and more. It is the imperious law of necessity. It is the sacred obligation of self-preservation."[77]

Cuban whites could not agree on how to resolve the problem of slavery. Much to their dismay, they learned that other free people in their society had already entered the debate.

4

The Free People of Color

It is true, we shall tell our people in this fable, that all of you in this land are brothers; but the god who fashioned you mixed gold in the composition of those among you who are fit to rule, so that they are of the most precious quality; and he put silver in the Auxiliaries, and iron and brass in the farmers and craftsmen. . . . The first and chief injunction laid by heaven upon the Rulers is that, among all the things of which they must show themselves good guardians, there is none that needs to be so carefully watched as the mixture of metals in the souls of the children. . . . Such is the story; can you think of any device to make them believe it?

PLATO, *The Republic*

Francisco Dionisio Vives governed Cuba from 1823 to 1832, longer than all but one other Captain-General and during the worst crisis in Spanish imperial history. He gained extraordinary powers and, without grossly abusing them, succeeded in keeping Cuba from following most of the rest of Spanish America into revolution. He broke up several separatist conspiracies; he installed the Military Commission; and while moving resolutely to centralize power in the office of the Captain-Generalcy, he wooed support for Spain from the Cuban patriciate by dispensing titles and favors. He was a capable manager with a keen if often mordant understanding of the complexities of Cuban society.[1]

When he returned to Spain in 1832, he responded to an official interrogatory about Cuba. On the specific question of the free people of color, he gave one of his lengthier and more sobering assessments. It would reflect not only the basic attitude of his immediate successors but that of many other members of Cuba's white community. To Vives the free people of color represented a dangerous problem without a ready solution. "The existence of free blacks and mulattoes in the middle of the enslavement of their comrades is an example that will be very prejudicial some day, if effective measures are not taken in order to prevent their [the slaves] constant and natural tendency toward emancipation, in which case they may attempt by themselves or with outside help to prevail over the white population." The measure Vives wanted to take was the expulsion of the entire free colored class from Cuba. But he knew that to attempt expulsion on such a scale would lead to even greater problems. "Having previously committed the error of not placing restrictions on their liberty to make it slow and difficult, and making matters worse by not paying attention to their propagation, it would be very difficult to want now to correct omissions and defects that could only be deplored, since it is not permissible to promote reform without stumbling into injustices that would awaken discontent and produce unfailingly the ruin of the country."[2]

Vives admitted that not all free people of color were equally dangerous. Many he considered "directly harmful," violent, perverse, and rebellious, capable of spreading their rebelliousness to others. But among those born in Cuba were also a number of "reputable artisans, good family men, who have urban estates and slaves." But even the ostensibly good and loyal he thought "indirectly dangerous," for in a general uprising of the people of color they would be "dragged along by the torrent."[3] Vives had little specific to recommend other than to sentence convicted free colored criminals to Spain's African prisons so their return to Cuba would be unlikely.

By 1840 success and opportunity had come to large numbers of free people of color, particularly in the port cities. The slave-based plantation economy had generated rapid economic growth. Free people of color marketed their skills and accumulated property, which could include slaves, and established communities with networks that ramified into the countryside. Yet with economic betterment during the sugar boom, they had become restive, increasingly frustrated by new discriminatory barriers that obstructed the fullest reach of their merit and by a color prejudice more virulent than they had known before. Those with talent and property had become its most convenient targets. While color prejudice was worsening, the aspirations of the free people of color, stimulated by Cuba's involvement in the world market, had probably never been higher. In an age of political awakening, notions of civil rights, equality, and human freedom would rouse free people of color as well as whites.

In the early 1840s Cuba had a sizable and internally stratified population of free people of color. During the sugar boom their numbers had quintupled from about 30,000 in 1774 to about 153,000 in 1841, of which slightly more than half were *pardos*. The proportion of free people of color in the total population during this period hovered fairly consistently at between 15 and 20 percent. Of all the slave societies in the Americas, only Brazil had a higher proportion of free people of color in its total population at a similar stage of economic development. No Anglo-American or Franco-American slave society approached such proportions. In Saint Domingue, for example, two years before its slave revolution, only 5 percent of the total population were free people of color. In Jamaica during the last quarter of the eighteenth century and in the antebellum southern United States, they comprised between 2 and 3 percent of the total population. When compared with the total free population, however, their numbers prove less exceptional. In the early 1840s free people of color were about 26 percent of the total free population in Cuba. Although they comprised only about 4.4 percent of the total free population in the southern United States in 1840, they comprised about 45 percent of the total free population in Saint Domingue in 1789 and about 25 percent in Jamaica in 1800.[4]

Within Cuba the numbers of free people of color varied markedly from east to west. In the early 1840s free people of color approached half of the total free population in the eastern department. They even outnumbered whites in the jurisdictions of Santiago de Cuba and Manzanillo. In the central and western departments their numbers diminished to little more than 20 percent of the total free population and outside of the major urban areas in the sugar-producing districts often to less than 10 percent.[5]

Wherever they settled in Cuba, free people of color entered the skilled trades and, indeed, had come to dominate many. Two years after La Escalera, according to an occupational distribution of the free population in the census of 1846, the majority of butchers, sawyers, masons, midwives, mineworkers, musicians, soapmakers, stonecutters, tailors, and wet nurses were free people of color. No whites were listed among the undertakers and almost none among the coachdrivers and cooks.[6] (See Table II.)

Well before 1840, free coloreds' service had extended to the defense of Cuba. Humiliations suffered during the Seven Years' War, the most grievous of which was Britain's capture of Havana, had prompted Spain to institute a series of military reforms that confirmed, first in Cuba and then elsewhere in the empire, the place of free coloreds in the military. With government support, companies of free colored militiamen with-

TABLE II. *Occupational Distribution of Cuba's Free Colored Population Selected Occupations in 1846*

Occupation	Number	All free colored workers (%)	All free workers in stated occupation (%)
Housewives	28,636	31.1	24.5
Farmers	18,252	19.8	25.1
Washerwomen	9,355	10.2	74.4
Seamstresses	7,648	8.3	38.2
Carpenters	2,510	2.7	49.4
Hatmakers	2,203	2.4	33.7
Tobacconists & Cigarmakers	2,138	2.3	26.4
Day-laborers & Servants	2,039	2.2	45.2
Shoemakers	1,970	2.1	59.6
Traders	1,939	2.1	19.2
Builders, Masons, & Plasterers	1,864	2.0	63.4
Tailors	1,696	1.8	72.0
Cattlemen	1,260	1.4	22.7
Administrators of their property	1,014	1.1	11.4
Peddlers	570	0.6	31.3
Blacksmiths	405	0.4	39.8
Estate Managers	363	0.4	11.7
Barbers and Bloodletters	361	0.4	51.1
Fishermen	321	0.3	13.0
Leatherworkers	305	0.3	62.5
Butchers	299	0.3	57.3
Cooks	294	0.3	98.7
Innkeepers	279	0.3	63.0
Sawyers	221	0.2	72.7
Coachdrivers	221	0.2	99.1
Musicians and Organists	216	0.2	53.7
Mineworkers	166	0.2	51.4
Stonecutters	61	0.1	55.5
Soapmakers	17	0.0	77.3
Undertakers	15	0.0	100.0
Wet nurses	11	0.0	68.8
Midwives	6	0.0	75.0

SOURCE: Cuba. Comisión de estadística. *Cuadro estadístico de la siempre fiel isla de Cuba, correspondiente al año de 1846* . . . (Havana, 1847).

stood the insults and discrimination of whites to grow into battalions with permanent staffing, formal training, and such benefits as the *fuero militar* (the right in certain cases to escape civil jurisdiction and to be tried by military courts), pensions, preferred employment, and preferred burial sites. The government made sure to give these units white commanders and to reinforce color lines by differentiating *pardos* from *morenos* in their uniforms, decorations, and pay. The privileges varied according to time, place, and military rank. At the end of the Seven Years' War, the Spanish

Crown permitted certain free colored militiamen to command the disposition of colored dockworkers in the cities, much as black *capitanes* had
commanded slave gangs in the gold mines of New Granada centuries
before. This privilege carried considerable prestige within the Afro-Cuban
community and higher-than-average payment from the commercial houses
that engaged the labor.[7]

By confirming the place of free colored militiamen in the defense of
Cuba, Spain had indirectly prepared them for leadership roles among their
people. During the sugar boom, free people of color had to seek government approval for many of their collective activities. When, for example,
the free *pardo* and free *moreno* communities of Matanzas sought to establish elementary schools for their children in 1828, two free colored militia
officers, one *pardo* and one *moreno,* presented the petition required to obtain licensing.[8]

Roles regularly overlapped for Cuba's free colored militiamen. Successful tradesmen commonly became low-ranking officers and, with age, were
often chosen to lead Afro-Cuban brotherhoods known as *cabildos,* which
administered to the spiritual and social needs of the Afro-Cuban community. These brotherhoods sprang up in other parts of Spanish America
and bear a distinct resemblance to the Negro *cofradías,* or fraternities, of
sixteenth-century Seville.[9] Their origin remains obscure but may in part
lie in the formal resemblance of the corporatist seigneurial institutions of
Spain to the communal political and religious institutions of West Africa.
Possibly even with a significantly altered social context, that formal resemblance proved attractive to the blacks themselves. More generally,
they paralleled societies of mutual support and opposition that arose in all
preindustrial shadow worlds.

Usually people of color of similar ancestry, both free and slave, joined
a *cabildo.* Carabalís, Congos, Lucumís, and other West African peoples
had their distinctive *cabildos,* usually in designated houses in the colored
quarters of the major cities and towns, with branches that could reach the
plantations. As far back as 1799, Captain-General Juan Procopio Basse-
court ordered Havana's Afro-Cuban *cabildos* restricted to outside the
walls, ostensibly because of the noise and disruption caused by their
observances. There they remained in 1840, most of them in the barrios of
Peñalver and Pueblo Nuevo.[10]

In promoting tribal cohesion, each *cabildo* served as a reservoir of
African culture by educating members in the rituals and theology of the
tribe. The leader of the *cabildo,* called a *capataz,* acted as a plenipoten-

tiary to white society. Should the *cabildo* or its members seek to register a grievance with Spanish authorities, the *capataz* represented them. Should members run afoul of the law, he assumed responsibility. Should they be fined, as custodian of the *cabildo* treasury he bailed them out. Some *cabildos* amassed considerable resources, which elicited jealousy and avarice from whites. *Cabildos* owned property in land and houses; they collected dues from members; they made profitable investments. All were needed: the sick needed care; the dead deserved decent burials; freedom for old and debilitated slaves required payment; justice often had to be bought.

On festival days the *cabildos* engaged in a communal reaffirmation of their African past, as modified by the New World setting. They celebrated their greatest festival on January 6 of each year, Epiphany to Catholics, perhaps because January 6 coincided with traditional African celebrations of the winter solstice or perhaps because on this day when Christ manifested himself to the Magi, one of them, Melchior, in his Christian depiction, resembled an African. On this "Day of Kings," Afro-Cubans dressed in a profusion of colors and costumes under banners distinctive to their tribal grouping and joined their respective *cabildos* where tribal elders led them onto the city streets in marches of ritual festivity. The Day of Kings and similar gatherings provided much more than entertainment. Amid the celebration, people of color traded information, communicated ancestral beliefs, and offered emotional support to one another.[11]

In 1840 in the free colored communities in Havana and the other major municipalities most people had contact with, if not membership in, Cuba's Afro-Cuban *cabildos*. They could boast of numerous talented and successful individuals: dentists Andrés Dodge, Pedro Pompé, and Carlos Blackely; musicians Claudio Brindis de Salas, Tomás Vuelta y Flores, and Ulpiano Estrada; phlebotomists Francisco Balmaseda and Tomás Vargas; undertaker Félix Barbosa; tailor Francisco Uribe; and dock gang captains José Agustín Ceballos and Marcelino Gamarra. Most were Cuban-born, although Pompé and Blackely had migrated to Cuba from Charleston, South Carolina. Most had accumulated property and wealth that amounted to thousands of dollars. Most had purchased the rank of officer in the *pardo* or *moreno* militia. Most knew each other and frequented the same social gatherings. They had families often interconnected by marriage.[12] All would be swept up in the process of La Escalera.

The free colored poets Juan Francisco Manzano and Gabriel de la
Concepción Valdés, alias Plácido, though neither achieved material success, had won great reputations in Cuba. Both would be caught up in the
process of La Escalera too. Manzano had weathered more than three decades of slavery before the quality of his verse moved members of the
Domingo Del Monte circle to raise the funds required to purchase his
freedom. At Del Monte's request, Manzano wrote his autobiography. Only
a first part has survived. A second was said to have been lost, perhaps
conveniently under the political pressure of the day, by Ramón de Palma,
a member of the Del Monte circle and one of David Turnbull's admitted
contacts. Students of Manzano may be right in thinking that the second
part reveals a more honest and aggressive Manzano on slavery, one less
restrained by the inferred guidelines of Del Monte and his followers, who
thought the portrayal of servile and degraded slaves more appropriate for
their purposes.[13] Part I passed into the hands of R. R. Madden during his
stay in Cuba. He took it to England along with Manzano's poetry for
translation into English and publication by the abolitionist press. In 1840
Madden introduced Manzano's words as the "most perfect picture of
Cuban slavery that has ever been given to the world."[14] They attracted
the attention of Victor Schoelcher, France's leading abolitionist, and he
translated portions into French. "Mis Treinta Años" [My thirty years],
Manzano's most moving condemnation of slavery in verse, was eventually
published in four languages: English, French, German, and Spanish, although publication in the last did not appear until almost a century later,
in 1937.[15]

Plácido was probably Cuba's most renowned person of color in 1840,
"the most inspired poet Cuba has ever seen," as Cirilo Villaverde put it.[16]
The illegitimate and orphaned son of a Spanish dancer and a *pardo* hair-
dresser, Plácido possessed an uncanny gift for lyrical improvisation. In
1834, at the age of twenty-five, he defeated twelve well-known white
opponents in a poetry contest held in Havana in honor of Francisco Martínez de la Rosa, then Spanish prime minister and a literary figure in his
own right. His victory made him the darling of white aristocrats. They
paid him to write poetry for baptisms, weddings, dances, and the like. Yet
for all his patronage and aptitude, Plácido never escaped poverty. A restless spirit drove him from job to job and place to place. He acquired
various skills and worked as a printer, silversmith, carpenter, and maker
of tortoiseshell combs—very chic at the time—but he never held any job

for long. He lived from hand to mouth, too often from the white man's hand to suit some of his contemporaries and some Cuban historians.

From 1836 until his execution, Plácido wrote his best compositions. He earned a meager income during much of that time from the Matanzas newspaper, *La Aurora,* which contracted to publish his poems on a regular basis. In 1839 and 1841 two collections of his verse, deeply informed by romantic themes and imagery, appeared in print. Whatever the debate about his genius—and in Cuba it has been fierce—his idealization of Cuba's natural beauty in *letrillas* (short poems intended to be set to music), his attention to medieval legend and to the noble savage of pre-Columbian America in narrative verse, and his thinly disguised attacks on tyranny in sonnets and *fábulas* (fables set to rhyme) were listened to and read by many Cubans of all colors. On the whole, they strongly argue for his place among Cuba's major protonationalist writers.[17]

The lives of these free people of color and the overall position of the free colored class in Cuba in 1840 suggest that Cuba's racial boundaries never hardened as they did in the antebellum United States. Why they continued to be more subtle and fluid, even by 1840, defies easy generalization, for color prejudice in Cuba has a long history, one which predates the sugar boom and which took shape under the influence of Spanish cultural antecedents.

The settlement of Cuba, like the settlement of the rest of Spanish America, proceeded from an essentially seigneurial system. A militant class of nobles, proportionally the largest in Western Europe, dominated an organic society in which Catholicism, military service, and "pure blood" opened the way to prestige and power. In the Spain of Ferdinand and Isabella, ancestry continued to matter more than merit, noteworthy gains by men of talent notwithstanding. Tradition, law, and an absolutist state enforced a hierarchical social order and sharpened the divisions between nonproductive and productive groups.

Spaniards rooted their seigneurial values in Cuba. As they acquired usufruct in land and rights to the labor first of Indians and then of imported Africans, their hidebound attitudes about pedigree, legitimacy, and the use of one's hands in manual and mechanical labor did not go away. Spanish disdain for these occupations, and the dearth of white colonists, especially of white females, made the early rise of a sizable free colored population in Cuba an unsurprising occurrence. Someone had to satisfy sexual appetites and undertake the skilled tasks essential to survival on a frontier. With the maturation of the plantation economy, the long-standing peninsular preoccupation with *limpieza de sangre* ("purity of the blood")—which originally had nothing to do with color but with the contamination of Islam, Judaism, and other heresies—gradually evolved into an unwritten law of purity of the skin to reinforce white supremacy in a society based on African slavery.[18]

Although the bulk of recent scholarship has rejected strict formulations of the thesis, most notably put forward by Frank Tannenbaum, of the relative benignity of Ibero-American slave systems, those Iberian traditions and institutions, as stressed by Tannenbaum, did shape social arrangements in ways significantly different from the social arrangements in the southern United States, even if they did not drastically ameliorate the physical conditions of slave life. Spain's lengthy experience with African slavery and darker-skinned peoples; its seigneurial customs and laws, which recognized rights of subjects in various degrees of servitude; and its centralized and authoritarian state, which withheld formal political power from a colonial slaveholding class, may have also acted to structure social arrangements toward more finely tuned gradations rather than polarization. Spanish colonists did come to Cuba better fitted than the Anglo-Saxon to relate to Africans, for a time-honored peninsular etiquette of dealing with peoples of different color and status had to some extent prepared them to control their prejudices within appropriate institutions and traditions.[19] For these reasons, a kind of relative harmony prevailed in Cuba during the sugar boom but largely on the surface where it could deceive even the most serious foreign observers.

J. G. F. Wurdemann, the South Carolina physician who was probably the most acute North American observer of Cuba's slave society, noted in 1846 that "Spanish courtesy throws a certain veil even over the features of the children of Afric [*sic*]. One, here, has so often to meet on an equal footing with those who are not of pure blood, even in the best society, that our Southern feelings, for the time, are thrown aside, and we play the Spaniard in his universal politeness." On close inspection Wurdemann discerned that social egalitarianism did not run deep. "It is remarkable . . . how very accomodating [*sic*] one's conscience is disposed to be in this Island. Indeed one would look quite *odd* to be sincere, and while here, I play the Spaniard I think not badly.[20]

Yet to say that the Spaniard had not the same antipathy to color as the Anglo-Saxon was not to say he had none. Rather, such assertions reflect primarily on the ferocity of Anglo-Saxon racism, which made the Cuban version, itself harsh enough, seem benign only by comparison.

In Cuba, to whiten meant to advance. A person *saltatrás,* or stepped back, by marrying someone of a darker skin. A child from the marriage of two mulattoes was called *"tente en el aire"*—literally, "holding oneself in the air."[21] Sexual relations between white males and nonwhite females had long been an accepted part of colonial Cuban culture, the more readily accepted when the colored female was free and part-white, even if the mulatto progeny represented a standing question of ancestry. The Cuban proverb "There is no sweet tamarind fruit, nor a virgin mulatto girl" reflects two realities: white male exploitative sexual behavior and the consequent vulnerability of mulatto girls. Cirilo Villaverde expressed a prevailing white image when he centered his celebrated antislavery novel on the sensuous quadroon Cecilia Valdés. Wedlock did occur, chiefly within class boundaries, but lower-class white males in the face of social stigma and a shortage of marriage-age white women defied custom most frequently by marrying free-born *pardas.* When not for love, free colored women coupled with white men because of coercion, economic necessity, the shortage of marriage-age men in their own class, or the possibility of social advancement for their children through whitening.[22]

A hint of the tensions that status and color prejudice could produce in Cuba's slave society comes from the letters of Juan Francisco Manzano. Domingo Del Monte's patronage had conferred on him some status, and he married a beautiful nineteen-year-old free *parda,* fathered by a white man. But the marriage had to bear up under what Manzano called "combat" from members of her family, who "complained about and even ridiculed her affection" for Manzano because, as his letters imply, his previous condition of servitude and his darker color had made him unworthy.[23] After visiting Cuba in 1843, the French journalist J. B. Rosemond de Beauvallon would contend that "in no country of the world, not even in aristocratic Spain is the division of social classes as clear or clean cut, as that in Havana."[24] He exaggerated but came closer to the truth than many of his fellow travelers who observed near color blindness among Cuba's inhabitants.

Boundaries between whites and free people of color became much more rigid during the first half of the nineteenth century, and to say that color had taken on added importance as a means of subordinating nonwhites in a burgeoning system of production based on African slave labor does not go far enough toward explaining what was happening to Manzano and other free people of color before 1840. What appears to have brought the racial situation closer to explosion was the introduction of two contradictory strains of liberal thinking into a preexisting and rigidifying color hierarchy. On one hand, the Enlightenment and the general secularization of Western thought in the eighteenth century had led to systematic investigations of humans and the origins of their diversity. These influences had reached Cuba during the sugar boom. As a result, explanations that cited innate, immutable factors of race were beginning to supersede environment, culture, or religion as rationale offered for differences among peoples. On the other hand, while schools of scientific racism were being introduced, the Age of Democratic Revolution was condemning slavery as a moral outrage, proclaiming the sacred natural right of all persons to freedom from arbitrary and despotic power, to have property in themselves.

At best, secular racism relegated people of color to a degenerative branch of the human family; at worst, it excluded them from the human family altogether. It appealed both to white reactionaries intent on substituting a racial chain of being for the medieval Catholic conception and to white liberals intent on escaping from the political implications of a revolutionary creed based on the equality and rights of man. White Cuban reactionaries used racism to reinforce the seigneurial notion that some were inferior to others; white Cuban liberals used racism to show that some individuals were not persons at all. As the eminent Caribbeanist Gordon Lewis has written:

To the modern reader there is an almost unbearable, indeed a tragic, tension between the need of the [proslavery] literature to show the slave as almost an animal in human form—for to admit his humanity would be to strike a mortal blow at the very basic principle of the system—and its need to defend the slave against the embrace of what the planters called the English "pseudo-philanthropists."[25]

Lewis could have added that the need to show the slave as worse than an inferior, as almost an animal in human form, began with urgency only at a particular historical moment when those English "pseudo-philanthropists" and the free-labor system from which they came had in the process of creating a new world order redefined humanity itself as something apart from dependence and hierarchy.

The Spaniards who colonized the New World and their immediate descendants could acknowledge the humanity of Indians, Africans, or anyone else, precisely because in a seigneurial society dependency on the wills of others defined humanity. Only belatedly, in the first half of the nineteenth century, did Cuban whites, with their own growing political aspirations and reflections on nationality, have to contemplate seriously the consequences of any generalized liberal-democratic movement and the prospect of admitting people of color, particularly members of a restive and talented free colored class, to participation in a reconstituted polity. In regard to manumission, for example, Cuban whites could have afforded a liberal manumission policy well before the first half of the nineteenth century, for manumission then did not necessarily endanger more fundamental social relationships. In the seigneurial world that developed with Spanish colonization in the Americas, human beings formed a vertical chain of dependencies. Freedom from slavery in such a world meant exchange of one dependent status for another.

Because Cuba's seigneurial past had bound superiors and inferiors in organic reciprocity, and because of long-standing traditions of interracial intimacy and ritualized interactions, some Cuban planters found it difficult to accept the banishment of people of color from the human race, as some of the more secular planters of the southern United States and "scientific" racists elsewhere were doing. "We cannot say, as the slaveowners of the Southern States of Am[eri]ca: 'Negroes are not men; they are a superior race of *orangoutans,* born to serve the whites, and, thus, promote civilization,'" wrote planter José del Castillo in 1843.[26] He was wrong and not just in his overstatement about Southern planters. Many liberal Cubans in pain from their own contradictions over slavery had to say it and did.

Some of the worst offenders were members of Domingo Del Monte's circle. When they derided Haiti for having a "stupid, insignificant, impotent government of orangutangs," discussed Britain's intention "to extract from slavery the *apes* imported from Africa," said that "even *orangoutangs* should be used [in the sugar plantations] were they susceptible of domestication," and shuddered at the thought of "despised humanity" in rebellion, they merely extended ideas enunciated by their ideological forefathers, like Voltaire in his *Essai sur les moeurs,* and Buffon in his *Histoire naturelle.*[27] A passage from one of Del Monte's essays on education, in which he repudiates the service of slaves in his proposed normal schools, suggests how race could be used to modify his liberalism in needed political ways: "The man who is born and raised a slave, whatever his color or race might be, precisely because of his condition, has to be vile, stupid, immoral . . . with due respect to human nature, certainly, there are races such as the Ethiopian, in which, some generous exceptions to the rule are encountered, but they do not begin to change it, because that would be to overturn the admirable order that Providence has put in place to govern the world."[28]

For Mariano Torrente, an archreactionary defender of slavery in Cuba, the special viciousness of liberal thinking on race argued for the superiority of the old ways, an ordered, paternalistic hierarchy that would not ban colored people from Cuban society, as the liberals would do, but would incorporate them within society as unequal partners.

How can any one, who prides himself on his sensibility, fail to become interested in those beings who appear to be repudiated by society, and who have been separated by some naturalists from the rest of the human family, as forming in their idea but a connecting link between man and the brute creation? Few surely are there, who do not reject so opprobrious a classification, and who would not be interested in making them participators in the benefits annexed to civilization. There will scarcely be found at the present time any one, however strongly opposed to the abolitionists, who does not nourish sentiments of real affection towards those beings who are withdrawn from a brutish and savage life.[29]

All American slave societies lived a supreme irony. Although white slaveholders could thank capitalist countries for providing a profitable world market for their staples, those same capitalist countries encouraged David Turnbulls with their revolutionary creeds of human freedom and civil rights. What made the capitalist world market of the first half of the nineteenth century so troublesome for slaveholders was the philosophical temper of the times. With the imports of goods from Europe came political radicals and a bold world view that challenged the social and political foundations of slaveholding countries. Democratic revolution is "an irresistible fact," wrote Alexis de Tocqueville in the 1840 volume of his classic *Democracy in America.* "Gradually the distinctions of rank are done away with; the barriers that once severed mankind are falling; property is divided, power is shared by many, the light of intelligence spreads, and the capacities of all classes tend toward equality."[30] With these words David Turnbull and certain of his free colored contacts would have identified.

Concentrated in the port cities, Cuba's free people of color were well positioned to come into contact with revolutionary ideas and people. The problem for Captain-General Valdés and his successors was how to contain them. "For the security of this Island, it is necessary to bear in mind that a multitude of men, schooled in revolutions and many of them in crimes, from all the nations of Europe seek refuge and take shelter [in

Cuba]," wrote Captain-General O'Donnell in 1844. Ever restless, they soon found their way into "all of the intrigues and in all of the commotions."[31] The small extent to which Cuba's free people of color reaped rewards from the world market and made foreign contacts meant not only that they might obtain a higher social position with all of its trappings, much as white plutocratic planters bought their way into the nobility, but that in the fashion of levelers in North and South America, France, and especially Saint Domingue, they might use their resources to topple hierarchy altogether, for, rewards aside, in Cuba's slave society they could not rid themselves of the stain of racial slavery. "They possess certain privileges, here called *freedom,* but which have little analogy to the European meaning of the word; they are unchained but the collar remains on their necks."[32]

Cuba's hardworking but stifled free colored class were people of ability and merit, in many ways the sansculottes of their society. The claim of Justo Reyes in 1832 that with six exceptions the elementary schools for people of color in Havana were "the most numerous, the better constituted, and the only ones in which are taught grammar and spelling" was probably meant to shame his fellow Creoles and the Spanish government into providing greater support for the education of whites.[33] But the point is many free people of color were educated. Some had learned to read and write, however crudely, as they needed to do for the kinds of middle-level jobs they were filling. They might put the learning to use, as their occupational counterparts had done on the mainland, in playing an active role in an independence movement. John Owen, the United States consul in Puerto Príncipe in 1833, the year Britain began its colonial emancipation program in the West Indies, was talking about the education some of Cuba's free people of color were getting when he expressed his fear of the "many enlightened" among them.[34]

Plácido's poetry speaks loudly to the heightened political awareness within the free colored community. In the sonnet "El Juramento" [The oath] Plácido stands by a tree of liberty at the foot of which is a spring whose water makes rebels of those who drink. He drinks. He begins "Décima" (a poem of ten lines) by asking whether or not Cubans are free. The feudal period, the time of oppression and darkness, has passed; around the world a cry rings. The poem ends: "Habaneros Libertad." His dedicatory sonnets "A Grecia" [To Greece] and "A Polonia" [To Poland] attest to a striking awareness of the revolutionary movements in the world around him. He praises the people of both countries for struggling to throw off the yoke of foreign tyranny.[35] That Plácido was urging Cubans, white and nonwhite, to do the same seems more than plausible.

At about the same time, Cirillo Villaverde described the clashing of values in the society of *Cecilia Valdés*. In one scene Leonardo Gamboa, the spoiled son of an affluent slave trader, meets with two fellow students named Diego and Pancho on a Havana street.

"What is the lesson for today?" asked Pancho.

"Govantes gave us the third chapter, which treats of personal rights," answered Diego. "Open the book and you'll see."

"I haven't even looked at the book," said Leonardo. "I only know that, according to law, there are persons and things. And that a good many things, although they speak and think, have no rights whatever. Pancho, for example, is a thing and not a person."

"I don't see why, for I am not a slave, which is what you meant."

"No, you are not a slave, but some of your ancestors must have been, and that amounts to the same thing. Your hair is suspicious."[36]

The net result of intellectual currents such as these by the early 1840s was to make Cuban whites and free people of color even more fearful and suspicious of each other. José del Castillo, who lived through the growing racial tensions of the early 1840s, believed those years were a turning point for the treatment of Cuba's people of color, that they signaled a general decline in paternalistic social relations and in the overall social authority of the old Creole families. He contrasted the situation after 1844 with that before:

When I was a child I heard blacks and mulattoes (of the kind we used to call Master Fulano and Master Zutano, although they were masters of nothing) boast of having been at a school with people of rank. One can still hear talk of the dances of the people of color in which the blacks and mulattoes wore various jewels loaned by those who had been their mother's master or mistress. Among those old families there were those famous for their inhumanity with their black slaves, but they were the exception not the rule.[37]

In areas of society where free people of color had struggled long and hard to make advances, they found themselves by the early 1840s under fierce attack, separated within society, not integrated into it. According to a Cuban adage of the time, a poor white man is worth infinitely more than a rich Negro, and, in the face of a rising class of free coloreds, whites wanted to keep it that way.

Although higher education had been largely an all-white vocation throughout the colonial period, elementary education became so only during the first half of the nineteenth century. In 1793 the majority of the thirty-nine elementary schools in Havana had free colored female instructors who taught racially mixed classes. Domingo Del Monte himself traced the elementary education of whites in Havana to a school for boys run in 1792 by a free colored instructor and officer in the *pardo* militia named Lorenzo Meléndez. Juana Pastor, a free *pardo* from the barrio of Jesús María, and Matías Velazco, the colored son of a white priest, had become highly regarded teachers of white children.[38] By 1840 the law was pressing for stricter segregation by color in education. This pressure reflected to a great extent the growing influence of the Havana Economic Society, whose education section, established in 1816, registered the calls of Del Monte and such other liberals and secular racists as Justo Reyes and José Antonio Saco to obey the distinctions "of nature" and to remove white children from colored classmates and colored instructors and to restrict the formal educational possibilities for free people of color.[39] A directive to officials in Havana of 17 June 1841, for example, explicitly forbade the mixing of white and colored pupils. From the end of the eighteenth century to the middle of the nineteenth the proportion of free colored elementary school students dropped from about 25 percent of the total to less than 5 percent.[40] According to the census of 1846, none of Cuba's 298 elementary school teachers, 36 music teachers, or 16 teachers of mathematics were free people of color.[41]

Since Spanish control of Cuba relied on African slavery, the state, by and large, supported worsening white color prejudice by enforcing new laws or not enforcing old ones. Despite some noteworthy exceptions, no person of color could become a priest, pharmacist, lawyer, doctor, or government bureaucrat. The occupational distribution in the census of 1846 suggests that those discriminatory laws were being strictly enforced before La Escalera. Of the 438 people listed as priests, none were free people of color. No printers were free people of color. None of the 270 pharmacists were free people of color. Neither were any of the 416 doctors and surgeons. None of the 208 holders of bachelor's degrees, 1,472 students of higher education, or 823 lawyers were free people of color. Only two of the 2,254 people listed as public employees were free people of color.[42] Even though free coloreds continued to enter middle-level trades and dominate many of them, certain whites saw this as a problem. In his well-known study of white vagrancy in Cuba, José Antonio Saco complained that "among the enormous evils that this miserable race has brought to our land, one of them is that of having separated our white population from the skilled trades."[43]

Largely in response to growing racial and political fears, the government passed a law in 1837, similar to one then in force in South Carolina,
that restricted the entrance of free people of color into Cuba. Authorities
remanded those who arrived in port to designated prisons until the vessel's departure, unless the captain or some other official posted bond so
that he could remain on board. Seeing this law in operation, the British
consul David Turnbull would say "the Havana is not a place where a person of colour, and a stranger, would choose to remain. Such . . . is the
dislike of the authorities to this class of persons; and such their anxiety to
discourage their arrival even when they are to remain all the time on
board their ship, that every possible obstacle is constantly interposed."[44]
Separation by color also occurred on Cuba's new railroads. Although free
people of color were not relegated to a Cuban equivalent of Jim Crow
cars, regulations in the 1840s did stipulate that only whites could sit in
first-class coaches.[45]

Captain-General Valdés reaffirmed the law of 1837 and imposed other
regulations on the people of color in his *Bando de Gobernación y Policía*.
No free person of color could work as a plantation overseer. All free people of color seeking work had to be licensed by the government. No persons
of color could carry the arms permitted to whites, except servants at the
behest of their master and drovers, who were allowed knives "without
point."[46] The Afro-Cuban *cabildos* could gather only on Sundays and ordained festival days and only outside the city walls. Except for the Day of
Kings, people of color could not walk city streets in the groupings of their
nation with banners or other symbols without the express permission of
the government. People of color could not sing or dance in "the style
of the nation to which they belong, nor of any other," in their houses, in
Christian altars, in funeral processions, or in other locations specified by
the government. The punishment of the free *pardo* Juan de la Cruz Valdés
in 1835 suggests how seriously the authorities took weapons violations.
For carrying a pistol he received fifty lashes and six years in prison.[47]

Richard Burleigh Kimball, a New York lawyer visiting Cuba in the
early 1840s, explained how Spanish law worked for another free person
of color. Kimball befriended a Mandinga washerwoman named Rosario
who had raised the money to purchase her freedom. "Since the patronage
of her former master was no longer hers, the petty exactions of the com-
missaries and sub-commissaries of the police ate up nearly all her earn-
ings." On a festival day she forgot to hang a lighted lantern outside her
door and was fined. A female servant who lived with Rosario neglected

to renew her work permit, so Rosario was fined for lodging an unlicensed person of color. When she tried to claim money owed her by a Spanish military officer for doing his wash, she had to borrow money to retain a lawyer, then plunged in "the ocean of Cuba law-suit." Thanks to the interposition of Kimball and a competent lawyer friend of his, Rosario won her claim. But *the expenses* [of the trial] . . . were far beyond the amount sued for; so that, upon the whole, it was understood and settled that poor Rosario should neither claim her bill nor pay any charges.[48] The victimization of Rosario does not appear to have been an isolated case, for Cuban whites themselves commented on how lesser Spanish officials without salaries attached to the police made a profession of preying upon free coloreds.

Laws in Cuba that promoted entrance into the free colored class by manumission have been seen as an important factor in the growth of the free colored class in Cuba and as a sign of a generally favorable racial climate.[49] These laws remained prominently on the books in 1840 but by then they neither explain the growth of the free colored population nor express a favorable racial climate. Cuban census data for the first half of the nineteenth century do not permit a detailed demographic analysis of the free colored population or, for that matter, of the white and slave populations. But the available numbers do sketch a structure favorable to the natural increase of the free colored population. Unlike the white or slave populations, the free people of color had more females than males, and more than half of its females were within the sixteen-to-forty age group—the group most likely to reproduce.[50] To some degree, manumissions did affect the age- and sex-specific peculiarities of the free colored population, for masters emancipated more female slaves than male.

Detailed manumission statistics probably do not exist for the 1840s, but those for the period 1858 to 1862 show females averaging 57.5 percent of those freed in a slave population that, according to the 1861 census, was 41.0 percent female.[51] The consistent bulking of males in the upper age groupings of the free colored population suggests that masters, when they manumitted males, were frequently relieving economic burdens; the consistent bulking of free colored females in the younger groupings suggests that masters, when they manumitted females, were frequently rewarding services in the bedroom and the kitchen. Color preference clearly figured in the pattern of manumission. Whereas *pardo* slaves formed less than 5 percent of the total slave population in 1846, they formed more than 23 percent of slaves manumitted from 1858 through 1862.[52] Slave children were manumitted in numbers that elicited notice but manumitted less frequently, it appears, than in the British West Indies. Manumission would seem to be far less significant than natural increase in explaining the growth of the free colored population during the sugar boom and why a markedly higher proportion of its people were under fifteen years of age than in the slave population.

Thus, despite the continued existence of liberal manumission laws, white class and racial fears prior to La Escalera appear to have markedly narrowed the slave's access to freedom. In 1818 the Havana town council went so far as to petition for an end to the government-sponsored lottery because slaves were winning and then buying their freedom. It reasoned that "the principal object of introducing blacks from Africa on our soil is the cultivation of the fields. . . . The blacks have not come here to be inhabitants of our cities nor to take part in the vices that in them abound, and the lottery produces this lamentable turnabout."[53] The petition failed, but complaints against the lottery for the chance it offered winning slaves to escape slavery continued. Although the lottery survived under Captain-General Valdés, his regulations restricted who could sell the tickets and where.

In their attitudes toward manumission and, by extension, the free colored class, Spanish authorities largely shared the growing fears and hostility of the white community. In 1843 José Joaquín de Agüero, a young liberal intellectual from Puerto Príncipe, came to the conclusion that a Christian could not own slaves and liberated eight of his own. Captain-General Valdés summoned Agüero directly to Havana for interrogation; so great was the political pressure that he fled to Philadelphia, all because, as Gaspar Betancourt Cisneros lamented, he had committed an act "that the laws not only do not prohibit but protect and celebrate."[54] Few of Agüero's countrymen followed his example. Not only did slaves have more value during the sugar boom, but the Spanish laws that promoted manumission now came to be seen by liberal whites as a tool to promote class rivalry and, thereby, to maintain imperial rule. A report of the Spanish government in 1846 estimated only five hundred manumissions per year; that would have been about half the number reported for Havana alone thirty-five years earlier.[55]

By 1840 changing white attitudes toward free people of color had brought about a slow but noticeable decline in the free colored militia. In the beginning, whites had generally looked with favor on a free colored militia as an outlet for class tensions by advancing some persons of color in both wealth and status. Division into *pardo* and *moreno* units could help to break up class alliances and reinforce the color-conscious social hierarchy. However, with the evacuation of its mainland colonies after the wars of liberation, Spain turned over an increasing share of Cuba's defense to regular troops. This change coincided with sugar prosperity and the full integration of a slave-based plantation economy into the wider world. As Cuba was transformed into a slave society, whites began to question the wisdom of arming a subordinate colored class that had already shown itself to be brave and capable in combat. During the early period of the sugar boom, Francisco Arango had repeatedly called for the elimination of the free colored militia precisely because of the potential threat it posed to white rule. The majority of his class, many of them militia officers themselves, did not take his warning seriously at the time; they knew the field value of these units and thought the barriers of color and status unlikely to be crossed. Then came the Conspiracy of Aponte in 1812 and discovery of the involvement of some of the *moreno* militiamen.[56]

In 1812 José Antonio Aponte, a talented woodworker and former commander of the *moreno* battalion of the Havana militia, organized in the Yoruban *cabildo* of which he was the head one of Cuba's most sophisticated and far-flung conspiracies of slaves and free coloreds. Napoleon's invasion of Spain in 1808 had set off separatist movements throughout Spanish America. Opportunistic Creoles in Cuba, as elsewhere, plotted to take control of their political future. Aponte had been one of the number of free colored militiamen who received approaches for support from white separatists in an aborted conspiracy of 1810. Aponte had great stature in the colored community. He used it to gather information on the liberal-democratic struggles in the wider world and on the political disarray of Spain's colonial empire.

French troops indirectly promoted Aponte's cause. The beleaguered regency had conceded parliamentary representation to the colonies at the emergency meeting of the Cortes at Cádiz. During one of its sessions, Miguel Guridi y Alcocer, a Mexican cleric, despite vigorous opposition from the Cuban delegation, pressed for a commitment on the abolition of the slave trade and slavery. People of color in Cuba and elsewhere picked up whispers, however imperfectly or inconsistently, from national or metropolitan debates on slavery elsewhere. The Saint Domingue Revolution had been fed by the rights-of-man debates in the French National Assembly, Denmark Vesey's conspiracy in 1822 by the congressional debates on the Missouri questions, the great Jamaican rebellion of 1831 by the emancipation debates in the British House of Commons. So too the Cortes debates reached Havana and Aponte and his followers, who seem to have propagated a version among the slaves of outlying regions in which slavery had already been abolished.

Aponte seems to have planned to stimulate an uprising of field slaves near certain cities, setting diversionary fires on plantations and in the suburbs to draw off regular troops, then propel himself to power by seizing key urban fortifications and armories. Aponte's surrogate in the eastern region, a Dominican veteran of the Saint Domingue Revolution named Hilario Herrera, counted on support from Haiti and its recently crowned king, Henry Christophe. Trouble came when two slaves betrayed the operations in Puerto Príncipe. Herrara fled to Santo Domingo, and the military rounded up many of his comrades for the usual whippings, imprisonments, and hangings. Resistance in Bayamo and other areas was smashed by the military. The Marqués de Someruelos, the Captain-General in Cuba, still had no inkling of the Havana connection until violence broke out on some nearby estates. Slaves razed the Peñas Altas sugar plantation, and killed several whites. A few days later, investigators learned of clandestine gatherings between Aponte and other men of color and searched their homes. In Aponte's house they found a large volume of illustrations that included African religious symbols, a battle scene between whites and people of color, and precise reproductions of greater Havana, indicating roads, plantations, warehouses, and military installations. On one of the walls hung a portrait of Aponte flanked by drawings of Henry Christophe, Toussaint L'Ouverture, and George Washington. They found incriminating documents also in the homes of Aponte's lieutenants.[57] Responding to an "urgent necessity to impose immediately prompt and exemplary punishment," the Marqués sentenced Aponte, five other free men of color, and three slaves to hang, their heads to be severed and exhibited in the "most convenient public places as a warning to others."[58] Aponte's head was posted at an entrance to Havana's principal colored ghettos.

Aponte's conspiracy was not the first such to be headed by a free person of color. In 1796 a free mulatto farmer, Nicolás Morales, influenced by the revolution in Saint Domingue, plotted with "various people of inferior status" to obtain certain reforms.[59] One year earlier, Charles IV had granted persons of part-Negro blood the right of *gracias al sacar,* that is, the right to buy legal whiteness. By paying a fee to the Spanish

Crown a mulatto could gain all the legal privileges enjoyed by whites: marriage with whites, entrance to the clergy, a university education, to mention a few. When the lieutenant-governor of Bayamo failed to publish the decree, Morales, heartened by stories that the mulattoes of Saint Domingue had attained equality with the whites, recruited supporters, including some whites who were complaining of high taxes, specifically the sales tax, and of encroachment by more powerful Bayamese planters on lands traditionally held in common or by the Crown. The conspirators intended to force the lieutenant-governor to present the decree of *gracias al sacar* and to petition King Charles to suspend the sales tax and redistribute land. Before the plan could be implemented, a member of the free colored militia denounced it to the lieutenant-governor, who promptly hanged Morales, jailed his underlings, and rewarded the apostate militiaman with a plot of land.

The Conspiracy of Aponte and subsequent instances of free colored unrest showed Cuban whites that there were dangerous political stirrings within the Afro-Cuban *cabildos.* From their beginnings in Cuba in the sixteenth century, the *cabildos* served as an instrument of ethnic cohesion. They had sustained rivalries, like that between Congo and Carabalí, and even rivalries within ethnicities. They had simplified communication between Spaniard and African and helped to adjust the *negros de naciones,* the recently imported victims of the African slave trade, to the ways of whites. They functioned only nominally as the agent to speed the religious conversion and instruction of slaves as originally intended when, in 1755, the Bishop of Cuba, Pedro Agustín Morell de Santa Cruz, had given the *cabildos* the official recognition of the Roman Catholic church. Rather, people of color turned them into a shelter for African ways and, robustly fed by the African slave trade during the sugar boom, they strengthened the differences between Afro-Cuban and Hispano-Cuban cultures. The weaker the identification with elements of the dominant white culture, the greater the difficulty in legitimating slaveholder power other than by brute force. Although by strengthening ethnic identification, the *cabildo* militated against the formation of any firm colored class solidarity, its members, as they entered the nineteenth century, appear to have occasionally put aside ethnic and intra-class color differences for revolutionary projects. The *cabildo* could be converted into a political hothouse. Indeed, conspiracies could grow within the urban, white-sanctioned associations of colored people.

The Military Commission, after its first session in 1825, prosecuted a steady stream of free people of color for uttering "subversive words," holding "secret gatherings," and committing "various excesses."[60] In 1837 it prosecuted an English mulatto "on the suspicion of having diffused pernicious doctrines" among the slaves. The man had in his possession assorted literature that included *The War in Texas; Instigated by Slaveholders, Land Speculators &c* and the *Memoir and Poems of Phillis Wheatley,* the black poet who had gently challenged North American whites to abandon their racism. One year later the Commission tried a *moreno* named Fernando Estrada for lecturing the good citizens of Bayamo from a pamphlet entitled *Ejemplo de la Libertad Civil* [The example of civil liberty]. The next year the authorities uncovered sundry writings about the establishment of constitutional government in the home of León Monzón, a captain of the *moreno* battalion of the Havana militia and a *cabildo* member. The Military Commission condemned Monzón and tens of other free people of color to prison, because "the grave evidence of this trial . . . is persuasive that plans of the conspiracy were hatched in the distinct societies [of the people of color] that without license or knowledge of the Governor met under the apparent pretext of dances and amusement."[61]

Proceedings against free colored militiamen prove common in the records of the Commission. In 1826 it tried Pedro Cortes, a former sergeant in the *pardo* militia, for spreading "subversive words," and José Emeterio Laza, a soldier in the *pardo* militia, for carrying a letter from Mexico; in 1827 it tried Domingo Suntas, a sergeant in the *moreno* militia, for holding "secret gatherings" and in 1837 Ignacio Hidalgo, a first sergeant in the *pardo* militia, for committing "various excesses." After the conviction of León Monzón in 1839, the Spanish Crown bade the Captain-General watch the free colored militia closely, and "in case its members show signs of seduction or desire for innovation, it is the royal will that you will proceed with full authority to destroy [them]."[62]

A constitutionalist *pronunciamiento* of General Manuel Lorenzo in 1836 shows that white fears of the free colored class were not confined to the western plantation districts. Taking his cue from liberal revolt in Spain, Lorenzo had pronounced against Captain-General Tacón to restore the Spanish Constitution of 1812 to Cuba. It began as a contest between two proud and ambitious men with different peninsular political loyalties. The liberal movement in Spain had split into two factions, each of which were cemented together by political patronage. Tacón owed his position in Cuba to the more conservative Moderado faction; Lorenzo owed his position to the more democratic Progresista faction. But soon the *pronunciamiento* attracted popular momentum. Lorenzo awakened long-standing regionalist discontent with Havana's political predominance and with imperial favoritism toward Havana and the western plantation districts.[63] Some of his lieutenants called for independence. But when Captain-General Tacón prepared for combat, previously enthusiastic men-of-property in and near Santiago faltered. Lorenzo's following included free colored troops. A protracted bloodletting endangered the social order by providing opportunities for them to advance their own interests. In consideration of its consul in Santiago and the British business interests to which he was tied, the British government acted to mediate a return to the status quo, contributing to the faintheartedness of the whites and Tacón's success. Captain Williams Jones of the British navy helped to convince Lorenzo to give up the struggle and board ship for safe passage to Spain by raising the larger issues: "Sir, no man conversant in the history of the times can be ignorant of the consequences of striking the first spark of Civil War in a Colony."[64]

Sandwiched between white masters and black slaves, free people of color might readily develop an ambivalent sense of loyalty. Many imbibed the prejudices of the culture to which they aspired and admitted their blackness as their guilt. The lighter and more Hispanicized people of color tended to stay away from the *cabildos,* preferring their own dances and celebrations to the street processions on the Day of Kings. José del Castillo, the Havana patrician, remembered that in the 1840s there were "many blacks and mulattos, some of them with abundant wealth who in their lifestyle, in their dress, and in their speech imitated those white gentlemen who still remained in Cuba, and among them no lack of people fond of reading serious books and even making verse."[65] Some imitated whites in slaveholding. An unnamed source, perhaps Turnbull or his aide Cocking, told the British Anti-Slavery Committee in 1842 that "many" free people of color owned slaves and treated them paternalistically.

They treat [their slaves] with the greatest kindness, they allow them the full Sunday and other holidays to work for themselves, provide them with decent clothes, and give them three reales weekly; the slaves consider such masters as their fathers. The free negroes who have acquired property, frequently purchase the freedom of the whole family from the grand-parents to the grand-children, and afterwards that of their friends who have come from the same town or village in Africa. They are decidedly in favour of the abolition of slavery.[66]

Yet, whether an internally divided free colored class aspired to be white, whether they acted "white," Creoles did not rest easy. Whites in tune with their age had contended for home rule; people of color could do the same. A racist Creole separatist, echoing the worst of his northern neighbors in terming African slaves apes and orangutangs and the free colored class "lazy and vicious," still had to fear that those inferior beings might obey the laws of mimicry too closely.

II

Cuba and Imperial Expansion

5

David Turnbull and the Crusade against Slavery

Slavery is the most vile and contemptible thing that can exist among men, because man, who is the most noble and free among all the creatures God made, is brought by means of it under the power of another, so that the other can make of him whatever he wishes, like any of the rest of his property, living or dead. And slavery is such a contemptible thing that whoever is subjected to it loses not only the power to make of himself what he wants, but he has not even the power over his own person, except by the order of his master.

Las Siete Partidas del rey Don
Alfonso el Sabio . . . ,
Part IV, Title V, c. 1263

Cuba's sugar boom came about during one of the most dramatic and profound shifts in moral sensibility in the making of the modern world, as history's first serious movement to rid the world of slavery gained support on both sides of the Atlantic. Great Britain had led the world in selling slaves from Africa to the Americas in the eighteenth century; in the nineteenth, it undertook a global crusade to end slavery.[1] After a series of hard-fought parliamentary struggles, the slave trade to Britain's colonies ended in 1807. Ten years later, Spain gave in to British pressure by signing a treaty to abolish its own colonial slave trade by 1820. But official corruption and the lure of gain frustrated diplomacy. Slave ships nimbly evaded British patrols in the Atlantic and the Caribbean. Cuba's hundreds of inlets were also the answer to a smuggler's prayer. Cuba imported more slaves in the 1830s than in any previous decade, and in all likelihood the 560,000 slaves imported in the first half of the century exceeded the total number imported to the North American mainland from the first landing in Virginia in 1619 to the legal end of the trade to the

United States in 1808.[2] Cuba's blatant contravention of the 1817 Treaty of Madrid set the stage for a long battle with the British government.

The British Emancipation Bill of 1833 heralded the end of the practice of slavery in the British West Indies. It also released the energies of abolitionists at home to maneuver against slaveholders in Brazil, the United States, and Cuba. In 1839 Joseph Sturge, a Quaker businessman, founded the British and Foreign Anti-Slavery Society to spread the gospel of abolitionism. One year later, Sturge and the Society organized the World Anti-Slavery Convention in London to map a comprehensive strategy. By constructing a trans-Atlantic network of activists in virtually every slaveholding region in the Americas politically well placed to procure and make public vital information on the operation of slavery as a system, they hoped to generate a tidal wave of moral revulsion.[3]

Among the Convention participants a forty-six-year-old Scot named David Turnbull figured as a rising star. He was admitted to the inner circles of the British and Foreign Anti-Slavery Society not by formal membership but by his previous service to the cause of human freedom. The only son of a Glasgow merchant, he was headstrong, humorless, often defensive, not the kind of man about whom someone could remain indifferent. Before his death in 1851, he would bedevil Cuba's planters and the trans-Atlantic diplomatic establishment as no abolitionist before or after him. Somehow neglected over the years since that have illuminated the roles of Sturge, Thomas Clarkson, Lewis Tappan, James Gillespie Birney, Harriet Martineau, and other leaders of the British abolitionist movement, Turnbull had earned acclamation from most of these in his own lifetime. His role needs to be reestablished.

Much of Turnbull's youth is mysterious. What is known suggests that early failures prepared him for radicalism. He had studied law at the University of Glasgow but was never graduated and, apparently, went bankrupt. His life picked up after the London *Times* hired him as a correspondent. In Paris, he fell in with a cosmopolitan group of liberal intellectuals, including French abolitionists, and wrote a partisan, eyewitness account of the July Revolution of 1830. In Spain, he reported sympathetically on what was perceived as a great liberal struggle against the Carlists; he greatly admired the efforts of George Villiers, Earl of Clarendon, to negotiate a more effective anti-slave-trade treaty. In 1837 he left the *Times* for a three-year tour of the Caribbean to search for evidence on what, for him, had already become truth: the superiority of free over slave labor. A British magistrate who accompanied Turnbull on an inspection of St. Vincent described him as a learned man, humane and penetrating, with a compelling vision "that we are passing for the last time through a country on the immediate eve of change, the most momentous which ever took place in any part of the world since the beginning of time."[4]

Turnbull spent the end of 1838 and early 1839 in Cuba, traveling about, questioning people of all ranks, writing down what he saw and heard. On his way back to Paris, he stopped briefly in the United States and, in New York, sat with Arthur Tappan, James G. Birney, and other members of the American Anti-Slavery Society in a March meeting of the executive committee. By February of 1840 he had completed his book *Travels in the West,* dedicated to Lord Clarendon; its central purpose was to go public with his plan to end Cuba's contraband slave trade. Lord Palmerston, Britain's foreign secretary, received a copy almost immediately, and Turnbull crossed over to London to carry on the bold interventions and brash salesmanship that would mark his career.[5]

Travels in the West touched off considerable discussion in the British press and among leading citizens and government officials at a time when the egalitarian elements of evangelical Protestantism had merged with the economics of the Manchester School into a coherent ideology, when free labor was substantiating Britain's claim to global preeminence. Debates on whether humanitarianism or naked self-interest motivated British abolitionism miss the point. Britain had redefined humanitarianism in a way compatible with British capitalism and the long-term projection of British power and in a way increasingly incompatible with slavery. Domestic clamor had mounted to end the slave trade and then to end slavery. Turnbull represented the new moral economy. He considered slavery criminal and called the slave trade "the greatest practical evil that ever afflicted mankind."[6] Having come to understand the inner workings of Cuba's slave system, he would now attempt to end its slave trade by exposing the duplicity by which certain parties concerted to circumvent international agreements.

As Turnbull and many other abolitionists were well aware, suppression of Cuba's slave trade was more apparent than real. The Treaty of Madrid had given the British the right to search suspected Spanish slavers and if slaves were on board to impound vessel and cargo. Special tribunals set up in Sierra Leone and Havana determined the fate of a seized vessel. Spain and Great Britain appointed to each tribunal one commissary judge and one commissioner of arbitration. If the judges disagreed, they were to draw lots to name one of the arbitrators to cast the deciding ballot. On a vote of guilty, the contraband slaves would be turned over to representatives of the government in whose territory the adjudication was made—ideally, to prepare them for freedom.[7]

Loopholes and lack of enforcement had, as noted earlier, undermined the treaty. Without the consent of all major nations to the British right to stop and board a ship to verify its nationality—in the language of international law, the right to search—vessels in the Cuban trade could switch flags to prevent it. Since seizure could only occur if slaves were discovered on board, empty outgoing ships blatantly outfitted for slaving could sail safely away. The greatest blame for the treaty's shortcomings, however, lay with susceptible Spanish officials. Various Captains-General and their underlings were known to receive money for each contraband slave landed, seeing it less as a bribe than a perquisite of office. Thus officials, made more vulnerable by low pay, who heard of an illicit landing of slaves investigated nominally or not at all. Elisha Atkins, a Boston sugar merchant who spent considerable time in Cuba, said slave traders would drill their African slaves to say "José" and cross themselves to pass the official inspection.[8] When evidence did reach the Court of Mixed Commissions, the Spanish members frequently winked at it. "In all the captures made by the English of Spanish vessels on these coasts and which have been adjudged in this city [Havana]," the Spanish merchant Pedro Diago confidently instructed one of his slave-trading captains in 1828, "there is not known a single instance of anyone having been punished; for all of them, owing to the assistance of friends, have succeeded in getting off."[9]

The slaves from captured slave ships, called *emancipados,* were to have received wages, religious instruction, and preparation for freedom in return for a term of service of about five years, which might be extended by no more than three years. Instead, they fell victim to Cuban labor demands and prejudice that cut short their lives in what often turned out to be a lifetime of bondage. Spanish authorities and many Cuban whites saw these men and women, neither slave nor free, as a nuisance, as an expense to maintain, and even as a threat to the social order. Cuba's whites had no wish to increase the ranks of the free people of color, and "news of their [the *emancipados'*] condition will surely give rise to reflection [and] contrasts, whose sad results would not be very difficult to predict.[10]

Under Captain-General Vives an ill-documented practice began of consigning *emancipados* for "donations" to "distinguished and honorable" citizens and to religious and educational institutions.[11] After discussions on how to get the *emancipados* out of Cuba, an accord with Britain in

1833 allowed them to be sent to Trinidad at Spanish expense. A few hundred were sent. But rising slave prices in the aftermath of a great cholera epidemic in 1833, more captured slaves, and the arrival in Cuba of Miguel Tacón in 1834 as Captain-General ended this practice. The purchase of their labor by planters for plantation work became an ordered and profitable business. Locations of *emancipados* and their terms of service were neglected or conveniently forgotten. An *emancipado* would abruptly "die," complete with a burial certificate from the parish priest, citing the identity of a truly dead slave; and, in a "reborn" life, remain a slave the rest of his life. A reckoning by the Spanish authorities themselves in 1841 put the number of *emancipados* at 9,020, more than 95 percent of whom had been rescued from slaving vessels captured between 1824 and 1836. Of that 95 percent, about one-third were counted as dead; another 2 percent could not be accounted for or had run away; and less than 2 percent had obtained freedom.[12]

Turnbull praised Lord Clarendon for wringing important concessions from Spain in an 1835 treaty. The regency of María Cristina, which had been installed in Madrid with British support, acceded to an "equipment clause," which allowed the seizure of vessels with merely the trappings of the trade, such as excess provisions, shackles, and hatches with gratings. The treaty, called the Clarendon Convention, transferred control of the *emancipados* to officials of the government whose cruisers made the capture—in effect, from Spanish to British hands.[13] By 1840 Great Britain had signed mutual search agreements with every major maritime power except the United States. Slave traders, therefore, resorted to United States registry and ran up United States flags. Even María Cristina herself invested in their lucrative operations. Many traders purchased swift Baltimore clippers, largely stripped of slaving gear, to elude British patrols and confound search.[14]

A legal officer of the *audiencia* of Puerto Rico testified in 1838 to the splitting of a thirty-dollar-per-head bribe from the slave traders by Cuba's chief officials: eight dollars went to the Captain-General, two dollars to his secretary, two dollars to his second in command, three dollars to the commander of the navy, one dollar to the harbor master, eight dollars to the intendant, and six dollars to unnamed others. Miguel Tacón reputedly retired in 1838 with 450,000 dollars of head-money, and the best estimates on the volume of the Cuban slave trade suggest the possibility of such a sum. Cuban slave traders never fared better than they did between the time of the Clarendon Treaty (1835) and the World Anti-Slavery

Convention (1840); they imported more than 20,000 slaves annually.[15]

Turnbull proposed to enforce the Anglo-Spanish agreements by expanding the power of the Court of Mixed Commission to include investigation of slaves already landed in Cuba. Since Great Britain lost any chance to free contraband slaves once they touched Cuba, Turnbull argued that the court should be invested with the power to institute a kind of *quo warranto* proceeding, in which masters could be summoned before the court and forced to prove that their slaves were held in accordance with earlier agreements. Distinctive social characteristics and physical markings, such as scars and tattoos, would make *bozales* (newly imported Africans) difficult to hide no matter what ruses slaveholders might employ. The court would also encourage slaves to institute proceedings on their own behalf. Turnbull thought to end the supply of slaves by scaring off demand. He doubted his plan would work perfectly. He understood that it would not be easily accepted in Spain nor, if accepted, easily implemented in Cuba. But the key was to have the invigorated Court of Mixed Commission, even if restricted in efficiency by its Spanish members, spread fear among Cuba's planters about the loss of their property. "It is by making the purchaser and possessor of an African slave insecure in the enjoyment of his unlawful acquisition that he is to be deterred from paying the price."[16] Turnbull knew that with low fertility and high mortality the slave population failed to reproduce itself naturally. Therefore, the majority of slaves in Cuba in 1840 had to have entered in the twenty or so years after the Treaty of Madrid. More than a project to end the slave trade, Turnbull offered *ipso facto* a virtual program of total abolition.

The Whig administration in which Lord Palmerston served as foreign secretary had heavily engaged itself in an aggressive and costly policy to suppress the slave trade as the preferred way to strike at the root of slavery. Turnbull knew this and on coming to London tried to get a hearing from Palmerston. His first letter failed to get a reply so another went off, this time to Lord Leveson, Palmerston's aide in the Foreign Office, in the hope of gaining an introduction. The appearance of the core ideas of Turnbull's plan in the London *Morning Chronicle* on March 9 may have helped, for the next day Leveson acknowledged Palmerston's receipt of Turnbull's letter, although with doubts about the efficacy of Turnbull's plan. Turnbull returned a lengthy explication that drew heavily from his book. Upon reflection, Palmerston saw some merit in what Turnbull had in mind and told Lord Leveson to go ahead and prepare a draft of a convention based on Turnbull's ideas for presentation to the Spanish government. Palmerston still considered any expectation of Spain's acceptance of the convention as "visionary" and assumed "that not one negro in a thousand would be brought up" before the Mixed Commission, but, as he confided to Leveson, "if carried into execution it would be useful both in Principle and in Practice."[17]

Turnbull waited in London while his ideas circulated in public. Their appearance in a column of the March 17 London *Times* prompted an invitation from the British and Foreign Anti-Slavery Society for Turnbull to give particulars. More invitations followed. Still not knowing that Palmerston was taking his plan seriously, Turnbull wrote Leveson with only slight coloring, that

The West India body, the British and Foreign Anti-Slavery Society, the African Colonization Society, and several other public bodies, some actuated by philanthropic, some perhaps by interested motives, have expressed themselves with remarkable unanimity in favor of the practicability of the plan. The subject has also occupied a large share of the attention of the press. Almost every existing journal has treated of it more or less minutely: not one of them, so far as I am aware, has withheld its approbation; and I venture thereupon to assume that the public voice has been declared in its favor.[18]

Shortly thereafter, *The Monthly Review,* another influential London journal, excerpted Turnbull's book and correctly predicted that his "disclosures and proposals . . . must force themselves upon the attention of the people of Great Britain, upon her senators, and rulers."[19]

Turnbull thought about returning to France but, with the opening of the World Anti-Slavery Convention near, he stayed on and came to play a prominent role in the proceedings. His long residence in Paris and his earlier association with French abolitionists, including François-André Isambert, Secretary of the French Anti-Slavery Society, made Turnbull the logical choice to introduce him and his small delegation to those attending. During the convention he took the podium to continue to campaign for his plan and later, behind closed doors, began another for himself as the logical candidate to implement it in Cuba.[20]

He had learned that Palmerston was going to open talks with Spanish officials about his plan. Aware that the British consulate in Havana had become vacant and that R. R. Madden, his fellow abolitionist and close friend from the Paris and Cuba days, had resigned his post as Superintendent of Liberated Africans, Turnbull now boldly proposed to Palmerston, more than once, that the Havana consulate should be combined with other offices, that it should be raised to the status of Consulate General, that vice-consulates should be established in ports actively involved in the slave trade, and that he himself should be the first person in whom the combined offices and power should rest.[21]

The continued agitation in the British press of one of Cuba's most celebrated violations of Spain's anti-slave-trade agreements no doubt helped Turnbull's candidacy. In 1839 fifty-three *bozales,* recently imported from Africa and bound for reshipment from Havana to Puerto Príncipe on the Baltimore-made schooner *Amistad,* revolted. They killed the captain and a cook, held two other whites captive, and tried to sail for Africa. When they approached Long Island by mistake, they were rounded up by the United States Coast Guard and jailed pending resolution in the courts. The *Amistad* affair became a cause célèbre for abolitionists on both sides of the Atlantic. In 1840 a final decision had not yet been handed down, and the British government had to consider what to do if the United States responded to the demands of Spain's minister in Washington to return the ship and the mutineers, illegally enslaved in the first place, to Cuba.[22]

Palmerston was not a crusader. Despite occasional lapses into personal vendettas, he predicated his foreign policy on hard military and geopolitical facts. The European balance of power concerned him far more than affairs in the Americas. But abolitionist values had taken hold in England, and Palmerston was well aware of the political power of the more organized bodies of abolitionists. He had drawn fire from some of their members in the 1830s for not supporting immediate abolition in the British West Indies.[23] Perhaps in compensation he had shown little reservation in attacking the evils of the Atlantic slave trade. Given his public pronouncements and the obvious violations of Anglo-Spanish agreements in Cuba, Palmerston may have considered the appointment of Turnbull in the wake of the World Anti-Slavery Convention as a firm statement to the Spanish and as smart domestic politics. After Turnbull had offered his candidacy, a high-ranking delegation from the British and Foreign Anti-Slavery Society met with Palmerston and most certainly discussed Turnbull and the Cuban situation. In August 1840 Palmerston appointed Turnbull to the combined positions of British consul to Cuba and Superintendent of Liberated Africans.[24] The Society had prepared the way for his acceptance with assurances of financial support. Turnbull had pledged to its members that he would "always be ready to promote the great objects to which they devote themselves by all the means in my power."[25] Now he stood in a position to translate his words into action.

A socially fragmented Spanish colony, rich in sugar and slaves, and coveted by imperialists in Britain and the United States, could ill afford the presence of an avowed abolitionist in a crucial diplomatic post. Turnbulls' reputation had preceded him. When he arrived to assume his duties in November, Cuba's ruling coalition of merchants, titled planters, and peninsular bureaucrats waited to obstruct his work and, indeed, to threaten his life. Rumors were swirling that Great Britain had succeeded in negotiating with Spain for the emancipation of all Cuba's slaves. Anxieties heightened about the threat posed by Turnbull to slave property. His coming roughly coincided with one more in an ever increasing number of slave revolts, this time in Cienfuegos province.[26]

Captain-General Pedro Téllez de Girón, the Prince of Anglona, a Spanish grandee with an unquestioned genealogy, was taking a per capita kickback from the slave trade at the time. He refused to grant Turnbull his exequatur, that is a written recognition of his office by the host country, then warned the metropolitan government to have Turnbull removed or risk colonial rebellion. Spokesmen for the two administrative councils that represented planter and merchant interests—the Junta de Fomento and the Tribunal de Comercio—echoed the prince with lengthy memorials beseeching the Spanish government to stem the assault on Cuba's labor system by Turnbull and anyone else or risk the simultaneous extirpation of Cuba's prosperity and its white population. María Cristina's regime owed too much to Britain financially and politically to do what was asked. It could only sympathize with the prince, concede the exequatur, and tell him to uphold the Treaty of 1835 while it maneuvered to persuade Palmerston to send a replacement.[27]

To many Cubans, Turnbull's presence actually capped a pile of outrages that they had suffered or were suffering at the hands of the British. They were bearing the indignity of the British hulk *Romney,* full of free colored soldiers from Britain's West Indian regiments, now anchored in Havana harbor in compliance with the Treaty of 1835 to take on *emancipados* released into British custody. Violence had broken out on shore between the soldiers and Cuban whites. Cubans charged that subversion was conducted from the ship; its colored soldiers, when they came ashore, were said to inspire Cuban slaves to rebel.[28] Cubans were hearing about officially approved abolitionist camp meetings in nearby Jamaica at which ardent Methodists and Anabaptists regularly forecast the slaveholder's day of reckoning.[29] In December 1840 Commander Joseph Denman of the British navy dealt a severe blow to Cuba's slave trading by razing one of its major West African emporia on the Gallinas River. Newspaper accounts put the loss of merchandise in the hundreds of thousands of dollars and of the slaves liberated by Denman at more than a thousand.[30] During the drawn-out legal and diplomatic proceedings of the *Amistad* affair, Madden traveled to the United States to give crucial testimony that established that the slaves had been abducted from Africa in violation of Spain's anti-slave-trade agreements. Against the demand of Spain's minister in Washington to return the ship and its mutineers to Cuba, the United States Supreme Court finally rendered a decision in 1841 to free the slaves.[31]

Anglophobia spread across the land in the early 1840s. To be British was to be a subversive. Poor Patrick Doherty, a British engineer on the Güines railway, made a mistake that caused a train collision; authorities jailed him for sabotage. James Joyce, another British transient, landed in a Cuban jail because he blustered over dinner to some sensitive Catalans, who denounced him for saying that Britain would come to rule Cuba and free the slaves.[32] J. G. F. Wurdemann, the perceptive South Carolina physician who was in Cuba recuperating from consumption, described how he and a countryman tried in vain to get the lieutenant-governor to change their passports so that they could travel to Matanzas. Only after a friendly Creole interceded did the lieutenant-governor relent. " 'He thought you were Englishmen,' he [the Creole] told us laughing, 'and did not half like your movements.' "[33] Gaspar Betancourt Cisneros, the influential Creole planter from Puerto Príncipe, wrote of his conversation with a lawyer and a noble kinsman several months after Turnbull took office, in which the lawyer proposed "to release an anonymous message to come to the attention of the English that here one hundred thousand men have sworn to assassinate every living Englishmen the moment England obtains a blank check in the business of our slavery."[34]

If Turnbull had practiced less immediacy he might have defused tensions. But crusaders rarely can. Seeing an opening, he practiced his abolitionist faith with both power and reckless abandon. José del Castillo, a well-educated Cuban notable, a slaveholder and a staunch Catholic, confessed in a letter of 1843 to the British and Foreign Anti-Slavery Society that he had been stirred from his mindless inertia about slavery only after coming into contact with David Turnbull.[35] Yet Turnbull provoked more native whites than he converted, and to the brink of violent retaliation, by his relentless probing into Cuba's slave system. He had inherited from Madden an extensive, if not always reliable, intelligence network of restive slaves and free coloreds, liberal Creoles, and paid informants. Turnbull learned not only of illicit slave landings but of infringements on the rights of *emancipados* and the whereabouts of people of color who had been spirited from British possessions to labor on Cuban sugar plantations. He did arrange the release of six colored victims of kidnapping shortly after his arrival and, for safekeeping, shipped them to the Bahamas, where in accordance with his "understanding of the general principle . . . [of] her Majesty's Government" they could help to firm up the "barriers against [North] American encroachment."[36] On most occasions, however, when he complained to the Prince of Anglona he met stiff resistance.

In the particular cases of an *emancipado* named Gavino and an enslaved British subject, Henry Shirley, Turnbull confronted the system head-on. Information from an antislavery Creole identified a Lucumí water-carrier named Gavino in a state tantamount to slavery sixteen summers and four masters after his release as an *emancipado* from a captured slave ship. Turnbull applied to the prince on Gavino's behalf for Gavino's release and payment of back wages. Gavino was Turnbull's test case "to place the iniquity of the whole system in a clear and striking light before the world."[37] Armed with considerable evidence and the knowledge that Gavino's present master would not muster a challenge, Turnbull hoped to score a judgment from the Captain-General that would recognize an independent right to police such matters within the island.[38] The prince rejected Turnbulls's presumptions: "I do not recognize in you the power to listen to complaints of this nature, and still less that of taking the name of the black in question, and of making representations in consequence, whether as British Consul or as Superintendent of Liberated Africans."[39]

The Cuban regime, like every other slaveholding regime, reacted with near hysteria to the slightest attack on slavery. The prince understood that Turnbull's activities in support of people of color were agitating a society that was already under severe internal stress. "This affair has a very serious bearing on the political administration of the affairs of this island," the prince admonished Turnbull, "because it supposes that you are qualified to listen to complaints and to offer protection to the people of color, and to support their pretensions. Such a state of things might loosen the ties of subordination and obedience."[40] Turnbull should desist or be handed his passport. In impassioned words that reveal much about him and the charged atmosphere in Cuba, Turnbull fired back:

Since the period when Your Excellency thought fit, under the influence of un-wise and dangerous councils, to refuse to receive me in the rank and station to which I have been raised by the favor of my Sovereign . . . I have been daily assailed with the darkest threats of deportation and murder. . . . But Your Excellency will permit me to suggest that if I am visited with deportation, the voice of the exile will be heard in every corner of Europe; that if I become the victim of assassination, while residing under the immediate protection of Your Excellency, the blood of the first Martyr which this fair Island shall have given to the Cause of Freedom will cry aloud for vengeance, and will serve to nourish and invigorate that glorious Tree of Liberty which first planted under the British Banner . . . is destined to spread like the Blessed Banyan until its shadow encircles the Earth throughout the whole extent of the broad Girdle of the Tropics.[41]

Turnbull addressed the plight of Henry Shirley with similar zeal. A disreputable Cuban smuggler named Le Desma had abducted Shirley along with five companions from Jamaica in 1830. Le Desma enslaved Shirley under an alias and set him to work in a small shop in the town of Santa Cruz. Somehow, nearly a decade later, Shirley managed to transmit a message to an aunt in Kingston that told her his location and condition. She notified Jamaica's Governor Metcalfe, who, in turn, relayed the information to Charles Tolmé, Turnbull's predecessor as consul. The proceedings would have stalled there had not Turnbull come into the consulate and taken personal charge of the case. With persistence and the weight of evidence on his side, he forced the prince to act. The Spanish auditor assigned to investigate, no doubt reflecting the prince's own commitment, brusquely reported that Shirley had simply vanished. When Turnbull pursued the issue and learned of Le Desma's flight with Shirley to Puerto Príncipe, another official probe yielded the dubious testimony of a fellow slave that Shirley was dead.

Turnbull bought none of it and resorted to other tactics. Since Metcalfe had uncovered witnesses to the kidnapping who could identify both Le Desma and Shirley, Turnbull decided to challenge Cuban authorities to hand over Le Desma so that he could be confronted by the witnesses, preferably in Jamaica but, if necessary, in Cuba. Le Desma might then be identified, perhaps punished for his crimes, or, at the very least, required to furnish information that would lead to Shirley's discovery. The prince adamantly refused to give up Le Desma. Spanish law prohibited such a confrontation of accused and accuser, and he reiterated that Turnbull had

David Turnbull (center), British consul in Havana, at 1840 World Anti-Slavery Convention in London. A radical abolitionist, he was convicted in 1844 in absentia as "prime mover" behind La Escalera. *Courtesy, National Portrait Gallery, London.*

(*Top*) Francisco Arango y Parreño,
prominent liberal planter; called the
father of Cuba's plantation system.
(*Bottom*) Gaspar Betancourt Cisneros,
influential Creole planter and advocate of ending the slave trade.

(*Top*) José Antonio Saco, liberal of the generation after Arango's, expelled from Cuba in 1834 for denunciation of slave trade. (*Bottom left*) Félix Tanco, Colombian-born abolitionist and author of antislavery novel, *Petrona y Rosalía,* one of Turnbull's contacts. (*Bottom right*) Domingo Del Monte, liberal intellectual and antislavery advocate implicated in the Conspiracy.

Gerónimo Valdés, Cuba's Captain-General, or chief executive, 1841–1843; he regarded slavery as crucial to Spanish rule. (*Right*) Beginning of advertisement in *Diario de la Habana*, 2 December 1843, listing 673 captured runaway slaves who were waiting to be claimed by their owners.

CONTADURIA
DE LA REAL JUNTA DE FOMENTO.

El domingo 3 de Diciembre próximo entrante, estarán reunidos en la casa de depósito, estramuros desde las 6 de la mañana hasta las 2 de la tarde todos los negros cimarrones existentes en las obras de calzadas comprendidos en la lista que a continuacion se inserta. Y se avisa al público para que los que tengan esclavos prófugos ocurran dicho dia al lugar designado a reconocerlos en donde estará abierto el despacho el tiempo acostumbrado para espedir las papeletas de entrega a favor de los que quieran estraer sus siervos.

2, Francisco congo, remitido de la cárcel.—3, Andres idem, remitido de Matanzas.—4, Anacleta mina, remitida de la Nueva Paz.—5, Miguel carabalí, remitido del Bayamo.—6, Pio gangá, remitido de Santi-Espíritu.—7, Luis carabalí, remitido de Guamutas.—8, Buenaventura idem, del Bayamo.—9, Merced conga, remitida de Guanajay.—10, Lorenzo carabalí, remitido de Matanzas.—11, Valeriana idem, aprehendida en la ciudad.—12, José criollo, de D. Francisco Hernandez, remitido de San Lázaro.—13 Juana conga, de Doña Juana Marente, remitida de Guadalupe.—14 José gangá, remitido de Villa-Clara.—15 José vivi, remitido del Guatao.—16 Celestino gangá, remitido de Puerto-Príncipe.—17 José carabalí, remitido de San Nicolas.—18 Hilario mandinga, remitido del Bayamo.—19 Antonio mina, remitido por el Sr. Mayor de Plaza—20 Carmen gangá, remitida de Rio-Blanco del Norte.—21 Canuto idem, remitido de Remedio.—22 Rafael idem, remitido de Villa-Clara.—23 José idem, remitido del Bayamo.—24 Patricio carabalí, de D. José Güen, remitido de Remedios.—25 Bartolomé congo, remitido de Puerto-Príncipe.—26 José mandinga, de doña Mariana Villalon, remitido de idem.—27 Ramon gangá, remitido de Villa-Clara.—28 Casimiro mina, idem de Cienfuegos.—29 Fernando congo, de D. Ramon Lazo, idem de Cayajabo.—30 Domingo idem, remitido del Bayamo.—31 Isabel idem, id. de Peudencias.—32 Ignacio gangá, de D. Pablo Pedroso, idem de Rio Blanco del N.—33 Socorro idem, de doña Francisca Perez, remitida del Horcon.—35 Rosario conga, idem de Alquizar.—36 José F. criollo, idem de Matanzas.—37 Felipe carabalí, idem de Quiebra Hacha.—38 Luisa mandinga, de D. Juan Martinez, idem de Jesus María.—39 Antonio congo, idem de Villa-Clara.—40 Genobeba lucumí, aprehendida en la ciudad—41 Josefa gangá, remitida de Guadalupe.—42 Antonio carabalí, aprehendido en la ciudad.—43 Antonio gangá, remitido de Villa-Clara.—44 Fabian congo, idem de Cienfuegos.—45 Merced idem, de D. Francisco de Sales, idem de Matanzas.—46 Nepomuceno idem, idem de Jibacoa.—47 Pantaleon idem, idem de Matanzas.—48 Cleto idem, idem de Cienfuegos.—49 Josefa carabalí, idem del Cerro.—50 Isabel conga, de Doña Viceuta de la Cora, idem del Bayamo.—52 Ramon lucumí, idem de Matanzas.—53 Pantaleon gangá, idem de idem.—54 María mina de D. Pablo Fernandez, aprehendida en San Lázaro.—56 Cayetano lucumí, remitido de Tapaste.—57 José gangá, idem del Mariel.—59 Merced lucumí, aprehendida en la ciudad.—60 José bámbara remitido de la Hanabana.—61 Elena carabalí, id. de Puerto-Príncipe.—62 Domingo congo, idem de idem.—63 Antonio idem, idem de Santi-Espíritu.—65 Carolina lucumí, idem de Matanzas.—66 Celestino idem, idem de idem.—67 Sotero carabalí, remitido de Madrugas.—68 Antonio mandinga, idem de Matanzas.—

(*Top*) José de la Luz y Caballero, director of Havana Economic Society, acquitted of involvement in La Escalera. (*Bottom left*) Father Félix Varela of Cuba's San Carlos Seminary, liberal activist, exiled to U.S. and suspected of involvement with Cuban dissidents. (*Bottom right*) General Narciso López, leader of the separatist, proslavery "American" party.

(*Top left*) John George F. Wurde-mann, South Carolina physician who wrote *Notes on Cuba* on colonial Cuban society while convalescing from consumption in the winter of 1843–44. *With the permission of Daniel M. Rogge* (*Top right*) Alexander Hill Everett, special U.S. envoy to Cuba in 1840; he opposed British abolition efforts and supported U.S. annexation of Cuba. (*Bottom*) Abel Upshur, native of Virginia and U.S. Secretary of State in President Tyler's proslavery administration; he worked to prevent "Africanization of Cuba," that is the domination of whites by people of color.

DIARIO DE LA HABANA

(*Left*) Advertisement for *"Esclavo prófugo,"* runaway slaves, *Diario de la Habana,* 12 September 1843. (*Right*) Cuban slave hunter (*rancheador*), with blood-hounds.

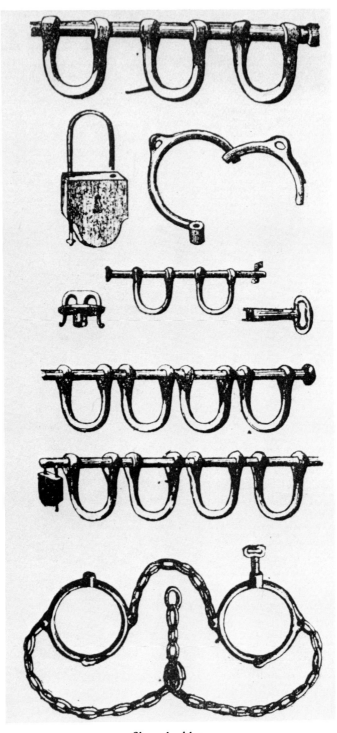

Slave shackles.

no authority to intervene in Spanish affairs. Turnbull lost patience and requested from Governor Metcalfe of Jamaica the strategic deployment of the British West Indian squadron to enlighten the prince, a request the governor ignored.[42]

Turnbull's defiance and relentless probing could seem to cast serious doubt on the wisdom of Palmerston's appointment. However much Palmerston favored the end of slavery in Cuba and wanted to extend British influence there, he had to work through and maintain Spain as the best way to achieve these goals given the countercheck of an aggressive, expansionist United States. His government, like the Spanish, foresaw Turnbull's possible precipitation of an incident that could move Cuba's Creoles toward independence and to look for help from the United States.

Cuba's slave-trading interest meanwhile "did not omit measures" to disparage Turnbull and to inflame Cuban whites against him. Francisco Jimeno, when asked to recall these days of which he was a part, described how the slave traders waged a verbal war against Turnbull and Great Britain. They spread "among the masses that the self-interest of the English was the only motive" for their insistence on the end of the slave trade. Printed works attacked Britain for attempting to destroy Cuba "in order to have the monopoly of the cultivation of [sugar] cane in the Indies" and for sending Turnbull, who was Britain's "agent in such iniquitous work." To Jimeno the charges of the slave traders were "ridiculous," but at the time "every idea contrary to slavery was seditious and the word abolitionist the greatest of crimes."[43] Mariano Torrente, a proslavery member of the Spanish Parliament, on the payroll of the slave traders, proclaimed that Turnbull's "presence is always an unfavorable omen, an inseparable obstacle to the tranquility of the country, and a banner under the shadow of which those persons ill-disposed towards the system at present in force, hope to mature the plans of their chimerical triumph."[44] Britain should remove Turnbull, and he could take the *Romney* with him.

Various Spanish ministers kept diplomatic channels humming in an effort to expel Turnbull, whom they considered a pharisee who was loosening Spain's hold on Cuba. Early in 1841 the Spanish government invested minister Antonio González with plenipotentiary powers and sent him to London solely to bargain for Turnbull's dismissal. The pattern of denunciation became monotonous. Turnbull was a "fanatic abolitionist," "inquisitor," and *agent provocateur,* who desired nothing less than the ascendancy of "his favorite black race."[45] Because of Turnbull, Spain even tightened its general policy for granting exequaturs in Cuba by ordering the authorities in Havana to file detailed reports on all individual applicants.[46]

With one eye on England's abolitionist party, Palmerston defended Turnbull, informing the ministers that Spain's inability to enforce the Treaty of 1835 had forced him to send a zealot to Cuba, that Turnbull's abolitionist views mirrored the beliefs of all British citizens. Unless specific crimes could be leveled against Turnbull, he would stay. But unbeknown to the Spanish government or the British public, Palmerston dispatched reprimands. He ordered Turnbull to eliminate "sneer and irony" from his communications and to exhibit proper respect in his dealings with both British and Spanish functionaries. Turnbull, characteristically indiscreet, had reminded Palmerston that "when your Lordship did me the honor to appoint me to this consulate it must have been foreseen that I was not exactly the person whose presence would be most welcome to local authorities."[47]

Turnbull clung to a principle, that "when a treaty or contract had . . . been violated, it was the undeniable right of the party aggrieved to choose its own agents, and to select its own mode of bringing the infraction under the notice of the other contracting party."[48] Frustrated by the Prince of Anglona in his personal attempt to extend the principle, he repeatedly prodded James Kennedy and Campbell J. Dalrymple, the two British members of the Court of Mixed Commissions, to take a more active role in protesting treaty violations and conducting investigations. To one official from the United States, Kennedy seemed to have "a personal feeling on the subject of slavery," but insufficiently strong, it seems, for R. R. Madden, who had warned Turnbull not to depend on either commissioner.[49] Both had availed themselves of the labor of *emancipados* and slaves; both shared the Spanish view that the court possessed no clear legal claim to engage in investigations; and, to Turnbull at least, both maintained their posts as little more than sinecures. Creoles dubbed them "priests who preach the morality they do not practice," and Turnbull's aide Francis Ross Cocking, in a letter to the British and Foreign Anti-Slavery Society, remarked caustically that "the one lives about 2 leagues in the country where his whole time is occupied in the study of Ornithology, and the other, *poor man,* is too simple to do good, and too innocent to do harm."[50] Turnbull's interventions, his unsubtle impugning of their integrity, evoked resentment from the men. And when Palmerston acted upon a memorial of the World Anti-Slavery Convention championed by Turnbull and ordered all British civil servants to divest themselves of direct or indirect interests in slave property, their resentment turned into hostility.

This issue may have played a part—a large part if Turnbull is to be believed—in the decision to remove Charles Tolmé, his predecessor. For a time, while consul, Tolmé had owned, or allowed his wife to own, a sugar plantation cultivated by slave labor. Havana during the sugar boom was one of the most expensive places in the hemisphere. A sixty-foot lot within Havana's walls in 1840 could sell for tens of thousands of dollars. Unlike Turnbull, who by choice located outside the walls, on the highway San Luis Gonzaga, within walking distance of the major colored barrios, Tolmé had chosen to live within the walls on the costly Calle de Obrapia. He had a big family and could not live well on the £300-per-annum salary provided by the Foreign Office. He supplemented his income by engaging in trade, which tainted him by association with elements of Cuba's slave-trading interest. He also owned slave domestics.[51] When Turnbull took over the consulate in 1840, he came with an increase in salary and instructions to police the new government policy to which he had contributed. Although Kennedy, a Palmerston client, appears not to have gotten along well with Tolmé, and claimed that he would never own slaves, he had hired them, and his British clerk on the Mixed Court not only had trafficked in them but employed *emancipado* servants. Thus, in the first in a series of rejections, the Court of Mixed Commissions said no to Turnbull's petition for a hearing on the Gavino question.[52]

Abolitionist prospects did improve somewhat, early in 1841, after a change in government in Spain led to the removal of the Prince of Anglona from Cuba. The overthrow of María Cristina by General Baldomero Espartero brought to Spain an avowed Anglophile as regent and to Cuba another Anglophile, the new Captain-General, Gerónimo Valdés. Valdés was a former provincial governor and a seasoned military man, in fact an "Ayacucho," one of the select group of several hundred Spanish officers on hand in Peru at General Rodil's surrender to Bolívar after the last great battle of the Spanish-American revolutions. He entered Cuba with a reputation for integrity and under orders to enforce the Treaty of 1835. His initial actions seemed to justify his reputation; he promptly called the major slave traders together and gave them six months to cease their activities; he closed Havana's public barracoons (the holding depots for contraband slaves), which had been barkering flesh for years within earshot of the suburban palace; and he disquieted the entire slaveholding community by commanding Cuba's leading institutions and individuals to submit reports that would assess the impact on Cuba of the emancipation of all slaves imported after 1820.[53]

Britain's abolitionists grew optimistic, but Turnbull lost his initial enthusiasm after hearing rumors that Valdés himself was taking a piece of slave-trading profits from the notorious firms of Martínez and Mazorra. In addition, the shutdown of the barracoons was accused of being a sham. Turnbull's sources charged Valdés with sending secret instructions to the slave traders, via local officials, to remove contraband slaves from the public view of the barracoons to the seclusion of *depósitos particulares,* planter- or merchant-owned buildings scattered in and around Havana. Turnbull could substantiate neither charge, try as he might. Kennedy and Dalrymple, after their own investigation, found Turnbull's suspicions groundless.[54]

Turnbull continued to put Valdés to the test in other ways. While barraging Valdés with protests that the slave trade continued unabated and doggedly pursuing freedom for various people of color wronged by the slave system, he renewed his quest for the release of Gavino and Shirley in the hope that the elusive right of denunciation and investigation by a British official could finally be attained. The results would prove mixed. By the end of June, Turnbull reported triumphantly to Palmerston, "Henry Shirley is free! After ten years of slavery in the province of Puerto Príncipe, he is now in the Havana and at my disposal."[55] But in the case of Gavino, Valdés led Turnbull over the same juridical trail taken by the Prince of Anglona. For Valdés, as for the prince, the Treaty of 1835 contained no specification of the name, rank, or quality of the agent to whom the duty of overseer would be assigned. When Turnbull thrust with a royal decree of 1826 that allowed anyone the right to denounce violations of Spain's anti-slave trade agreements, Valdés parried twice. First, he said, by law only the members of the Mixed Commission had the right to "watch over" (*velar sobre*) the exact performance of the Treaty of 1835. Second, whereas Spanish law recognized the right of all to denounce Treaty infractions, Turnbull as a foreign official could not exercise the official role of public accuser in the legal proceedings. Valdés added to his lecture in a later communication to Turnbull by saying:

I have never denied, nor do I deny now, to one high contracting party the right they may have of procuring from the other the fulfillment of Treaties by the means pointed out by the laws of nations. But I will say and repeat that the Captain-General of the Island of Cuba has no other superior but her Majesty's Government on which he is dependent and so long as that Government does not authorize me to recognize those or other faculties in you, I neither could nor ought to recognize them without failing in the most sacred of my duties.[56]

The reality that Turnbull stubbornly refused to heed was that no Cuban Captain-General, no matter what his political sensibilities, could willingly bestow on a foreign official, least of all an abolitionist, the investigatory power Turnbull sought. Nor would Cuba's Creoles, including those opposed to the slave trade, consent to a proceeding that called into question their very right to property. These facts Turnbull's British critics had pointed out all along. A regime, unless suicidal, must secure order; all other questions naturally follow. Any doubts that Valdés may have entertained, Espartero erased. Yet a world frenzied by democratic revolution and bound together by international economics intruded into the ordained relations of nation and colony and complicated the instrumentalities of order.

By 1840 Spain's economic dependence on Cuba rivaled Cuba's political dependence on Spain. As the Earl of Clarendon had learned in hard negotiations: "Cuba is the pride and joy of Spain. It is cherished as the only fraction left of the world which once owned Spain as mistress. Cuba is the place whence revenue comes *ad libitum.*"[57] The nineteenth-century sugar boom had made Cuba a treasure trove, and successive peninsular ministries relied on the island to pay their creditors, of which Great Britain was the largest. Britain had heard of Spanish offers to sell Cuba and had considered a lien against it to get previous loans to Spain repaid. Outright possession of Cuba, if ever in Palmerston's dreams, could not be easily effected without driving Britain into war with the United States and possibly France. But the flow of credit enabled Britain to extend its authority with the regime in power at Madrid and through it to extend more safely its unwelcome influence in Cuba. Thus, Valdés had to juggle the contradictory demands of two vital props for the regime: Cuba's planter class, which though amorphous and without formal political power closed ranks on the question of immediate abolition; and a liberal British administration that seemed to many Cubans and other observers bent on imposing it. Had Valdés had his way, he would have invoked article 7 of the Treaty of 1835, which gave Spain the right to change the location of the Court of Mixed Commission, to effect a transfer from Cuba to the less charged atmosphere of Puerto Rico, where the *Romney* and, possibly, Turnbull would follow. But Palmerston resisted the suggestion, and Espartero's regime preferred not to anger Britain by pressing on.[58]

Valdés did not play patron to the slave trade, but neither did he, as a staunch foe of liberal reform in the colonies, deserve the praise that British liberals—or recent writers—would lavish on him. He was not liberal, anti-slavery, or sentimental. A confidential report of 3 November 1841, in response to an order from Madrid for information on how best to meet Cuba's labor requirements given Spanish compliance with its anti-slave-trade treaties, reveals Valdés to have been an extremely able and perceptive servant of the Spanish state and a canny politician. He began by addressing the problem of the development of the white population, whether free white labor could replace black slavery in the countryside and, if so, how white immigration into Cuba could be encouraged. He knew the Cubans to be deeply involved in this matter and not usually with Spanish interests in mind. Valdés concluded that Cuban agriculture could not and should not be left to white labor. He repeated the familiar argument about the enervating effect on white labor of a tropical climate, the susceptibility of whites to fevers and other maladies. He adduced numbers to show how the use of free white labor would raise the planters' cost of production beyond what they could afford. He pointed out the cultural taboos: "To see a white man bent under the weight of fieldwork at the side of slaves clashes with established ideas in this country; and this favorable attitude to the white, is not easy, is not possible, to extinguish with a mandate."[59]

Like Captains-General before and after him, Valdés saw the maintenance of slavery as crucial to Spanish rule in Cuba. Cuban loyalty to Spain, he stressed, flowed neither from "the singular virtue of its [white] natives nor their favorable disposition toward the interests of the mother country because I consider the natives of this island as addicted to political emancipation as those born in Peru or in Mexico." The presence of Spanish troops had less to do with keeping Cuban whites submissive than with their fear of "the black and colored race." Leading Creoles "constantly clamor for the promotion of the white population because they know that if the day comes when it is superabundant, they would be able to say without risk an everlasting good-bye to Spain." Since continuation of the contraband slave trade encouraged British interference in Cuba, Valdés proposed a government policy to maintain slavery by stimulating the natural reproduction of slaves. He looked to the southern United States as a model.

Cuban plantations had to redress their sexual imbalance, encourage marriages, relieve the burdens for pregnant slaves, improve hygiene and supervision for newborn slaves, and "finally, to adopt rules that seem best able to reduce mortality."[60]

Valdés closed his report by offering what he considered to be five sacred maxims for the better government of Cuba. First, Spain should choose Captains-General with the greatest possible care. For any future crisis in Cuba, Valdés explained, the stakes had risen. "Here a more vital question is discussed, which is that of the eternal separation from the rest of the Monarchy." Second, Spain should keep power in Cuba concentrated in the hands of the Captain-General. Third, it should leave the promotion of the white population in Cuba to individual interests. Fourth, it should work to keep the black and colored population in balance with the white population "not precisely in number, but by strength and importance, procuring the increase and conservation of said [black] race by all the means within the capacity of the Government and not in opposition to the strict observance of the letter of the [anti-slave-trade] treaties." Fifth, Spain should adhere strictly to the Laws of the Indies (a seventeenth-century legal code and the most comprehensive and detailed legal code ever produced by Spain for its overseas possessions) so as to avoid "dangerous innovations" and to provide for more efficient imperial administration.[61]

In the summer of 1842 a deputation of prominent citizens from the Spanish port city of Santander, at least some of whom can be identified as investors in the slave trade, petitioned for Valdés's removal on the grounds of his apparent inability to secure Cuba from Britain's government-sponsored policy of abolitionist intervention. In reply Valdés reminded Spain's Foreign Ministry that the general deterioration in relations with Britain came about precisely because British complaints against the slave trade had some basis in fact. When he arrived in Cuba, he said, violations of the Anglo-Spanish treaties were "so little concealed that inside the very entrance-ways of the Capital [i.e., Havana] the barracoons destined to sell human flesh were in full public view." The British commissioners denounced them at the time, and also the open provisioning of slave ships for the journey to the African coast, although their denunciations paled in number and intensity compared to those of David Turnbull, a "man of violent passions and the most hotheaded of the abolitionists."[62] Furthermore, Valdés noted, the drumbeat of complaints from Britain's minister to Spain warned of direct British intervention unless something was done.

Valdés had no doubt that the Santander deputation was being funded by the slave-trading interests. He also warned that such petitioning to the government posed the dangers of excess democracy:

The right of petition exercised on this island and other overseas possessions would be lamentable. . . . Admit the precedent of the Deputation of Santander; tolerate this first step, and we have sown the seed of our own destruction. Today without foreseeing the consequences, let the conduct of a powerful nation and of a Captain-General be reproached, and tomorrow there will be clamor for provincial deputations, for elective town councils, for national representation, for liberty of the press, and for everything that may cause the inevitable loss of that which we possess in America and Asia.[63]

Throughout his rule, Valdés applied a restricting hand to the slave trade that slowed human imports. A drop in sugar prices, Captain Denman's arson of slave-trading facilities at Gallinas, and planters' fear that Spain would submit to Turnbull's emancipation plan all contributed to the slowdown. His rule coincided with the first capture of a slave ship by a Spanish cruiser.[64] But had he zealously confined all suspected slavers to port, he would have choked off also much of the legitimate and semilegitimate business that brought a healthy flow of money into government coffers. By conceding to Great Britain the political principle that might eventually permit de facto abolition, he might have fomented Creole rebellion. General Espartero, the regent, and Valdés were left with the fundamental problem of how to reconcile slavery with the needs and obligations of the regime itself, Cuba's planters, and Palmerston's government. At least in the short run, the longer Turnbull remained in Cuba, the more improbable that reconciliation would be.

Happily for Spanish interests, by the end of the summer of 1841, Turnbull had become increasingly isolated. The British members of the Mixed Commission had joined British businessmen in Cuba, Spanish officials, and the slave-trading interest in the attack on Turnbull. They maligned him to Valdés, Palmerston, and visiting dignitaries; they continued to refuse to hear certain cases brought by him to the court; and fostered rumors of his impending dismissal. As Turnbull moaned to eighty-one-year-old Thomas Clarkson, one of abolitionism's founding fathers: "I expected of course to meet at every step with the most determinate opposition on the part of the Spanish Authorities but I confess to you I was not prepared for the rancorous hostility with which all my efforts are counteracted by the gentlemen of the Mixed Commission and more especially by the English members of the Court."[65]

Palmerston warned Turnbull "that unless you change your course of conduct towards those with whom you have intercourse, and leave off getting into needless Quarrels with every Body with whom you have to deal, your further continuance at Cuba can be of no use whatever either to her Majesty's Government, or to that cause for the Promotion of which you were sent to Havana."[66] His standing plummeted to new lows after the abolitionist party broke with Palmerston over his support for free trade in sugar. The Whig ministry collapsed; the Tories took power with Lord Aberdeen as Palmerston's replacement, and Aberdeen had less tolerance for Turnbull's conduct even than Palmerston. To counteract some of the criticism and to shore up political support, Turnbull's clerk, Francis Ross Cocking, had periodically conveyed to the British and Foreign Anti-Slavery Society unduly sanguine reports on Turnbull's exertions. The Society published many of the letters, unsigned, in the *British and Foreign Anti-Slavery Reporter.* Spanish officials detected them, attributed them to Turnbull, and cited them as evidence of abolitionist intrigue.

In this uncertain climate small disruptions invariably became larger. Several months after Turnbull's arrival someone in Havana opened up a crate of English crockery to find it inscribed with representations of blacks dancing around the flag of liberty. "The excitement caused thereby has been so great, that it is believed the Custom House will cause every crate of English Earthen Ware, which may exist in the place, or may arrive here after, to be opened and examined."[67] Hyperemotional planters contributed to the uncertainty with protests and talk of assassination. To them, Turnbull's plan of emancipation looked like imminent disaster. Turnbull the man then became the convenient target for the projection of all anxieties generated by the slave system. Projection begat an evil image of Turnbull, which with a succession of slave, free colored, and Creole agitations, mediated by post hoc reasoning, produced the conviction that abolitionist-inspired conspiracies were rampant.

An October 1841 uprising of some forty slaves employed in the construction of a Havana palace for the Spanish-born planter Domingo Aldama fortified that conviction. Valdés reported that the slaves involved were Lucumís (Yorubas), "militant and insubordinate by nature." They had refused to work and disobeyed authority, including the commands of Aldama himself. Troops were called out and opened fire. Six slaves were killed; ten were wounded. "This action," Valdés explained, "has been in the final analysis extremely useful in this capital, where the voices of emancipation spread by some agent of the British abolitionists, encouraged in the blacks their irresistible propensity to rise up and to throw off the yoke." Valdés believed that such a display of arms, which had become familiar in the countryside "as frequent as the uprisings were there," was needed in Havana also not only to restore respect for authority but to reassure white residents of their security. For the sake of public tranquility, he proceeded to ask that General Espartero be reminded of "the urgent necessity to eject from this country the British Consul Mr. David Turnbull."[68]

The Creole planter Gaspar Betancourt Cisneros, long an advocate of an end to the slave trade, described the situation in Puerto Príncipe in December 1841, as "so bad . . . that one cannot even speak rationally, because he is labeled a rebel—or an abolitionist, which is now worse than a rebel."[69] Turnbull admitted that "if a negro insurrection should unhappily arise, I am deliberately of the opinion that I cannot hope to escape the unreasoning impulse of the fury of that wretched portion of the community which desires the perpetuation of the Slave Trade."[70]

Domestic politics and death threats notwithstanding, Turnbull remained on the offensive with new investigations and thus continued to feed hopes of amelioration of conditions, or even freedom on the part of the colored population, and fears of subversive activity on the part of Spanish officials and Cuban planters. He set out in November in the company of a compatriot named Goff to search the coffee plantation Santa María in Cárdenas province to check out charges that an emigré Englishman named Forbes, who had recently died, had transshipped about 120 Bahamian blacks there after the passage of the 1833 Emancipation Bill. While en route, Turnbull and Goff stayed in the Hotel de Comercio in Matanzas, in which, according to previous intelligence, two or three of Forbes's former slaves worked. Turnbull began to question the colored employees in his room about where they were born, how were they treated, and so forth. "Persons were not lacking who watched the Consul and on becoming suspicious of his conduct immediately informed the Governor."[71] The governor, Antonio García Oña, an owner of an *ingenio* himself, ordered agents to the scene who mistook Goff for a British military officer, seized his passport, and because Turnbull failed to produce one, pointed him back to Havana.[72]

On his return, Turnbull had to set aside the Forbes case temporarily to aid James Thompson, a Bahamian black kidnapped and sold into Cuban slavery, who had sought out the British consulate after hearing about Turnbull on Havana's docks. Requests for information from Bahamian officials bore fruit when a witness to the kidnapping turned up there. Turnbull brought him to Cuba for examination by Spanish authorities. One of the Captain-General's legal advisers heard the testimony but then informed Turnbull that three witnesses, not one, were necessary to overcome the presumption against the liberty of a person of color.[73]

These incidents, combined with Turnbull's recurrent complaints of Spanish inefficiency in dealing with slavers and his attacks on British capitalists who were said to be tied to Cuban slave-trading firms, were a matter of concern to Aberdeen. He had notified Spain's minister in London in February 1842 that Great Britain did "not intend at present to press upon the government of Spain the question of a convention, for the purpose of examining generally into the condition of the negroes in Cuba."[74] Spanish officials continued to seek Turnbull's removal, finding Aberdeen far more friendly and conciliatory than Palmerston on the question. In March, Aberdeen finally resolved to bridle Turnbull by separating his commissions as consul and as Superintendent of Liberated Africans. "The reasons assigned for this separation," Turnbull confided to Joseph Sturge, "are that the union has not accomplished the purpose contemplated by Her Majesty's Government; that information has reached Lord Aberdeen that British interests in Cuba have suffered in consequence; and that my conduct as Consul has not been marked by the necessary degree of 'Moderation and Discretion.' "[75] Arthur Aston, Britain's minister in Madrid, explained to Antonio González that the interests of British merchants as well as the public interest had led to the decision to separate Turnbull from the consulate.[76] The decision effectively isolated Turnbull, for only the consulship was recognized by Spain. As mere Superintendent, Turnbull lacked the official capacity to contact the Captain-General and lost the protection afforded by the consulship. With assassination looming larger as a possible result, Turnbull took the advice of Creole friends and moved on board the *Romney* in Havana harbor.[77]

The prospect of carrying out a crusade in a minor post from the deck of a ship could not have satisfied Turnbull, but he hoped that Sturge and the British and Foreign Anti-Slavery Society would again intervene and get him a more substantial post elsewhere. A lieutenant-governorship in one of the British West Indian Islands or the consulship in Peru seemed appropriate. To enhance his chances he provided Sturge with a mildly romanticized synopsis of his accomplishments:

I feel that I have given a stimulus to the cause of Freedom among the native population, which cannot fail, in due season, to lead to beneficial results. I have enabled a number of intelligent negroes, nominally free, to emigrate to a land of true freedom in the British West Indies, from whence they are constantly writing to their friends of the happy change they have made. I have recovered and sent home within the year seven English negroes who had been kidnapped in Jamaica, the Bahamas, and Sierra Leone, and sold here as Slaves. And I have procured for upwards of a hundred of the unhappy and degraded "emancipados," the practical recognition and enjoyment of their freedom. . . . All this has served to inspire the Slaves of this Island with Hope, which next to the positive enjoyment of Liberty, is perhaps the greatest good which could have been obtained for them. Above all the rich Creoles have arrived at the conclusion that their own freedom, that is their expectation of sharing in the management of their own affairs, is inseparably bound up with the extinction of the Slave Trade and the personal freedom of the Slaves now existing in the Island.[78]

On those infrequent occasions in which Turnbull dared to return to the island, an armed escort chaperoned him. He kept abreast of what was happening on shore largely through the efforts of an old faithful black servant named Bernis and his assistant Francis Ross Cocking and readied himself for a new offensive against the Forbes estate.

Joseph Tucker Crawford, a veteran diplomat who had served in the Lisbon and Tampico consulates, arrived in June to replace Turnbull. He had just begun to take up his duties when Turnbull briefed him on, among other things, the case of the slaves on cafetal Santa María, and pleaded with him to use the power of the consular office to extract the passport Turnbull needed for another trip to Cárdenas. Crawford, though a responsible antislavery man, did not burn with Turnbull's fever, and Lord Aberdeen may have transferred him to Cuba for precisely that reason. He questioned the utility of Turnbull's adventurism and refused the services of his auxiliaries. Many words passed between Turnbull and Crawford on the subject of the passport before Crawford reluctantly applied to Valdés. To no one's surprise, Valdés denied the request on the grounds that Turnbull held no commission to search the Forbes plantation.[79]

Following this setback, a personal crisis induced Turnbull to relinquish the Superintendency and leave Cuba altogether. His wife Elinor, whom he had married in northern Ireland sixteen years before, had become distraught under the pressure and needed to get away to more serene surroundings. Turnbull told Crawford, and in August booked passage for New Providence (Nassau) in the Bahamas. The slave traders and their allies breathed easier, for now they thought they could, in Gaspar Betancourt's words, "deceive the English government and continue the contraband slave trade."[80]

Crawford disliked Turnbull, and he, like many British businessmen in Cuba, gave thanks to see Turnbull leave. Turnbull had mysteriously continued to ignore weeks of Crawford's pleas to turn over the consular archives. In October 1842 Crawford described Turnbull to the Foreign Office as off "playing philanthropy" in Nassau. "There is no bearing the man's nonsense, and I hope that shewing up his infamous deception and the falseness of his character . . . will satisfy you, if that were wanting, how wise it was to remove him from office and put a stop to his figuring in any way as connected with Her Majesty's Government."[81]

But neither Crawford nor the slave traders had seen the last of Turnbull. Less than two months later, he reappeared in the city of Gibara on the eastern end of Cuba. While in the Bahamas, he had gathered testimony that several hundred ex-Bahamian slaves had been shipped to Cuba to labor as slaves on plantations owned by British subjects in an area between Gibara and Holguín commonly referred to as "English Cuba." Turnbull managed to get a passport from the ingenuous son of the Spanish consul in New Providence; he chartered a small vessel captained by a convicted smuggler, Thomas Catto, and crewed in part by free coloreds; and attempted to reclaim the liberty of those victimized. Local authorities refused to cooperate and instead seized Turnbull, his black servant, and his belongings, and forced him to go south to Holguín. The lieutenant-governor there informed Valdés, who had both Turnbull and his servant transferred to Havana. Among the belongings of Turnbull's black servant, Valdés's examiners discovered what appear to have been fifty-nine handbills of the Baptist Missionary Society with the disturbing opening words "Proclaim the Fiftieth Year. Leviticus 25:10."[82] In referring to their Bibles, Valdés's examiners would have read the Spanish version of this:

And ye shall hallow the fiftieth year, and proclaim liberty throughout all the land unto all the inhabitants thereof: it shall be a jubilee unto you; and ye shall return every man unto his possession, and ye shall return every man unto his family.

That Turnbull was bold, courageous, daring, eager, and committed to the crusade against slavery even critics might concede. Yet precipitate idealism often makes familiar script for tragedies. The self-righteous rarely concern themselves with consequences. Turnbull, with his unauthorized descent on Cuba, had placed not only himself in jeopardy but his objectives and British policy to maintain Spanish rule in Cuba as well. Captain-

General Valdés and the Spanish government might be convinced, with difficulty, that Turnbull had acted on his own to free a handful of slaves, allegedly former British subjects, without the sanction or knowledge of the British government. But Cuba's planters, enraged over Turnbull's audacious landfall, declared otherwise, that Turnbull and Britain were contriving to stir up a slave rebellion. Any softness by the authorities in prosecuting Turnbull or resisting British interference in the slave system would convince more and more planters that their interest lay outside of the Spanish empire, perhaps with the United States and its Southern leadership, and therefore against the prevailing British policy to maintain Spanish rule.

To Captain-General Valdés, what Turnbull had done did qualify as subversion:

Such an act however simple it may seem is an offense against the social order of the island of Cuba, because every act intended to introduce disorder among the slave gangs on the estates, indisposing the slaves with respect to their overseers and masters, and giving occasion by his general declaration "that many others had a right to their liberty," at which all the gangs might rise, does not merit any other qualifications.[83]

On the matter of punishment, Valdés, to his eventual cost, had to stop short of the planters' call for execution. But he expelled Turnbull with the warning that if he returned "he will be dealt with as a disturber of the public peace."[84] Spanish authorities escorted him for embarkation aboard the steamer *Thames* on November 6 as "thousands turned out to see the fellow off."[85] At his departure he was reported to have pledged that he would yet be martyred to the cause. "Depend upon it," Crawford predicted to the Foreign Office after Turnbull's departure, "he will not long be still where he is but will meddle with what does not concern him very soon or make some exaggerated and offensive misrepresentation of some one or some thing which will give trouble."[86]

Spanish agents watched Turnbull closely thereafter. He retained powerful friends in England. Probably in recognition of this, Lord Aberdeen acted over the protests of the Spanish minister in London, to appoint Turnbull to a judgeship in Jamaica on the Court of Mixed Commissions established in accordance with a slave-trade treaty with Portugal. In a letter of 15 November 1842, informing Turnbull of his decision, Aberdeen explained that Turnbull's removal from Havana "was demanded by a regard for the public service," although he had never been insensitive to Turnbull's "great zeal and ability" in pursuing an end to the slave trade.

Aberdeen regretted he had not been able to fill Turnbull's request for the consular office in Lima, but had fully intended to give him "the first suitable employment," with this caveat:

> You will pardon me, if I take the liberty on this occasion, and with reference to the highly responsible situation in which you are about to be placed, strongly to impress upon your mind the necessity of calmness, impartiality, and discretion in your conduct. The absence of these qualities, in your former Office, have sometimes been noticed by my Predecessor, as well as by Myself.[87]

Cuban planters had reacted against Turnbull to prevent a slave revolution like the one that had occurred in Saint Domingue. They lived in a world that he could not tolerate nor with which he could compromise. He had added to their insecurity of property, just as he had calculated, and that insecurity had eventually forced him out of Cuba. But if no longer in Cuba, the man whom Spanish authorities and Cuban whites regarded as an "inquisitor" was still close by in Jamaica. If Turnbull had demonstrated anything, it had been a reckless perseverance in pursuit of a cause. Those at the top of the Spanish imperial system had to worry not only about what he might do next but about the international movement he represented.

6

Francis Ross Cocking
and International Conspiracy

I believe that the primary substance of all things is existence; the rest is secondary. Let us then see to it that we exist, for all our shortcomings and difficulties, since in the end it is always better to be than not to be.

SIMÓN BOLIVAR,
Letter to General Francisco
de Paula Santander, 1822

When David Turnbull was removed from the Havana consulate he left behind a network of informants and his chief aide, Francis Ross Cocking. Through Cocking much of the information about Cuba's troubled slave society passed to Turnbull and others. He became Turnbull's chief spy and the man around whom, for a short time, dissident elements within Cuba seemed to draw closer to each other.

Cocking had hoped to ride on Turnbull's coattails to a job in the British Foreign Service. He came to Cuba in 1839 from New Orleans to work as a humble bookkeeper for the Drake Brothers merchant house. He accepted a more lucrative offer from another merchant, who dismissed him once he had expeditiously disentangled the company ledgers. Cocking turned to the British consulate and David Turnbull to help plead his case before Spanish justice, only to end up unrequited and unemployed. Turnbull rescued him and his family from impending destitution by giving him a job. Cocking spoke Spanish like a native, thanks to more than ten years' residence in Venezuela. His Venezuelan wife and his contacts in Cuba's mercantile community enabled him to gather intelligence where Turnbull could not.

Cocking became an abolitionist with suspicious alacrity after he engaged himself with Turnbull: In January 1841 he contacted Turnbull for the first time; in February he joined the consulate; in April he was running errands in the name of African freedom. If he had any serious commitment to abolitionism before 1841, he had swallowed it when in 1839 he signed on with the Drakes, a transplanted British family who had built a business empire in Cuba in less than two generations by investing in the production and marketing of slave-grown staples.[1]

Félix Tanco, a Colombian-born Cuban nationalist, and probably the most intense member of Domingo Del Monte's politico-literary *tertulias,* discussed Cocking in a letter to Del Monte of 18 April 1841. Turnbull had not yet met Del Monte, and since Tanco was a friend in common he had sent Cocking to Tanco to obtain a letter of introduction and a copy of Del Monte's latest anti-slave-trade paper. Cocking's intelligence and fluent Spanish impressed Tanco, as did his claim of affiliation with the British and Foreign Anti-Slavery Society. During their conversation, Cocking asserted that resistance to the abolition of slavery in Cuba would cause *"unfortunate consequences"*—words that Tanco, although a passionate critic of the slave trade, feared might indicate "a plan already made and decreed in England against the island of Cuba, if here one thinks or is stupid enough to think of resisting."[2]

Cocking spoke the truth about his connection with the British and Foreign Anti-Slavery Society, although Tanco inferred too much. Soon after starting work for Turnbull, Cocking volunteered to channel a steady stream of intelligence on Cuba to the Society headquarters in London. Most of the news about Cuba in the 1841 and 1842 editions of *The Anti-Slavery Reporter,* the Society's newspaper, derived from Cocking, not Turnbull. For Cocking, exertions on behalf of the Society held out tangible rewards. The Society would pay for the costs of gathering intelligence, and, if grateful, it could use its influence to land him a substantial diplomatic post. Response from the Society boded well: "To possess so intelligent and valuable a correspondent as yourself in Cuba, they [the members of the Society] not only feel to be a great advantage to themselves, but of essential importance to the cause of suffering and oppressed humanity."[3]

But months of legwork and spying for both Turnbull and the Society yielded only disappointment. Cocking had no official capacity with the Foreign Office, and although called vice-consul by Turnbull and looked upon as such by prominent Cubans, Cocking could be more accurately described as Turnbull's clerk and not as an official of the Foreign Office. Lord Palmerston disregarded Turnbull's repeated endorsement of Cocking for a consular post in the city of Matanzas, and with the fall of the

Whigs and the succession of a Tory ministry in the summer of 1841, what slight influence Turnbull may have had with the Foreign Office vanished. Cocking hoped for better from the Society and in his correspondence angled clumsily for patronage. In a by-the-way in one of his letters, he told John Scoble, the Society's secretary, that Turnbull had recommended him "very warmly" to the late Whig ministry, "but being personally unknown to the new Foreign Minister [Lord Aberdeen] he is naturally unwilling to press the subject for the present; although in his official report on the Trade of the Island he has demonstrated that a Consul or Vice-Consul of Matanzas is absolutely required."[4] Whether from a lack of effort or political influence with the Tories or for some other reason, the Society never obtained an office for Cocking.

Upon learning of Aberdeen's decision to detach Turnbull from the consulship, Cocking became desperate. He had never felt adequately remunerated for his service and now the coming of a new consul placed even that small income in jeopardy. Joseph Crawford arrived in June 1842, and Turnbull dutifully solicited him to retain Cocking. Crawford's answer: He had "sufficient assistance."[5]

Cocking anguished, once more at the brink of destitution. Turnbull urged him to go to Jamaica, where officials stood ready to interview him for a job as an immigration agent. Since slavery had ended in the British West Indies, a political turnabout had taken place between former slaveholders and abolitionists. Jamaican planters led by an *arriviste* Scot named Alexander Barclay were undertaking immigration projects to address labor shortages in the aftermath of slave emancipation, since a number of Jamaican freedmen and women had chosen not to remain on the plantation. Cocking had letters of introduction from Turnbull with which to meet Lord Elgin, the governor-general; Dr. John Ewart, the first chief of Jamaica's immigration agency; and Richard Hill, a gifted abolitionist politician and the first colored stipendiary magistrate in Jamaica.

That the physical conditions of life for contract laborers, African, European, Asian, or West Indian, were rarely an improvement over those for slaves mattered less to the abolitionists like Turnbull than the simple fact of the contract laborer's nominal freedom. Successful immigration would also help British West Indian plantations return to a competitiveness that might challenge slavery in Cuba and Brazil. Like his friend R. R. Madden, Turnbull looked favorably on the immigration of free people of color into the British West Indies; he had previously sounded out Charles Metcalfe, a former governor-general of Jamaica, on a plan to use that labor-hungry island as a terminus for the removal of people of color from Cuba. Since Spain would never willingly cooperate, the plan called for an agent acclimated to Cuba who could maneuver with stealth and discretion to promote emigration.[6]

Crawford approved the venture, but Turnbull had problems in getting Cocking to make the trip. Cocking wanted money but preferred not to leave his family. Turnbull offered money, but only to underwrite the expenses of the trip. After a false start in which trouble with the steam packet returned Cocking to port, Turnbull notified Crawford that Cocking "now hesitates about prosecuting his journey to Jamaica; and as it was only in view of his going there, and of combining his personal interest with the promotion of a great national object that I agreed to request of you to advance him $300, I hope you will do me the favor to see that the equivalent . . . is really applied to the purpose originally intended."[7]

Cocking finally completed the journey in August 1842, the same month that Turnbull had to leave Cuba for the Bahamas. Cocking was embittered at Turnbull's parsimony, and that bitterness surfaced in his correspondence with the British and Foreign Anti-Slavery Society. Whereas Crawford, the new consul, seemed "true to his principles and firm in his adherence to the cause of humanity . . . [and] too much of a politician to descend to personal invective and insult which can tend to no good," Turnbull "was ever as ready to insult his friend as his foe, and he has left the Island execrated by his enemies, and despised by those who were his friends, and who continue to be, truly and sincerely, friends to the cause of humanity."[8]

The Society must have grimaced at Cocking's words, for this personal scuffling was a needless distraction from the cause of abolitionism. Cocking had not wished to upset his patrons, so he assured them that the matter was purely private. "That although I shall ever feel indignation towards the man who has tried to injure me . . . so sincere is my desire to serve the cause of African Freedom, that even with him would I cooperate, if by doing so I could in any manner whatsoever serve the cause."[9]

In Jamaica, Cocking fared miserably. Despite letters of introduction from both Turnbull and Crawford, he failed to convince Lord Elgin, Metcalfe's Tory replacement, and other high officials to endorse the project. Cocking sailed back to Cuba in September worse off than when he left, for Spanish agents were shadowing him. He apprised the British and Foreign Anti-Slavery Society that

I am already suspected and indeed accused of being the author of many letters which have appeared in the Anti-Slavery Reporter. I have Government spies all around me, wherever I go I am sure to meet with a spy. I have been watched at Jamaica, and within a hour after my arrival at Santiago de Cuba a Lieutenant Colonel of the Spanish army was sent to my hotel to take up his lodgings and to endeavor to find out what I was about.

Since Mr. Turnbull gave up the Consulate I have been without anything to do to gain a living. My friends in the Island are few, my enemies are many, and I have now nothing to depend upon or to appeal to, but the circumstances of my being a British subject.[10]

Cocking lingered on in Cuba for several months until he secured sufficient passage money from Crawford to take himself and his family to England. London was readying itself in 1843 for the second World Anti-Slavery Convention, and Cocking probably judged that he could best seek support there. Once in London, he pressed the British and Foreign Anti-Slavery Society for money. In a melodramatic letter he blamed his impoverishment on his service to the cause of African freedom, which had heaped upon him "the odium of almost all the white population of the Island of Cuba, including Foreigners of all nations." Ever since Crawford had taken office, his own life had deteriorated. He had become friendless and penniless: "The finger of Scorn has been pointed at me as a declared enemy to Cuban prosperity, and had it not been for the assistance afforded me by two Gentlemen at Havana, natives of the place, whose names I am not authorised to mention, myself and my family would have succumbed to desperate necessity."[11]

With the Society's verdict pending, he attended the Anti-Slavery Convention as its Cuban expert. A member of Parliament in attendance questioned whether David Turnbull had truly served abolitionist interests, for the official correspondence had convinced him that Turnbull's conduct has been "more calculated to embitter the feelings of Cuba and Spain than anything else that could have been done." John Scoble, the Society's secretary, vigorously defended Turnbull by pointing to Cuban enormities and to Turnbull's courage in the defense of humanity. Cocking, with a request of £100 in the balance, rested his enmity and proclaimed Turnbull's "extraordinary exertions" as the reason for the abatement in Cuba's slave trade.[12]

One week after the end of the Convention, with the Society's decision still pending, Cocking decided to refresh its memory with another graphic appeal for aid. He needed money to go back to Caracas, where he had "relations and friends who are able and willing to assist me."[13] Scoble finally responded: The Society refused his request for £100, but in recognition of his services, it would grant him half the sum. Cocking took it and managed to ship himself and his family back to Venezuela. Had his Latin relations or friends lived up to his expectations—or pretensions— history would have relegated him to obscurity. But poverty hounded him in Caracas, as it had in Havana and London. He scratched out a living teaching "English and Mathematics to Persons possessed of too little energy to learn, and Spanish to some foreigners."[14] By 1846 he was working as a clerk for Bedford Hinton Wilson, the British chargé d'affaires in Caracas. In a desperate bid to salvage some personal advantage from his career in Cuba, he tried to peddle a confession, to the British in 1846, of his entanglement in a Cuban conspiracy to overthrow the Spanish government and to emancipate the slaves.[15]

Again, five years later, in 1851, he tried to interest the Spanish in buying it. He foolishly allowed a written confession and corroborating documents to be kept overnight by the Spanish chargé d'affaires in Caracas, who told him that he would have to judge their worth before any money could change hands. Thanks to the chargé's speed of wit and quill, copies reached Spain, free of charge, to lend substance to indictments of official British misconduct and abolitionist intrigue in Cuba.[16]

Cocking opened his confession with an account of events in Havana in 1841 and 1842. He and a group of "wealthy, talented, and influential" Creoles, including South Americans, had come together to look into the feasibility of Cuban independence and slave emancipation. They agreed on the desirability of separation from Spain but split on the question of emancipation. He claimed to have worked energetically at repair of the split and well enough to secure their consent to a separatist manifesto of six parts: First, the whites would cooperate with the people of color to promote Cuba's independence. Second, the rebels would publish a declaration of independence to justify their movement and to brand all nonsupporters as traitors. Much of this declaration, according to Cocking, appeared as the "Address to the London Anti-Slavery Society," written at his request in 1841 by a certain Pedro María Morilla. Third, all slaves who joined the fight for independence would obtain freedom, and "as soon as the island should be tranquilized, her Independence acknowledged, and the treasury in shape," their masters would be compensated. Fourth, any slave who took up arms against his master would be guilty of treason and "dealt with accordingly." Fifth, plans would be drawn up for total emancipation but in such a way as to ensure the safety of the masters. Sixth, a special envoy would be sent to the British government to present the rebel case and to seek British assistance in the establishment of civil and political rights in Cuba for "all classes and colours of men."

Before Cocking and the Creoles had put the finishing touches to their project, his confession said, Crawford replaced Turnbull in the British consulate. Cocking went to Crawford and detailed "faithfully, even unto the very minutia" what he had done, "under Mr. Turnbull's directions." Crawford surprised him by approving his conduct, or so Cocking said. Cocking then called a meeting of the committee, "or rather two committees . . . one composed of white men, and another composed of Mulatto and Black Men," between which, according to Cocking, he was "the only organ of Communication, save on special occasions when by stealth one or the other of the coloured men would communicate with one or other of the white men," although Cocking said he had helped to arrange those meetings too. Both of the committees had become dispirited by Turnbull's dismissal as consul, so he revived them with the news of the posture Crawford had taken, news that seemed especially to animate the people of color, who "in less than eight days [sent out] Emissaries . . . to almost every part of the Island." Cocking believed that "at this particular period, if I had had a 10 Gun Brig under my command, a few thousand stand of arms, and a mere handful of men to effect a landing, with these arms, at such a place as I could have pointed out, I should have been enabled to establish the Independence of the Island, and the consequent freedom of the slaves; for there were thousands and tens of thousands ready and prepared to flock, armed, to the place of disembarcation."

While colored agents were attempting to build an island-wide movement, Cocking said, he went to Jamaica but only ostensibly to interview for the job of immigration agent. In Jamaica, with Turnbull's letters of introduction, he tried unsuccessfully to convince prominent officials to back the rebel movement. Heeding prior advice from his Creole co-conspirators, Cocking also searched out General Santiago Mariño, a former ally and rival of Simón Bolívar during the liberation of Venezuela and current exile in Kingston.[17] Cocking briefed Mariño on the conspiracy and tested his willingness to take command of the movement. More than willing, Mariño reportedly was enthusiastic about the prospect.

Not only was he willing and desirous to place himself at the head of the movement in Cuba, but . . . he was prepared to carry out my particular views with respect to the freedom of the Slaves, having had, as he himself stated to me, a proposition made to him to that effect by certain "Agents of an Anti-Slavery Society in London" (these were his very words) a short time previous to my application to him being made.[18]

Cocking rethreaded the Jamaica Channel to the eastern end of Cuba to meet with sympathetic Creoles. In Santiago, the center of General Lorenzo's constitutionalist movement of 1836, he found to his delight the "most influential native inhabitants, among whom were military men (Colonels and Captains); Public Functionaries (two 'Alcaldes' and a Judge), and other gentlemen of Independent Fortune," ready to venture "life and fortune in the hope of gaining their political and civil rights," much more so in fact than Havana's Creoles. They drew back only when Cocking mentioned slave emancipation, although he left with an understanding that they could raise ten thousand men in rebellion. From Santiago, Cocking shipped to Manzanillo, Trinidad, and Cienfuegos, before reanchoring in Havana. There, he soon perceived, the fervor for rebellion among his white "Coadjutors" had diminished. They "had even come to the resolution of not admitting native born slaves to bear arms in the Struggle for Independence." Cocking inveighed against them before accusing United States agents of seducing them away with the credo of independence without emancipation. As evidence, he recalled the movement of diplomatic personnel: Robert Campbell had replaced James Calhoun as the United States consul in Havana; other officials, mostly military or naval officials, had disembarked to assume consular posts in the out-ports; and the majority of these officials were known to have contacted millionaire slaveholder José María Martínez de Campos, Conde de Santovenia.

To check out his suspicions, Cocking met with Andrés Fernández de Lara, the count's nephew, and asked whether it would be wise to gather funds to recruit revolutionaries in the United States. He replied that "agents had already arrived from the United States . . . to treat with the Natives of Cuba on the subject of their Independence." According to Cocking, Fernández de Lara dropped the name of a major in the United States Army—Cocking thought the name was Coss—who was authorized to offer the Creoles clandestine men and arms for their fight for independence "on the condition, sine qua non, that Cuba should continue to be a Slave Holding State." In calling the plan "madness," Cocking put Fernández de Lara on his guard, and in their next meeting, in the presence of

Pedro María Morilla, Fernández de Lara backtracked from his previous words, saying that the major spoke for himself and not with any official instructions from the U.S. government. Later, however, Cocking heard a different story from a former captain in the Spanish army, identified as Pedro P. Piernas y Larrin, who claimed to have refused the request of the "Independence Party" for his support. The captain was said to have told Cocking of the long-standing communication on the subject of Cuban independence between U.S. government officials and Antonio de Frías, a prominent slaveholder who had been educated along with two more famous brothers in the United States. Not only did many prominent Creoles back Frías, according to Cocking, but some influential and Anglophobic peninsular Spaniards did as well. The home of the Conde de Fernandina (José María Herrera) secreted one meeting attended by the Conde de Santovenia, several other big planters, and the United States consul— apparently, Robert Campbell.[19]

Cocking also identified as an attendant Frías's brother-in-law, the soon-to-be-notorious Narciso López. Like Domingo Del Monte a Venezuelan by birth, López had fought for the royalists during the war for liberation and distinguished himself against Bolívar's forces. In defeat, he evacuated to Cuba in 1823, began his romance with the beautiful Dolores de Frías, and became acquainted with and, apparently, somewhat sympathetic to Creole dissatisfaction with imperial rule. His military career resumed its ascent in Spain soon thereafter. Against the Carlists, he again distinguished himself in the field and in one instance saved the life of Gerónimo Valdés. With Valdés's patronage, López went on to hold several important political posts in Spain, including that of military governor of Valencia. Evidence exists to show that while in Spain he continued to maintain relations with Creole dissidents. The appointment of Valdés to the Captain-Generalcy of Cuba directed López back to Cuba, and under Valdés he became governor of Trinidad and head of the Military Commission.[20] His friendship with Valdés appears not to have translated into unquestioned loyalty to Spain, however, according to Cocking, who said that in the meeting at the home of the Conde de Fernandina, López had "pledged himself to embrace the cause of independence on the terms proposed by the United States."[21]

Despite the defection of whites, the eagerness of the people of color to revolt remained strong. The "social position" of the free people of color, Cocking explained, "is the very lowest that can be imagined, and the constraint that is imposed on all their actions, have awakened them to a sense of their degraded condition, and to their honour be it said, they are ready to risk their lives and all they possess in an attempt to gain for themselves and their still more degraded brethren, that Liberty, which . . . as men they deserve to enjoy." As for the slaves, "no pen can describe or language portray the intensity of their sufferings." Cocking discovered on his return to Havana that "the Coloured Committee, who had Agents travelling all over the Island, had raised a spirit of revolt which it was not easy to prevent from breaking out." This committee gave Cocking a signed petition so he could forward it to the Reverend J. M. Trew, secretary of the recently formed Society for the Extinction of the Slave Trade and for the Civilization of Africa, with the "sole object" of getting funds for arms and munitions for General Mariño and the projected revolution.[22] But Trew's answer, as Cocking recounted, proved empty.

Cocking swore that at this juncture he did "every thing Man could do" to dissuade them, telling them that an uprising at this time was premature, "unsupported as they then were by the Wealth and Power of the White Natives." He ascribed a major slave revolt in March of 1843 in Cárdenas province to one "head-strong" colored chieftain. Cocking admitted failure, his plan gone awry and his situation now tenuous. The whites had defected; the people of color appeared out of control; and both factions now distrusted him. The Creoles, "with the exception of my noble friend Don Domingo Del Monte," wanted him to go to Mexico, but Crawford counseled him to leave for England instead. With his arrival in London on 17 May 1843, the confession ended.

Cocking's confession is not new. A defective Spanish translation of it appeared in the *Boletín* of the National Archive of Cuba in 1904. Cuban scholars who have examined the Conspiracy of La Escalera have divided on whether any or all of it can be trusted. Although the 1846 version in the records of the British Foreign Office does contain significantly more detail, by itself it cannot sustain the argument for the existence of an abolitionist conspiracy to foment slave rebellion and emancipation. David Murray gives Cocking far more credit than he deserves in calling him a "committed abolitionist."[23] He emerges as a down-at-heel opportunist—the Spanish chargé in Caracas called him a "miserable adventurer." Such men can rarely lead gangsters, much less nationalist rebels. That Cocking may have acted as a go-between and informant for a range of political factions seems closer to the truth. The significant question is not whether Cocking told the whole truth—he did not—but what threads of truth can be extracted from the ambiguities, embellishments, and pre-varications.

Other sources bring the events into sharper focus. Joseph Crawford's correspondence with the British Foreign Office would appear to acquit him of Cocking's imputation that he approved a conspiracy. It indicates that he agreed to the creation of an immigration agency but says nothing about his support of Cocking's master plot. Since Crawford had taken over the consulate at the command of Lord Aberdeen, who, unlike Lord Palmerston, was endeavoring to smooth out Anglo-Spanish relations, he would have defied all reasonable expectations of personal loyalty, diplomatic procedure, or political self-preservation had he sanctioned the conspiratorial activities of a former British official without Aberdeen's consent.[24]

Crawford's consular dispatches do prove beyond a shade of doubt that Creoles and Afro-Cubans were mulling schemes to overthrow the Spanish government and that Cocking had entangled himself in them. In August 1842 Crawford informed Aberdeen of the existence in Cuba of "several" revolutionary cabals, "all the particulars of which, I am told, have been long known to Mr. Turnbull."[25] Back in 1841, according to Crawford, a fragile understanding seemed to have formed between white and colored separatists on the basis of an independence movement that was pro-British and pro-emancipation. That understanding, however, was breaking down under the weight of the slavery question and intrigue from the United States. Crawford passed along a translation of a secret communication of October 1841 in which white separatists begged Claudio Martínez de Pinillos, the Conde de Villaneuva, to take charge of their movement. The count represented planter interests and for sixteen years as intendant had served as the highest-ranking Cuban-born official until General Espartero, the Spanish regent, had him, in the words of the Charleston *Courier*, "most unceremoniously" replaced, about one month before the communication.[26]

From what Crawford could determine, the people of color remained wedded to the original understanding, but the Creoles had been edging toward independence without emancipation ever since the visit in 1840 of United States special envoy Alexander Hill Everett. The expressed purpose of Everett's mission was to investigate the alleged ties between the contraband slave trade and Nicholas Trist, then United States consul in Havana. But Crawford's unnamed sources accused Everett of clandestine missionary work among the Creoles. Other intelligence accused no less a personage than Father Félix Varela—the man who, Luz y Caballero would say, "taught Cubans how to think," and who was in exile in New York City for his liberal activism—of being the "Emissary of this party" and of having negotiated assurances of support for Creole rebellion from high government officials in the United States.[27] Moreover, to the list of prospective field commanders of this separatist movement, Crawford offered another name:

> They [the rebel Creoles] count upon some show of assistance from the Main and have, it is said, invited a certain General Samana, who is commanding the Revolutionary Troops at Tabasco against Mexico and is a Creole of this Island, to make a descent with a few followers somewhere on the South side, if near to Santiago de Cuba, so much the better.[28]

Crawford had insufficient knowledge to record perfectly for Lord Aberdeen the name he had heard; authorities in Cuba with some intelligence on the events in Tabasco knew this "certain General" too well.

Cuban-born "General Samana" was Francisco de Sentmanat, a general, yes, of a fashion, and an adventurer worthy of a picaresque novel. Although largely forgotten by historians, Sentmanat was something of a living legend in the circum-Caribbean region, dashing and charismatic, power-hungry and reckless, utterly contemptuous of death, and a crack shot with a trail of dueling victims from New Orleans to Villahermosa, the kind of man every revolution needs but ultimately consumes. He had trained for the military in Spain under the auspices of two well-positioned uncles and proved sufficiently attractive or intimidating to have married high—twice, it appears: first into the noble Cuban family of Armenteros and subsequently into the New Orleans Creole family of Bernard de Marigny.[29] For his participation in the 1820 constitutionalist *pronunciamiento* of Riego against Ferdinand VII, Sentmanat was held in a prison cell in Ceuta. He broke out, fled across the Atlantic, and ended in Mexico in the service of General Antonio López de Santa Anna. In 1825, at the age of twenty-three, Sentmanat, with Santa Anna's backing, led—but eventually had to abort—a joint Colombian-Mexican expedition designed to strike a spectacular first blow for Cuban independence by knocking out the Morro fortress in Havana harbor. As a consequence of his separatist plotting with fellow Cubans in a masonic society known as the Great Legion of the Black Eagle at the end of the decade he was jailed again and nearly executed. Released in celebration of the birth of the future Queen Isabel, he passed back to Mexico, to a country rapidly disintegrating by revolution, to become one of Santa Anna's warlords. By the time of Crawford's dispatch, Sentmanat had taken hold of the entire state of Tabasco as its governor-general.[30] His presence in Mexico may explain the part of Cocking's confession about why certain of his Creole co-conspirators wanted him to proceed there. Del Monte, Luz y Caballero, and other prominent liberal Cubans knew Sentmanat because they had studied together in the classes on constitutional government taught by Félix Varela at the famed San Carlos Seminary. In 1823 Sentmanat along with Del Monte and more than forty other graduates of Varela's classes had signed a petition that was read before the Spanish Cortes in support of imperial political reform and constitutional government.[31]

On 1 October 1842 Crawford offered other news. He was aching to get Cocking out of Cuba: "I fear he is up to his neck in the Revolutionary schemes of the Creoles."[32] Cuba seemed closer to rebellion, and only the internal division within the Creoles, their fear of the people of color and abolition, was keeping the lid on. A short time later, two unnamed white men, one in a military uniform and the other in civilian dress, called upon him as representatives of a party of Creoles who were plotting to rid Cuba of both slavery and Spanish rule. No doubt because of what happened to General Lorenzo's separatist movement in 1836, they asked Crawford what action the British government might take upon the outbreak of rebellion. Another Cuban revolutionary party, they pointed out, had allied itself with the United States and in opposition to abolition. Since they considered liberty and emancipation inseparable, they looked to Great Britain for "favorable considerations."[33] Before departing, they alluded to plans for rebellion that could be implemented within several months.

These disclosures seem to have taken Crawford aback. As he told Aberdeen, "I answered that I was sorry they had thought fit to ask such an interview that being accredited as a British Officer to the Authorities of her Majesty the Queen of Spain in Cuba, I could not and ought not to listen to such things." Crawford could not speak for the British government, but he affirmed that "every human person" should deplore a violent upheaval in Cuba.[34] He felt sure that the British government would never countenance a rebellion to end slavery in Cuba, that it was seeking a peaceful solution only.

Crawford included another disclosure. Captain-General Valdés had been alerted to the existence of anti-Spanish plotting as well as to the presence in Jamaica of "a certain Colombian General Mariño, who is likely to take command in the projected Revolution."[35] Valdés had ordered authorities in the port towns to be vigilant. Should Mariño attempt a crossing, they were to arrest him on sight.

Crawford was incorrect about Mariño's national origin but not on his whereabouts. His past would not have allowed Spanish officials to take him lightly either. He was in Jamaica and, by all accounts, in need, having been expelled from Venezuela after leading a failed rebellion with separatist overtones in 1836, the so-called Revolution of the Reforms. He eventually took refuge in Santo Domingo, where he appears to have found quiet support from Jean-Pierre Boyer, Haiti's mulatto president, for a paramilitary adventure against Puerto Rico. Intelligence had reached Spain in 1837 that Mariño's intention was "to proceed with about Eight hundred men, a large proportion of them officers, with as many arms as he can obtain, and to proclaim an abolition of slavery and division of the land amongst the Negroes."[36] The expedition never took place. If it had, Cuba's Captain-General had orders to aid his Puerto Rican counterpart in smashing it.[37] To Spanish imperialists and all those with a major stake in upholding the slave system, personalist, warrior-adventurers like Mariño and Sentmanat posed dangers far greater than the protracted bounds of their own ambition, for in an Age of Democratic Revolution, the political and ideological patterns of recruitment could advance social revolution in step with the individual pursuit of power.

Crawford's December missives thickened the plot. They identified that shadowy military man from the United States whom Cocking accused of being a secret agent as Major John Cooke; like Cocking, Crawford said that Cooke had been using the cover of consul to steal about, communicating promises of United States assistance to antiabolition Creole separatists via Andrés Fernández de Lara and his uncle, the Conde de Santovenia. Official correspondence between Havana and Madrid reveals that Crawford had denounced Major Cooke to Captain-General Valdés but that Valdés and other Spanish officials had their own worries and were under orders to reduce the number and influence of all foreign agents in Cuba. Thus they refused to grant the exequatur Cooke needed to take up the consular post in Gibara.[38] Hard evidence to prove that Cooke was working behind the scenes to promote annexation has not yet turned up, although as a native Virginian he must have at least brought up the subject during his social communions with leading Creoles.[39]

A free mulatto activist "of great intelligence" named "Gigot" apprised Crawford of his receipt from the Conde de Santovenia of an overture on the linking of free coloreds with whites in a proslavery independence movement, an overture that was "apparently acceded to in order to get from the American party the extent of their plans and professions."[40] One of Crawford's dispatches contains a list of principals of the so-called American party. Not all of the names are legible, complete, or spelled correctly, but those that can be deciphered read like a social register: Joaquín Gómez, Wenceslao de Villurrutia, Joaquín Aizpurúa, Domingo Goicouría, Juan Antonio Isaguirre, Roque Jacinto Llopart, Salvador Samá, and Miguel Biada, all big merchants or merchant-planters; the Conde de Santovenia (José María Martínez de Campos), the Conde de Fernandina (José María Herrera), the Marqués de Arcos (Ignacio Peñalver), the Marqués de Esteva de los Delicias (José Buenaventura Esteva), the Conde de Peñalver (Nicolás Peñalver), a Montalvo (probably Juan), Manuel Del Monte (nephew of Domingo Del Monte), Antonio de Frías, and General Narciso López (brother-in-law of Frías), all big planters or tied by family to big planters. According to Crawford, Frías had just returned from the United States, where "he had many private interviews with that government."[41]

From what Crawford could uncover after the start of the new year, the proabolition Creole party had temporarily postponed its rebellion. Valdés, in the meantime, had called out the Military Commission to interrogate suspicious characters, but it had directed its attention "only to plots amongst the Negroes."[42] One case, that of Joseph Mitchell, an English-speaking free person of color arrested in December 1842 for possessing seditious documents, did generate some excitement. The authorities at first thought Mitchell was from Jamaica. As it turned out, he was born in Africa and had long been a resident of Cuba. The Military Commission accused Mitchell of being an abolitionist agent of David Turnbull and questioned Crawford about him. Crawford wrote home that while the Spanish government seemed to have adopted a strategy designed to polarize relations between Creoles and free people of color, partisans of France and the United States were busily engaged in the dissemination of antiabolitionist propaganda.[43]

Not until April 1843 did Crawford have significant new information. Another rebel had paid him a visit—this time an impassioned representative of a conspiratorial faction of the people of color named Juan Rodríguez. He delivered a handwritten message to Crawford, who dispatched it to Aberdeen along with a summation of their conversation. Rodríguez wrote that on 4 April 1842 he had "put into the hand" of David Turnbull, a petition to "be placed at the feet of Her Majesty the Queen . . . asking for aid in munitions and armament."[44] According to Rodríguez, Turnbull promised not only to send the petition but to effect the actual transfer of munitions and armaments by March of the following year. March had come and gone without consummation, and since the colored rebels were becoming restless, Rodríguez turned to Crawford for assistance.

Please write to Her Majesty, to the Lords, my Lords and the Society of Quakers and also to the Superintendent of Africa [i.e., Turnbull], the Guardian of Liberty, or to whomever else you think most proper so as that we may be properly directed under our present circumstances and that I may be able to provide for the tranquility and repose of these men who live in a dying state.[45]

Rodríguez also mentioned how in November of the previous year he had entrusted Francis Ross Cocking to deliver a document to Crawford. Cocking never did, but decided to send it on; to where, Rodríguez did not say. He begged Crawford not to trust Cocking any further.

Crawford tried to convince Rodríguez of the futility of rebellion. If Rodríguez was telling the truth, Turnbull had deluded him and had made promises he could not possibly keep. The British wanted a negotiated end to slavery in Cuba "without violence or an open and disastrous war of Castes." According to Crawford, Rodríguez "expressed very great doubts whether the delegates from other parts of the Island now here in Havana, would be persuaded to abandon or could induce their people to give up the project, as it was the general opinion amongst them, that if they were all sacrificed it would be preferable to their present state of existence."[46] Like Cocking, Rodríguez referred to the plantation district of Cárdenas province where one overeager member of the colored faction had led an ill-fated insurrection, an insurrection that proves that this movement was not solely confined to the free people of color but had included slaves as well.

Other meetings followed. Crawford told Aberdeen in May that Rodríguez had reasserted the people of color's determination to revolt "on or about the 31st Instant at points simultaneously." Crawford again pleaded with Rodríguez for restraint by pointing out

the dreadful situation in which these men are about to place themselves, without arms and exposed to the action of a disciplined army, but they reckon upon their inaccessibility, the approach of the rainy season, consequent sickness amongst the troops from exposure in such a climate and the impassable state of the inland Roads as well as the distracted attention of the Military to so many points, enabling them to hold out, until sympathy shall bring them assistance from abroad.[47]

Rodríguez's statements coincide with parts of Cocking's testimony. They would verify his story that the people of color had put together an elaborate and extensive revolutionary organization with which Cocking had fallen into disfavor. They suggest strongly that Turnbull had some relations with the conspirators, perhaps not as the head of a colored movement to extirpate Spanish oppression, but as a contact point, in any case, and a symbol around which the people of color could rally for their political liberation.

Turnbull was pursuing his new duties as Commissioner of the Mixed Court in Jamaica when Lord Aberdeen confronted him with Crawford's revelations. Turnbull denied everything, denied ever having laid eyes on Juan Rodríguez or his application for arms and munitions. "It is perfectly well known at the Havana," he contended, "that however strongly attached to the cause of human freedom, my feelings are utterly abhorrent to such a violent mode of accomplishing any measure of emancipation."[48] Of course, admission of even the barest contact with a rebel movement of Cuba's people of color might have ruined him with the Foreign Office, for how could it excuse his official silence about the movement as consul?

That Turnbull had some contact with Juan Rodríguez seems likely. Rodríguez had no obvious reason to lie to Crawford. The fate of the second document, the one Rodríguez claimed to have entrusted to Cocking, and which Cocking claimed to have forwarded to J. M. Trew of the Society for the Civilization of Africa, points in the same direction. The document did exist, for Trew's acknowledgement of it is filed near Cocking's confession in the records of the British Foreign Office.[49] Why Cocking would choose to bypass Crawford and to send the document to Trew proves puzzling unless Crawford disapproved of what was going on and Turnbull, who is listed as a participant in the Society for the Civilization of Africa's organizational meeting, had counseled Cocking somewhere along the line about the reasonableness of the course. While David Murray is probably correct in asserting that the British and Foreign Anti-Slavery Society knew nothing about the plotting in Cuba, the Society for the Civilization of Africa must have, although apparently giving neither it nor Cocking countenance.[50]

Cocking's confession does point to evidence against Turnbull. Cocking credits himself with having persuaded a Pedro María Morilla to set down the fundamentals of white separatism in the "Address to the London Anti-Slavery Society." The address does exist in the Foreign Office records and was published without attribution in the British Parliamentary Papers as the "Address of the Young Creoles to the London Anti-Slavery Society."[51] But, suspiciously, Cocking, the man who claimed to have personally requested the address, errs in naming its author. Instead of Pedro María Morilla, he could have meant José María Morilla, a liberal intellectual from Santo Domingo who was practicing law in Havana, or Pedro José Morillas, also a lawyer, a member of the Del Monte circle, and one of Turnbull's admitted acquaintances.[52]

A dispatch in 1853 from the United States consul in Havana contains the definitive answer in this sworn statement from Pedro José Morillas:

I attest on my word, the most solemn oath, if it may be necessary, that having been solicited by the English Consul in this city [Havana], Mr. Turnbull, he said to me that the powerful and influential abolitionist societies of England at whose head was Prince Albert [i.e., the Society For the Extinction of the Slave Trade and the Civilization of Africa] offered to the natives of this Island whatever resources of money, arms, boats, and men that might be needed to acquire their independence from Spain, provided they would proceed at the same time to emancipate the slaves. A seductive proposition that I rejected immediately on the ground that although the principle of liberty of all men is based on the immutable and holy law of nature, it is in our present circumstances opposed to another natural law, no less sacred, of self preservation; and I concluded by proposing that if the philanthropic principles of said societies were honest and rational, they would use their power in liberating first the whites from the heavy tyranny of Spain, and afterwards, the manumission of the slaves in a gradual and prudent manner for the benefit of both races. The Consul invited me to write a memorial on the subject and having done so upon the said basis, he sent it to England, where, it is said, it was published but without any result. Lastly I am aware of the fact that the said consul called and made similar propositions to various persons, natives of the country, whom he thought influential and disposed to admit his dazzling offer, which was rejected by all.[53]

At least during the first year or so of Turnbull's consulship, these young Creoles had good reason to maintain cordial relations with Great Britain. However much thinking Cubans separated the issues of slavery and the slave trade and disagreed with Turnbull's specific proposal, they did agree that the slave trade to Cuba must end as soon as possible. Like R. R. Madden before him, Turnbull solicited information from liberal

Cuban whites on Cuban society and politics. They, in turn, carefully informed Turnbull in the hope of having their predicament told in Britain, thereby to reinforce British exertions to have Spain abide by its anti-slave-trade agreements, if the means to that end did not simultaneously undo slavery. Those represented by Morillas in his "Address to the Young Creoles to the London Anti-Slavery Society" saw larger opportunities, at least in October 1841. By working through Turnbull and the British abolitionists, they tried to sway the British government with promises of commercial advantages and a program of gradual emancipation into covering their separatist movement with a protectorate and thereby guaranteeing a quick and relatively painless ascendancy without the potentialities of social revolution inherent in a protracted war of liberation.[54]

Before his expulsion, Turnbull, in a letter to Lord Palmerston, listed nineteen "enlightened" Creoles with whom he was in regular communication, "either directly or indirectly," on the subjects of slavery and the slave trade. Only the "fear of exposing them to personal danger" dissuaded him from the pursuit of closer relations. The nineteen formed the core of Cuba's intellectual and literary life. All nineteen could be said to have been dissatisfied with Spanish authoritarian rule; some, such as Porfirio Valiente, had previously engaged in more open separatist activity.

Turnbull's Admitted Contacts

1. Domingo Del Monte	11. José Antonio Echevarría
2. José de la Luz y Caballero	12. Rafael Leopoldo Palomino
3. Félix Tanco	13. Juan Francisco Funes
4. Cirilo Villaverde	14. Francisco Muñoz del Monte
5. Porfirio Valiente	15. José del Castillo
6. Manuel de Castro Palomino	16. Victoriano Betancourt
7. Ramón de Palma	17. Francisco Valdés Herrera
8. José Zacarías González del Valle	18. Pedro del Arroyo
9. Pedro José Morillas	19. José Ramón Ruíz
10. José Luis Alfonso	

Most of these nineteen were between twenty-five and forty-five years of age; most were lawyers by training; all were born in Spanish America but not all in Cuba; many had studied at the famous San Carlos Seminary under Father Félix Varela.[55]

Relations with Turnbull proceeded with considerable risk, for, as Domingo Del Monte informed him in a letter that announced a forthcoming delivery of a paper on the reasons for the continuation of the slave trade,

"Although I have signed it, you know very well that the publication of my name, at the foot of such a paper, would be more than sufficient to draw down on my head proscription and even death."[56]

Turnbull's subsequent correspondence from Jamaica contains more to substantiate some of Cocking's confession and shows his continuing involvement in Cuba's internal affairs. Perhaps chastened by Lord Aberdeen's inquiry, Turnbull while at his new post in Jamaica took care to report approaches by three expatriates from South America, Antonio Falques, Juan José Nieto, and General Santiago Mariño, on matters that included the abolition of slavery and the status of Cuba. Falques had just returned from Cuba and "did not conceal his desire to promote its independence." Turnbull requested them to prepare a memorandum for presentation to Lord Elgin, but, according to Turnbull, he declined to see them or their memorandum, "in consequence chiefly I believe of the allusion to the present state of the Island of Cuba, as to which he [Elgin] had received the special instructions of the Secretary of State for the Colonies to abstain from all interference."[57] Following Elgin's lead, Turnbull said, he declined to have any further contact with Mariño or the others.

The reference in Cocking's confession to a slave revolt in Cárdenas as an abortive outgrowth of a conspiracy of the people of color also conforms with the words of Juan Rodríguez. Both men were referring to the slave uprising of March 1843 in the district of Cimarrones in Cuba's sugar heartland. Cuban whites had no idea of its ramifications at the time, although its uncommon size and sophistication terrified them. It occurred on March 26 on *ingenio* Alcancía, one of the largest in the region, owned by Joaquín Peñalver, an absentee Creole patrician, and administered by a "superannuated, weak and withall an intemperate man."[58] At one o'clock in the morning watchmen were changing shifts. Drums began to beat, slaves revolted, killed the mill engineer and two other employees, and destroyed property. Slaves of both sexes gathered together to the sound of drums and moved on "in military order, clad in their holiday clothes, with colours flying, and holding leathern shields" to recruit on neighboring estates.[59] Slaves who were working nearby on a railroad line were locked up in Cárdenas but got out and inflated the number of rebels to between five hundred and one thousand. The local soldiery and well-armed bands of *monteros* battled the insurgents and eventually drove them into the hills around the village of Bemba (now Jovellanos), inflicting, according to various speculations, tens or hundreds of casualties.

Captain-General Valdés, on hearing the news, ordered four companies of crack troops and one hundred lancers to speed to the scene. On passing through Cimarrones, the commanding officer, Turnbull's old antagonist Antonio García Oña, governor of Matanzas, reported a "great loss of property, by fire, on five sugar plantations, four white persons have been killed and two severely wounded . . . many blacks have been shot, and as many more hung by the white inhabitants and soldiery."[60] García Oña and a portion of his regulars remained in the area for some time, using bloodhounds to round up the fugitives. The Charleston physician J. G. F. Wurdemann, on hand in Cárdenas shortly after the bloodshed, found the inhabitants "still under considerable excitement. . . . Each man had a tale of prowess to relate of himself or his friend, and . . . a drunken Irishman, who had charged singly into a crowd of the insurgents, was still an object of interest to the citizens, although only one, and he a foreigner, gave him a shelter and food."[61]

Wurdemann could afford a sense of humor. Captain-General Valdés could not. Talk of imminent rebellion in Cuba had been reaching peninsular officials for some time. From what direction it might come, they could only guess. Abolitionists, annexationists, Francophiles, soldiers of fortune, free coloreds, slaves, and Creoles all merited government surveillance.

More slave revolts broke out in the western countryside in the late spring and summer of 1843. In May slaves rose up on *ingenios* Santa Rosa and Majagua, both owned by Domingo Aldama, and destroyed much property. In June *ingenios* Ácana and Concepción suffered disturbances, which were reported to involve a group of about fifty blacks led by two free mulattoes. Later that month, also in the district of Guamacaro, about three hundred slaves rose up on *ingenio* Flor de Cuba. In July about forty Lucumí slaves revolted on *ingenio* Arratía.[62]

The case of José Dolores, the leader of a band of runaway slaves, suggests how the patterns of resistance were changing. He appears to have been a creole slave who ran away from a plantation in the district of Limonar. In 1843 he became a hero to the plantation slaves of Cuba's western countryside, a fright to their masters, and an item in the trans-Atlantic press not for occasional raids for necessities from the relative safety of a *palenque* but for maneuvering his male and female followers around the countryside to launch strikes in the hit-and-run style of a modern guerrilla. Sometime after March of 1843, José Dolores actually moved his band eastward in an unsuccessful attempt to liberate those rebel slaves who had been imprisoned as a result of the failed uprising on *ingenio* Alcancía.[63]

A general perception persisted, apparently shared even by Consul Crawford, that "for the want of energy" Captain-General Valdés might act slowly in a crisis.[64] But even though Valdés took confidence from the forces at his disposal and from what he called the "contradictions" within the ranks of those Cuban whites who aspired for independence that the projects of adventurers would not be realized, he hardly dallied. Between Turnbull's expulsion in November 1842 and the middle of 1843, Valdés alerted security forces, collected intelligence, shuffled troops, forbade the issuance of passports to any free persons of color born in Spanish territory who intended to travel to a foreign land, and ordered strict compliance with article 25 of the slave code on estate security. The Spanish vice-consul in Kingston, Jamaica, had been sending regular communications to Valdés on the movement of the local adventurers and abolitionists.[65] That Spanish agents had shadowed Cocking seems not only possible but likely.

At the same time, Cuban whites, ever more insecure, tensed to strike out at somebody. The powerful slave-trading interest was blaming Valdés for the beginning of the trade's recession and were agitating in Spain and in Cuba to have him removed. The best estimates indicate that in 1842 the volume of Cuba's slave trade had dipped to about one-third of its 1840 level, and in 1843 to about one-half that level. Despite frustratingly vague orders from Spain and at least one official caution against "excessive zeal" in the enforcement of the anti-slave-trade agreements, Valdés proved more dutiful than Turnbull had thought, and an uncertain future and low sugar prices put slaveholders in no mood to buy.[66]

Gaspar Betancourt's letters of 1842 and 1843 to Domingo Del Monte testify to the caldron of rumor and tension that Cuba had become. The perceived massing of abolitionist forces inside and outside of Cuba at a time of increasingly authoritarian rule by a Spanish government, deeply in debt to England from where the most vocal and politically powerful abolitionists came, had implanted in Cuba's planters insecurity about the future of their slave property. Their insecurity directed their attention away from paternalistic behavior to a strategy of quick return at the physical expense of their slaves. Near the end of 1842 he told of the "stupidity and swagger" that was rampant in response to the "stories of Turnbull, Haity [*sic*], and the Bando [de Gobernación] and all the rest." He became "convinced that the most talented men, of most learning, and

even virtue, have become rattled here by the subject of slavery or the African trade, like the hidalgo from La Mancha [i.e., Don Quixote], who
when it came to the subject of chivalry lost his head."[67]

Also in December he wrote:

Our horror-mongers [i.e., the slaveholders] are alarmed by the matters of
Turnbull, Haiti, and the *Bando de Gobernación y Policía* that will take effect
starting in 1843. The flayers of flesh [*hombres de arrancapellejo*] are resolved
not to comply with articles 6 and 12 and all those that favor the blacks, because, for the very reason that there are abolitionists, Haiti, and England in
the world, it is necessary to correct them severely, to make them bend their
backs, and to whip them, which is what truly tames them, and [the slave-
holders] are quite ready to work this way.

As for Haiti now you see that it is a stupid, insignificant, impotent government of orangutangs which in two kicks fly to the mountains to eat *jobos* [a
Cuban fruit] and guava. So a lawyer has told us, and he is not the stupidest
one we have. The reconquest of Saint Domingue is not a problem for Don
Quixote.[68]

And in January of 1843:

I have read a letter which says that the emissaries, missionaries, and diplomatic
agents of England go from *door to door* (these are the exact words) *offering
us independence in exchange for emancipation*. What a terrible condition.
. . . It is said that the metropolitan government has sold out to the guineas
and interests of England. What rogues are those English. They have proposed
to ruin us and in one way or another they will succeed.[69]

In tightening its security network, the Spanish government netted for
subversion José Mitchell along with four other free people of color who,
by their own words, had been listening to Turnbull and then encouraging
people of color to emigrate from Cuba.[70] The alarming documents that
Spanish authorities discovered in Mitchell's hat were probably passports
obtained illegally for them by Turnbull and literature on Turnbull's
scheme for emigration. Mitchell's four friends had sojourned in Jamaica
to experience life under British freedom first hand so that they could con-
vey their impressions to their fellows back in Cuba. Spain's vice-consul in
Kingston sighted the quartet and alerted Valdés, who had them seized
upon their return.[71] Valdés claimed that the documents found on Mitchell
"alluded to a conspiracy among the people of color."[72]

From the point of view of liberal-minded Britons, Mitchell deserved
far less than the initial sentence of death by garroting that the Military
Commission under Narciso López handed down or the later commutation
to life imprisonment. The promotion of emigration from a land of slav-

ery to a land of freedom, even if done unlawfully, could not be labeled a revolutionary conspiracy. But the battle between British abolitionists and Spanish bureaucrats amounted to a battle of systems and world views. Great Britain epitomized the new: a nation raised to the pinnacle of world power by free men and markets. Spain represented the old: a nation staggering and stumbling to escape the legacy of its seigneurial past yet supported by a prosperous colony of slaves and masters. To Spanish regimes that subsisted off Cuba, freedom became sedition and the men who preached it, subversives.

The events of the spring of 1843 engendered hectic government retaliation. The Military Commission busied itself with the trials of slaves and free coloreds implicated in the Cárdenas uprising. It arraigned various other Afro-Cubans for slandering the government, inciting disturbances, and acting suspiciously. Authorities in the town of Villa Clara, the strategic center of Cuba, arrested the celebrated poet Plácido with two others, one a white man and convicted Cuban separatist, for being suspicious characters.[73] In June the dithering governor of Cienfuegos asked Captain-General Valdés to ban festival drum-beating not only because he detested the sound but because the slaves were using it to assemble surreptitiously.[74] Crawford told of the extensive movement of troops and their deployment among the plantations. Charles Clarke, the British consul in Santiago, reported that Count Mirasol, the intendant of Cuba, had arrived in May in a Spanish warship with soldiers and munitions after having inspected the fortification of the town of Baracoa.[75] In March, the month of the slave revolt in Cárdenas, Governor Juan Tello of Santiago sent Captain-General Valdés a copy of the Jamaican *Morning Journal* that announced the landing of David Turnbull. Other communications from officials in Cienfuegos, Trinidad, and Puerto Príncipe linked political turmoil in Haiti and Santo Domingo to the intrigues of abolitionists in Jamaica. Letters from Spanish citizens in Jamaica warned Valdés of probable collusion between Turnbull and General Mariño.[76]

To separate truth from all the hearsay and conjecture, Valdés ordered a special agent Eduardo Fesser, to Jamaica. Valdés instructed him explicitly to identify the leaders of the abolitionists and their allies; to assess the likelihood of invasion; and, if likely, to discover the invasion's point of departure, size, composition, and equipage. Mariño, and other South Americans would come under strict surveillance, as would Turnbull and General Jean-Pierre Boyer, who had just been deposed as president of Haiti and was rumored to be in Jamaica. Valdés also ordered an investigation of Carlos Duquesnay, the Spanish vice-consul in Kingston, who had been regularly sending intelligence to him about a possible invasion, to check his reliability and character.

Under the code name "Lino," Valdés's confidant imparted some comforting news in June of 1843. The number of South Americans in Jamaica proved small, probably no more than forty or fifty. He did not find "the least indication" of an abolitionist invasion from Jamaica, and he did not observe communication between Turnbull and adventurers from Colombia and Venezuela. Vice-consul Duquesnay seemed honest but of limited talent. Fesser actually roomed in the same house in which Turnbull had stayed for the first few weeks after his arrival. The owner, a "respectable person" who "did not have a good opinion" of Turnbull, told Fesser that he never saw Turnbull speak with any South Americans.[77] Turnbull lived some distance away at present and it was certain that he had met with Boyer. Because Boyer was more than seventy years of age, however, Fesser depreciated his capacity for adventures. He thought Turnbull himself wildly dangerous, but since he and the abolitionist society lacked funds, they seemed unlikely to do anything. For the time being, Spanish rule in Cuba seemed safe from external threat.

7

Africanization or Annexation to the United States?

━━━━━◆•◆━━━━━

> But when the planets
> In evil mixture to disorder wander,
> What plagues and what portents! What Mutiny!
> What raging of the sea! Shaking of earth!
> Commotion in the winds! frights, changes, horrors,
> Divert and crack, rend and deracinate
> The unity and married calm of states
> Quite from their fixture! Oh when degree is shaked
> Which is the ladder to all high designs,
> The enterprise is sick!
>
> SHAKESPEARE, *Troilus and Cressida*

Any movement of forces that might affect Cuba's status had to concern the United States. As one of many nations locked in a struggle for advantage in an international market, it could scarcely ignore the "bulwark of the Antilles," the "key to the New World." Cuba sits astride the Straits of Florida, the Yucatan Channel, and the Windward Passage, three narrows that unlock entrances to the Gulf of Mexico. A power that commands Cuba could command the Caribbean. A power so situated, a short hundred miles from the Florida Keys, could threaten the security of the United States.

International rivalries precluded bold action by the United States to annex Cuba. Great Britain, for one, saw Cuba as a barrier to the southward expansion of the United States and throughout the antebellum period used its supremacy at sea as an effective counterpoise. U.S. aggression to wrest Cuba from Spain could bring about the British ascendancy it was designed to avoid. President James Madison and his immediate successors settled on a policy of mutual understanding with Great Britain

183

to uphold Spanish sovereignty in Cuba.[1] They hoped thereby to buy time for that future day when the United States could confront Britain on better terms. Each side nevertheless monitored the other's hemispheric activity with distrust. Now leading the anti-slave-trade campaign, Great Britain could, consciously or not, continue its expansion of power, in Cuba, Texas, or Brazil, in the guise of humanitarianism. Political realists pointed out that the series of mutual right-to-search agreements, from which the United States had prudently abstained, enhanced Great Britain's maritime and commercial might at others' expense.[2] In Britain's search of suspected slavers, it could (and on occasion did) use the right to search as a pretext to obstruct commerce and impress seamen.

Emancipation in the British West Indies had demonstrated that behind the movement to abolish the slave trade stood forces that intended to abolish slavery as well. The British government had allied with those forces and seemed bent on bringing about emancipation in Cuba. Whether truly humanitarian or practical reasons dictated British policy made little difference to those classes whose self-interest ran counter to it. By and large, officials who pursued abolitionist policies, David Turnbull, for example, truly believed in their humanitarianism. But the British had redefined it according to a new set of values consistent with British capitalism. Abolitionism enhanced British power by giving Britain a moral force that transcended immediate economic calculation and, at the same time, helped prepare for a world in which British capitalism and all other national capitalisms could thrive.

John Calhoun, the consummate spokesman for Southern slaveholders, conceded that humanity played a part in abolitionism, but "as is not unusual with fanaticism," he saw philanthropy combined inextricably with power and profit.[3] After Calhoun, arguments narrowed. Since slave emancipation had accelerated the decline of the British West Indies, British West Indian sugar producers would be served if rivals were forced to compete on a more equal basis. A plan like Turnbull's for emancipation would destroy Cuba's plantation economy if it ignited racial conflict similar to the one that had occurred in Saint Domingue. "Africanization" of Cuba would add one more link to a chain of territories to the south of the United States populated by free blacks and indebted to Britain for their freedom—a chain that could obstruct United States expansion and also endanger slavery in the South. Nicholas Trist, United States consul in Havana from 1833 to 1841, expressed his fear of abolitionism as an instrument of British imperialism when he reported "a deep excitement [in Cuba among the Creoles] with a corresponding degree of alarm (which cannot fail to grow with every revolving day) in regard to the supposed designs of the British Government respecting the extention [*sic*] of its modern Colonial System—for the *West* Indies—to this Island."[4] Cuba's future seemed to absorb the leadership of South Carolina more deeply than other states of the South. Among the slaveholding states, South Carolina possessed most of the largest plantations, land with the highest density of slaves, and a white minority. Not by coincidence, South Carolina produced the South's least democratic state and the most mature, intimate, and powerful ruling class of slaveholders. "Nowhere else in America," William Freehling has written, "did the wealthy class so successfully conspire to keep power away from the common man."[5] South Carolinians led the way in constructing an ideology of Southern nationalism that promoted slavery as a positive good, as the very essence of civilization. "You know my policy," Simms would tell Hammond in 1848, "to use Uncle Sam at large and all his resources, for those acquisitions, which in the event of a dissolution will enure wholly to the South."[6] Charleston to Havana in 1840 could take less than a week in good weather, and the several ships that booked passage every month freighted back the latest political news along with recovering invalids. John Calhoun had long pressed for the acquisition of Cuba to stave off the British and prevent a repetition of Saint Domingue. Such South Carolinian stalwarts and William Gilmore Simms and James Henry Hammond shared Calhoun's concern.[7] Joel Roberts Poinsett, a South Carolinian planter, diplomat, and politician, remembered in 1850: "The annexation of Cuba to the United States, or if that were found to be impossible, its independence under the protection and ample guaranty of our government, have been the frequent subject of my day dreams ever since I visited that island in 1822 [1823]."[8] Although as United States minister to Mexico from 1825 to 1829 Poinsett seems to have abided by administration instructions to help keep Cuba in Spanish hands by discouraging Mexican ventures to liberate it, and although as a staunch unionist, he never predicated his interest in annexation on slavery or narrow sectional interests, his hosting of prominent Cuban exiles like Father Félix Varela and introductions of them to expansionists indirectly served sectional interests by heightening awareness of the Cuban question among leading slaveholders. By 1840 Poinsett was well aware of the growing fears within Cuba of British abolitionism and the possibility of Africanization by slave revolution.[9]

In the early 1840s Southern sectionalists like Simms and Hammond were beginning to contemplate Cuba's annexation seriously. Southern travelers generally reported Cuban society hospitable to their values. Many would have agreed with Thomas Worthington King, a Northerner who had settled in New Orleans, when he told his mother on her return from Cuba in 1844: "Your observations with regard to the manners of the Cubans is just what I expected and corresponds with my own ideas of the Spaniards, who however inferior to the Yankees in Education, really possess more good feeling and more good manners than our fellow citizens of the U States."[10] J. G. F. Wurdemann of Charleston, the physician who frequented Cuba for his health in the early 1840s, wrote at Simms's prompting an exceptionally acute description of colonial Cuban society. "The subject of this volume," said Reverend Daniel Whitaker, the expansionist editor of the Charleston-based *Southern Quarterly Review,* "must be of deep interest to our countrymen— more especially of the Southern States. . . . Let it once appear that the old Castilian grasp is about to be released—and Cuba is an independent government—or ours forever, whatever England, or Europe itself, may advance to the contrary. This is the natural and necessary course of things."[11]

Southern slaveholders' interest in Cuba specifically and in expansionism generally reflected both anxiety and confidence within a society increasingly troubled and introspective. Slaveholders recoiled at the worldwide abolitionist onslaught. They shuddered at the image of a Denmark Vesey or Nat Turner overturning the Southern way of life. They believed, as only a self-conscious, tightly knit, and deeply entrenched ruling class can, that their society had set a standard for others to follow. Simms's defense of slavery in the abstract against the attack by abolitionist Harriet Martineau in 1839 and a similar defense by Hammond against that of Thomas Clarkson in 1845 showed such confident self-consciousness.[12] The concept of expansion of slavery across national boundaries thus was simultaneously both offensive and defensive, above all, a Southern conception, contemplated seriously in South Carolina, and impracticable in slaveholding countries in which slaveholders lacked formal political power.

Should Great Britain and its antislavery missionaries succeed in extending its influence in Cuba as the champion of free labor, the North stood to suffer along with the South. Economic ties with Cuba had multiplied with the sugar boom and the concomitant liberalization of Spanish trade regulations. By 1840 the United States had become Cuba's biggest trading partner, and only Britain and France exceeded Cuba in the total value of trade (both exports and imports) with the United States. The U.S. consumed more Cuban sugar than any other country and sent lumber, foodstuffs, and manufactured goods in return. Sugar, its distillable by-products, coffee, and tobacco found ready markets as working-class ingestibles in an industrializing economy. The career of Moses Taylor, that prim New York entrepreneur, attests to the fortunes made by North Americans in the shipping and marketing of Cuba's slave-grown staples.[13]

In the early 1840s newspapers were actively promoting economic and political interest in Cuba by depicting Cuba as a land upon which a bounteous heaven had lavished gifts. The *New York Herald,* reporting on the October 1842 arrest of David Turnbull by Spanish authorities, added: "Cuba is one of the most fertile, healthy, beautiful, rich and lovely islands on the face of the earth. It is a perfect paradise. . . . These foreign attempts to interfere with its peculiar institutions are causing great discontent; and the prospect of following the example of the United States, of Texas, of all Spanish South America, is getting stronger and stronger every day."[14] The *Daily Picayune* of New Orleans in June 1843, after providing its readers with statistics on Cuba, said "the extent and condition of the population of this fruitful Island, the spot on which the British fanatics have fastened their pestiferous regards (!!) and whose government waits but for time and tide to second and support their designs,—the key to the Gulf of Mexico—the outlet of the ponderous wealth of the great Valley of the Mississippi . . . holding, like our own Southern States, an immense slave property, cannot but excite the most intense interest with the politician and the statesman of all countries, especially our own."[15] *Hunt's Merchants Magazine* of New York alerted its readers to the creeping menace of Britain, "insidiously advancing to the possession of Cuba. . . . Cuba is the garden of the world; and under an independent, republican government, would ultimately rival England, in power and wealth."[16]

Although ownership of Cuban plantations would remain largely in Cuban hands until the twentieth century, by 1840 migrants from the United States were prospecting for wealth there. About a thousand had settled permanently in Cuba, the majority in Havana and on the fertile clays of Matanzas and Cárdenas provinces. Perhaps a thousand more filled the demand for skilled laborers as artisans, machinists, and engi-

neers in the sugarmill complex. In the eastern end of Cuba, North Americans supplied labor, capital, and expertise for mining copper and iron ore
and for constructing railroads.[17] Taken together, these connections hardly
spelled Yankee domination of the Cuban economy, but they did lend
substance to a vision in both North and South, increasingly fostered by
the press, that Cuba belonged in the North American orbit. As Secretary
of State John Quincy Adams had hoped in 1823,

Cuba, almost in sight of our shores, from a multitude of considerations has
become an object of transcendent importance to the political and commercial
interests of our Union. Its commanding position with reference to the Gulf of
Mexico, and the West India seas; the character of its population; its situation
midway between our southern coast, and the island of San Domingo; its safe
and capacious harbor of Havana, fronting a long line of our shores destitute
of the same advantage; the nature of its productions and of its wants, furnish-
ing the supplies and needing the returns of a commerce immensely profitable
and mutually beneficial: give it an importance in the sum of our national interests, with which that of no other foreign territory can be compared, and
little inferior to that which binds the different members of this union together . . . if an apple severed by the tempest from its native tree cannot
but fall to the ground, Cuba, forcibly disjoined from its own unnatural connection with Spain, and incapable of self support, can gravitate only towards
the North American Union.[18]

During the administration of Martin Van Buren (1837–1841), the
United States continued to interpret the national interest in Cuba as the
preservation of the status quo. Still recovering from the Panic of 1837,
it could not afford a confrontation with Great Britain over Cuba or anything else. Yet intermittent reports suggested that debt-ridden Spain
was on the verge of selling or mortgaging Cuba to Britain. Britain's
funding of the Liberal victory in the first Carlist War had made a deal
more than possible, notwithstanding Lord Palmerston's firm denials. The
case of the Africans' mutiny on the Cuban slave schooner *Amistad*
handed Britain a conspicuous violation of its anti-slave-trade agreements
with Spain and a pretext for extending its influence in Cuba.[19] The
Amistad affair and abolitionist intrigue in Cuba, even before Turnbull
and apparently with Britain's blessing, prompted the United States
chargé d'affaires in Madrid, at the behest of Secretary of State John
Forsyth, a Georgian slaveholder, to caution Britain and assure Spain that
"in no event [could the United States] permit the occupation of Cuba by
British Agents or forces, upon whatever pretext undertaken; and that, in
the event of any attempt to wrest from Spain this portion of her terri-

tory . . . [it] might securely depend upon the military and naval re-sources of the United States to aid her in preserving or recovering it."[20]

At about the same time, Palmerston and the abolitionists accused U.S. consul in Havana Nicholas Trist of annexationist intrigue and com-plicity in Cuba's contraband slave trade. The ubiquitous R. R. Madden hurled charges against Trist which set off a minor sensation in the North-ern press and led to British inquiries into the scope of U.S. influence in Cuba. Cuban slave traders did use swift Baltimore clippers with United States flags and registry to escape British cruisers. And, among other things, the irascible and Anglophobic Trist, with personal investments in at least one Cuban sugar plantation, proved altogether too generous in legitimizing the sale of ships to U.S. citizens in Cuba who acted as front men for slave traders. Because Trist had to return to the States to defend himself, Van Buren ordered an agent to Cuba to superintend the affairs of the consulate and investigate the allegations. He also directed the agent to make a discreet reading of Cuba's political climate.[21] He felt confident that Great Britain would not take over Cuba, but he would have wanted sufficient intelligence to draw up contingency plans in case of the worst.

To execute the mission Van Buren handpicked Alexander Everett, a man particularly suited to gather information in Cuba. Everett was a veteran diplomat, a versatile intellect and a Harvard graduate, and a noted Hispanophile as well as the issue of an old Massachusetts family. He had served at the courts of Russia, the Netherlands, and Spain; he had edited the highly regarded *North American Review;* he had culti-vated, with his good friends George Ticknor, Washington Irving, and William Hickling Prescott, a North American school of Spanish studies; he numbered among his many Spanish acquaintances Cuba's Captain-General in 1840, the Prince of Anglona.[22]

Everett believed in Manifest Destiny. He, unlike his younger brother Edward, had staked his political fortune in the Democratic party and consorted with such leading party expansionists as John L. O'Sullivan, the writer-publisher to whom the expression Manifest Destiny is com-monly attributed. As minister to Spain during the presidency of his men-tor, John Quincy Adams, he had initiated, on his own, informal conversa-tions with Spanish officials to forward a scheme to acquire sovereignty over Cuba. In a secret letter to Adams, which was never deposited in the archives of the State Department, Everett premised his scheme by, in ef-fect, parroting Adams's words on the geopolitical reasons why "Cuba must at one time or another belong to us."[23] Spain's quixotic refusal to recognize the independence of its former colonies had added to the risk that they would live up to promises of striking back by liberating Cuba. A detached or unstable Cuba might prove irresistible plucking to a European power, particularly Britain, since Adams's acquisition of Florida by treaty in 1821 had increased Britain's interest in securing a Gibraltar in the Gulf of Mexico.

To Everett, Cuba formed "properly an appendage of the Floridas. . . . The American Government could not consent to any change in the political situation of Cuba other than one which should place it under the jurisdiction of the United States."[24] He hoped to take advantage of the financial plight of the Spanish Crown by offering a massive loan guaranteed by the "temporary" cession of Cuba to the United States. This way Spain would save face by retaining nominal control of Cuba and could reclaim sovereignty if the loan was repaid. Everett doubted, however, that Spain could ever repay it.[25] His negotiations, needless to say, never got far, but his interest in the annexation of Cuba continued.

Everett revered the United States as the agent of liberty and democracy and its institutions as the great hope of mankind. The government of the United States, he would proclaim in O'Sullivan's *Democratic Review*, "exemplifies more fully than it has ever been exemplified before, and probably to as great an extent as it can be reduced to practice, the beautiful idea of perpetual Peace. . . . It is obvious that such a system has no necessary territorial limits excepting those which are imposed by considerations of mere physical convenience."[26] Slavery tarnished this image, but Everett, an outspoken anti-Malthusian, abided by a version of the safety-valve thesis. According to this thesis, slavery in the United States would eventually expire by a process of internal disintegration. Expansionism would help by siphoning off slaves from the exhausted soils of the border and Atlantic Seaboard states and by restricting them to more productive western regions, which, in time, would also decline. Final abolition would then occur, ideally with the freed slaves moving across the border into Mexico.[27]

Everett went to Cuba twice in 1840 and used his spring trip to inquire into the Trist matter. His search brought him into contact with British officials, Spanish authorities, and prominent Creoles. He maintained cordial relations with the British and consulted James Kennedy of the Mixed Commission about Trist on several occasions. After depositing the results of his investigation in Washington, without establishing either Trist's guilt or innocence, he embarked in the fall from

New York to return to Cuba. Aboard ship, as if by some cynical twisting of fate, he met David Turnbull in transit to assume his consular duties in Havana. Each had heard of the other; each was curious.[28] Turnbull would write later:

It was not very likely that a person, of the high rank and attainments of Mr. Alexander Everett . . . should be sent to the Havanna to inquire into the conduct of a mere consul; and as Mr. Everett was observed to court the society of many of the leading creole proprietors, and to seek the intimacy of persons entertaining the most exalted and enthusiastic ideas upon the subject of Cuban independence, his long sojourn in the island, on more than one occasion, leads pretty clearly to the inference, that the true object of his mission was to feel the pulse of the people on the subject of annexation.[29]

Once in Cuba, Turnbull watched Everett closely and conveyed his impressions to Palmerston. The more Everett moved about asking questions, the more Turnbull became convinced "that the designs of the United States on this magnificent Island . . . are fast approaching maturity."[30] Everett met Turnbull several times and was struck by his intensity. Turnbull wasted no time in bringing news to Everett that Cuban miscreants had enslaved a free person of color from the United States. He urged Everett to join forces with him to free other people of color held unlawfully and, as if to convert an unbeliever, followed up with a tour of the *Romney* to show him the condition of a recent consignment of *emancipados*. Everett needed no conversion. "The whole business," he recounted to his wife, "is a mass of *abominations*."[31]

To Turnbull's chagrin, however, Everett impressed the Creoles. Amid lavish dinner parties and exchanges about John Locke's political philosophy and José Zorilla's poetry, Everett formed a lasting friendship with Domingo Del Monte. On both trips Everett mined Del Monte for information on Cuba. Indeed, the required report on Cuba's political situation that he subsequently prepared for the government relied almost entirely on Del Monte and materials he provided. In return, Everett put Del Monte in touch with literati in the United States and personally carried writings by him and other Creoles there so that they could inform the appropriate circles.[32] Everett perceived that through Del Monte he could project a positive image of the Creoles to expansionists and, at the same time, supply badly needed facts about Cuba.

Everett left Cuba in February 1841 satisfied that he had established vital contacts. The diary he kept during the Cuban trips makes clear that the subject of annexation did crop up during his many fraternizations with the Creoles. "The interference of the British in the Slavery Question has created a general sentiment among the inhabitants in favor of union with the U.S." And in his entry of 2 December 1840 he predicted a "complete political revolution" in Cuba."[33]

Turnbull carried on an intense vigil and on news of Everett's departure hurriedly notified the British consul in New Orleans, Britain's minister in Washington, Commodore Douglas of the British West Indian squadron, and Lord Palmerston. He felt certain "that the mission of Mr. Everett . . . has an important political object in view," and he promised Palmerston that if Everett returned he would not cease "to persevere in the system of observation I have thought it my duty to pursue."[34]

Everett expected to return to Cuba but never did. The political complexion in Washington had changed. Martin Van Buren lost in his bid for reelection. The opposition Whigs assumed power in 1841, briefly under William Henry Harrison and then under John Tyler. Although Tyler was a special case, the Whigs, in addition to their predominant distaste for Andrew Jackson, tended to deplore expansionism, at least for the short run, so as to avoid the issue of slavery's extension and hence to prevent disunion. Politically out of favor, Everett decided to accept an offer to become president of newly formed and short-lived Jefferson College in Louisiana.[35] Everett kept abreast of events in Cuba. He wrote to Del Monte, thanked him for his loan of books and manuscripts, and invited him to compose a brief history of Cuba that would cover the principal political and economic events of the last two decades. In ways that would presage the arguments for Cuba's annexation by the expansionist Young America movement in the 1850s, Everett resolved to show that Cuba and its whites were worthy of what he thought was their inevitable absorption by the United States.

Everett used a manuscript by Del Monte and a published paper by José de la Luz y Caballero as the basis for a review essay on the "State of Education and Learning in Cuba" for the first volume of the *Southern Quarterly Review*.[36] It was a useful place. The *Review* catered to the section of the country most sensitive to what transpired in Cuba; its Charleston headquarters made it readily accessible to the cream of Southern leadership; and Daniel Whitaker, the expansionist editor, would see to its proper circulation.

The piece itself opened in good liberal fashion by connecting Cuba's "rapid progress . . . in almost every particular" and, specifically, its increased interest in the development of human capital, to the end of Spanish mercantilism and the beginning of free trade. It praised Del

Monte, Luz y Caballero, and other Creoles for struggling against an oppressive government to promote public education, though, as his quotes of Del Monte make clear, the improvements in Cuban education had been marginal. They were largely confined to Havana and a few other cities; the situation in the countryside and especially in the plantation districts continued to be a wretched mess. Everett said nothing about slavery and blamed instead "the continuance of the present political system."[37] He closed with a sermon:

We have been led to make these remarks . . . by the interest which now extends itself in this country to every thing connected with the situation and fortunes of Cuba. That superb island, the Queen, as she is proudly called by her sons, of the Western Indies, politically still in an embryo state, contains within herself, in her vast resources, fine climate, and eminently fortunate geographical position, the germs, should circumstances prove at all favourable, of future greatness.

But he warned of British imperial ambitions.

Another island, far away in the German Ocean [North Sea], less extensive and much less favored by nature than Cuba, not content with the possession of half the continents and islands on the globe, is casting a longing eye upon the orange groves and sunny lawns of the Great Antilla. It is much to be feared, that the extreme zeal which now animates the British Government for the emancipation of half a million slaves in Cuba, is prompted, in part at least, we trust not entirely, by the same spirit which has led them to rivet the fetters of a more galling slavery upon the limbs of a hundred million Hindoos, and which is urging them to the slaughter and subjugation of three hundred million Chinese—the lust for universal dominion. But this grasping spirit, which has succeeded in so many enterprises, apparently of greater difficulty, will probably fail in its attempts on Cuba. The island whenever it may separate from the mother country, will not revolve as a satellite round the orb of any other European power, but will take its place as a new and brilliant star in our American constellation.[38]

A response from the New Orleans *Daily Picayune* could speak for much of the South. In commenting on this issue of the *Southern Quarterly Review*, it asserted that Everett's article "will attract much attention." A "growing anxiety" existed in the South about Cuba. The anticipated separation from Spain now seemed only a few years distant. Since Cuba's future status largely depended on the Cubans themselves and, according to the *Picayune*, the "most intelligent portion of the population" favored annexation to the United States, "the public mind in the south is anxiously bent upon the state of society in Cuba, and all information tending to shed light upon the subject is greedily snatched up."[39]

While Everett and the *Picayune* preached Manifest Destiny, Daniel Webster, Tyler's secretary of state, had set out to improve Anglo-American relations. He inherited trouble on several fronts: violence in disputed territory between Maine and Canada; persistent British affronts connected with the right to search suspected slavers on the high seas; and tension over the destiny of Texas. Turnbull's provocations added Cuba to the list. Webster disclaimed any administration plans to take control of Cuba and wanted Great Britain to do the same. The instructions to Aaron Vail, the chargé d'affaires in Madrid, made clear Webster's intention to maintain the status quo in Cuba. By the fall of 1841, stories about pending British intervention in Cuba to bring about the emancipation of slaves had surfaced in the European press to such an extent that Vail confronted Antonio González, the Spanish minister of foreign affairs, about them. Spain had no intention of relinquishing Cuba, González said. By the sale of the islands of Fernando Po and Annobón in the Gulf of Guinea, Spain had lessened its financial obligation to Great Britain; and with the change in ministry from Palmerston to Lord Aberdeen, Britain seemed more content with Spanish attempts to suppress the slave trade. Vail asked González point-blank if Great Britain had demanded the immediate emancipation of all slaves that had been introduced fraudulently. He received a strategic reply, as Vail reported it to Webster: "Of the secret wishes of Great Britain, he could not undertake to speak."[40] The rumors had started when the Spanish government acceded to a request by Great Britain to determine the number of slaves that had entered in violation of the Treaty of Madrid. True to the Spanish tradition of "I obey, but do not comply," Spain never intended to hand those figures over to Britain.

The inflammatory stories in the European press about British interference in Cuba had their counterparts in the expansionist press of the United States. The 1 October 1841 issue of the *New York Herald* reported the solicitation, under British pressure, by Captain-General Valdés of local opinion on Turnbull's plan to emancipate all slaves imported since 1820. Like Turnbull, the *Herald* understood that emancipating contraband slaves would mean the virtual end of slavery in Cuba. "It may be pure philanthropy [on Britain's part] . . . but we doubt it very much. And in the movement it is easily to be seen, that England aims at the heart of our southern States, and is determined to possess herself of Cuba."[41]

As Pedro de Alcántara Argaiz, Spain's minister to Washington, would tell Spanish officials, the perceived situation from press reports, particularly the October item in the *Herald,* induced a delegation of politicians, principally from the South, to confront him. They conveyed a simple message: The United States would respect Spain's authority in Cuba but only if Spain withstood British pretensions. Should Spain lose control of Cuba, the United States would have no other choice than to join with those Cubans who would move to protect their lives and property. Argaiz related the delegation's claim that "many of the principal *European* landholders in that Island, as well as the Creoles and resident Anglo-Americans" had been in regular communication with the United States government about British designs since the winter of 1841.[42] In another communication, he recalled a debate in the House of Representatives in which two Southerners, the louder of whom appears to have been Waddy Thompson of South Carolina, became so enraged over British influence in Cuba that they questioned Spain's capacity to rule, then declared that the United States would happily oppose Britain by contriving with restive Creoles "to convert the Island into a new state of the Anglo-American Confederation."[43]

Argaiz, conferring with Webster, was told that the administration had been approached on the subject of annexation by Cuban landholders and merchants who feared Spain's abandonment of them to Britain. Webster said that he had rebuffed the overtures and would continue to do so as long as Spain intended to keep Cuba Spanish.[44]

Spain could comfort the United States by promising to resist Great Britain and the United States could do the same for Spain by pledging support if needed, but neither Spain nor the United States could feel secure in the knowledge that Turnbull or the slaves might trigger a disaster from which only Great Britain could prosper. Because persistent rumors struck people prone to conspiracy theories, the reality of social ferment in Cuba, stark as it was, would never match the magnitude of its perception. Perhaps the Spanish regime of General Espartero itself contributed to the creation of the British bogey. Espartero's mouthpiece, the *Eco del Comercio,* for example, published stories on the British threat as did the opposition press.[45] Caught between the demands of an abolitionist ally and the financial dependency on a slave economy, his regime needed to play the United States in an international game of checks and balances. U.S. support of a Spanish rather than a British Cuba checked Great Britain from making extraordinary demands on Cuba without the

Espartero regime's risking the alienation of its ally by a direct rejection of those demands. Conversely, stories about U.S. encroachment in Cuba brought Britain to the defense of Spain. The danger remained that the game might get out of hand.

James S. Calhoun, the Whig successor to Nicholas Trist in the Havana consulate, submitted a lengthy report to Webster early in 1842 on the existence of widespread tension. A slave revolt had broken out near Baracoa in the eastern end of Cuba. Rumors were flying that blacks had slaughtered whites in Jamaica. Calhoun believed the British government to be blameless, but he accused David Turnbull of being "perfectly willing to engage in *any scheme,* having for its object the abolition of Slavery *here* or *elsewhere.*"[46] Periodically therafter, he updated Webster on Turnbull's peregrinations.

The subject of Cuba continued to excite Southern congressmen and the Democratic press in 1842, much to the dismay of Minister Argaiz. He might have seen a prominent advertisement in the *New York Herald*—which later apologized for printing it—by an unidentified Cuban patriot who was clearly attempting to arouse public support in the United States for Cuba's independence from what he described as an exploitative, undemocratic Spanish regime sold out to British abolitionism.[47] Although the questions of Texas and Mexico commanded much more interest, Cuba and British interference in Cuba could be seen to intertwine. Alexander Everett received private information from the head of a United States commercial firm in Havana that Turnbull and the slavery question were stirring up trouble. Everett mentioned this to Del Monte in a letter of September 1842. He confessed that he found Turnbull "not blessed with a very large share of the valuable quality [discretion] just alluded to" and solicited further information from Del Monte.[48]

Del Monte replied on 20 November 1842 that a cataclysm impended in Cuba: "England has decreed our ruin, and Spain does not *know* or does not *want* to know this, and the Spanish authorities on the Island do not want or do not know how to weather the tempest."[49] Britain, exasperated with the endlessness of the contraband slave trade, had unleashed the abolitionists to act as a "most adequate instrument of punishment and vengeance." The societies had scattered agents throughout Cuba, offering independence to the Creoles if they would join with free coloreds to abolish slavery. The abolitionists and their allies counted on naval and military support from Jamaica. They had two great warships at their disposal and were dealing with the exiled Venezuelan *caudillo,* then in Kingston, Santiago Mariño, to put him at the head of an invasion. An insurrection of slaves, free coloreds, and deluded Creoles would follow Mariño's invasion. If the abolitionists triumphed, Del Monte predicted, British influence would know no bounds in the Western Hemisphere. With the support of 600,000 blacks in Cuba and 800,000 more in the British West Indies, Great Britain could close the Caribbean to United States shipping and strike a death blow to slavery in the South. White Cubans preferred an alliance with the United States, so it must act now to protect itself and its "lesser sister of the great Western Confederation of the Caucasian Peoples of America" by girding Cuba with warships.

Everett hastened to promise Del Monte that he would do all he could to "turn the communication to the best account."[50] He held a generally dismal opinion of President Tyler and his ability to act in a crisis, but after consultation with friends, decided to send the contents of the communication, without identifying its source, to Secretary of State Daniel Webster. Everett related how Webster in a terse acknowledgment promised to tell the president but expressed doubt that " 'the British Government would countenance a project of the kind developed in your letter.' "[51] When weeks passed, and Everett had heard nothing further, he asked Caleb Cushing of the Committee of Foreign Affairs of the House of Representatives, who said little more than that Webster had other intelligence to the same effect. Because neither man seemed to attach sufficient weight to Del Monte's revelations, Everett turned to Senator John C. Calhoun of South Carolina, a man "better qualified by situation and character, than almost any person, to say and do whatever the occasion might appear to require." According to Everett, Calhoun promptly replied that he considered the informer's story to be "of the highest interest, and that he had written to the President upon the subject."[52] This and subsequent communications by Everett had the effect of making his connection with Del Monte a major bridge of Cuban influence on foreign policy decisions within the Tyler administration.[53]

Unknown to Everett, months before, another letter had already alerted Tyler to the danger of a British-backed slave revolution in Cuba, a letter that may well explain the heated temper of Southern congressmen face to face with Minister Argaiz. It was written by Waddy Thompson to William Butler, also a South Carolinian congressman, in November 1841. On his way to Alabama Thompson had crossed paths with an "accomplished spaniard" named Miguel de Sylve [Silva], who was heading for Cuba to carry out an important mission.

The spanish Government have received the most satisfactory evidence that there is a deeply laid scheme of insurrection in Cuba—stimulated and fomented by the Brittish Government through the agency of the Brittish Consul [David Turnbull] and emissaries from Jamaica. This gentleman is charged with the suppression of it. I saw his papers & authority. He informs me that the French Government which is in close alliance with one of the parties in spain is hostile to the movement and has ordered a portion of her navy to that region to watch these movements and give aid if need be. I have long been satisfied that Great Brittain is anxious to extirpate slavery in the West Indies and everywhere else—not from motives of philanthropy but from others purely commercial [.] She has lost her market for her manufactures on the continent of Europe & is losing it on this. Her last recourse for the maintenance of her purely artificial & factitious [indus]trial system is to build up in the West Indies both a market for her manufactures and supply of her raw materials. The first step towards this is to crush slave labor—The great rival in the production of the latter. I can think of no movement more vitally interesting to us of the south—Little less so indeed than to the people of Cuba—for if this movement succeeds with our immediate neighborhood of Cuba & immense commerce with that Island it would be in vain to attempt to keep out the contagion.[54]

Thompson urged Butler to forward his letter to either Tyler or Webster. Tyler received it on 15 December 1841. Three months before, he had been warned about British intrigue and "abolitionist fanaticism" by Nicholas Trist before his leaving the Havana consulate. On December 16 Tyler ordered intelligence on what was going on in Cuba.[55]

Also unknown to Everett, Webster had initiated diplomatic inquiries. He directed special agent Thomas Cookendorfer to Havana with a summation of the Del Monte letter and confidential instructions to General Robert Campbell, a former congressman from South Carolina, who in October 1842 had succeeded James Calhoun as the United States consul in Havana. Webster wanted Campbell to gain as much intelligence as possible as quickly as possible so that an "exceedingly anxious" Tyler could be well informed.[56] Another summation with instructions went to Washington Irving, the noted author and new minister to Spain:

In thus communicating to you the substance of the statements of this writer, you will distinctly understand that your Government neither adopts nor rejects his [Del Monte's] speculations. It is with his statement of supposed facts that it concerns itself; and it is expected that you will examine and report upon them with scrupulous care, and with as much promptness as strict secrecy and discretion will permit. . . . It is quite obvious, that any attempt, on the part of England, to employ force in Cuba, for any purpose, would bring on a war, involving, possibly, all Europe as well as the United States;

and as she can hardly fail to see this, and probably does not desire it, there may be reason to doubt the accuracy of the information we have received, to the extent to which it proceeds. But many causes of excitement and alarm exist; and the great magnitude of the subject makes it the duty of the Government of the United States to disregard no intimations of such intended proceedings which bear the least aspect of probability.[57]

In one of the periodic meetings on reclamations concerning the *Amistad* affair, Webster revealed details of the alleged plot to Minister Argaiz and proposed to send ships and men to intervene on Spain's behalf should the report of a conspiracy prove true. Argaiz received copies of the letter, which were speedily conveyed to authorities in Havana and Madrid.[58]

The relation of Argaiz to the United States injected one more variable into the equation. Argaiz rather loosely adhered to a political faction called the *Moderados* which opposed Espartero. Although descended from the same liberal parentage as Espartero's *Progresista* party, the *Moderados* looked to France rather than Great Britain for inspiration. On the whole, its members represented the propertied and educated elements of Spanish society and espoused a liberal conservatism. They resembled the Orleanists or, better, recalled the Girondists. Argaiz had retained his ministerial post after Espartero's ascendancy but as he became increasingly insulated from the mainstream of the regime, he had warmed up to the United States. In October 1841 in Spain, Espartero, amid some anxious moments, throttled a *Moderado* uprising. Argaiz learned through Webster that, during the crisis, Espartero considered transplanting his regime to Cuba and in the months that followed he heard that Espartero was contriving to barter Cuba for British protection. Such "perfidious plans" wounded his national pride and stimulated his factional loyalty. By working with the United States, Argaiz hoped to frustrate any plot to detach Cuba from Spain.[59]

In his tense correspondence with the metropolitan government on the putative conspiracy, Argaiz included a declaration to seek United States help if Captain-General Valdés proved unable to preserve Spanish rule in Cuba. The official response could only have left Argaiz more suspicious of Valdés and the Espartero regime. On the one hand, Valdés, suspicious that the slave-trading interest was undermining him, contradicted the Del Monte letter by claiming tranquility in Cuba and downplaying the possibility of a white conspiracy with colored support to foment revolution. On the other hand, the Spanish government rejected Webster's offer and prohibited Argaiz from reaching any agreement on Cuba with the United States. Should an emergency arise in Cuba, Spain authorized the Captain-General alone to seek outside assistance. Argaiz had failed to sense the extent to which the Espartero regime distrusted the United States. News of the projected invasion, emanating from Jamaica, came as no surprise, for Valdés and Spain's vice-consul in Kingston had been gathering intelligence all along. The questions were: Was Great Britain or the United States backing it, and of what elements was it composed? Spain's *Progresista* minister in London, General Sancho, had transmitted information, ultimately derived from the British consulate in Havana, that United States agents were engineering the conspiracy.[60] While Minister Argaiz was courting the United States to protect Cuba from Great Britain, Minister Sancho was courting Great Britain to protect Cuba from the United States.

By the spring of 1843 a period of watchful waiting had ensued. Campbell and Irving had fulfilled Webster's directives by then, and their reports indicated that the unnamed informer (Del Monte) had overstated his case. According to Irving, Spain seemed confident in its own ability to handle any crisis. And since it "did not at present entertain serious apprehensions in regard to the Island," it gratefully refused Webster's offer of military aid.[61] Campbell, although leery of the abolitionists, doubted British preparedness to take Cuba. Webster must have breathed easier and could devote more time to the pressing problems of Oregon and Texas. But Campbell would remain in full confidential communication with Valdés, for as Webster told Irving, "Enough . . . of danger and alarm still exists in that quarter to render caution and vigilance, on the part of this Government, indispensably necessary."[62]

From what Alexander Everett could determine, Del Monte's worst fears seemed unfounded. He had sent another copy of the Del Monte letter, this time to his younger brother Edward, President Tyler's minister to England. Edward Everett conferred with General Sancho and returned the following assessment:

He seems to be aware that Cuba is the object of the exertions of the Abolitionists, both of England and the United States, but he did not appear to think that this Government [i.e., Britain's] gave them any countenance. . . . As it must know that France and the United States would resist to the utter most any attempt to appropriate Cuba, I hardly think it would choose to disturb the peace of the world by any projects against that island.[63]

Alexander Everett shared this news with Del Monte, whose situation in Cuba had become precarious. Under pressure from the slave traders and the Spanish authorities because of his anti-slave trade activity, he had left Cuba with his family for a forced vacation in the United States. He stopped briefly at Charleston, where Daniel Whitaker dressed him properly with letters of introduction to Webster and Abel Upshur, Secretary of the Navy. From there, he set up a temporary residence in Philadelphia, a traditional refuge of Cuban dissidents as well as a stronghold of removed Southern planters and their Northern sympathizers.[64] He informed Everett of his whereabouts, then added that the apprehended peril had been postponed thanks to his own success in disrupting the machinations "of one of the most active agents from London" (probably Cocking) and forcing him to leave for England. In a subsequent letter to Everett, Del Monte would claim that he worked through Joseph Crawford to get "the agent" out of Cuba. Both statements recall the part of Cocking's confession in which his "noble friend" Del Monte was prominent in convincing him not to go to Mexico as certain unnamed Creoles had urged. "But this partial triumph," Del Monte added, "is of no value for the tranquility and security of the island, if, with the most inexcusable blindness, the traffic of African slaves—sinister source and exclusive and necessary element of the ultimate ruin of that beautiful island—continues."[65]

Edward Everett's optimistic assessment reached Del Monte in Philadelphia and prompted further correspondence. What General Sancho said had left Del Monte totally unsatisfied. Sancho was Britain's ally and Cuba's enemy, he told Everett. "Like all those members of the *exaltado* [radical liberal] party of Spain," Sancho understood almost nothing about Cuba except its functioning as a "mere sugar factory" to be exploited for the benefit of the metropolitan treasury. That Everett had apprised Senator Calhoun of the events in Cuba was more encouraging from Del Monte's point of view, for Calhoun, as a slaveholder, would likely see what Edward Everett had not, that Cuba by a revolution of the slaves could pass into British hands virtually, if not formally. With a few abolitionists, several small boats, clandestine shipments of arms and munitions from Jamaica or New Providence in the Bahamas, and supporters from Haiti, a rebellion might succeed, according to Del Monte. He predicted that Great Britain would then be on hand to hail the flag of the new black nation and, according to the law of nations, bind Cuba to it with treaties of alliance and commerce so strict that "not even Puffendorf himself could add to or detract from them."[66]

The reasoning made perfect sense to Alexander Everett, who had repeatedly indicted the Whigs for misplacing their trust in Great Britain. Had Van Buren or Calhoun been president, he confided to Del Monte, "the matter would be viewed in a rather different light at head quarters; but even then, in the present state of public opinion on the subject of slavery, it would be extremely difficult to adopt a decided course."[67] Everett rightly sensed that the national preoccupation with Oregon and Texas would defer Cuba's annexation for several decades. Until that time, the United States had to limit Britain's influence there. Everett chose as his best course to lay all of Del Monte's intelligence in front of Calhoun. "I cannot but lament," Everett wrote Del Monte, "that a territory, so highly favored by nature, and so admirably situated for a full and rapid development of its resources, should be involved in any way in the tempestuous politics of Europe. Although appearances in this country are not at present very favorable . . . I must still hope and believe that the time is not far distant, when . . . the Great Antilla will add another bright star to the flag of our Confederacy."[68]

Happily for Everett, domestic politics were acting in his favor by giving Calhoun greater influence over foreign policy. Tyler had broken with his fellow Whigs in 1841 by vetoing legislation sponsored by the party's de facto head, Henry Clay. With an eye to the 1844 election, Tyler then set about to build, through patronage, a Southern-based, states-rights party of his own. His movement needed national appeal, so he initiated plans in the spring of 1843 to annex Texas. In May, Secretary of State Webster, a longtime opponent of annexation, resigned and was replaced by Abel Upshur, a native Virginian, Calhoun's friend and ideological disciple, and a man who had already endorsed the notion of slavery as a positive good.[69] Since Upshur agreed with Calhoun that any slaveholding country lost to abolitionism would further isolate and weaken the South, he expended considerably more energy than Webster not only on Texas's annexation but on trying to ensure Cuba's autonomy from the British. "My only object," Upshur would instruct Minister to Spain Washington Irving, "is to obtain full and accurate information in regard to every movement which England may make, with reference to Cuba, whether designed to obtain a transfer of that Island to herself, or to obtain a control over the policy of Spain in regard to it—or to affect the institution of African slavery now existing there."[70]

In Spain, the struggle against Espartero was reaching a climax. Important *Progresistas* had defected to the *Moderado* opposition. Newspapers and private sources indicated that Espartero would soon abandon

Spain and, with the support of Great Britain and his clients in Cuba, set up a regime in exile. Minister Argaiz himself informed Upshur of the possibility. In July a coalition of *Moderados* and estranged *Progresistas* finally ousted Espartero, and he fled Spain in a British warship for an undisclosed location.[71]

From Consul Robert Monroe Harrison in Kingston, Jamaica, Upshur obtained news of the arrival of the "Notorious Turnbull" and his contact with ex-president Boyer of Haiti and various other potential subversives. Harrison felt sure that Turnbull would continue his plotting to raise Cuba's slaves. Harrison's initial fear, which drove him to recommend the revival of Southern militias and to write letters of warning to Southern governors, receded somewhat when intelligence indicated the adjournment, perhaps abandonment, of Turnbull's plan because of the want of money, the vigilance of Spanish authorities in Cuba, Boyer's downfall in Haiti, and internal dissension.[72] On the same subject, Consul Robert Campbell in Havana wrote:

The Consul at Jamaica seems quite alarmed at the machinations of the arch fiend Turnbull, he is not the first to whom he has appeared as a raw head and bloody bones. His true character is briefly this, a Glasgow bankrupt, with some talent, more pretension, a great fanatic, and regardless of truth. . . . I have seen a plan drawn by him in Jamaica for revolution in this Island, and the relative stations which the emancipated were to occupy, but knowing it to be futile and that this Government were apprised of it I did not deem it of sufficient consequence to mention.[73]

Having lived one country away from Nat Turner's rebellion, Upshur did deem the plan of sufficient consequence.

The reports of Harrison and Campbell came while Duff Green, an outspoken expansionist and proslavery advocate, was informing Upshur, the Tyler administration, and the expansionist public about the dangers of British policy. Green, on a business trip to Paris in 1842, and a diplomatic mission in Europe for Tyler in 1843, was sending back reports explaining how the British government was using its antislavery crusade to expand its world empire and encircle the United States in the process. His ideas repeatedly appeared in leading newspapers in the last months of 1843 where they stirred up, as he had calculated, further support for the annexation of Texas.[74]

Sectional interests would take precedence in Upshur's conduct of foreign policy, but the extent of his success would be determined by how well he could package the needs of the South as the needs of the nation.

Abolitionists in and near Cuba, political instability in Spain, the status of Texas, and British policy in general posed formidable threats to the Southern way of life. Upshur understood what the future would hold for the South with the emancipated slaves of two British client states on Southern doorsteps. The annexation of Texas presented itself as the number-one priority for Tyler's reshuffled, pro-Southern administration. Whether Britain admitted as much or not, abolitionism was a subtle instrument for neocolonialism. "It is worse than childish," Upshur declared in words that could just as easily have been Calhoun's, "to suppose that she [Great Britain] meditates the great movement, simply from an impulse of philanthropy."[75]

Yet if the South needed no more evidence of the darker side of British policy, the North seemed to, and the annexation of Texas could never result without bi-sectional support. Upshur had to secure it by getting Northern merchants and manufacturers to see their stake in annexation too. What was happening in Cuba did have the benefit of enhancing Upshur's capacity to convince them of the "practical operation" of abolitionism, of the economic calculation behind Britain's alleged philanthropy. Just as the destruction of slavery in Cuba could be readily linked to the declining fortune of Britain's West Indian plantations, so too could British influence in Texas be linked with commercial advantages, the capturing of markets, and the dumping of surplus manufactures.

Because of the gravity of the situation for the South, Upshur sought Calhoun's advice forthwith. "My own mind is very disturbed on the subject of Texas. . . . There can be no doubt, I think, that England is determined to abolish slavery throughout the American continent and islands if she can."[76] To Calhoun, Britain combined the "ambition of Rome and the avarice of Carthage." He applauded Upshur for his concern: "You do not in my opinion attach too much importance to the designs of Great Britain in Texas." Then, under the influence of Everett's communication, he added, "Connected with this subject, Cuba deserves attention. Great Britain is at work there, as well as in Texas, and both are very important to our safety." To preserve Southern safety, Calhoun outlined a policy for Upshur. With regard to Cuba Calhoun asked, "would it not be well for our govt. & that of France to enter into a guaranty of its possession to Spain, against the interference of any other power?"[77]

A felicitous embrace with the Spanish minister Argaiz prepared Upshur to proceeed with Calhoun's recommendation. Upshur wanted to preempt Britain and abolitionism in Cuba; Argaiz wished to guarantee the orderly transfer of power in Cuba to the pro-French *Moderados*. Thus, Argaiz consented to help Upshur form a tripartite alliance of Spain, France, and the United States to defend Cuba from Great Britain. With the support of Argaiz and, as Alexander Everett would eventually learn from President Tyler, "chiefly on the strength" of the Del Monte letter of 20 November 1842, Upshur ordered two sloops of war and a brig to Havana.[78] Had Argaiz not learned that General Leopoldo O'Donnell had successfully supplanted Valdés as Captain-General, he would have embarked with the squadron to oversee affairs in Cuba personally. As it was, he gave the commander a letter of introduction and official communications to take to O'Donnell. Upshur instructed commanding officer J. S. Chauncey to recognize only O'Donnell as Captain-General and, should violence break out, to place the warships at his disposal.[79] On 8 November 1843, only a few weeks after O'Donnell had taken command of Cuba, Chauncey's squadron plowed into Havana harbor.

Free *moreno* militiaman; fear about arming subordinate class led to decreased use of free colored militiamen in 1840s.

Plantation sites of conspiracy: (*Top*) In the background, beyond the city of Matanzas, plantations where rebellions occurred in 1843–44. (*Bottom*) Santísima Trinidad sugar plantation; in December 1843 Esteban Santa Cruz de Oviedo learned of a conspiracy there from his slave and concubine, Polonia. *Courtesy, Library of Congress.*

Map with triangles indicating *ingenios,* sugar plantations outside Matanzas, where slaves were involved in conspiracy.

(*Top*) Leopoldo O'Donnell, successor to Valdés as Captain-General, who empowered Military Commission to investigate and quell the Conspiracy. *Escoto Collection, by permission of the Houghton Library, Harvard University.* (*Bottom*) News story of first sentences of the Matanzas branch of the Military Commission, 5 July 1844.

Sentencia pronunciada por la Seccion de la Comision militar establecida en la ciudad de Matanzas para conocer de la causa de conspiracion de la gente de color.

PRIMER CUADERNO.

Don *Félix Maria Callejas, teniente del regimiento infanteria de Tarragona, 3.° ligero Peninsular, secretario de la Seccion de la Comision militar, y como tal actuando con el teniente coronel D. Felipe Arango.*

Certifico: Que en la causa seguida contra los autores y cómplices del incendio ocurrido en el ingenio titulado Encanto, de la propiedad de D. Baudilio Piqué, el dia primero de Marzo próximo pasado, y sublevacion intentada por parte de su dotacion y las de otras fincas colindantes, se encuentran á las fojas que al márgen se espresan la sentencia y demas actos siguientes:

Sentencia á foja 351.—Visto el decreto del Sr. Brigadier de infanteria D. José Falgueras, presidente de la Comision mili-

(*Top*) Santiago Mariño, soldier and adventurer exiled from Venezuela after leading a failed revolution there; he was suspected of inciting rebellion in Cuba in early 1840s. (*Bottom*) Francisco de Sentmanat, Cuban nationalist and adventurer suspected of involvement in the Conspiracy; he was captured in 1844 invasion of Tabasco, Mexico, "his Head cut off and fried in boiling oil."

La Escalera, or "the Ladder" to which slave suspects were bound before interrogation by the lash.

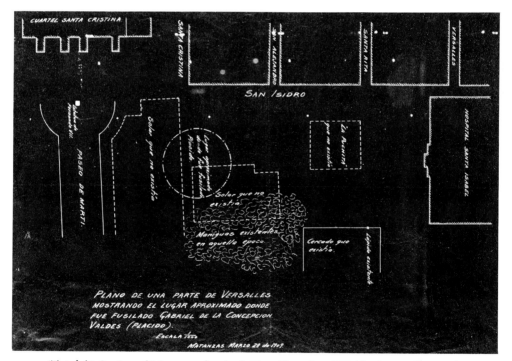

De la *Aurora de Matanzas* del 28 y 29
del corrriente copiamos lo que sigue.

Matanzas 28 de Junio.

En nuestra Adicion de ayer publica-
m.s lo siguiente:

AL PUBLICO.

Se han puesto hoy en capilla los reos
Gabriel de la Concepcion Valdes, alias Placido, Jorje Lopez, Santiago Pimienta, José
Miguel Roman, Andres Jose Pimienta, José
Torres, Manuel Quiñones, Antonio Abad,
esclavo del comerciante Sr. D. José Baro,
Jose de la O, alias Chiquito, del hacendado
Sr. D. Francisco de la O. García, Bruno
del Sr. Dr. D. Santiago de la Huerta, y
Miguel, del Sr. D. Juan José Naranjo;
no habiéndose verificado lo mismo en los
reos Luis Guigot y Antonio Bernoqui, por
hallarse el primero prófugo, y haberse sus-
pendido la sentencia del segundo hasta la
resolucion de S. M.

Acusados y convencidos estos desgra-
ciados del delito de instigadores en la causa
que se sigue contra ellos sobre levantamien-
to de la gente de color, se les ha condenado
á que mañana sufran la pena de ser pasados
por las armas.

Hé aquí el fin que espera á todos aquellos, que en su obcecacion, no temen atraer
sobre sus cabezas la inexorable espada de
la ley. No era posible que sucediese de o'ra
manera: la temeridad y loca intentona á que
iban á lanzarse estos infelices, no era mas
que el preludio de su infausta suerte, la pro-
funda cima que iba á tragar para siempre........

Son tales los elementos de seguridad
con que cuenta la Isla de Cuba, que solo vi-
sionarios sin educacion, en el estado mas
abyecto de barbarie é inmoralidad, seduci-
dos por almas viles, pueden desear promo-
ver conmociones, tan pronto ideadas como
estinguidas.

(*Top left*) Section of Matanzas, *barrio de Versalles,* where Plácido, free mulatto and popular Cuban poet, was executed in 1844. (*Top right*) Beginning of story informing public of impending execution of Plácido and referring to suspension of Antonio Bernoqui's death sentence, *Diario de la Habana,* 30 June 1844. (*Bottom*) Plan showing exact location in *barrio de Versalles* where Plácido was shot on 28 June 1844.
Escoto Collection, by permission of the Houghton Library, Harvard University.

Plácido

(*Top*) Gabriel de la Concepción
Valdés, alias Plácido, the Cuban poet
who was executed as ringleader of the
Conspiracy. (*Right*) Modern sculpture
of Plácido in the city of Matanzas.

III

Conjuncture

8

The Year of the Lash

Upon this a question arises; whether it be better to be loved than feared or feared than loved? It may be answered that one should wish to be both, but, because it is difficult to unite them in one person, it is much safer to be feared than loved, when, of the two, either must be dispensed with.

MACHIAVELLI, The Prince

At thirty-four the youngest of the eleven Captains-General who had come through Havana since 1800, General Leopoldo O'Donnell looked less the laureled warrior than a bureaucratic factotum. He was stiff and balding, sleepy-eyed and callow-faced. Yet he had survived the high-stakes game of peninsular war and politics, a worthy descendant of Donegal, whose forefathers had tendered their swords to the Spanish Crown.

His rise in the military had been swift. From a ten-year-old sublieutenant he had progressed to captain at nineteen and to colonel at twenty-four. During the first Carlist War, he led liberal troops to a string of victories, the greatest of which, at Lucena, earned him a promotion to general and the nickname "The Leopard." The war's end brought General Espartero to the regency and factionalization to the liberals. O'Donnell sided with the *Moderados,* Espartero's conservative opposition, and in 1841 led an ill-fated coup from the Basque country. The dissolution of Espartero's regime two years later allowed O'Donnell to emerge from asylum in France. *Moderado* leaders gave him the Captain-Generalcy of Cuba largely to rid themselves of a potential rival for power.[1]

He had scarcely settled in his Havana palace before there was a rebellion of slaves on a plantation in the sugar district of Sabanilla in Matanzas province. On 5 November 1843, slaves on the Triunvirato sugar plantation ravaged it, then crossed to the neighboring Ácana plantation, which still had slaves in shackles for rebelling a few months earlier. There they burned property, killed six whites—three women, two men, and a child—and wounded others. Some of the slaves of Ácana hesitated to join in. The Triunvirato slaves responded by dragging them along after burning their possessions, including huts and animals, as well as the estate buildings.

As news of the uprising spread, a band of *monteros* under the command of the district magistrate rode to the nearby Concepción sugar plantation, whose administrator had prepared for an attack by shutting all his slaves except thirty he trusted in the plantation purging house. At three o'clock in the morning the Triunvirato rebels arrived; the *monteros* were driven off; the rebels set fire to the plantation and were joined by the thirty trust-worthy slaves. On another, the San Miguel sugar plantation, whites were supported by "faithful and loyal blacks," and the rebels retreated after tak-ing "whatever could be carried and was of use to the estate."[2] *Ingenio* San Lorenzo was burned on their next stop; some of its slaves joined the rebels, and a force, now numbering three hundred men, women, and children, proceeded on to *ingenio* San Rafael, where an ambush by *monteros* and a detachment of lancers sent from Matanzas by Governor García Oña was waiting. After a battle of several hours the rebels broke rank and fled, leaving fifty-four dead and sixty-seven captured; almost half their total number. The whites had few casualties.

The slaves, in their several forays against the sugar plantations, inflicted far more damage to property than to people. Canefields and mill houses where slaves had worked, smoldered in ruin. Losses on *ingenio* Triunvirato were estimated at $80,000. Slave revolts had happened before, but not with the size and frequency of those in 1843. In between the major revolts of March in Cárdenas and November in Matanzas fires and slave unrest had occurred on the *ingenios* Santa Rosa and Majagua in May, distur-bances on *ingenios* Ácana, Concepción, and Flor de Cuba in June; and re-volt and fire on *ingenio* Arratía in July. Greater "insolence," "insubordina-tion," and "indifference" to white slave owners and overseers showed even among their most trusted house slaves, and greater "arrogance" and "dis-respect" also from free people of color.[3]

Because the March revolt in Cárdenas had implicated slave railroad workers, some planters believed that white carters and muleteers, threat-ened with the loss of their jobs by modernization, had instigated the vio-lence. According to Domingo Del Monte, "This opinion was strengthened by the subsequent conflagration of the plantation Santa Rosa, belonging to Don Domingo de Aldama, he and his brothers-in-law, the Alfonsos, being the largest stockholders in the rail-road from Havana to Matanzas."[4]

By the time of the violence in Matanzas, planters concluded that the Cárdenas and Matanzas uprisings had been connected and were not mere isolated instances. From what Del Monte could learn from sources in Cuba,
"Instead of being prompted, as they formerly were, by the accidental severity of some overseer of whom the blacks wished to rid themselves, they
are now the result of a settled conviction by the slaves of their own rights
and those of their race."[5] The slaughter of the Triunvirato rebels had not silenced the slaves in Sabanilla. José Luis Alfonso, the nephew of the owner
of Triunvirato and himself a prominent planter, disclosed to Domingo
Del Monte in early December two more slave disturbances that were
put down "without effusion of blood." More and more the slaves exhibited
"greater firmness . . . a greater tendency to rebel and to contend forcibly
for their rights."[6]

The planters demanded protection; bands of *monteros* would not do.
They believed that the government should either establish a permanent
rural militia or else billet regular troops in the countryside. Harvest time
was approaching, and continued slave violence would be costly.

Near the end of November, ninety-three well-to-do but untitled Matanzas planters signed a memorial to acquaint the new Captain-General
with the specifics of their emergency. They pleaded for a "measure of protection and security" and for the eradication of the African slave trade, the
perceived root of all their present danger.

The memorial presented fresh population estimates, no doubt projected
from the manipulated census of 1841, that placed the number of people
of color at 660,000, almost 500,000 of whom were slaves. Any sensible
man, it warned, would "know where the consequences of the preponder-
ance of that colored population, slave and free, may reach. If only nearby
Haiti did not present so horrifying an example, but one that should never
be disregarded so that the second edition of the same book does not come
to be." The memorial blamed the uprisings in Cárdenas and Matanzas on
the inspiration of the Saint Domingue revolution, the abolition of slavery
in Jamaica, and "the emissaries sent not only from those islands but also
by persons and societies, multiplying in the soil of Cuba, whose existence
our wise government is not unaware." It entreated Captain-General O'Donnell to rid Cuba of the contraband slave trade, "that affront to our civilization, that horrible cavern where our hopes of security and future well-
being are buried, that hydra that frightens the capitalists who come to
establish themselves in our soil."[7]

The petitioners commissioned a delegation to present the memorial to

Governor García Oña. They expected him to transmit it to O'Donnell, but García Oña read it, then shredded it before their eyes. "It was the most friendly act he could do for them," he was reported to have said, "as such a petition was an insult to the Government, and they would be looked upon as conspirators."[8]

Centralization of political power within an aged, authoritarian, imperial edifice, not without flexibility but lacking in democratic forms and substance, meant that, to a great extent, Cuba's internal governance would reflect the personality of its Captain-General. O'Donnell, according to the anecdotes told after his rule in Cuba, was another Tacón, a man quick to rage if, for example, Havana's citizens failed to doff their hats when he passed.[9] He treated dissent as insubordination. The memorialists professed loyalty to Spain; O'Donnell questioned how loyal the Creoles truly were. Spain's painful lesson with revolution in its former colonies in South America had taught government officials not to trust such protestations.

Benigno Gener, one of the memorialists, chose to bypass García Oña. He sent O'Donnell a copy of the memorial with a personal plea. In consideration of what O'Donnell called "the lightness of Gener's letter, he restrained himself in response. His correspondence makes abundantly clear that he would be unwilling to tolerate any repetition of a petition like Gener's. The law prohibited such petitions, in any case, lest they promote conspiratorial associations. Even though O'Donnell conceded the thinking behind them might be reasonable, they could tend "to alter the tranquility of the country and the territorial integrity of the Spanish monarchy." O'Donnell gave his permission to Governor García Oña to adopt "the measures that you deem convenient against the promoters of this class of expositions."[10]

O'Donnell strongly suspected that the anti-slave-trade Creoles really yearned for independence. The majority, on the contrary, wanted neither abolitionism, nor annexationism by the United States, nor even separatism. They preferred reform within the Spanish empire. But with Spain tenuously holding on to Cuba and the *Moderados* tenuously holding on to Spain, an ambitious young martinet could not endure any internal criticism of whatever motivation.

The dramatic appearance by the squadron dispatched from the United States by Secretary of State Upshur in Havana harbor on November 8, only a few days after the Sabanilla slave revolt, added to the tension and uncertainty. True, Captain Chauncey, the squadron's commander, brought the results of Spanish minister Argaiz's unauthorized negotiations with the United States to defend Cuba from British machinations. The presence of United States warships might deter the British or a British-backed Espartero from designs on Cuba. But, in diplomacy, as in life generally, generosity happens too rarely to be presumed upon. O'Donnell seems to have understood the risks of a lingering United States presence; it could provoke British intervention; it could exploit slave rebellion as a pretext for permanent intervention in Cuba. O'Donnell thanked Captain Chauncey and Havana consul Robert Campbell for their country's consideration, but insisted that Cuba was under control.[11]

Weeks later, Argaiz was abruptly removed from his post. Secretary of State Upshur wanted to know why. Minister to Spain Washington Irving found Madrid curiously quiet on the subject, but an undisclosed source told him only:

The [Spanish] government had considered his [Argaiz's] application to the United States precipitate and uncalled for, and made with a view to atone for past devotion to Espartero by a striking exhibition of zeal in the cause of his successors. It had also been displeased with his irregular proceeding in communicating the fact [before O'Donnell's arrival] by letter to the second person in command in the island of Cuba, instead of the first (Genl Valdez) as though he thought the latter in league with the enemy. The consequence had been contradictory rumours and suspicions in the island, one party asserting the grasping intentions of the English upon Cuba, and another, in which was the British Consul [Joseph Crawford], asserting the design of the United States to send vessels of war to take possession of the island.[12]

O'Donnell rejected the Creoles' notion of a permanent rural militia, for it posed unacceptable political risks. He did, however, pledge to send regular troops to the countryside with the proviso that the planters would share the expense.[13] The planters bitterly complained, in private, at this condition. José Luis Alfonso spoke for many when he called it "unjust and outrageous." They were already shouldering oppressive economic burdens. Sugar prices had dropped "so low that they did not leave the landholder a profit . . . and what is more, even when we [the Creoles] pay more than two-and-a-half million pesos annually for the maintenance of troops, it is still demanded that we sweat blood for public employees and bayonets that are even more disposed to assassinate us than to assassinate the slaves themselves."[14]

At the dedication of a branch of the Havana railroad, Alfonso complained to two of Cuba's more powerful officials: the Conde de Villaneuva, the recently reappointed, proslavery, Cuban-born intendant, and Antonio Javier de Ulloa, Cuba's chief naval officer. Alfonso appealed for government troops in the countryside and an end to the slave trade. The count and Ulloa assured him that they would relay his message to O'Donnell.[15] Alfonso then gathered with other substantial Matanzas planters to formulate a political strategy. Juan Poey, Cuba's noted sugar agronomist and owner of the Las Canas sugar plantation proposed the organization of a secret network of Creoles throughout Cuba in the misplaced hope that sustained, systematic, and anonymous exposure of illicit imports of slaves would scare off prospective buyers and lead to effective government enforcement of its anti-slave-trade treaties. Poey's proposal was shelved in favor of another memorial to be drawn up by Alfonso and José Ricardo O'Farrill and signed not only by the Matanzas planters, but by three members of Cuba's high nobility: José María Herrera, Conde de Fernandina; O'Farrill's father, Rafael, a colonel in the royal Army and patriarch of the family greatly responsible for the eighteenth-century liberalization of the slave trade; and Juan Montalvo, decorated colonel of the Matanzas cavalry and brother of the Conde de Casa-Montalvo.[16]

But before Alfonso could finish his work, a sugar planter, Esteban Santa Cruz de Oviedo, uncovered a "conspiracy" that implicated slaves from his Santísima Trinidad plantation and the surrounding region. A slave woman named Polonia, one of Santa Cruz de Oviedo's concubines, had betrayed the conspiracy. Santa Cruz de Oviedo said he had confirmed her testimony by hiding in the slave quarters and overhearing slave discussion of plans for an uprising.[17]

Santa Cruz de Oviedo had not signed the Matanzas memorial; he was involved in the contraband slave trade himself and had no interest in abolition. A genuine slave revolt would be immensely costly for him. Slave executions inevitably followed slave conspiracies; in sheer pesos and centavos a conspiracy on his plantation would be punishing.

Santa Cruz de Oviedo had, nevertheless, given his slaves ample reason to plot and rebel. He appears to have run his three plantations like a Simon Legree. Of the three plantations, two he had inherited from a slave-trading father; the third, Santísima Trinidad, he had developed into one of the largest and most technologically advanced in Cuba. By the 1850s Santísima Trinidad was notorious for breeding slaves, as Oviedo himself had done by siring at least twenty-six mulatto children.[18] Many planters charged him with sexual abuse of his female slaves. Creole Francisco Jimeno remembered him as "an ignorant man, of limited intellectual powers, a refugee from the company of rational people, living on his estate in complete isolation, delivered over to the false enjoyment of his harem of slaves, and reputedly cruel in the treatment of his slaves."[19] In the aftermath of the November uprising on *ingenio* Triunvirato, rumors circulated about unrest on Santa Cruz de Oviedo's Jesús María plantation. They deeply concerned Miguel Aldama, Domingo Del Monte's brother-in-law, whose family had extensive contiguous holdings. A letter from Aldama to Del Monte told how he had weighed whether or not to respond to these rumors by leaving Havana to join his father and brother on the family plantations. He decided to go, for "it would be by no means strange that Oviedo's slaves would rise in rebellion because of the cruelties and horrible tyranny of their owner."[20]

In response to Santa Cruz de Oviedo's revelation of a conspiracy, Governor García Oña, with O'Donnell's approval, ordered troops into Sabanilla and instructed government agents to extract the truth. Slaves from Santísima Trinidad and neighboring plantations confessed under torture to timing a rebellion for Christmas Eve. Whereupon the authorities sentenced more than a hundred slaves to prison and rounded up more than a thousand to watch the execution of sixteen who were identified as ringleaders. The executed included two privileged *criollo* slaves from the Aldama plantation Santa Rosa, the same Santa Rosa that had caught fire in May after the uprising in Cárdenas. Miguel Aldama, who witnessed the investigations, in a tone of disbelief informed Del Monte that one of the "principal chiefs" was Florencio, " 'The most trusted black' " on Santa Rosa, and another was Ciprián, a venerable slave driver.[21] What Aldama saw in Sabanilla also evoked this extraordinary confession.

If the plans of the slaves were horrible, even more horrible have been the punishments handed out to these unfortunate beings, true martyrs of liberty. My misfortune was that I had to watch them while my very nature recoiled without being able to help them in any way, to see them suffer under the torment of the lash, inflicted by men who are called civilized. It is true that now the question is life or death that our slaves, roused by the new system established on the estates and animated by ideas that the English agents have infused in them, are subjected only with difficulty to the conditions in which our barbarity has cast them. Now we see them crude and haughty, defying armed force, (since we have lost the moral force entirely); Now we see them all united that want to champion the sacred cause of liberty, and among them there no longer exists either [negros de] naciones or [ethnic] rivalries. Everyone has sworn an oath to triumph or die—an oath that not even the cruel lash can break.[22]

To planters of the Matanzas black belt, survival had eclipsed economic expediency. "It is remarkable," reported Joseph Crawford in December, expressing the fear of the slaveholders, "that those who have been executed acknowledge that they were well treated, well clothed and well fed; but said confessing their intentions, as they did, that they would be slaves no longer!"[23] White vigilantes began to patrol the countryside. Many planters confined their families to their townhouses rather than risk the annual Christmas pilgrimage to the plantation for the holiday celebrations. "The better you treat Negroes," José del Castillo kept hearing, "the worse for you."[24]

The behavior of the slaves on Santísima Trinidad and other Sabanilla sugar plantations also sharpened the prose of Alfonso's memorial of December, 1843. In response to the vital labor question: Did Cuba's plantation system require constant imports of African slaves? it shouted no. The plantations of the southern United States had survived without an external slave trade by stimulating natural reproduction. And technological innovation in the sugar industry, it argued implausibly, might lessen planter dependence on slaves by making whites more employable. But "if such measures might not be enough to augment or sustain the production of the island in its present state, of what importance is that in comparison to the ruin and general desolation that is awaiting us under the present system?"[25] What the earlier Matanzas memorial had stated, Alfonso's reiterated. The disproportion between white and colored was growing in Cuba and particularly in the black-belt districts of the west. "Uprisings that were previously isolated and only produced desolation and death within the narrow circle in which they were born," Alfonso wrote, "present today a character of gravity" by their "great frequency," "premeditation," and "organization." Years of importing thousands of unacculturated Africans were undoing the social fabric. Planters had lost the "moral force" over their slaves; "physical force" alone restrained the slave's "bellicose spirit." The memorial closed with an appeal *"to destroy effectively, once and for all, the contraband trade in African slaves* and to secure the tranquility of our country along with the lives and haciendas of these loyal inhabitants."[26]

O'Donnell moved to secure Cuba but in a style not wholly gratifying to those loyal inhabitants. The conspiracy in Sabanilla and the general international uncertainty had stiffened his resolve to crack down on all of Cuba's dissidents. He toured Matanzas and stationed troops in rural localities. Not satisfied that the lashings in Sabanilla had uncovered the "true origin of so many disturbances in the countryside," he ordered his legal representatives (*fiscales*) in Matanzas to expand the circle of their

investigation. With O'Donnell's permission, Governor García Oña commissioned Santa Cruz de Oviedo and his cousin, Francisco Hernández
Morejón, also a planter and a tough, veteran rural policeman nicknamed
"Pancho Machete" by his detractors, to conduct "extra-judicial procedures"—a wonderful euphemism for state-sanctioned torture. Santa Cruz
de Oviedo initially declined to go on the hunt because of illness and
concern for his own estates, although many months later he would conduct some investigations.[27]

The extrajudicial procedures were effective. In early January 1844
Hernández Morejón offered new testimony from a slave of "ten or twelve
years" with purported corroboration from four other slaves that convinced
Governor García Oña—who in turn convinced Captain-General O'Donnell—of the existence of a "vast plan . . . directed by agents who had
used the slaves as tools to extend it and execute it to the ruin and desolation of the country."[28] Anastasio Carrillo y Arango, a prominent lawyer
and sugar planter from the district of Cimarrones, an area still unsettled
by the March uprising of 1843, gained Hernández Morejón's signature to
a request for permission to conduct extrajudicial procedures on his own
estate. O'Donnell approved and went further by bestowing the privilege
on other Matanzas landholders. In January of 1844, José Jáuregui,
owner of *ingenio* La Andrea in the district of Macurijes, near the origin
of the March 1843 uprising, wrote Hernández Morejón of the discovery
of a conspiracy on his plantation and that his slaves had been in communication with the slaves who had conspired in Sabanilla. He requested
an armed force to assist in further interrogation. The testimony extracted
from the slaves of La Andrea provided what the government perceived
to be clear indications of the complicity of the free people of color.[29]

The new year would be ominous not only for people of color but also
for the Creoles. With the slave-trading lobby offering money to O'Donnell, and with his own racial prejudice stimulating his doubts that people
of color could hatch a sophisticated plot unaided, O'Donnell began to
scent the "true origin" of internal disorder among the Creoles and particularly among anti–slave trade advocates. José Luis Alfonso observed
his suspicions and backed away from the plan to present the memorial.
"The business of the memorial," he wrote, "has taken a bad turn. The
slave traders have the ear of the new Captain-General to whom their
special interest has opened his ears and closed his eyes. The representation
will not be presented now, because it will displease him, and he has tried
to intimidate those that oppose his intentions; our magnates have been

cowed, and meanwhile blacks enter and will continue to enter until God's will be done."[30]

O'Donnell had not climbed to where he was by blissfully accepting coincidences. Nor could any tough, politically ambitious, young officer basically ignorant of Cuba yet newly arrived to guard it as Spain's remaining Crown jewel, leave unanswered simple, seemingly unrelated, challenges to his authority. In the first months of 1844 he had no clear idea about the origins of the unrest or its ramifications. He saw dangers all around. His suspicion naturally fell on public acts of disobedience. Too many events remained unexplained.

During the traditional pre-Lenten celebrations, O'Donnell had imposed an eleven-o'clock curfew on all places of public entertainment near the Tacón Theater in response to the solicitations of Francisco "Pancho" Martí y Torrens, the theater's director and manager. He exempted cafés associated with the theater and owned by Martí that served "amusement within and ices without, both of the worst quality and at the highest price," according to the Cuban correspondent of *The Republic,* a short-lived New York daily.[31] Martí was a master huckster, one Catalan for whom the Cuban stereotype fitted like skin. He dealt in slaves but had started out selling fish. By contributions to the right people he came to exercise a monopoly over the entire Havana fish market. He had won the post of managing the Tacón Theater by making large contributions for its construction to its namesake. In the early 1840s rumors spread that the theater was losing money. Habaneros did not worry, for Martí the fishmonger seemed to have an inexhaustible supply of floating capital.[32] When the Havana town council was hard-pressed to pay certain debts, Martí offered to do so from money he expected to make from a dance during *carnaval,* using an exclusive privilege conceded to him in 1840 that for twenty-five years he could present six masquerades per year. To secure his personal profit, Martí apparently sought to influence O'Donnell's wife, also a Catalan. He persuaded O'Donnell to impose the curfew. Several young patrons of a café near the theater repeatedly refused to obey. When they answered the demands to leave put by Fernando O'Reilly, a deputy alcalde and patrician planter, by hurling a bowl of *ponche de leche* (a kind of Cuban eggnog) over his head, much to the amusement of a gathering crowd, O'Donnell had had enough. He rode to the scene with an escort and, with fixed bayonets, arrested the troublemakers. Some of those arrested had a history of outspoken anti-

Spanish opinions; they appear to have, on occasion, spoken out against slavery. One had openly denounced the sentencing of José Mitchell, Turnbull's alleged free colored agent, for which the authorities had earlier reprimanded him.[33] But the Havana correspondent for *The Daily Picayune* of New Orleans thought the onslaught was overreaction.

A great state of excitement here. . . . Last night [February 20] the troops, headed by the Captain General, under pretence of dispersing a mob, made a furious assault, with fixed bayonets on all the orange and candy stands, and old women with their "milk punch" for the refreshment of the masqueraders, and it is said that a large number of gallons of this latter, and we know not how many oranges, have been destroyed. . . . We heard of no incident, except that one fat gentleman in his eager haste jumped into the fosse of the city walls and made a tremendous rent in his pants. Several ragged boys were arrested for making "sight" at the soldiers—that is, applying the thumb to the olfactory proboscis and gyrating the digits. The people are highly indignant and your spirit knows not what will be the result.[34]

According to another account of the incident, which has gone down in Cuban lore as the Battle of Ponche de Leche, O'Donnell in riding to the scene encountered the celebrated Francisco de Sentmanat, who had turned and declared against the Mexican president Santa Anna with the purpose of making Tabasco a separate state; Sentmanat had been overpowered and ousted by a General Ampudia, another of Santa Anna's Cuban-born warlords. Sentmanat, the story says, challenged O'Donnell to a duel. O'Donnell prudently declined but ordered Sentmanat to prison, then expelled him from the country.[35] Sentmanat went to New Orleans, not-so-quietly rounded up a band of adventurers, and in June, from a ship called the *William A. Turner*, descended on Tabasco, where they were expected. Surrounded by troops, all except Sentmanat surrendered without a shot. He was captured and later executed, "his Head cut off & Fried in boiling oil put on a Spike hung up in an Iron Cage & exhibited in the public square for days." Ampudia explained that he wanted to rest assured of Sentmanat's death.[36] Sentmanat's exact purpose in Havana is a mystery. But he had appeared there when a dissident leader was expected, and as a leader with a history of separatist activity, he made O'Donnell and other Cuban authorities quite nervous. How nervous would come out in the questions asked of suspected conspirators in the interrogations to come.

From early January to the end of March throughout Cuba's sugar heartland, the most intense period of search, seizure, torture, confession, trial, and punishment ensued. O'Donnell freed the Military Commission from constraints, and its agents, joined by frightened planters, inflicted a bloodbath on the colored population. O'Donnell empowered Fulgencio Salas, the president of the Commission and from early February to mid-March the interim governor of Matanzas while García Oña was recuperating from an illness, to extend the use of violent means to the interrogation of the free people of color, for, as he would tell Salas in February and as Salas would relay verbatim to agents in the field, "when one deals with the security of the country and of crimes against the State, any means is legal and permitted, if beforehand the moral conviction exists that the desired result will be produced and that the public welfare demands it."[37]

Testimony extorted by threats and torture in various districts implicated others until cells in the city of Matanzas overflowed with prisoners, most of them brown or black. With concern for the planters' economic interests, O'Donnell had ordered only leaders of the plot to face the Military Commission.[38] Unknown numbers died while being transported to Matanzas jails. Hundreds, at least, of accused people of color, as the judgments of the Matanzas branch of the Military Commission themselves make clear, died in prison during the proceedings or were too sick to attend court in their own defense. Lengthy imprisonment was virtually inevitable under the Spanish legal system, because prisoners could not be bailed for serious crimes, nor would they learn the charge until their initial court appearance.[39]

Richard Burleigh Kimball, a New York lawyer visiting Cuba in 1844, sent back a grisly account of the affair to *Knickerbocker* magazine. He described the agents of the Military Commission as "most sordid, brutal and sanguinary." Their method of interrogation presupposed the answers to be given and was "accompanied by the most violent chastisement, often inflicted in such a manner as sooner or later to produce death."[40] If free people of color wanted mercy, they usually had to buy it. One accomplished sadist named Ramón González

ordered his victims to be taken to a room which had been white-washed, and whose sides were besmeared with blood and small pieces of flesh, from the wretches who had preceded them. . . . There stood a bloody ladder, where the accused were tied, with their heads downward, and whether free or slave, if they would not avow what the fiscal officer insinuated, were whipped to death. . . . They were scourged with leather straps, having at the end a small destructive button, made of fine wire. . . . Their deaths were made to appear, by certificates from physicians, as having been caused by diarrhoea.[41]

Another *fiscal* flogged a free person of color, then bound him hands-to-feet; he was hung bleeding overnight from the ceiling of a house. Juan Costa, an officer, whipped to death forty-two free people of color and fifty-four slaves during his investigations. *Fiscal* José del Peso "found sport in hanging the accused victims on a tree, and then cutting the ropes to see them fall to the ground in bunches." So scandalous did the "numberless robberies, extortions of money, and all kinds of wickedness" of the *fiscales* become that a few were eventually jailed.[42]

Lest Kimball's avowed liberal sensibilities accuse him of untruth, Francisco Jimeno, a Matanzas Creole fresh from college in 1844, remembered a farm near the south side of his city in which people of color were incarcerated and tortured. "There the fiscals used pain to exact confessions; there scenes were enacted comparable only to those set down in the annals of the Inquisition and those hair-raising scenes from Dante's Inferno." Carts transported survivors of the torture to a makeshift hospital in Matanzas and "daily two or three bodies exited for the cemetery."[43] Registers recorded the cause of death as diarrhea.

A frenzy had gripped Cuba, British Commissioner James Kennedy reported. Fires had broken out in the countryside, and government spies had flooded Havana. He heard that "A French merchant at Matanzas has come to this place, giving as a reason to his friends, that he could not endure the sights he had to witness there, and specifying the cartloads of bodies he saw carried to the burying place torn by the lash."[44] In the town of Güines he heard about mass floggings of people of color before large crowds.[45] Some government agents reported an increase in slave runaways and in "the spirit of insubordination" of those who remained. Suicides of slaves and free coloreds appeared to increase as well. The authorities launched offensives against maroons, including those of El Espinal in Matanzas province, suspecting they were involved in the conspiracy. By the end of February, the celebrated maroon guerrilla José Dolores had been reported captured and executed.[46]

To compound problems, there was a terrible drought in the countryside. Grassland dried up, and as it did some planters had to resort to molasses and corn husks to feed their cattle. Even so, thousands died along with poultry. Vegetables withered on the vine. Next year's sugar crop seemed in danger.[47] Cubans must have thought the curse of heaven was on the land.

Government agents moved into *ingenio* Arroyo, between Matanzas and Cárdenas, to conduct investigations and lashed slaves indiscrimi-

nately. When, a few days later 350 acres went up in flames, the plantation managers reported the cause as an accident no doubt to prevent a
new double loss of property, slaves as well as cane.[48] In the town of
Cárdenas the nightly whippings of colored prisoners kept others from
sleeping. "Prisons were full, & the depot of the Railroad was taken to be
used as a place of Confinement. . . . Patrols paraded the Streets by
Night, all communication with the country was stopped, & business entirely stagnated."[49] One resident of Matanzas watched through a window
as slave prisoners were driven through the streets with "welted flesh . . .
and leaving lines of blood in their tracks."[50] Thomas M. Rodney, the
United States consul in Matanzas, informed Secretary of State John Calhoun in April that he stood on the best of terms with the Spanish government and that what he was about to say caused him pain, but that a
terror was overspreading Cuba. Like Jimeno, Rodney likened the Military
Commission to the Inquisition. Free people of color had died under the
lash, and given the "exquisite torture," he understood why they might
say anything to free themselves from suffering.[51]

William Norwood, an Episcopalian clergyman from Virginia, sojourn-
ing on the Mt. Vernon estate in Matanzas in 1844, kept a diary from
January to April. On February 15, he noted that the Negroes were restive
and that conditions in general were "not very pleasant." A few days later
he heard the bell clanging on a neighboring estate. The slaves of Mt.
Vernon grew excited. Norwood and some others armed themselves, rode
over, and found a fire. On February 26, he recorded the "Military Commission at work all around us making investigations & ordering arrests.
The prisons at Matanzas full & a large house hired for a prison." What
he saw himself and heard from eyewitnesses underscores the severity of
the investigations. His entry for March 8–10 speaks of trouble on the
estate of Sebastian Hernández. "He has 700 negroes—100 in irons. Several have died under the lash. 10 who were engaged in a former conspiracy to be executed. The mulatto sons of Padre Chavis [Nicolás González de Chávez] implicated in the conspiracy. Rome when will thy
abominations cease!!"[52]

In April Norwood heard more terrifying news.

Several weeks ago 25 arobas [sic] of arsenic [more than 600 pounds!] were
found in the houses of some free negroes. Enough to poison the whole white
population & no doubt intended for that purpose. An attempt was also made
to poison the whole garrison of 8000. The bread is all furnished them by one
bakery & the negroes who work in the establishment had poisoned it all. The
fact was discovered just before the bread was to have been sent to the barracks.

A new African slave not let into the secret asked the proprietor if he was looking for that which they put into the bread. He answered yes & was shown a quantity of arsenic which had been left & hid. Another attempt was made yesterday to poison one of the first families of the city by putting arsenic in their soup. The dose was so strong that it was tasted by the first of the family who tasted the soup & one mouthful made her sick.[53]

Whether what Norwood heard was true or exaggerated cannot be definitively established. At least one arrested slave testified to the authorities that whites were going to be poisoned since poison was "better than war."[54] A few poisonings did occur, and they set off a scare among the white population. As late as June of 1844, the Havana correspondent of *The Republic,* a New York newspaper, reported that the fear of being poisoned had reached the point where "in many good houses in this country, people live solely on eggs, which they eat from the shell" rather than eat what their colored cooks had prepared.[55]

The courage shown under interrogation by some people of color made a deep impression on Norwood. In March he wrote that "During a late examination by a military commis[sioner] a negro was asked how he could expect his freedom as his master had purchased him with his money. He replied that the money was obtained by the labor of Negroes. Another who possessed $1,200 was asked why if he wished for freedom he did not purchase it. He answered I will keep my money & owe my freedom to this arm, extending his right arm."[56] His observation of the continued militancy of the slaves even while undergoing torture accords with other witnesses. Ramón Flores de Apodaca, who was ordered to bring order to the plantations of the district of Alacranes, reported that slaves had died under the lash and died "rabid" on seeing their plans foiled.[57]

Some of the confessions implicated whites, including foreign technicians and liberal Creoles. A manager for a branch of the Drake Brothers merchant house in Matanzas nervously reported to a New York associate that "the appearance of things have been somewhat alarming so far as it relates to the interests of our Planters, & to Cap the Climax our Government have interfered & taking extorted confessions of Negroes under the rack who have brought accusations against Whites. Some 8 or 10 of our Planters have been most unceremoniously arrested & thrown into prison under close confinement."[58] Domingo Del Monte and José de la Luz y Caballero, who were abroad, temporarily escaped arrest. Gertrudis Gómez de Avellaneda, also abroad, also avoided arrest but at home her books *Sab* and *Dos mujeres* [Two women] were banned by the censor, "the first for containing doctrines subversive of the system of slavery in the island and being contrary to morality and good habits, the second for being infested with immoral doctrines."[59] Benigno Gener fled to England to escape arrest. Félix Tanco, Manuel Martínez Serrano, and Manuel de Castro Palomino had no such luck and were imprisoned. For those of his color, Consul Thomas Rodney despaired: "I am perfectly aware that in the present state of turmoil in this island energetic measures are required, but it does seem most strange and unnatural that the testimony of a simple black man of bad character should be taken up against persons of the first respectability, whose interests are identified with the island's and whose personal character is above suspicion."[60]

In March Félix Tanco was suspended from his job as administrator of the Matanzas mails on the basis of "confidential intelligence from respectable persons" that he was spreading politically dangerous ideas and that his house was a center for their dissemination. Before Tanco's arrest, Matanzas governor García Oña had received orders from O'Donnell to keep him under surveillance. According to O'Donnell, Tanco professed ideas "neither favorable to the order and tranquility of the island nor to its dependency and union with the Metropolis."[61] O'Donnell refused to allow Tanco to continue in his job. Former Captain-General Tacón, O'Donnell said, had had a bad opinion of Tanco and once called him to Havana for questioning.

Andrés Fernández de Lara and his uncle, the Conde de Santovenia, who were proindependence and proslavery, took passage to New Orleans in February, possibly fearful that O'Donnell's crackdown might touch them, possibly to continue discussions with annexationists, but, in any case, not only to enjoy the racing season as had been reported.[62] William Norwood, the Episcopalian clergyman who was visiting in Matanzas, wrote in his diary that "clubs have been lately held where republican principles have been advocated & revolution discussed. Senor ———— one of the leaders in this matter was sent for day before yesterday (13th) [of April] & told that if he would leave the country in 24 hours he might escape with his life. The Governor's recommendation of fresh air & travelling was followed without delay."[63] He could have been referring to a trip similar to Fernández de Lara's.

About a score of British subjects, many of them sugar plantation mechanics and engineers, were arrested. Daniel Downing, an Irish engineer on a Cárdenas sugar plantation, was seized and confined at Cárdenas with about forty prisoners, most of them colored. "The room was in a terrible State of filth and the Stench from the Excrement of so many being allowed to remain in the room during the heat of the day made our situation dreadful." A "hoary-headed old Savage called the jailer" placed Downing in the stocks for six days and nights. Only when he bribed his keepers did he receive better treatment. He learned the reason for his imprisonment days later when slaves under flogging testified they had heard Downing say to another "ingles" something about killing Spaniards. Downing pleaded, "I can't speak scarcely a word of Spanish except Sufficient to get along with the opperation of Cain grinding with the Mayoral and Negroes and surely the little Conversation I used to have with Poor Elkins was in English therefore the Negroes could not understand us."[64]

Spanish authorities also seized Elkins, who was a British machinist employed on a sugar plantation, and confined him under conditions that one eyewitness compared to the Black Hole of Calcutta. He was accused of contacts with David Turnbull and other abolitionists and of being the trustee of an as yet undiscovered munitions shipment from England. The Spanish authorities accused him foolishly of such correspondence, one of his friends said, for Elkins could neither read nor write.[65]

Joseph Leaming and Patrick O'Rourke died shortly after release from imprisonment. The British government demanded an investigation. They learned that Leaming had been in jail for more than three months and O'Rourke for ten days. Leaming had contracted a fever and remained unattended. The witnesses produced by Spanish authorities in the investigation denied any connection between the deaths of either man and their imprisonment.[66]

One of the most graphic testimonies came from Theodore Phinney, a sugar planter in Cárdenas province. Phinney had quarreled with Lieutenant-Governor Javier Quintairo of Cárdenas province over the behavior of Phinney's overseer, Augustín Contrera. Because Contrera drank too much liquor and abused Phinney's slaves, Phinney had fired him. Contrera begged for a second chance, and Phinney relented, but Contrera did not reform so Phinney fired him again. This time Lieutenant-Governor Quintairo interceded, protesting, according to Phinney, that Contrera's "severity with the negroes was his chief recommendation." When Phinney reluctantly consented to rehire him, but not as the overseer, Quintairo mounted his horse in a rage and threatened, " 'That is the only way to keep the negroes in Subjection & Contrera is the only man who can do it! If you dismiss him, & there should be any disorder on the place afterwards, I will come with my troops & cut down every man on it!' "[67]

In March lancers rode to Phinney's estate with an order from Quin-tairo to enlist Contrera in interrogation of the slaves. Phinney described the aftermath:

Stripped naked & lashed to a ladder on the ground with a rope around each wrist so tight that the blood could scarsely circulate, and the whole arm drawn above the head till the shoulder joints fairly cracked, while the ropes were secured to the top of the ladder, the feet and legs stretched in the same man-ner, and fastened to the lower part with a double turn round the loins and back, binding the whole trunk of the body immoveably to the rounds of the ladder, in this position, the poor negro was thought to be ready to commence his declaration! . . . Good God! is it in the nineteenth Century that we live? or the palmy days of the Inquisition once more returned?[68]

Seven of Phinney's slaves died under the whip. One young male was severely lashed on one day and was returned to the ladder on the next day.

The first question was, "what more do you know than you told yesterday?"—"Nothing"—"You lie you black scamp; you know that"—mentioning the name of a free black man in Cárdenas—"you know that he told you all the negroes of the Island were going to rise against their Masters & become free, & if you don't confess it, you shall be flogged to death!" . . . The flogging went on till the men stopped to rest their arms which were tired with the blows given, & again the negro was asked the same as above. The reply "no Senor, No!" . . . It soon became apparent that his strength was going fast, & his unwill-ingness to tell a lie yielded with his strength,—"Spare me," he could scarcely articulate, "& I will confess anything you say!"—They stopped.[69]

Phinney appears to have attracted the anger of slaveholders of neigh-boring plantations for treating his slaves too leniently. In 1837 an up-rising had broken out on one of Phinney's estates, and in 1844 a number of Cuban planters from Cárdenas province testified that Phinney's estates were badly governed. One reported that "his slaves were as free."[70] Span-ish authorities gathered testimony and accused Phinney's favorite slave, a creole named Nicolás, of being a conspiratorial leader and executed him.

Phinney's carpenter, Samuel Moffat, and engineer, William Bisby, both suspected by Contrera of informing on him, were two of a small group of U.S. citizens to become embroiled in the process of La Escalera. Thomas Savage, an engineer who had worked on an *ingenio* for the Marqués Duquesne, was picked out of a lineup of six *monteros* in their native smocks and trousers and a U.S. sailor in uniform by a tortured slave. The slave said he had been promised money by an "inglés" if he would help stir up the slaves.[71]

Dr. Wurdemann of South Carolina, who was in Cuba during the tumultuous winter of 1843–1844 convalescing from consumption, discussed these events at the end of his *Notes on Cuba*. His explanation, which closely corresponds to the early Creole interpretation, accepted the existence of a conspiracy and assumed it was led by the free colored poet Plácido. "Many of the whites were to have been flayed and broiled while alive," Wurdemann wrote, "and with the exception of the young women, reserved for a worse fate, all, without discrimination of age or sex, were to have been massacred." Still, the viciousness of the investigations and the punishments disgusted him. He singled out Lieutenant-Governor Quintairo for "the most outrageous acts." "A thousand lashes were in many cases inflicted on a single negro; a great number died under this continued torture, and still more from spasms, and gangrene of the wounds." Wurdemann did not discount the subversive activity of "the notorious David Turnbull," deploring "the wild efforts of the abolitionist to force the freedom of the negro, which have only curtailed his privileges, and thwarted the measures employed by his master for his civilization."[72] But he did challenge the government's emphasis on outside instigators. Planter absenteeism and ignorant overseers, he believed, deserved much of the blame for the Conspiracy.

The price of slaves acted as a slight check on the number of slave executions; ironically, the lives of the free people of color cost less. "It is generally supposed," reported T. M. Rodney, U.S. consul in Matanzas, "that the free mulattoes and blacks engaged in this affair, and it seems they are all engaged without an exception, will either be executed or driven from the island, the slaves will be dealt with severely but only the prominent leaders executed."[73] Rodney knew some of these free people of color well. Indeed, Andrés Dodge, the London-educated dentist said to be one of the leaders of the Conspiracy, had once operated on the teeth of Rodney's wife. Rodney told his wife in March of Dodge's arrest. He "refuses to say anything and is to receive 'Boca abajo' until he does; some of the most respectable mulattos in town, even owning sugar estates, have to undergo 'Boca abajo' on mere suspicion."[74] About a week later, Rodney wrote that "George, a free mulatto who wished me to hire him, was whipped to death, and tomorrow if Dodge does not confess he is to undergo the same punishment." He did, and Rodney may have watched. "They say this morning that Dodge died of his whipping. I hardly believe it for he only received a hundred tho' he fainted three times under it; however the whip is a severe one now, having its end bound with wire."[75] The rumor was mistaken, for Dodge survived the whip. He was executed later.

In the city of Matanzas merchants were worried because the government was sweeping the free colored stevedores into jail. Reports to Governor García Oña from the field convinced him that his white troops were insufficient to put down a major revolt. In March, therefore, he stripped the free colored militia of its weapons; several months later O'Donnell would dissolve the free colored militia. In April, O'Donnell gave all male, adult, foreign-born, free people of color fifteen days to leave Cuba. From 10 March 1844 to 30 June 1845, according to Cuban historian Pedro Deschamps Chapeaux, at least 739 free people of color fled: 416 of them went to Mexico, ninety-two to Africa, forty to the United States, and the rest to Jamaica, Brazil, and Europe. Surveillance by Spanish agents continued in Mexico and elsewhere to prevent their return to Cuba. Eventually a royal order prohibited any free person of color, or *emancipado,* from entering Cuba.[76]

Many members of Cuba's native-born, free colored, petite bourgeoisie saved themselves from torture or death only by flight or by acquiescing in the intimidations and extortions of officials that were instigated or sanctioned by white business competitors. "Some among those executed this morning," Thomas Rodney observed, "were worth their 30, 40, and $50,000, all this is confiscated to the state; these people are doing a first rate business in the way of picking and stealings, never was there such a harvest before, and you may rest assured they will gather in to the last grain."[77]

At best, the most prominent free colored artists and businessmen spent time in prison and lost their hard-earned property. Several such imprisonments silenced the poetic voice of Juan Francisco Manzano. Claudio Brindis de Salas, a musician, fled Cuba after he left prison. An undertaker, Félix Barbosa, emerged from prison to find much of his wealth plundered. A respected tailor, Francisco Uribe, committed suicide in his cell. Augustín Ceballos, the giant captain of the dock gangs, wasted to death in a prison in Cárdenas. Tomás Vargas, a phlebotomist, Andrés Dodge, and Plácido were taken from jail to face a firing squad.[78]

One compilation of sentences from the records of the Matanzas branch

TABLE III. *Sentences of Matanzas Branch of Military Commission, 1844*

	Slaves	Free Coloreds	Whites	Total
Executions, including one black woman	39	38	1	78
Imprisonment (10 years)	202	126	0	328
Imprisonment (8 years)	303	345	4	652
Imprisonment (6 months to 1 year)	38	272	2	312
Banishments	0	433	2	435
Workhouses	0	17	0	17*
Lighter punishments	8	1	5	14
Acquitted, including 10 women	193	955	82	1,230
TOTALS	783	2,187	96	3,066

SOURCE: Morales y Morales, *Inciadores y primeros mártires de la revolución cubana* (Havana, 1901), 173.
* adjusted for error in enumeration

of the Military Commission showed just over 1,800 killed or imprisoned or banished. (See Table III.) It accounts for only a portion of the sentences.

The seventy-eight said to have been executed were judged to be leaders or instigators of a projected revolution. Of the thirty-eight free people of color executed, half appear to be *pardos,* or mulattoes, and half *morenos,* or blacks. The slaves imprisoned to await the proceedings of the Military Commission came from 230 plantations (186 sugar plantations and 44 coffee plantations) in twenty-five districts, the majority in the districts of Lagunillas, Guamacaro, Alacranes, Yumurí, Macuriges, and Cimarrones. Almost all of these plantations fell within the jurisdictions of Havana, Matanzas, and Cárdenas, where, according to the census of 1846, more than 40 percent of Cuba's slave population lived.[79]

The reign of terror, the extent of which official figures on punishments only hint at, caused an outpouring of condemnation from Western Europe, with Great Britain in the lead, and the northern United States. The London *Times* published eyewitness accounts to denounce "the shocking cruelties inflicted lately on the slaves in Cuba."[80] The *British and Foreign Anti-Slavery Reporter* followed the events closely and by August "hoped that, with this fearful deluge of blood, the atrocities by which this island has been desolated will be terminated."[81] The Philadelphia *North American,* after reporting on "the horrible cruelties perpetrated by Gov. O'Donnell, and the military commissioner at Matanzas," added, "It seems a reproach to Christendom that monsters such as O'Donnell are tolerated."[82]

The slave trade to Cuba appeared to be growing again. O'Donnell's administration had returned defenders of the slave trade to high political office, and whispers had begun flying around Havana in November 1843, only one month after O'Donnell's arrival, that he was pocketing the customary per-head payoff from the slave traders.[83] Campbell Dalrymple and James Kennedy, members of the Mixed Commission, complained to Lord Aberdeen in January 1844 that under O'Donnell the Cuban slave trade "revives with nearly its former activity.[84] The best recent estimates of the Cuban slave trade show an upward trend during O'Donnell's first year from about 7,000 imports in 1843 to about 10,000 in 1844. Reports from Madrid explained that O'Donnell was watching over the slave-trading investment of his adored Queen Isabel.

British consul Joseph Crawford and O'Donnell exchanged testy messages, reminiscent of those between Turnbull and Valdés, on the subjects of *emancipado* freedom, on the imprisonment of so-called British subversives, and on the slave trade itself. Crawford resented O'Donnell's condescension and his apparent corruption. As masses of diplomatic correspondence reveal, O'Donnell's francophilia, short temper, and suspicions that British agents were behind the Conspiracy inclined him to forget diplomatic courtesy in dealing with Crawford. Lord Aberdeen responded angrily to what he heard and read and pressured Spain to remove O'Donnell immediately. "Let them make him Captain-General of Madrid or anything else they please," he said to his minister to Spain, "but let them only send a man who is determined to execute the Treaty [of 1835], & who is able to resist the Bribes of the Slave Dealers."[85]

O'Donnell justified his actions with a simple logic. His prosperity and that of the *Moderado* regime depended on Cuban prosperity; Cuban prosperity depended on the plantation economy; white plantation laborers wilted under a tropical sun; and Cuba's slave population could not yet reproduce itself naturally. Hence, Cuba had to maintain slavery, and, to maintain slavery, Cuba had to maintain the contraband slave trade.[86] His argument was similar to that of the Portuguese in the late sixteenth and early seventeenth centuries, when northeastern Brazil boomed with slaves and sugar plantations: "no slaves, no sugar, no Brazil." O'Donnell might well have said "no Cuba" and, indeed, "no Spain."

O'Donnell counterattacked by arranging for his supporters to send pro-O'Donnell memorials to the queen during the height of the La Escalera terror. Joaquín Gómez, one of the most notorious slave traders of the day, collected signatures door-to-door from the most conservative

individuals and corporations in Cuba. Another memorial requested that
O'Donnell be honored with the title of Conde de la Salvación de Cuba.[87]
Gómez and more than three hundred "títulos de Castilla, property owners,
merchants, and other notable persons of Havana" endorsed another such
memorial; addressed to the queen, it was published under their names
in the Havana newspapers: "The enemies, Señora, of the tranquility and
prosperity of this Island are many and of various kinds and colors, and
it would not be strange that within Your Majesty's own court some are
sheltered in order to direct better their machinations to the detestable
end of losing it [Cuba], beginning their work by putting Your Majesty's government in disagreement with this captain-general."[88]

The Junta de Fomento, the planter-merchant organization for promoting Cuban prosperity, sent an encomium to the queen:

The slaves of our countryside, stirred up and promoted by the free and emancipated in the cities, have plotted an extensive, vast and horrible uprising. A
conspiracy, which in its combination encompassed the entire island, which
ramified into foreign countries and plainly counted on outside auxiliaries of
the same color, which was conceived with the most perfect cunning and whose
secret up until now has not been violated by any of those complicated, was
about to break out and might have effected the most frightful ravages and,
simultaneously, destroyed the lives and fortunes of these inhabitants, if the
finger of Divine Providence, which securely protects us, had not inspired your
Majesty with the happy thought of putting the command of this Island in
the expert and diligent hands of the distinguished individual who governs
today.[89]

The fifteen signatures at the bottom of the memorial identify such big
merchants as Julián de Zulueta, Domingo Goicouría, Joaquín Andreu,
and Nicolás Galeran and such titled nobles as the Marqués Duquesne,
the Marqués de la Cañada Tirry, the Conde de Romero, and the Conde
de Santovenia.

O'Donnell and the Junta de Fomento also combined to draw up new
and more stringent measures that officially superseded Valdes's 1842
police regulations on the slaves and free people of color (see Appendix II). O'Donnell's measures sanctioned the "full power" of masters,
leaving the severity of slave punishment to the master's discretion. One
article affirmed the government's intention to enforce previous laws governing the movements of free people of color; another stipulated that
any person, white, free colored, or slave, would be arrested if found on
a plantation without "a letter or paper signed by the person who sent
him"; another stipulated one white employee for every twenty slaves on

a plantation; another responded to the widespread rumors and testimony about plans of the people of color to poison whites by forbidding the employment of people of color in drug shops or in making "even the simplest prescription"; still another banned the sale of liquor in the countryside.

O'Donnell had achieved all for which Spain could have hoped. His measures worked with the divisions within the conspirators themselves to give Spanish rule in Cuba a reprieve of several decades from the forces of an age beyond its control. By the end of the summer of 1844 Cuba had returned to satisfactory order. Arrests and trials would continue well into the next year, but the worst of the fury had passed. With renewed confidence O'Donnell could boast, "With a guitar, a fighting cock, and playing cards the government and peace is assured in this land."[90] "All is apparently tranquil here," said one British correspondent in August 1844, *"but it is the tranquility of terror."*[91]

During the first week of October, a hurricane hit Cuba. The old ones could not remember another one like it. It battered the ground where La Escalera had taken place. In the countryside, plantations and towns were flattened. Cattle died. Bridges were swept away. Already sick coffee estates succumbed. The town of Cárdenas, according to one correspondent, was "wholly destroyed." Water flooded over Matanzas and ruined thousands of boxes of sugar. Twenty-nine vessels in port went under or were driven ashore. In the interior, the Matanzas newspaper *Aurora* reported, "The villages of Sabanilla, Limonar, and Santa Ana no longer exist."[92] In Havana many ships at anchor also sank or were driven ashore. Floodwater covered streets. The public promenade and many other places lost their trees. Part of the Tacón theater flew off into space. Even the Morro fortress was damaged. As the storm abated, O'Donnell had to call out troops to control roving bands of people of color who were looting property and assaulting whites. People mentioned Plácido. Had he not promised divine retribution for the crimes committed? To them, it was an unearthly coincidence that the hurricane wrought its worst devastation in western Cuba on October 5, the day of Plácido's patron saint.[93]

9

La Escalera Reexamined

Haití de su dulzura enmarañada
extrae pétalos patéticos
rectitud de jardines, edificios
de la grandeza, arrulla
el mar comon un abuelo oscuro
su antigua dignidad de piel y espacio.

Out of its own tangled sweetness
Haiti raises mournful petals,
and elaborate gardens, magnificent
structures, and rocks the sea
as a dark grandfather rocks
his ancient dignity of skin and space.

PABLO NERUDA,
"Toussaint L'Ouverture"

Whether there was or was not a conspiracy before there was the terror, and if so, who was guilty and who was innocent, are questions requiring historical analysis. Conflicting and missing evidence has produced much speculation that the Conspiracy of La Escalera was a fraud, a strategy devised by O'Donnell and his agents to justify a brutal policy of colonial repression. José Gutiérrez de la Concha, Captain-General of Cuba, six years after La Escalera in 1850, was to say,

The judgments of the Military Commission produced the execution, confiscation of property, and the expulsion from the island of many persons of color, but without their having been found with arms, munitions, papers, or other incriminating evidence that confirmed the conspiracy, or to even make it presumable, at least on the large scale embraced by the judicial investigations.[1]

His words raise questions about the propriety of what O'Donnell had done, even as they allow for the existence of a conspiracy.

The extent of the brutal repression and the punishments are not at issue in the records. The fury of the investigations undoubtedly caught up innocents. Juan Francisco Manzano went to jail initially because his color and surname matched those of one accused conspirator and because he, like Plácido, was a poet. He stayed there even longer because of his association with Domingo Del Monte.[2] Thomas Savage, the white sugar engineer, had the misfortune of being caught in the wrong place by the wrong person at the wrong time. Some slaves may have knowingly perjured themselves against whites to escape further torture: some slaves may have consciously implicated innocent white sugar plantation workers in recompense for some previous offense or simply because they were white.

One *emancipado* received four years in prison for predicting that the whites would trade places with the slaves one day. Free Negro Rita Domínguez, in a moment of indiscretion, proclaimed her desire to see all white men shot. She received one year's labor in a hospital. Antonia, the cook on the coffee estate of Pedro Domech, was shot for preparing to use poison on him, and Tomás Robaina was shot for bringing it to her. But no poison was ever found. The slave José was also shot for "entrusting frogs and salamanders as ingredients for the preparation and elaboration" of witchcraft. The trial of the slave Narciso Carabalí revealed that he had not run away from *ingenio* Botino to participate in a conspiracy but had been induced to run away by two white men, one of whom was his former overseer, in order to get the present overseer fired. The Military Commission even admitted a mistake in the case of the slave Matías Gangá. Matías threatened to kill whites, but it had nothing to do with a revolutionary conspiracy. The overseer's son appeared to have had improper dealings with Matías's wife.[3]

Liberal Creoles, clearly innocent of involvement in the Conspiracy of La Escalera but guilty of speaking out against the government and the slave trade, were jailed or bullied into silence. Domingo Del Monte, for one, was branded by the slave trading interest as a conspirator and Spain's most dangerous enemy. The crying of conspiracy settled many old scores, as the story of Contrera, the overseer, shows. Venal officials extorted wealth from free people of color, and members of the white petite bourgeoisie eliminated free colored competitors, like the dentist Carlos Blackely and his protégés. British Consul Crawford pointed to the *fiscales* as "very young officers" many of whom charged money to exempt slaves from the lash.[4] James Kennedy, the British commissioner, thought O'Donnell's entourage included military officers who, knowing and caring little about Cuba, manufactured crimes to further their purses and their careers. Lawyers accompanied these military men and, as lawyers will do, used "every device" to despoil the accused.[5] Pedro Salazar, one of the most notorious of the government's investigators, eventually went to jail for six years for myriad abuses of his office with the Military Commission, including destruction of documents related to the proceedings against persons convicted of conspiracy.[6]

The mistakes and excesses do not add up to deny the existence of the Conspiracy of La Escalera. If O'Donnell and his subordinates had concocted it or had purposely exaggerated a minor plot or a local disturbance as a Machiavellian tactic to reassert imperial rule, then the official correspondence ought to show at least a hint of such activity.

The archives of the British Foreign Office hold a record of the proceedings that were initiated by Spanish authorities near the end of 1844 in response to Theodore Phinney's complaints against the agents who conducted the investigations on his La Sonora estate in Cárdenas province. For this investigation the government gathered testimony from almost fifty white planters, merchants, and professionals, mostly from the sugar districts of Lagunillas but also from the districts of Cimarrones, Palmillas, Macurijes, and Guamutas. Many of the planters, if they had not interrogated their slaves themselves, had witnessed interrogation by the *fiscales.* One of the questions asked of each of these planters was whether an extensive conspiracy of slaves had truly been uncovered. None doubted that an elaborate conspiracy had existed among the slaves of these plantations.[7]

Scores of missives in which Captain-General O'Donnell, local officials, and the *fiscales* communicate about the matter survive in the Houghton Library of Harvard University, part of the remarkable collection of José Escoto, the Matanzas bibliophile and investigator of La Escalera.[8] They cover in detail the crucial period from early January to late March of 1844. They concur that the authorities did not concoct a conspiracy or exaggerate it as a ruse. The letters are serious and urgent. They reveal how their suspicion about the island-wide ramifications of unrest in the Matanzas countryside became conviction as local officials and agents in the field, acting separately, sent in information that coincided at various points and with other sources.

Francisco González del Valle and other students of La Escalera have blamed Esteban Santa Cruz de Oviedo for unduly swaying O'Donnell about the ramifications of what had been discovered on the plantations of Sabanilla. But although O'Donnell did want Santa Cruz de Oviedo to participate in subsequent investigations in the field, he, in fact, declined because of illness and returned to his estates.[9] Nor does Francisco Hernández Morejón, who is often blamed as well, appear decisively influential, judging from the evidence in the Escoto Collection. While he did journey to many estates in and around the district of Sabanilla to establish order, extract testimony, and provide his superiors with information, he often did so after the planters themselves had obtained preliminary confessions or had observed activity they considered suspicious. Moreover, Hernández Morejón was not the only stream of information to O'Donnell. Officials of Santa Ana, Cimarrones, Alacranes, Macurijes, and many other districts had sent in intelligence at about the same time of possible connections between David Turnbull, Haiti, free people of color, and discontented slaves in the countryside.[10] Nor did Pedro Salazar, the *fiscal* convicted of abuse of his office with the Military Commission, become a significant figure until after March 13, when the broad outlines of plotting had been detected, when in the city of Matanzas he was directed to pursue leads in the confession of José Erice, the free *moreno* militiaman.[11]

In rooting out the Conspiracy, O'Donnell and his men understood that excesses would result from their methods. Indeed, they admitted some of them. But they felt justified precisely because they believed in the gravity of the situation and worried about their own weakness in the face of it.[12]

In response to the first indications of trouble, O'Donnell made clear what he intended to do, "namely to return the slaves to their habitual state of discipline and servitude without grave damage to the proprietors, and at the same time to punish in a severe and exemplary manner the chiefs [of the slaves] and the white and free people of color who have introduced this germ of unrest and insubordination."[13] O'Donnell wrote these words in the beginning of February. From then until the end of March he received numerous reports of disturbances in the western plantation districts. Slaves were running away, setting fires, manifesting a "spirit of indiscipline" or "symptoms and demonstrations of insurrection" and, in a few cases, they were rebelling.[14] O'Donnell sent cavalry into the affected zones. What Pedro Cruces reported to Governor García Oña in March after observing the situation in the district of Alacranes, other government agents approximated in similar communications.

The result of the declarations obtained, the confessions of the slaves themselves, and the denunciations they make linking some estates with others produces the firm conviction that in the said district of Alacranes there is not a sugar estate, coffee estate, big or small ranch, farm, general store, private house nor even a single hut in which there is a black that is unaware of the plan of insurrection.[15]

Eventually the government pieced together a vast map of unrest, linking rural and urban, slave and free colored. Documentation in the Escoto Collection sheds considerable light on how this happened. Word of the discovery of a plot on José Jáuregui's La Andrea estate in the district of Macurijes brought Hernández Morejón there in the middle of January to carry on with the investigations. There he became much more aware of the magnitude of the plotting and the difficulties ahead of him in finding its origins, for slaves, some of them under torture, implicated many more estates in different districts.[16]

On La Andrea, according to Hernández Morejón, a slave driver named Marcelino led the conspiracy he had plotted with slaves on neighboring estates. For the projected uprising he had hidden away weapons made of wood, which apparently were burned when he was seized for questioning. Persico Criollo, a mulatto slave, confessed that certain free people of color had used magic to seduce the slaves into a conspiracy. His confession led to the arrest, interrogation, and eventual execution of Luis Morgado, a free *pardo*.[17] O'Donnell received intelligence from Hernández Morejón and told García Oña in a letter of January 26 that he had found the declaration of a black slave named Germán on La Andrea to be particularly revealing since it presented "higher ideas" than the slaves would be expected to possess.[18]

About a week later, the district magistrate of Guamacaro received evidence of collusion between slaves of various estates under his jurisdiction to rise up, led by the slaves Simón and Domingo Criollo, José Gangá, and Ventura Lucumí.[19] On February 8 Rafael Mariscal reported that the declarations of the slaves on José Govin's sugar plantation had identified a free *moreno* named José María Mondejar and several other free people of color as the most active promoters of insurrection in the districts of Sabanilla and Alacranes. O'Donnell considered the testimony eventually extracted from Mondejar especially significant for the light it shed on the "extension and antiquity" of plotting and ordered it to be vigorously pursued in the hope of finding the source of the conspiracy.[20]

Hernández Morejón and a government agent named Pedro Cruces followed Mariscal with more information about free colored subversion in the western plantation districts. Not only were free people of color acting as the "intermediaries of seduction," but, to the astonishment of planters, investigations were implicating many of their most trusted and advantaged slaves.[21] Slaves confessed to plotting to kill whites and take possession of the land. At least some of them were said to have counted on outside help from England and Haiti. By the end of February, after lengthy investigations, Cruces had linked Havana's colored coachmen to unrest in the countryside.[22]

In the district of Alacranes, Ramón Flores de Apodaca believed the Conspiracy had "vast ramifications" and recommended prohibitions on the movement of free people of color in the countryside to prevent them from "developing their talents as Plácido."[23] He eventually pinpointed Manuel López, a free *pardo,* as one of the chief agents of conspiracy in Alacranes. Testimony gathered in the district of Macurijes also identified free people of color as the chief troublemakers. According to the summation of one official, the plot was years in gestation and led by a free black named Jacinto Roque. Free people of color had seduced the slaves with magic and various promises, among them that English boats with arms and munitions and black soldiers would support the insurrection. If the revolution failed, the boats would be on hand to take the rebels away. Fires would initiate the revolt and signal the other estates to join in.[24]

As the investigations spread out from Sabanilla and Macurijes well into the jurisdiction of Cárdenas, investigations there led to the belief that a "chain of conspiracy" had formed with its first link in Sabanilla. By the end of March, the authorities had arrested an English-speaking free *pardo* named Luis Segui as a leader of the conspiracy in Cárdenas.[25] Government agents had a difficult time making connections in Cárdenas and elsewhere, for many slaves were only loosely aware of a general plan. Only a few supplied details. José María Velasco, for example, after investigating six estates in his district, called those involved "very subaltern."[26] They knew an insurrection was coming but only that when it started on other estates they were to get their machetes and join in.

At the end of February O'Donnell was feeling more confident about the situation in the countryside. He attributed improvement to the movement of cavalry, the vigilance of the government's agents, and the prudent conduct of the plantation owners themselves. He had already ordered all of those slaves judged to be leaders of the conspiracy to be removed from the plantations for further proceedings in Matanzas in order to instill in those who remained behind "a salutary fear."[27]

The results of the interrogation of the coach drivers Julián and Toribio Gangá in early March of 1844 provided what O'Donnell called a "clear and accessible path" to the principals of the insurrection.[28] By this time the attention of the authorities was rapidly shifting into urban areas. On March 13 José Erice, the decorated free *moreno* militiaman from Matanzas, offered to exchange what he knew about the conspiracy for lenient treatment. Before committing suicide—according to one newspaper report by hanging himself with a pocket handkerchief and the cords of his suspenders—he implicated Luis Gigaut, a free *pardo* carpenter, and Miguel Flores, a free *moreno* leatherworker, both said to be from Havana.[29] Flores was arrested in Havana about a week later; Gigaut was never located. According to Mariano Fortun, the official who received Erice's declaration, Erice made clear that the conspirators counted on support from David Turnbull and Haiti.[30]

At about the time of Erice's confession, a mulatto coachman named Bruno Izquierdo added to the list of declarations against Plácido, who had been jailed in late January and held incommunicado for many weeks. Izquierdo's testimony also led to the imprisonment of three unnamed people of color and one white considered to be members of the "Junta Superior" of Matanzas.[31] O'Donnell's letter to Fulgencio Salas of March 14 indicates that an investigation of the slaves who worked for the many sugar warehouses in Matanzas was well under way when he received news of Izquierdo's revelations. He considered Erice's suicide "a calamity" for the continuing investigations into the origin of the conspiracy.[32] But subsequently Antonio Lara presented to García Oña revelations of a mulatto slave owned by Blas de la Cruz who admitted to being involved in the plot. Plácido had spoken to him about it and compromised him in it. The slave also named a person of color named Marcos Ruíz as a principal leader of the conspiracy in Matanzas. Ruíz was charged with organizing and heading a cavalry unit intended for strategic application in the projected insurrection. To this end he had used his house to recruit many of Matanzas's colored coachmen, including as his second in command the coachman of Governor García Oña himself. Lara's investigations of the slave gangs that worked the docks for the various sugar merchants convinced him that hundreds were under the command of a slave named Domingo Lucumí.[33]

Testimony of the mulatto slave of Blas de la Cruz was corroborated by a *moreno* slave named Antonio Abad, who implicated himself and fifteen other people of color. Those of the first culpability included the *pardos* Plácido, Antonio Bernoqui, Jorge López, Santiago Pimienta, and Bruno Izquierdo and the *morenos* Marcos Ruiz, Manuel Quiñones, José Erice, and José de la O. García. Ramón González examined the accused and on

March 23 informed García Oña that the testimony of Bernoqui tied together with that of Jorge López and Santiago Pimienta.[34]

At the end of March the royal prison of Matanzas alone contained
more than four hundred persons alleged to be principals in the conspiracy,
including fourteen whites and seven black women. As a further precaution, O'Donnell approved the disarming of the free colored militia and
urgently sought permission from Madrid to increase the number of regular troops. One *norteamericano* who entered Havana in May probably did
not realize how perceptive he was when he wrote, "Every place, every
pass, finally the whole city is guarded, it seems to me just as if they were
afraid the island will be taken from them."[35]

Power, as Balzac has written, shows up not by striking hard or often
but by striking true. Because many scattered streams of intelligence had
identified free people of color to be the major source of the trouble, and
on the advice of such agents in the field as Ramón Flores de Apodaca,
O'Donnell sanctioned the use of "all vigor and severity" to destroy them
as a class. "The grave and extensive conspiracy discovered in this island in
which the majority of the race of free people of color were involved," explained O'Donnell to Spain's minister to Mexico so that he would understand the exodus of Cuba's free people of color there, "made me consider
as a very important object for the future of this country, the diminution
of this caste."[36] He unsuccessfully sought Madrid's approval to begin massive, forced deportations.

In dealing with the emergency, O'Donnell fashioned a special branch
of the Military Commission in Matanzas. It held seventy-one sessions and
passed thousands of sentences. Its close attention to punishment, to mu-
tilating the remains of many of those executed for exhibition in precisely
specified locations, argues strongly for the existence in the authorities of
an honest fear of revolutionary violence. One proceeding against more
than seventy people of color from the district of Alacranes for plotting to
exterminate whites and to raze the district's many plantations resulted in
almost wholesale convictions. Punishments ranged from years of imprisonment or of hard labor in irons to deportation and execution. Five free
people of color, four of them free *morenos,* and four slaves were executed; their heads were cut off and displayed.

That of the first [Manuel López] [was displayed] on the royal road in front of
the house in which he lived; that of the second [Bonifacio Berson] in the
mill yard of the San Ignacio sugar plantation; that of the third [Rafael Ca-
ballero] in the plantain field of the San Benito sugar plantation next to the

hut of the watchman; that of the fourth [Cayetano Soría] on the royal road in front of the house in which he lived (in barrio Gonzalo); that of the fifth [José Cambon] in the mill yard of the San José el Naciente sugar plantation; that of the sixth [Feliciano Criollo] and seventh [Carlos Gangá] in the same spot on the San Lorenzo sugar plantation; that of the eighth [José María Lucumí] in the same spot on the San Benito sugar plantation; and that of the last [Rafael Gangá] on the tobacco farm that was in his charge, there to remain until they be consumed by time.[37]

The Military Commission concluded that "not the least doubt" remained as to the guilt of David Turnbull in being "either by himself or with others of his colleagues, if not the individual who conceived the destructive idea, at least the prime mover and focal point, from where the present plan of conspiracy and several other projects for the desolation of this country emanated." It convicted him of playing upon the aspirations of the free people of color, particularly the *pardos,* by "inculcating in them the idea of liberty" and by plying them with toxic visions of a happier future, and then, proceeding to the next step, by sending handpicked agents throughout Cuba to convince other people of color of England's favor in a struggle for emancipation. Turnbull, it said, imported "Luis Guigot, a rather intelligent *pardo,*" for this purpose. The report said that in the house of Jorge López, a free *pardo* carpenter and lieutenant in the *pardo* militia, Guigot met with López, Plácido, Santiago Pimienta, Antonio Bernoqui, and several other prominent *pardos* and in two sessions got them to accept "the ideas of the ex-consul Turnbull." They then went out to various parts of the island to "water the seed of rebellion by making converts."[38]

The official version went on that since Havana held out "great impediments" to the *pardos,* the central junta was formed in Matanzas. The location and lay of the land made it easily accessible by land or sea, and the surrounding plantations contained more potential recruits than any others. The junta deliberated and selected Plácido as president, Santiago Pimienta as treasurer, Tomás Vargas as general, and the multilingual Andrés Dodge as ambassador. It goes on to say that two distinct factions, one mostly composed of moderate *pardos* and the other, much larger and more radical, of *morenos,* eventually clashed on the direction and goals of the movement. Miguel Flores, a free colored leatherworker, said to be an agent of David Turnbull, labored in Matanzas to reconcile the two factions. He united the *pardos* and *morenos* and persuaded them to undertake "a project of furious insurrection and bloodshed and extermination of all whites, the moderate party of *pardos,* without a doubt, having de-

cided to agree to such terms by having judged that it could not resist
the furious and violent state of the blacks because of their far greater
strength."[39] Then, under Plácido's orders, the report said, the united *pardo*
and *moreno* conspirators formed secondary juntas in other localities; conspirators from Havana held meetings in the town of Güines because of
its relative privacy and its proximity to the railroad and the plantations.
Dances in certain cities celebrated cooperation between various rebel
groups and concealed further plotting. Information passed in "the cockpits, the streets, and the dances," and the conspirators took a terrible
"death oath" to maintain the strictest secrecy.[40] Word widely circulated of
arms and other assistance to be forthcoming from Haiti and England
or England's agent Turnbull. While slave insurrection in the countryside was drawing off government troops, urban conspirators would seize
control of key strongholds. In Matanzas, the government convicted coachmen of preparing themselves to become a rebel cavalry and slave dock-
workers of plotting to cross over the mouth of the San Juan River
from their place of work among the sugar warehouses to seize the fortress
of La Vigía.[41]

Lines of communication to the plantations used runners, slave drivers,
and rural free people of color. Some rural free people of color, regularly
hired as seasonal skilled labor, according to the government, acted as
agents of the conspiracy. They recruited the most influential slaves on the
plantation, usually the drivers, to lead the gangs in a general insurrection,
"offering them the guarantee that they would be free, that they would
mate with white women, and that they would be owners of the land."[42]
In sentencing more than 170 people of color from Madruga and adjacent
districts southwest of Matanzas, the Commission declared,

The principal conspirators used the free people of color to propagate the revolutionary project who on the pretext of performing their crafts or jobs entered the villages and estates for the purpose of seduction. They gave dances
or took advantage of their occurrence with the same object in mind. They
offered jobs and the distribution of land; demanded oaths; threatened death
to those who did not take part in the uprising; promised liberty to the slaves;
and gave hope to everyone that they would be aided by the blacks of Guarico
[Haiti or the region around Cap Haitien] and some foreigners.[43]

The means of animating the plantation masses were said to include the
widespread use of *brujería,* that is, magico-religious objects and rituals,
supposed to ward off the white man's power. For their involvement in
plotting to raise the slaves of the districts of Rancho Veloz and Quemado

de Güines, Juan Congo, alias Candela ("the Light"), and Juan Carabalí received ten years of hard labor in irons on their masters' plantations after fifty lashes in front of the slaves of all the involved estates "to discredit among the Africans the notion of the immense power that they attribute to the so-called *brujerías* and which they have widely used to excite and inspire security and confidence in the realization of their plans."[44] In the case of the alleged effort to poison Pedro Domech on his Buena Esperanza coffee plantation and the projected uprising of its slaves and of those on neighboring plantations, the court sentenced Agustín Domínguez, a free Negro, to six years in prison for selling *brujería* after "taking into consideration the prejudicial use that the free people of color have made of such charlatanry to urge on and move the African slaves, who by their lack of civilization, place so much value in these hoaxes as is proved in every part of this conspiracy trial."[45] Marcos Mandinga, a slave sexagenarian on the coffee plantation Madamita, promoted the conspiracy of the people of color in the districts of Lagunillas and Cimarrones, according to the Military Commission, by holding meetings in a cave on Madamita where he practiced *brujería,* passing out "potions and amulets" to be used by his followers "against all manner of dangers with which they might be threatened."[46]

The proceedings against more than sixty people of color charged with involvement in planning an uprising of several plantation districts near Havana resulted in the execution of a free mulatto named José Amores; his body was mutilated, and his head posted in "the most public place" of the town of his birth for what the tribunal called the most despicable crime of turning what was holy into a means to recruit at least one slave into a plot to destroy whites. Amores appears to have been the sacristan for the church of the hamlet of San Pablo de Bainoa.

Not content with adding to his converts by means of ordinary oaths and threats of death, he trampled on one of those things most sacred and respected by every Christian. He had the audacity to take from the holy ciborium the chalice for the Holy Communion from the church of San Pablo de Bainoa, and making a slave kiss it, he made him swear his allegiance to the exterminator party, to promise secrecy and to die before revealing anything to the whites.[47]

In two of its proceedings, the Military Commission pointed to a history of "seditions movements" by the people of color in districts where the current round of rebellion had taken firm hold, as if to posit years of significant preconditioning by what might be called a tradition of violent resistance.[48] In the districts of Macurijes and Cimarrones, the Commission observed, "revolutionary plans" had proceeded "with the greatest energy." These districts, with slaves more than 70 percent of the population according to the census of 1841, had experienced four disturbances in the previous two years. The slave uprising of March 1843 in these districts of Cárdenas province—to which both Cocking and Juan Rodríguez had referred in different contexts as connected to the revolutionary plotting of the people of color—had unsettled whites the most "as much by the force and material of which it was composed as by a certain order and regularity in its course."[49] In sentencing people of color in the district of Guamacaro, the Commission looked farther back in time. "Seditious movements have repeatedly occurred" there since 1825, and in that year a major slave uprising had killed whites and destroyed plantations. "The boldness of the revolutionaries reached the point of confronting whites with supplies of firearms, which they managed with some skill."[50] By 1844, the Commission indicated, the district's planters had still not fully recovered from this trauma.

The government noted in one of its summations its reliance on the testimony provided by José Erice. The suicide of a star witness would tend to diminish confidence in the Military Commission's case, and those who look for the analogue of a modern legal proof in the records will be disappointed. The absence of a modern legal proof does not, of course, in itself, disprove the existence of the Conspiracy. When the charges against Turnbull became public, the British legation in Spain demanded proof and the Spanish government ordered O'Donnell to provide it. He shipped back reams of documentation, certified copies of which went to the British Foreign Office.[51] Few of the many students of La Escalera have delved into the thick bundles of testimony upon which the judgments of the Military Commission were based.[52] Some, like Manuel Sanguily, in the spirit of *épater le droit,* argue for the total fraudulence or purposive exaggeration of a conspiracy; they dismiss the records of interrogation as at worst manufactured by O'Donnell and his underlings or at best untrustworthy given the reliance on torture and other brutality in extracting confessions.

A careful examination of the interrogation records in O'Donnell's *expedientes* and the Escoto Collection raises doubts whether all evidence was indeed lies extorted by torture. Thousands of interrogations took place. They were conducted over months at different locations by different officials of different interests and character. Not every *fiscal* was a

Pedro Salazar. It is difficult to dismiss the pattern of evidence. Indeed, what is striking is the frequency with which negative answers from those interrogated are recorded to questions that for fraudulent officials would have best been answered in the affirmative. Could the wealth of detail be manufactured by the officials? Could it be made to cohere? The results of the interrogations do contain discrepancies and contradictions, and the fear of torture surely pressured some of the accused to say what the interrogator wanted as it may have pressured others to tell the truth. Instances of fraud by certain officials in obtaining declarations can be demonstrated. Yet, in general, the conclusion drawn from the interrogations appears to be supported by other evidence that the government had caught a revolution in the making.

What the Military Commission claimed about David Turnbull he had admitted himself in a general way. The Commission contended that Turnbull was the "prime mover," the man who was inciting the people of color with subversive notions of liberty and a better future. Turnbull said in a letter to Joseph Sturge in 1842 that his efforts had "served to inspire the slaves of this Island with Hope, which next to the positive enjoyment of Liberty, is perhaps the greatest good which could have been obtained for them."[53] He added that some of those people of color whom he had helped to free and leave Cuba were writing back to their friends and telling them of the virtues of freedom. The message handed over to Joseph Crawford by Juan Rodríguez, that obscure person of color who had met with Crawford on the subject of promised munition shipments from England, calls Turnbull the "Guardian of Liberty" and clearly indicates that both Turnbull and England had become a rod that drew the flash of lightning.[54]

Also, Turnbull had numerous contacts with Cuba's people of color. Living where he did in Havana on the highway San Luis Gonzaga, he could hardly have avoided them. His great popularity among them even has a witness in Captain-General Valdés.[55] To Lord Palmerston Turnbull admitted ominously that while he had been circumspect "to a most inconvenient extreme" in dealing with people of color, they had their own ideas.

In this country, it is not unusual for slaves to go about, with or without the sanction of their masters, seeking a purchaser of themselves, to their own liking. Such applications are frequently addressed to me, in general with the sincere and unaffected purpose on the part of the applicants of bettering their condition; but on one or two occasions, involuntarily communicating the impression, of their being sent by others, either to discover my sentiments on subjects connected with the coloured classes, or to entrap me into the commission of some act of indiscretion.[56]

In presenting Spain's evidence against Turnbull to Lord Aberdeen, the Duque de Sotomayor stressed how remarkable it was "that even those culprits who have uniformly refused to own to their participation in the crime, on being charged with some inculpatory facts take shelter under the publicness of the conspiracy and denounce Mr. Turnbull as its notorious and avowed author."[57] In what precise way Turnbull did author the Conspiracy the mass of evidence presented does not establish. But his presence in Havana, his antislavery sentiments, and his efforts on behalf of slaves and *emancipados* had become notorious in the colored population, and that population believed that behind Turnbull stood the mighty British nation. Plácido, for one, while repeatedly denying under interrogation his involvement in the Conspiracy, acknowledged that the people of color looked to Turnbull as their "liberator and protector."[58] Would various authorities in recording individual depositions all falsify what people of color such as Plácido had said about Turnbull and not also falsify their denials of conspiratorial involvement?

The Military Commission identified as agents of David Turnbull two mystery men, Luis Guigot and Miguel Flores, and assigned them key roles in the organization of the Conspiracy. Francisco Jimeno, the Creole who lived during La Escalera and researched it afterwards, doubted the existence of a Guigot. "No one knew him; no one saw him; they only knew of him by the sentence and for the inhabitants of Matanzas he is a myth."[59] For this reason and others, Jimeno doubted the reality of the Conspiracy and attributed the slave insurrection of 1843 to local causes.

But Guigot did exist. His real name was probably Gigaut or Gigaud. He appears to have traveled widely in the circum-Caribbean region. The testimony of Antonio Bernoqui, a free *pardo* carpenter, before the Military Commission in Matanzas mentions that Gigaut once worked in Veracruz as a translator. He appears to have come to Cuba from Haiti by way of New Orleans, the last port of call of Francis Ross Cocking on his way to Cuba, and to have worked as a wood craftsman.[60] In 1842 Consul Joseph Crawford refers to a highly intelligent free person of color named "Gigot" as his source of information on the attempt by the Conde de Santovenia to court free colored support for his independence schemes. He says "Gigot" had a brother.[61] On 16 September 1844 an incarcerated

Manuel de Castro Palomino wrote Domingo Del Monte that "the mulatto Gigaud, as a clever man, opportunely saved himself and no one knows his whereabouts. Consequently, he had never declared against you or me."[62]

José Escoto spent years around the turn of the century researching the question of a conspiracy. One of his correspondents, a mulatto named Manuel Federico D'Aure, remembered that at his mother's home Plácido had met with "his friends" Luis Gigaut and Ramón Ponce. "Luis Gigaut had received an accomplished education in Switzerland, birthplace of his father and his godfather, Luis Monte . . . [He] was a friend in Matanzas to all the people of color who then had position and education and whose houses he visited."[63] Passenger lists for the arrival of vessels at New Orleans show that in 1828 a "Louis Guillaut" arrived from Havana in the company of no less a personage than Francisco de Sentmanat.[64] Since Francis Ross Cocking must have known Gigaut, a Gigaut-Sentmanat connection could have been one more reason why in 1843 Cocking considered fleeing to Mexico.

Under interrogation, Plácido, Juan Francisco Manzano, and virtually every prominent free colored suspect admitted to knowing or knowing of Gigaut. Miguel Flores, who during his reexamination for the trial of Pedro Salazar denied almost everything he was alleged to have said previously, did admit to having overheard regular talk about Gigaut among the people of color.[65] Also, under interrogation, Félix Tanco admitted to knowing Gigaut.[66] Gigaut almost certainly fled Cuba at the time of La Escalera. The Military Commission sentenced him to death *in absentia*. The government did have success in capturing one of Gigaut's intimates, a *pardo* named Antonio Acosta, who had been previously implicated in a masonic conspiracy of 1823.[67]

A letter from Turnbull to Lord Aberdeen in 1846 confirms that Turnbull had had earlier Haitian connections. In this year, when rivalry in Texas, Oregon, and elsewhere threatened another war between Britain and the United States, Turnbull recalled that, in 1838 during his first tour of the Caribbean, he had visited Haiti and conversed with "some of the most intelligent and influential of the citizens," including then President Jean-Pierre Boyer, about how "much valuable assistance to the cause of freedom and humanity" Haiti might give. If war between Britain and the United States broke out, Turnbull proposed, in 1846, to help in the dismemberment of the United States at the vital point of New Orleans by calling on Haitian troops to raise Louisiana's slaves and free people of color.

If one or two of our West India Regiments, supported by a Haytian legion of some 10,000 men, and an adequate Steam Squadron . . . were entrusted with the means of arming the two oppressed classes of the native inhabitants, [the slaves and free-coloreds of Louisiana] the disaster of the last war at New Orleans [during the War of 1812] would in all probability be redressed.[68]

Thus Turnbull discussed abolitionism with prominent Haitians before his consulship in Havana. He might have first met Gigaut and General Santiago Mariño or drawn Haitians to Cuba. Contrary to what he said when cornered by Aberdeen in 1843, Turnbull, under some circumstances, would condone the use of violence as a means of forwarding abolitionism.

On the basis of José Erice's confession, Miguel Flores, the second of Turnbull's alleged agents, was convicted by the Military Commission of surreptitious movement to and from the British consulate. Erice did tell the truth about this. Flores worked in Havana as a free *moreno* leather-worker and operated under an alias. Consul Crawford knew him. Flores, as it turns out, was none other than Juan Rodríguez, the rebel who had visited him in 1843 about Turnbull and a petition for arms and munitions.[69]

Government authorities captured Flores, and, under interrogation, he implicated José de Luz y Caballero. The role in the Conspiracy by the liberal Creoles, in general, and Luz y Caballero, in particular, has undergone an energetic and largely successful critique by Francisco González del Valle. José Erice first implicated Luz y Caballero along with several other prominent liberal Creoles. Flores followed with accusations, although he almost certainly lied under the pressure of Pedro Salazar, the ruthless *fiscal,* who wanted corroboration of Erice's testimony. In later examinations by other officials, Flores denied most of what he was supposed to have initially declared to Salazar. González del Valle noted that for any white to have engaged in a conspiracy that, in the words of the Military Commission itself, aimed at "furious insurrection and bloodshed and extermination of all whites," defies reason.[70] Nor would Turnbull for all his abolitionist passion have embraced a conspiracy on these terms. The results in Matanzas of the Commission's proceedings against the accused whites testify to the weaknesses of these charges. Of the ninety-six whites brought before the Commission, eighty-two were acquitted, six received prison sentences that ranged from six months to eight years, five received lighter punishments, two were exiled, and only one was executed.[71]

The Military Commission and González del Valle failed to understand that the Conspiracy of La Escalera was not one "Conspiracy" but several conspiracies, each many years in gestation; each was volatile, each had its own distinct character, but they converged. Although Francis Ross Cocking may have exaggerated the importance of his own activities in Cuba and later lied about those of Consul Crawford, groups of dissident whites and people of color did indeed form by late 1841 or early 1842, and Cocking may well have tried to act as "an organ of communication" to join such forces. The key moment for the conjunction of these groups into a separatist movement would have come in 1841 and 1842, with Turnbull in the British consulate, with Palmerston and his ministry aggressively exerting pressure on a vulnerable Spanish regime to enact Turnbull's plan of emancipation, and with increasing slave resistance perceived to be tied to abolitionist maneuverings. Feeling backed into a corner, the white elite, not just those liberal intellectuals opposed to the slave trade, contemplated desperate measures and desperate alliances to save themselves and the slave property from which they profited. The external forces beyond their control seemed to be heading them to the realization of their omnipresent class and racial fears. If Cocking had stirred up the people of color with the prospect of white support, he would have disappointed them by the winter of 1842–1843, for no support was forthcoming. With Turnbull removed, Palmerston's ministry fallen, and reassurances forthcoming from Spanish officials, the external situation seemed much less threatening. Cuban whites regained some confidence in Spain's ability to secure life and property, and class and racial fears resumed their restraining influence on separatism.

Domingo Del Monte told bits of the story to Alexander Everett. In one letter of 12 July 1843, a few months after Cocking had left for England, Del Monte said he had "managed to break up the machinations of one of London's most active abolitionist agents."[72] In another letter, of 28 June 1844, he said:

The subsequent events have confirmed the precision of my calculations. In my letter to you of 20 November 1842, you have seen how an English agent wanted to compromise me greatly by communicating to me the fatal secret of their plans in order to raise our slaves; how he offered to make me chief of the revolution; how I, of course, not only rejected such a wild proposition but tried to dissuade the said agent [Cocking] from his diabolical plan, proving to him the impossibility of its success, and how mistaken he was in judging me capable of committing the madness of sacrificing the tranquility of my country and the existence of my race, to the liberty of the blacks; and how, in short, in the sorrowful impossibility in which I found myself of revealing these tremendous secrets with impunity to the executive authority of my country because of the lack of individual security, which is experienced within its institutions. I went to you so that by this means the President of the United States might know, and he might inform our government but without the source of the discovery even being remotely suspected, for I was also running the risk of being assassinated by any one of the conspirators. I did more: I dissuaded with my arguments some rash [white] youths whom that agent also wanted to compromise. I endeavored by means of the present British consul, Mr. Crawford, to expel the agent, now without resources, without hope, from the island as far too dangerous an uninvited guest. He actually left, and I even believed that everyone was now helped, because I also saw that Captain-General Valdés had taken prudent measures in order to impede the [slave] trade and the communications between Jamaica and Cuba. I consider these measures as beneficial results of my letter to you. But the seeds of rebellion that the agent had sown among the rash population of color—victim of the intrigues of the English—bore fruit or, better said, aborted in the way that you may know.[73]

From his prison cell, Manuel de Castro Palomino, in the same letter in which he mentions Gigaut, exclaimed:

The scoundrel Coking has been so lucky up until now that no one has mentioned him. . . . He will of course be very far from here laughing at all of us. God forgive him if he deserves it, he who in my view bears the greatest blame for all that is happening.[74]

Cocking's fall from favor with the people of color probably stemmed from his failure to deliver on promises he made for white support and shipment of munitions. The connections of Cocking and Turnbull to dissident Cubans, white or colored, once they left Cuba, Turnbull in 1842, Cocking in 1843, would seem to have been limited and, in Cocking's case, probably nonexistent. They had, however, stimulated a movement or, as Cocking admitted, several movements, which once in motion had lives of their own.

Who the rash young Creoles were, Domingo Del Monte did not say. But likely one of them would be Félix Tanco. Although his letters do not seem to have remained with the British and Foreign Anti-Slavery Society, Tanco along with several other Cuban liberals corresponded with it. The agent of transmission on at least one occasion was Consul Crawford, who explained to the Reverend J. H. Hinton, chief editor of the *British and Foreign Anti-Slavery Reporter,* "Mr. Ferrer at Santiago & Mr. Tanco at Matanzas are afraid of the risk of theirs [correspondence] being transmitted thro' the Island post office."[75] Letters from Tanco to Del Monte survive. They show him to be an ardent nationalist and antislavery advocate, frustrated by Creole passivity under Spanish rule and, for a time, in contact with Turnbull and Cocking. To Tanco, Spain was the most immoral and shameless of governments. He wholly despaired of the likelihood of the contraband slave trade ending under Spanish rule and began to question the efficacy of moral suasion in changing prevailing attitudes. Tanco told Del Monte after receiving a copy of the anti-slave-trade treaty of 1835 hammered out by Lord Clarendon,

What hope is there Señor Don Domingo that our land may be improved with literature, or with new town councils, or with civil governors, or with provincial deputations, or with assemblies, neither this nonsense or that nonsense, while they are stuffing us full of blacks everywhere. . . . May God permit that all these tribes of blacks be converted into tigers, bears, serpents and into every carnivorous and ravenous animal and not leave alive any of the wicked white race that lives in the Island.[76]

The government's claim of division within the free colored class between a smaller group of more moderate *pardos* and a larger group of more radical *morenos* seems clear. Cocking's confession points out that the "self constituted Committee at Havana to examine into the possibility of giving Independence to the Island of Cuba and thereby insure to the slave population their immediate emancipation from bondage" was actually "two Committees, there being one composed of white men, and another composed of Mulatto and Black Men."[77] Given the system of stratification by class and color in Cuba's slave society, rebels of whatever hue would have had to overcome formidable obstacles to recruit and mobilize forces. *Pardos* and *morenos* had a well-documented history of antagonism and separate development, much of it promoted by the Spanish government.[78] *Pardos* more closely identified with white culture and attitudes toward property; *morenos* generally had closer ties to the slaves.

The shared misery of Spanish rule made various alliances of color and class possible. But whites, *pardos,* and *morenos* would not have agreed on what should replace Spanish rule, to what extent change would extend beyond the Spaniards in power or the forms of imperial governance to the structure of society itself. Would change be confined to political elites? Or would the social hierarchy be torn down? Revolutionary movements invariably consist of a conjunction of disaffected social groups. Such questions furnish the rocks on which such movements can be dashed whether in the Europe of 1848 or the Cuba of 1844.

During the years of Turnbull's consulship, Cuban whites, both for and against slave emancipation, moved closer toward separatism, and the disposition of the free people of color in the struggle for liberation would

bear heavily on the outcome. The more conservative sensibilities of propertied free *pardos* made them a potential asset to white separatists interested in recruits and in trying to restrain the colored ranks as a whole.
Whites had actively sought free colored support in previous separatist
conspiracies, including the Black Eagle Conspiracy of 1829.[79] The approach of the Conde de Santovenia to Luis Gigaut in 1842, Consul Crawford reported to the Foreign Office in December of that year, appears to
have had no other purpose than to sound out a key free colored leader
about a political deal. Joseph Crawford had some sense of what was going on when he told Aberdeen that

> Many of the influential Creoles fearful of a deterioration in the value of their
> properties have had their principles of humanity overcome by their avarice
> and cannot resolve to emancipate altho' decided whenever they can to free
> themselves of Spanish Rule. Such men are assiduously trying to get the Brown
> free population to join in their projects and I am sorry to say that in some
> instances they have been successful.[80]

But Gigaut and his supporters showed little interest in separatism without emancipation. Liberal ideology had shaped their politics, and, encouraged by Turnbull and Cocking, they had early hopes of joining forces
with liberal whites like Del Monte and Luz y Caballero. In response to
government questions, Juan Francisco Manzano alluded to what Gigaut
was preaching to win colored converts, namely that Turnbull "in the
name of his government projected freedom for the slaves and the giving
to all people of color the rights that nature had given them."[81]

The events of late 1842 and early 1843 had to confront the free *pardos*
with hard political choices. Turnbull had gone; Cocking had failed to deliver: expectations of white support had proved empty. Boyer's regime
had fallen in Haiti and in the process had exposed great tensions there
between mulattoes and blacks. The free *pardos* could abandon their struggle for rights and an improved status or pursue them by coming to an understanding with the more radical *morenos,* as the government contended
they did. Still, the relations between the free *pardos* and *morenos* and
their relations with the slaves must have remained unsteady. Witness the
statements of the *moreno* Miguel Flores, alias Juan Rodríguez, as reported to Joseph Crawford in 1843, on the problems he had in control-
ling the movement, and on the unauthorized insurrection of one rebel
leader, apparently a slave, in the Cimarrones district of Cárdenas province
in March of that year.

The Military Commission specifically credited, in addition to José Erice,

Antonio Bernoqui with providing key details that allowed it to comprehend the broad outline of the conspiracy. That Bernoqui had close relations with Plácido and other prominent free people of color cannot be denied. Indeed, what makes his testimony particularly interesting is his connection with Plácido at the time of Plácido's arrest in Villa Clara in 1843. Among those documents the authorities said they discovered in his possession is the brief letter of introduction into which some scholars have read pregnant references to a conspiracy. It is addressed, as noted earlier, to a man named Martínez and thanks him for his interest "in the little affair" and tells him that "better days are soon coming." The author of that letter, as it turns out, is Antonio Bernoqui, who calls Plácido a "person of my friendship and confidence."[82]

At least a partial record of Bernoqui's testimony before the Military Commission went with the files of material shipped by O'Donnell to Spain and, from there, to the British Foreign Office. Upon close examination, it yields striking information on the course of relations between *pardos* and *morenos*. Bernoqui said he had been introduced to Luis Gigaut by Plácido in late 1841 or 1842, and that Gigaut had come to Matanzas as a self-professed agent of Turnbull to recruit fellow *pardos* to work for slave emancipation. He stayed in Matanzas a short time, spent most of it with Plácido, then returned to Havana. After Gigaut, the *moreno* Miguel Flores arrived in Matanzas around the middle of 1843 to meet with the same people. According to Bernoqui, a gathering of *pardos,* Bernoqui included, heard Flores say,

that his arrival had been with the same end that had brought the *pardo* Luis Jigó some time ago, but that he wanted to get together with all the people of color to see the number on whom he could count so that those who were encharged by Luis Jigó to unite people of color, this information would be given them in time to prepare the *pronunciamiento,* with the hope that no white would remain since they were going to bring down all those who might be in their way, that he had blank diplomas to reward those who might most distinguish themselves, that people and resources were counted on outside of this Island, supplied by the consul who had been here for three years, called Mr. Turnbull, and by others, and that these people and resources were made ready in order to support the conspiracy, as soon as it was pronounced. To such proposals all those in attendance told him that they were not entering such a project, since they had dealt with Luis Jigó on quite different matters.[83]

Flores returned to Havana, but the *pardos* of Matanzas noticed with discomfort growing unrest among the blacks. Bernoqui claimed that Flores had close relations with José Erice and that the two of them had spoken to the blacks about the revolutionary project. Bernoqui then went to Havana, saw Flores, and advised him not to return to Matanzas. Flores called the *pardos* stupid for their moderation. When asked if he had seen Gigaut in Havana, Bernoqui admitted he had and had told him of Flores's solicitations in Matanzas. Gigaut's reply, according to Bernoqui, had been that "Those are the affairs of blacks and in no way was he doing anything other than what he had previously arranged, that it should be so expressed to the others, and that he would go to Matanzas."[84]

Bernoqui could not say if Gigaut had lived up to his promise to return to Matanzas. When asked "if he thought there were many *pardos* and *morenos* comprehended in the projected revolution," Bernoqui replied: "The time has come to declare that by the conversations that he had had with Jigó he thought the plan is extensive and that there were enough people to count on, although on the part of the *pardos* the end is not so dreadful as those of the blacks who are many and generally agitated. For that reason there has not been nor can there be considered between both classes the necessary unity to proceed in accord, each following diametrically opposed paths."[85] When asked why the *pardos* had contemplated resistance at all, Bernoqui answered that the "little consideration they enjoyed in society" had moved them to form a conspiracy, that it was done to gain concessions from the whites "for destroying the blacks or balancing the forces," and that never did they have in mind to ally with the *morenos* "who by their ferocious disposition are enemies of all colors not their own."[86]

Bernoqui exaggerated, for a number of free *pardos* failed to follow the example of the Matanzas leadership. A *pardo-moreno* alliance did form, albeit weakened by *pardo* dropouts. What plan of action such an alliance had, as suggested by more than the government's documents, recalls Aponte's plan of 1812. If the free people of color were to have any chance of success, they had to seek support from the slaves, especially in the western districts where the proportions of free people of color were considerably less than in the east or in Cuba as a whole. A mass rising of the slaves in the Havana-Matanzas-Cárdenas black belt would draw troops away from the municipalities. Thus, rebel *pardos* and *morenos* would have extended the lines of communication to the countryside. There talk would have passed between leaders and potential recruits about land, liberty, riches, and power, since such demands would reflect the need to confer immediate and concrete benefits to followers of a mass movement.

On the plantations of every American slave society, the slave driver was the most prestigious field hand, a recognized authority within the slave quarters, a chief agent of acculturation for incoming Africans, and thus a logical instrument of recruitment.[87] That slave drivers functioned as the key instrument to raise the masses of African-born slaves is evidenced by what happened in November 1843 on Triunvirato and other plantations of the Sabanilla district.

The language used by people of color in their testimony to the Military Commission, the way they used such words as *libertad* (liberty), *derechos que la naturaleza les concede* (natural rights), *ciudadano* (citizen), *nación* (nation), *república* (republic), has a distinctly modern quality and hints at the kind of world the rebel leadership wanted to build in the aftermath of a successful revolution.

The declaration of Valentín Espinosa, a free *moreno,* is credible in what he says about Gigaut and Miguel Flores, about their contact with the British consulate, and about how the people of color had made a representation to the British government. It is corroborated in the independent testimony of Joseph Crawford to the British Foreign Office. Espinosa confessed that he knew of a conspiracy and that Miguel Flores had told him of Great Britain's working for Cuba's people of color "to make them prosper and to enjoy the rights of citizens." According to Espinosa, Flores saw the arrival of a British warship in Cuba as a sign that Britain was looking into the condition of the people of color and that it soon would help them take possession of "their legitimate rights."[88]

Félix Ponce, a free *pardo* carpenter, said he had been seduced into the conspiracy by Santiago Chávez, that is, Santiago Pimienta, the free mulatto son of Father Nicolás González de Chávez. Pimienta owned slaves and a ranch, La Paciencia, in Matanzas province. His brother-in-law was Andrés Dodge. That Pimienta knew Luis Gigaut well and had invited him to his house in the early 1840s can be established independently of the records of the Military Commission. Ponce knew that Pimienta was a rich man but one who "was disposed to sacrifice all his wealth for the liberty of slaves and to constitute this Island into a Republic equal to that in Santo Domingo."[89]

When people of color met they talked about politics both in their own country and the wider world. Jacobo Fernández, a free *pardo* mason, while accusing Turnbull of agitation, also refers to a gathering of free people of color in which discussions about the republics of South America, Santo Domingo, and Jamaica took place. Francisco Uribes, a free *pardo* tailor, apparently advised caution about the kind of freedom Turnbull was espousing, for "from letters that he had received from Jamaica he knew that those of color there were not pleased with their liberty and preferred slavery."[90]

Mobilization of the plantation slaves need not have and, for the most part, did not have the conversion of the African-born slave masses to those liberal-democratic notions that were influencing the colored leadership. A successful revolution does not require of a class what it requires of a vanguard. The followers of Miguel Flores showed themselves to be, as any successful revolutionary leadership must, simultaneously forward-looking and backward-looking. On one hand, they talked of forming a republic "where the blacks and mulattoes would form the laws."[91] Some intended to call the republic "Hatuey," like Haiti an Indian name, that of an Indian chief whose resistance to the Spanish conquest of Cuba got him burned at the stake. On the other hand, the followers of Miguel Flores in the countryside and on the plantations had to use the past to raise support. The primacy of *brujería* in plantation recruitment, referred to in the testimony of many slaves to the Military Commission, would be understandable since many African-born slaves would have blamed sorcery for their enslavement and thus would have looked to sorcery to undo it.[92]

The use of voodoo and voodoo priests by Toussaint L'Ouverture, not to mention his eventual move to put them down once he was in power, demonstrates both the possibilities and the dangers; why great revolutions are always a lengthy process. Had the people of color become sufficiently unified and powerful to execute a revolution in Cuba, the traditional, Africanized outlook and habits of the plantation soldiery, once unleashed, would undoubtedly have proved difficult for colored leaders of a more secular, Eurocentric vision to control. This would be especially true while factions vied for political ascendancy, and if certain leaders, reminiscent of Toussaint, had attempted to retain a plantation regime as essential for the economics of nation-building in opposition to a likely vision of freedom of the slave rank and file to reconstitute itself as a peasantry—to borrow Sidney Mintz's familiar concept—with a widespread distribution of land.[93]

The troubled relations between *pardos* and *morenos* in Cuba places the death of Plácido in a different perspective. The debate that has raged about him for so many years has tended to oscillate between extremes. "Is Plácido," as Emilio Roig de Leuchsenring wondered in 1944, "the eminent lyric poet, conspirator and propagandist of independence, civic patriot and man of dignity and decency or the contrary, a mediocre and servile poet, adulator of the whites and disdainful and depreciative of the blacks, a racist of little worth, against whom Spain committed a great crime, shooting an innocent."[94]

Plácido may not have led the Conspiracy of La Escalera or any other project but between the extremes are numerous other possibilities. No definitive answer can be reached from the existing evidence about precisely what relation Plácido had to the Conspiracy of La Escalera. Although one can question the credibility of the government's witnesses, certain circumstantial evidence bolsters the possibility of his involvement: the expression of nationalist and separatist sentiment in his poetry; his curious movements in the interior of western Cuba in 1843; his arrest in Villa Clara that year on the suspicion of subversion, along with Ramón Morejón, one of the two white men to be exiled by the Matanzas branch of the Military Commission and a man who would eventually return to Cuba as a follower of Narciso López.[95]

Francisco Jimeno, when asked for an opinion decades after La Escalera by Manuel Sanguily, scoffed at the Commission's judgment. Plácido may have had poetic genius; his poetry may evidence revolutionary sensibilities; and his marriage *saltatrás,* or down the social ladder, to a *moreno* woman in 1842 may have had some political meaning, but Plácido had not the stuff of which leaders or even soldiers are made. He may have had incidental contact with conspirators; he may have had incidental involvement in a conspiracy. But president of it—unlikely. According to Jimeno, Plácido was "weak and indolent," docile, a suckler of favor and money from elite whites.[96] Others who knew Plácido and who were more sympathetic than either Jimeno or Sanguily remember a "kindly" or "light-hearted" man, although they divide on whether Plácido was actually involved in La Escalera.[97] One white, whose prominent family hosted Plácido many times, remembered that he showed "respect to all those persons whom he considered socially superior" but was "a storehouse of hidden melancholy that in vain those who surrounded him daily tried to keep hidden."[98]

The acute analysis of Plácido's poetry by Jorge Castellanos and Enildo García should erase any doubts about Plácido's political imperative. The *fábula* "El Hombre y el Canario" [The man and the canary], tells of a caged canary who must deceive his enslaver to survive because to survive is to live to find the moment to free itself.[99] His dedicatory poem to the Mexican General Andrés de la Flor, given to him on his de-

parture from Cuba in 1839, explicitly connects Plácido to separatist politics. De la Flor was a Cuban by birth, from Matanzas, who in the early
1830s was sentenced to prison by the Military Commission along with
Francisco de Sentmanat for involvement in the Black Eagle Conspiracy.
Amid the words of praise and glorification of de la Flor, Plácido speaks
of the thousands of strong and intelligent men in Cuba "plunged into
inactivity and slavery," who "with courage and sword" could become
heroes of the Fatherland.[100] The reference at the end of the poem to
de la Flor's being "the heir of the spirit of Hatuey" represents the influence on Plácido—and if on Plácido probably other educated people of
color involved in La Escalera—of the so-called siboney literary movement, which took hold among Plácido's young, educated white countrymen and which served by its selection and romanticization of Indian
themes to attack Spanish rule and to inspire anticolonial thinking and
an indigenous nationalism.[101] This movement may explain why at least
some members of the colored leadership contemplated a nation called
"Hatuey." The presence of favorite sibonist words in the language of
the conspirators strongly suggests at least the indirect influence of Plácido. Ramón Vélez Herrera, alias El Vate, was a white contemporary of
Plácido and one of the leading figures in the sibonist movement. According to Juan Remos, a Cuban literary historian, Vélez Herrera "was
the true discoverer of the exceptional qualities of Plácido and encouraged
him and lent him books."[102]

Plácido may have had more fortitude than Jimeno and other com-
mentators understood. The evidence places him in close association with
Luis Gigaut. Plácido opened his home to him, attended parties with him,
and escorted him around Matanzas. Under interrogation, Plácido admitted
"that he had always been friends with Jigo [sic] but circumspect because
his expressed ideas coincided . . . with those of Domingo Del Monte
and the British consul."[103] He denied that he had any knowledge of
conspiratorial activity. The Military Commission confronted Plácido with
Bernoqui's testimony about attending the meeting in the house of Jorge
López, the free pardo painter, in which Gigaut defined his antislavery
mission. Plácido answered "that he had formed the best opinion of his
friend Bernoqui to the extreme of not doubting a point of his veracity
but that Gigaut could have very well acted in those terms without his
hearing it or his fixing his attention on that subject."[104] For Plácido to
have lived with Gigaut as close friends without any such knowledge
would have seemed as doubtful if not implausible to an impartial jury
as it did to the Military Commission.

Credible evidence exists that Plácido had some involvement with Gigaut and his activities but insufficient evidence exists that Plácido was guilty of the Commission's charges. Plácido denied them up to the moment of his execution. He could have done so with a clear conscience, for the kind of conspiracy the government charged him with leading— a racist "project of furious insurrection and bloodshed and extermination of all whites"—was not his way. Plácido had shown no obvious racial hatred of whites. Indeed, he was mostly white himself and spent much time with white intellectuals and patrons and had many white friends. If anything, his politics, like Gigaut's, desired to ally liberal whites with *pardos* to end slavery and win Cuba's independence. To judge by his poetry, Plácido was motivated far more by feelings of nationalism, of *cubanidad,* than by color prejudice.[105]

To be sure, Plácido had ties to the *moreno* community. Indeed, María Gila Morales, his *morena* wife, was the sister-in-law of José Erice, the free *moreno* militiaman who had given such important testimony before his suicide.[106] How much Plácido knew of the activities of the *moreno* conspirators is unclear, and he may well have parted company with them after their radicalization. Under interrogation, he denied explicitly any association with Miguel Flores.[107]

There were references to Plácido by thirty-two government witnesses. Plácido was the most famous person of color in Cuba. Plantation slaves and rural free people of color who were interrogated made clear that they knew the name of Plácido even if they had never seen him. His name would have proven valuable to rebel agents in their recruitment drives. His reputation and ability to move around Cuba would certainly have qualified him to be a courier or messenger, as the documents found on him after his arrest in Villa Clara in 1843 strongly suggest. What role Plácido had could have been exaggerated or distorted as months passed, the relations between *pardos* and *morenos* shifted, and word of the plotting traveled from mouth to mouth. Certainly Plácido's fame made him a prime target for government officials bent on teaching an unforgettable lesson to the people of color. Following Plácido's release from a jail in Trinidad, where he had been transferred after his arrest in Villa Clara, the region's governor had warned Garciá Oña in a letter of 15 November 1843 to watch Plácido carefully because he was a suspicious character dangerous to Spanish rule. As early as 1 February 1844 government agents had talked about the need to suppress his poetry.[108]

While in the hands of the Military Commission, Plácido was said to have given a lengthy revelation, naming names, fifty-five names to be exact, among them Domingo Del Monte, José de la Luz y Caballero, Benigno Gener, Félix Tanco, "El Consul Inglés," and "Gigot," the *pardo,* but, significantly, not Miguel Flores or Flores's alias, Juan Rodríguez. He talked, critics charge, without having a lash put to him and for an empty promise to be spared execution. Domingo Del Monte and his fellow white liberals blamed Plácido for their subsequent troubles with the authorities. Subsequent generations of interpreters picked up the denunciations of Plácido. Francisco Jimeno believed that Plácido incriminated Del Monte and members of his circle because that circle, "where the flower and cream of our writers gathered," held Plácido in contempt for his deficiencies of character and unjustifiably proclaimed Juan Francisco Manzano's poetry superior to his.[109]

Plácido deserves better. He made his revelation under severe pressure, most likely from the notorious *fiscal* Pedro Salazar. It is dated 23 June 1844, five days before his execution and almost five months after his original detainment. He had already undergone numerous interrogations, lived incommunicado for months in a miserable cell, and knew execution to be coming in days.[110] Even if he revealed what is attributed to him without taking stripes, he would have done so under extreme physical and psychological duress.

The records sent by O'Donnell to Spain leave an impression of Plácido's character that differs markedly from that suggested by Jimeno. Plácido seems to have been evasive during many interrogations before June 23. He admitted to a knowledge of the antislavery ideas of Turnbull and Gigaut and thought Del Monte shared these ideas. He knew of Del Monte's contact with Turnbull but said that he had turned down Del Monte's solicitation of a poem that would "praise the British government for the humane role it was playing in seeking the end of slavery."[111] Interrogation of Plácido began only in March, after Antonio Bernoqui and several other people of color had talked. Bernoqui was spared execution. Plácido was not. O'Donnell refused to suspend Plácido's death sentence because he deemed his revelation to be unimportant. "I only see in that writing," he told García Oña, "a stubborn man who insists on his innocence despite the superabundant proof of thirty-two witnesses who have testified against him in the proceedings."[112]

For all the debate about Plácido's fortitude, about his execution and how he faced death, the words of T. M. Rodney, the United States consul in Matanzas demand quoting for he was an eyewitness and hardly the most sympathetic one: "Mr. Cross and I went out to see some 11 poor wretches shot this morning. Placido was one, he sustained himself like a man and died true game, the first fire he received three balls but did not kill him and he sang out tira (fire) (adios mundo) good by world."[113]

The circumstances under which Plácido gave testimony raise questions about whether his revelation or anything in it can be taken at face value, whether the words are Plácido's or Pedro Salazar's. The content itself offers clues. It is less a precise, coherent delineation of plotting and plotters than a rambling mélange of recollections of many years that attest to the long-standing discontent of several Cuban social groups. The very imprecision and disjointedness of his revelation, the choice of words and the details of the recollections, and his continued and total maintenance of his innocence suggest that Salazar could have done better. Thus, by and large, Plácido is speaking.

Despite disjointedness and, at times, unintelligibility, the testimony admits to the existence of widespread plotting and fractious relations among several distinct but intertwined groups. It begins by thanking Salazar for his "generous offer" to intercede with Captain-General O'Donnell on Plácido's behalf in exchange for his knowledge about the conspiracy but adds in the next paragraph:

It will be useless, Sir, in my opinion, however much energy the Government may employ in order to find the prime mover of these events in the classes of *pardos* and *morenos*. They are nothing more than some blind instruments of older and more profound machinations managed by hands much more powerful and capable than those of these automatons.

The confession goes on to say that white separatists had actively sought the support of the free *pardos* and has Domingo Del Monte in several meetings with Plácido, in effect to recruit Plácido, and with Plácido, the *pardos,* to the latest in a series of white efforts to raise Cuba in a revolt for independence. It recalls Francisco de Sentmanat's activity in the 1820s to ignite an independence movement and his dramatic appearance in Havana in 1843.

The appearance of Sentmanat in Havana precisely fourteen days before the uprising of the blacks [in Sabanilla in November 1843] when it was said that a general of known valor and reputation was coming to put himself in charge of the affairs: Will the blacks and mulattoes be the ones who had coordinated these events? Would Plácido, who in order to transport himself to Matanzas had to sell six chickens that he brought to give for lack of money, be the one who might be connected with men who still do not count on the *pardos* for their plans? Ah, Sir! There is here a strong and masterful hand. How many cups of Champagne will be consumed now in praise of the victims who will be sacrificed in order to exasperate these classes [of *pardos* and *morenos*] which neither can unite among themselves by the natural antipathy that they profess for each other nor ally themselves in any hidden machination by the impossibility that exists of their keeping a secret among themselves.

The revelation has an explicit denial of Plácido's ever having mixed with slaves. It charges that the "true seducers" of the people of color were "those ideas of equality." Talk "of the time when hierarchies would disappear," when people of color could enter a public café "as men who were without any other difference than the accident of their color" had also proved compelling.

The result of all this is that Jorge Bernoqui, Santiago [Pimienta], and perhaps some others whom I don't know, deluded by Gigo into thinking that the up-risings of the slaves might put the whites in the necessity of giving to the *pardos* the betterment that they sought, always uniting themselves to the whites because they could not doubt that with the blacks any type of agreement was impossible. . . . It seems that [José] Erice and his [*moreno*] comrades had designed a bloody plan worthy of them, and perhaps influenced by the English consul [David Turnbull], very different from the one of the *pardos*—who in this one would be the first victims. My relations with Jorge Bernoqui and Pimienta and the fatal reputation that my verse had given me has made some firmly believe that I was director, and others, being certain that it is not this way, it is convenient for them to say they believe it. The result is that all say it, and the Government, which did not find anyone else in whom to fix the blame with greater probability and convinced by what the proceedings [of the Military Commission] brought forth, will say judiciously that if anyone was the head of this thing, it is I. From what has been said one can deduce that six [five] plans existed, namely, the abolitionist, which is more of a religious sect than a hostile party; the independents; the *pardos* deceived by them; the free blacks who have formed themselves from information gathered without any other support other than their strong desire to destroy everyone; and the slaves who want to be free.[114]

Del Monte learned of Plácido's revelation after he had left the United States for Paris. Along with the slander of the slave traders it was causing much trouble for the relatives Del Monte left behind in Cuba. José Luis Alfonso, Del Monte's brother-in-law, told him that "your friendship and relations with this accursed Englishman [Turnbull] not only have compromised you to the point of closing the doors of this country to you permanently but has exposed all of us who bear the name Alfonso or Aldama to the most unjust persecution."[115] Del Monte went to a Paris newspaper with a letter defending himself and his family against the accusations and rumors. He neatly omitted any reference to Francis Ross Cocking or contact with any English agents. He never mentioned how he dissuaded rash young Creoles from involvement in a conspiracy. He explained, truly enough, that he, his wife, his family, his friends were white, among the elite of Cuba, people who drew their economic life-blood from the plantation system. He was not a lunatic, and only lunacy would explain why he would instigate people of color to overthrow the social order with fire and sword, to kill white men and ravish white women, as he had been accused. To be sure, he championed the end of Cuba's slave trade and advocated the use of free white labor.

But I also know that this grand ideal cannot be secured with either violence or the precipitation of revolutionary measures, that the spirit of morality, religion, philosophy will gradually gain ground in the souls of the Spanish Cubans, and they must hope that the Queen of the Antilles would not be another Haiti, another Jamaica, condemned by an evil fate to be eternally inhabited and possessed by one of the most backward races of the human family. . . . I do not want my country to have slaves and even less that these slaves be blacks, that is from such a savage branch of the human family.[116]

The evidence against him, Del Monte added, hardly qualified as such since it had been extracted under torture. As for Plácido, his chief accuser, Del Monte claimed to have met him once and only once, in 1835, when Plácido sought to borrow money.[117]

Unlike Plácido, Del Monte did win acquittal, in 1846, but he never returned to his beloved Cuba. He died in Madrid in 1853. One of his letters to Alexander Everett suggests at least a partial explanation of why he stayed away: "the fear of assassination by some black who believed me a traitor to a cause to which I never belonged."[118]

The evidence does not permit the ending of all uncertainty about the events of La Escalera and the people entangled in them. One might hope that Luis Gigaut had kept a record of his activities in Cuba and that one day someone will find it. What can be said now with reasonable certainty is that the "Conspiracy of La Escalera" existed as several conspiracies, each having distinct cores of whites, *pardos, morenos,* or slaves, each overlapping, if only in some cases at the margin, each dilating or contracting at particular times between 1841 and 1844. British abolitionism and abolitionists, as reflections of a new world order based upon free labor, directly and indirectly inspired and hence encouraged the formation of all the conspiracies. Spanish authorities and Cuban planters saw the resultant unrest as a single conspiracy and as a real threat to the existing social and imperial arrangements.

Even if the entire mountain of testimony gathered by the Military Commission is dismissed as being tainted by the indisputable corruption of some government officials and their savage methods of interrogation, the words of Domingo Del Monte to Alexander Everett, the sworn testimony of Pedro José Morillas to the United States government, and the many letters of Consul Joseph Crawford to Lord Aberdeen remain. Testimony from Francis Ross Cocking corroborated by the statements of Miguel Flores, alias Juan Rodríguez, to Consul Crawford establishes a connection between country-wide plotting of the people of color and the March 1843 plantation uprising in Cárdenas province. The proximity in time and place of the various outbreaks of resistance in the Sabanilla district in November and December of 1843 and their proximity, in turn, in time and place to the Cárdenas uprising, strongly suggest a similar connection. Numerous bits of evidence, some from eyewitnesses, indicate that the character of the resistance had changed. In 1843 and 1844 colored rebels were sounding different from the past; they were acting different. Normally antagonistic ethnic groups had now suppressed their differences. Talk of natural rights, citizenship, and liberty came from their lips. David Turnbull and the liberal-democratic ideas for which he stood had indeed inspired the people of color to seek to control their own destiny. Joseph Bidwell of the British Foreign Office, who knew Turnbull well, concluded, "there is no Evidence to prove that Mr. David Turnbull was not cognizant of and did not encourage Mr. Cocking in his Labours. It is believed that he did encourage the movement: Altho' he denies it."[119]

Spain emerged from the events of 1844 with its hold on Cuba tightened for several decades. The slave system remained intact and profitable. Sugar production recovered and the average annual output for the 1850s more than doubled the level for 1840. After 1844, government officials and slave traders had to rethink the African slave trade seriously, and fewer than two thousand slaves per year entered Cuba in the next four years. Traders and planters would try to replace slaves by importing poor whites and indentured Chinese. But by 1853 the slave trade returned to the level of 1840 and would again soar to more than 20,000 slave imports per year by the last years of the decade. By 1860 a prime male *bozal* had almost tripled his 1840 value to more than $1,000.[120] Economic indicators for the 1850s say that Cuba's slave system was not disintegrating and that La Escalera had little lasting effect on its economic performance. But they hardly tell the whole story.

How much O'Donnell's decimation of Cuba's colored leadership contributed to a twenty-year period of relative calm can only be speculated upon. But like the economy, the free colored class would recover and the social tensions and ideological contradictions revealed in 1844 would again resurface after 1868 during thirty years of political and military struggle for Cuban independence. La Escalera's dead would be resurrected as protomartyrs. Plácido's poetry lived on to the dismay of future authorities, who tried to suppress it as subversive of the imperial order. For decades after his death, as Bernardo Costales recalled, the government considered it a crime "to recite his verses, to pronounce his name, to consecrate his memory."[121] The exigencies of war forced Spain into implementing a program of gradual emancipation. The Moret Law of 1870 granted freedom to all slaves born after 1868 and to all slaves more than sixty years old. Eventually slavery was replaced by a patronage system whereby slaves, now called *patrocinados,* worked for stipends to be used for gradual self-purchase. If the program had worked as intended, all *patrocinados* would have become free men and women in 1888. But because of the initiatives of the slaves themselves, the authorities could not fully control the process. The royal decree of 7 October 1886 recognized that fact by freeing the few remaining *patrocinados.*[122]

Outside of Cuba, the events of La Escalera would add weight to the arguments of Northern expansionists like Alexander Everett and Southern particularists, like John C. Calhoun, against the imperialist designs of Britain and for the immediate annexation of Texas. Southerners worried about the Africanization of Cuba would find it easier to talk to equally worried Creoles about annexation. Persons in touch with the events of La Escalera from both Cuba and the United States would reappear as principals in the filibustering adventures of Narciso López at the end of the decade. Narciso López's design for Cuban annexation by the U.S. emerged during the process of La Escalera and, contrary to what many scholars have believed, before the coming of Leopoldo O'Donnell ended López's tenure of Cuban offices. Both Esteban Santa Cruz de Oviedo and Francisco Hernández Morejón would eventually become involved in the annexationist movement and be arrested for it.[128] British and United States abolitionists would mine the events of La Escalera to fuel their attacks against slavery and to claim homage for Cuba's colored martyrs for freedom. David Turnbull would continue to campaign against the evils of the Cuban slave trade and Cuban slavery as a judge on the Court of Mixed Commission in Jamaica, a post he appears to have held until shortly before his death in Paris in 1851.[124] Martin Delany, an early antebellum champion of black nationalism, would use Plácido and Cuba as the centerpiece of his novel *Blake*. First published in its entirety as a serial in 1861, it depicts the Africanization of Cuba by a revolution of the people of color as part of an international struggle of black people for freedom and dignity.[125] As the Conspiracy of La Escalera had international roots, so did it have international results.

APPENDIX I

The Slave Code of 1842

1. Every slaveholder shall instruct his slaves in the principles of the Holy Roman Catholic Apostolic Religion so that those who have not been baptized may be baptized, and in case of the danger of death, he shall baptize them, since it is known that in such cases anyone is authorized to do so.

2. The aforesaid instruction shall be given at night at the end of work, and immediately afterwards the slave shall recite the rosary or some other devout prayers.

3. On Sundays and feast days of obligation after fulfilling their religious obligations, slaveholders or those in charge of the estates shall employ the slaves for two hours to clean the houses and workshops, but no longer, nor occupy them in the labors of the landed property, except in harvest time when delay is impossible. In such cases they shall work the same as on week days.

4. [Slaveholders] shall heed their responsibility to those slaves already baptized who have arrived at the proper age to administer the sacraments to them, whenever the Holy Mother Church requires it or whenever it may be necessary.

5. [Slaveholders] shall put forth the greatest attention and diligence possible in making them [the slaves] understand the obedience that they owe to the constituted authorities, the obligation to show reverence to the clergy, to respect white persons, to behave well with the people of color, and to live harmoniously with their companions.

6. Masters shall necessarily give their slaves in the country two or three meals a day as they may think best, provided that they may be sufficient to maintain them and restore them from their fatigues, keeping in mind that six or eight plantains or its equivalent in sweet potatoes, yams, yuccas, and other edible roots, eight ounces of meat or salt fish, four ounces of rice or other pottage or meal is standardized as daily food and of absolute necessity for each individual.

7. [Masters] shall give them two suits of clothes a year in the months of December and May, each consisting of a shirt and pants of nankin or linen, a cap or hat, and handkerchief; in December shall be added alternatively a flannel shirt one year and a blanket for protection during the winter the next.

8. Newly-born or small slave children, whose mothers are sent to work in the field, shall be fed very light food such as soups, *atoles* [a pap made from corn flour], milk, and similar substances until they are weaned entirely and have finished teething.

9. While the mothers are at work, all children shall remain in a house or room that all sugar estates and coffee estates should have, which shall be under the care of one or more female slaves, as the master or administrator may deem necessary, according to the number of children.

10. If [slave children] shall become sick during the lactation period, they shall be nursed by the breasts of their own mothers, who shall be exempted from fieldwork and applied to domestic duties.

11. Until they reach the age of three years, [slave children] shall have shirts of striped gingham; from age three to six they may be of nankin. The girls of six to ten shall be given skirts or long dresses, and the boys of six to fourteen shall be provided with trousers. After these ages the dress shall be like the adults.

12. In ordinary times slaves shall work nine or ten hours daily, the master arranging these hours as best he can. On sugar plantations during harvest time, the hours shall be sixteen, arranged in such a way that the slave shall have two hours in the day to rest and six at night to sleep.

13. On Sundays and on feast days of obligation and in the hours of rest during the week days, slaves shall be permitted to employ themselves within the estate in mechanical labors or occupations, the product of which shall be for their own benefit in order to be able to acquire the means to purchase their freedom.

14. Male and female slaves older than sixty years or less than seventeen shall not be obliged to do strenuous work, nor shall any of these classes be employed in work not appropriate to their age, sex, strength, and constitution.

15. Those slaves who because of their age or because of sickness are not fit for work shall be maintained by their owners, who shall not be permitted to give them their freedom in order to get rid of them, unless they provide them with sufficient means, according to the dictates of justice and the determination of the *procurador síndico,* so that they may be able to support themselves without need of other assistance.

16. Every estate shall have a depository reserved for the placement of the instruments of labor, the key of which shall never be entrusted to a slave.

17. On leaving for work each slave shall be given the instrument he needs for the labor of the day, and later, as he returns, it will be taken from him and locked up in the depository.

18. No slave shall leave the property with any instrument of labor, much less arms of any kind, unless accompanied by his master or overseer or the family of either, in which case he may carry his machete and nothing more.

19. Slaves of one estate shall not be able to visit those of another without the express consent of the masters or overseers of both. When they have to go to another estate or leave their own, they shall take a written pass from the owner or overseer with the description of the slave, the date of the day, month, and year, the declaration of his destination, and the time he must return.

20. Any individual of whatever class, color, and condition he may be is authorized to arrest any slave if he is met outside of the house or lands of his master; if he does not present the written license he is obliged to carry; or if, on the presentation, it shows that the bearer has manifestly changed the route or direction described or the leave of absence has expired. The individual shall conduct said slave to the nearest estate, whose owner shall receive him and secure him and notify the slave's master, should he be from the same district, or the *pedaneo* [district magistrate], so that he may give notice to the interested party in order that the fugitive slave may be recovered by the person to whom he belongs.

21. Owners and overseers of the plantations shall not receive any remuneration for the fugitive slaves that they shall apprehend or deliver according to the aforesaid article, since it is a service that the proprietors are reciprocally obliged to loan and redounds to their private advantage.

22. The master shall have to pay, besides the cost of food, the cost of medical treatment, should it be necessary, and all other costs, as expressed in the same fugitive slave law.

23. Masters shall permit their slaves modest amusement and recreation on festival days after they [the slaves] have complied with their religious obligations, but without leaving the plantation or joining with slaves of any others. They shall make do in open places and in full view of their owners, overseers or foremen, until sunset or until the bell rings for evening prayer and no longer.

24. Owners and overseers shall be charged particularly to watch vigilantly in order to restrain excessive drinking [among the slaves] and the introduction of slaves from another estate and free men of color into the amusements.

25. Masters shall take great care to construct for unmarried slaves spacious dwellings in a dry and ventilated area, with separation of the two sexes, well closed and secured with key, in which a light shall be kept burning all night. Where means permit, they shall have a separate dwelling for each married couple.

26. At the sleeping hour (which in a long night shall be at eight and in a short one at nine) the slaves' roll shall be called so that only the watchmen shall remain outside, one of which shall be appointed to see to it that everyone keeps silent and to inform the master or overseer of any disturbance on the part of his companions, of any intruders, or of any other important occurrence.

27. On each plantation there shall be a room well-closed and secured for each sex and two others besides for contagious diseases where slaves who may fall sick shall be attended in severe cases by physicians and in slight cases, where household remedies are sufficient, by male or female nurses, but always with good medicine, proper food, and with the greatest cleanliness.

28. The sick shall be placed, where it is possible, in separate beds that consist of a straw mattress, mat, or *petate* [a mat made of palm leaves], pillow, blanket, and sheet, or on boards sufficiently convenient for the healing of individuals that lie on them, but in all cases raised from the floor.

29. Masters of slaves shall avoid the illicit contact of both sexes and encourage marriages. They shall not prevent marriages made with slaves of other owners, and they shall give to married couples the means of living under the same roof.

30. To accomplish this end and so that the consorts may fulfill the ends of matrimony, the wife shall follow the husband whose master shall buy her at a price that may be suitable to both sides or else by arbiters appointed by both sides or by a third party in case of disagreement. If the master of the husband does not want to buy the wife, then her owner shall have the power to buy the husband. In the event that neither of the owners want to make the purchase, then the married slaves shall be sold together to a third party.

31. When the master of the married male slave buys the wife, he shall also buy all her children under three years old, since according to law the mothers are obliged to suckle and nurse them until they attain that age.

32. Masters shall be obliged by the magistrates to sell their slaves when they have injured them, badly treated them, or committed other excesses contrary to humanity and the rational way with which they should be treated. The sale shall be made in these cases at the price fixed by the arbiters of both sides, or by a magistrate in case one of these should refuse to name a price, or by a third person in case of disagreement, when it may be necessary. But if there is a buyer who wants to purchase them without arbitration at the price fixed by the master, then the sale shall be made in his favor.

33. When masters sell their slaves for their own convenience or at their own determination, they shall be at liberty to fix any price that pleases them, according to the greater or lesser estimation of them.

34. No master shall oppose the *coartación* of his slaves if they present at least fifty pesos of their price on account.

35. Slaves *coartados* shall not be sold for a higher price than that fixed in the last *coartación,* and this condition shall pass from buyer to buyer. However, if the slave desires to be sold against the will of his master without just cause or by his bad conduct gives cause to be sold, the master may add to the price the amount of the sales tax and the cost of the deed of sale.

36. As the benefit of *coartación* is very personal, the children of the moth-

ers *coartadas* cannot be participants in it, and they can be sold like any other slave.

37. Masters shall free their slaves as soon as they put together the amount of their evaluation as legitimately fixed. The price, in case the interested parties do not agree, shall be named by an arbiter appointed by the owner of the slave or in his absence by a magistrate, another by the *procurador síndico* representing the slave, and a third chosen by said magistrate in case of disagreement.

38. The slave who may discover any conspiracy plotted by another of his class or by any persons of free condition to disturb the public order shall receive his freedom and besides a reward of five hundred pesos.

If the informers should be many and present themselves in such a way as to show that the last ones did not know that the disclosure had already been made, then all such informers shall receive their freedom, and the reward of five hundred pesos shall be divided equally among them.

When the denunciation makes reference to a conspiracy of slaves or to the project of some cunning slave or free man against the owner, his wife, children, relations, the administrator, or overseer on the estate, owners are recommended to be generous with the servant or servants who have so well fulfilled the duties of a good and faithful servant, as it is much to their advantage to offer an encouragement to loyalty.

39. The price of freedom and the reward referred to in the first paragraph of the previous article shall be taken from the fund that results from fines imposed by infractions of this law or any others ordered by the government.

40. Slaves shall also acquire their freedom when it is granted them in a will or by any other legally justified means that proceeds from an honest and praiseworthy motive.

41. Slaves shall be obliged to obey and respect their owners, administrators, overseers, and all other superiors as heads of the family and to fulfill the tasks and works given them. He that shall fail in any of these obligations shall be and ought to be punished by whomever is in charge of the plantation according to the type of failing or transgression, with imprisonment, shackles, cudgel, or stocks, which shall confine by the feet and never the head, or with flogging, which must never exceed twenty-five lashes.

42. When a slave shall commit grave excesses or some crime for which the penalties referred to in the previous article may not be sufficient, he shall be bound and presented before the magistrate so that in the presence of his master, should he not give him up to justice, or before the *procurador síndico,* should he give him up and chooses not to continue the proceedings, [the slave] may be proceeded against according to law. In case the owner did not relinquish or submit the slave to justice, and he is condemned to the payment of damages and costs toward a third party, the owner shall be responsible for

the same, which will not exempt the slave from bodily punishment or another type as the crime may merit.

43. Only owners, administrators, or overseers shall be able to punish slaves, with the moderation and under the penalties aforesaid. Any other person who may do so without the express mandate of the owner or against his will and cause any wound or injury shall become liable under the penalties established by the laws. The case may be opened at the instance of the owner or in his absence at the instance of the *procurador síndico,* as the protector of slaves, unless the transgression should be such as to affect the public good, or, officially, if it should pertain to this last category.

44. The owner in charge or his subordinate on the estate who may disobey or infringe any of these rules shall be fined twenty to fifty pesos the first time, from forty to one hundred pesos the second time, and from eighty to two hundred pesos the third time, according to the greater or lesser importance of the infringed article.

45. Fines shall be paid by the owner of the estate or person who has been guilty of the negligence or infraction. In case he is not able to pay because of lack of funds, he shall suffer a day in jail for each peso that he has been fined.

46. If the offense of the owners or those encharged to manage slavery on the estates should consist of the excessive use of punishment causing slaves grave contusions, wounds, or mutilation of limbs, or other serious injury, besides the monetary fines already cited, the person who may have caused the injury shall be prosecuted criminally at the instance of the *procurador síndico,* or officially, so as to impose on him the penalty commensurate with the crimes committed. The owner shall be obliged to sell the slave, if he is still able to work, or to give him his freedom, if he is disabled, and to pay him during his lifetime a daily stipend which the magistrate shall determine sufficient for his food and clothing, payable monthly in advance.

47. Fines shall be applied in this manner: a third part of their amount to the magistrate or judge who imposes them and the remaining two-thirds to the fund that is to be formed in the political administration of each district for the cases named in article thirty-eight, to be delivered under receipt, to the secretary's office at that administration.

48. The lieutenant-governors, magistrates, and *pedaneos* shall see to the punctual observance of these regulations and shall be inevitably responsible for any omissions or excesses.

Source: Translated from the *Bando de gobernación y policía de la isla de Cuba . . .* (Havana, 1844), 59–68.

Slave Regulations of 1844

PART A (ESTATE REGULATIONS):

1. The owners of slaves destined for agricultural labor shall take care that those [slaves] under their dominion are instructed by the administrator, overseer, or steward of each estate in the principles and mysteries of our holy religion, that they comply properly with the precepts of the church, and that they receive the blessed sacraments from the parish priest.

2. Said masters, using completely the full authority that the laws give them over their slaves, as the only means to keep them in subjection, shall order that through the said employees [i.e., administrators, overseers, or stewards] they [the slaves] shall be given food, clothing, and assistance during their sickness to the extent that individual prudence deems suitable. Likewise said slaves may be punished when delinquent, with the lash or imprisonment in the quantity and for the time that the employee or person encharged considers consonant with the instructions that for each case he has received from the master, who in no case should apply the lash himself and who upon ordering it, should incline to moderation rather than excess.

3. They [the owners] shall instruct said administrators, overseers, or stewards: 1) to close doors or door-jambs after prayers every night of the year until dawn and to place on the estate a patrol, commanded by a white man; 2) not to leave the estate any day of the year, except to discharge some business of the owner or except with the express permission of the owner; 3) to arrest and send to the district judge any person of color, free or slave, and any suspicious-looking white man who comes on to the estate without a letter or paper signed by the person who sent him and the same for any peddlers; 4) to watch vigilantly, under the strictest responsibility of the employees of the estates, the conduct of the free people of color.

4. When any death, wound, or symptom of insurrection occurs on the estate, they [the owners] shall order said administrators, overseers, and stewards to notify the district magistrate immediately so that he can make the necessary preliminary investigation of the incident.

5. They [the owners] shall order only whites to be employed as carters,

muleteers, porters, and as any other person who, in the business of the estate, has to leave its boundaries.

6. They [the owners] shall have on each estate, however large it may be, a number of white employees corresponding to five percent of its colored laborers.

PART B (GENERAL REGULATIONS):

1. All *emancipados* on the island who have finished their civil and religious education and instruction shall be taken by the government as soon as they have been placed in liberty in order to furnish them with the provisions and means to leave the country in the same manner and form that Her Majesty, who shall be informed, decides.

2. There shall be a general investigation of the free men of color who live in the Island and who do not have employment, property, or a known means of subsistence so that they may be judged by special tribunals as vagrants, prejudicial to society.

3. After a given length of time, all foreign-born free people of color shall be expelled.

4. There shall be punctual and rigorous compliance with the existing prohibition on the disembarkation of any person of color, free or slave.

5. The local authorities shall watch vigilantly the conduct of the people of color who rent land in the country.

6. The prohibition on people of color who gather together without the permission of the local authority shall be strictly observed, and any crime that they commit against the whites shall be severely punished.

7. On no account shall people of color be employed in the apothecaries, nor even make the simplest prescription.

8. In the country, in accordance with the investigation and report of the respective local authorities, all taverns that for their bad local situation, the lack of invested or liquid capital, show themselves incapable of contributing to the public utility shall be suppressed, after I [i.e., the Captain-General] have been advised and given my permission.

9. The sale of aguardiente in the country, wholesale or in any other way, is prohibited and is only permitted in urban areas.

10. The owners of estates contiguous to each other shall be urged to employ clergymen of known virtue to instruct their respective blacks in our holy religion and in the obligations of morality, obedience, and submission, which the laws and society impose on them and oblige them to defend.

Source: Translated from José María Zamora y Coronado, *Biblioteca de legislación ultramarina en forma de diccionario alfabético,* 7 vols. (Madrid, 1844–49), 3:139–141.

Notes

Archives and Collections

AGI	Archivo General de Indias, Seville
AHN	Archivo Histórico Nacional, Madrid
Estado	Sección de Estado
Ultramar	Sección de Ultramar
AMAE	Archivo del Ministerio de Asuntos Exteriores, Madrid
ARC	Amistad Research Center, New Orleans
ACC	Amistad Case Collection
BL	Bancroft Library, University of California, Berkeley
FSPC	Francis Samuel Philbrick Collection
BM	British Museum, London
BPL	Boston Public Library
CIH	Centro de Investigaciones Históricas, Universidad de Puerto Rico
EMHL	Eleutherian Mills Historical Library, Greenville, Delaware
HL	Houghton Library, Harvard University
EC	Escoto Collection
ECS	Escoto Collection Supplement
HML	Hill Memorial Library, Louisiana State University
HSD	Historical Society of Delaware, Wilmington
RC	Rodney Collection
HSP	Historical Society of Pennsylvania, Philadelphia
HTML	Howard-Tilton Memorial Library, Tulane University
HUL	Huntington Library, San Marino, California
LC	Library of Congress, Washington, D.C.
DDC	Domingo Del Monte Collection
MHS	Massachusetts Historical Society, Boston

AEP	Alexander Hill Everett Papers
ENP	Everett-Noble Papers
NYHS	New-York Historical Society, New York City
NYPL	New York Public Library, New York City
SC	Schomburg Collection
PL	Perkins Library, Duke University
PRO	Public Record Office, Kew, England
CO	Colonial Office Records
FO	Foreign Office Records
RHL	Rhodes House Library, Oxford University
BFASP	British and Foreign Anti-Slavery Society Papers
USNA	United States National Archives
DC	Despatches from United States Consuls
DISM	Diplomatic Instructions of the Department of State. Special Missions
MLDS	Miscellaneous Letters of the Department of State
VHS	Virginia Historical Society, Richmond

Journals

BAN	Boletín del Archivo Nacional (Havana)
GC	Gaceta del Caribe
HAHR	Hispanic American Historical Review
JGSWGL	Jahrbuch fuer Geschichte von Staat, Wirtschaft und Gesellschaft Lateinamerikas
JIH	Journal of Interdisciplinary History
RBC	Revista bimestre cubana
RBNJM	Revista de la Biblioteca Nacional José Martí
RC	Revista cubana
RH	Revista de la Habana
RJ	Revista de jurisprudencia
RUH	Revista de la Universidad de la Habana
USMDR	United States Magazine and Democratic Review
WMQ	William and Mary Quarterly

Terms for Describing Archival and
Documentary Material

exp.	expediente (file)

leg.   legajo (bundle)
RG   Record Group

INTRODUCTION:
LA ESCALERA AND THE HISTORIANS

1. Clara Cutler Chapin, "Plácido: Centenary of a Cuban Poet," *Bulletin of the Pan American Union* 78 (June 1944):318; *Scott Standard Postage Stamp Catalogue,* 139th ed., 4 vols. (New York, 1982), 2:648.
2. *Granma,* 28 July 1974. Translations, unless otherwise stated, are the author's.
3. Joaquín Llaverías, "Introducción," in *Diccionario geográfico de la isla de Cuba* by José de J. Márquez (Havana, 1926), 5–18; Francisco Calcagno, *Diccionario biográfico cubano* (New York, 1878–1886), 404–5; Ramón Eduardo Ruiz, *Cuba: The Making of a Revolution* (New York, 1970), 119.
4. José de J. Márquez, "Plácido y los conspiradores de 1844," RC 20 (1894): 35–51, 97–121, 247–64, esp. 35–47.
5. José Ferrer de Couto, *Los negros en sus diversos estados y condiciones; tales como son, como se supone que son, y como deben ser* (New York, 1864), 74–80; José de Ahumada y Centurión, *Memoria histórico política de la isla de Cuba* (Havana, 1874), 235–43; Justo Zaragoza, *Las insurreciones en Cuba: Apuntes para la historia política de esta isla en el presente siglo,* 2 vols. (Madrid, 1872–1873), 1:536–51.
6. Manuel Sanguily, "Un improvisador cubano (el poeta Plácido y el juicio de Menéndez Pelayo)," *Hojas literarias* 3 (February 1894): 93–120; idem, "Otra vez Plácido y Menéndez Pelayo (reparos á censuras apasionadas)," *Hojas literarias* 3 (March 1894):227–54. See also idem, *José de la Luz y Caballero (estudio crítico)* (Havana, 1890). For biographical information on Sanguily, see José Antonio Rodríguez García, *Manuel Sanguily* (Havana, [1926]).
7. Manuel Sanguily, "Una opinión en contra de Plácido (notas críticas)," *Hojas literaria* 4 (August 1984):425–35, esp. 435.
8. For criticism of Sanguily's view of Plácido, see, e.g., Tomás Carrión, *A vuela pluma. Haití, Plácido y Manuel Sanguily* (Havana, 1894), 13–40.
9. Vidal Morales y Morales, *Iniciadores y primeros mártires de la revolución cubana* (Havana, 1901), 129–77, esp. 147–77.
10. Ibid., 154.
11. Cf. his "Examen del proyecto de inmigración de aprendices africanos," RJ 1 (1856):157–58, 163 with his "Plácido," RC 2 (December 1885):547–61, esp. 555. On his family connections to Vidal Morales, see Francisco Xavier de Santa Cruz y Mallén, *Historia de familias cubanas,* 8 vols. (Havana and Miami, 1940–1986), 1:216, 223; 3:63–64.
12. Ibid., 1:223; Vidal Morales to Francisco Jimeno, 11 August 1882, EC, box 20, HL; fragment of letter, Morales to Jimeno, [?], EC, box 20.
13. See Jimeno to Sanguily, 22 January 1886 and [?] April 1886 (copies), SC, NYPL. These letters are reprinted in Ángel César Pinto Albiol, *El pensamiento filosófico de José Martí y la revolución cubana* (Havana, 1946), 137–76.
14. Jimeno to Morales, 23 July 1882, in Pinto, *Pensamiento,* 149–59. See Santa

Cruz y Mallén, *Familias cubanas,* 4:399–400; Fermín Peraza Sarausa, *Diccionario biográfico cubano,* 2nd ed., 14 vols. (Gainesville and Coral Gables, Fla., 1965–1966), 12:45–46, for biographical information on Jimeno.

15. Morales to Jimeno, 11 August 1882, EC, box 20, HL.

16. Joaquín Llaverías, *Historia de los archivos de Cuba,* 2nd ed. (Havana, 1949), 165–67; Robert Freeman Smith, "Twentieth-Century Cuban Historiography," HAHR 44 (February 1964):47.

17. Calcagno, *Diccionario,* 437; Academia de la Historia, *Centón epistolario de Domingo Del Monte,* 7 vols. (Havana, 1923–1957), 1:x; Peraza, *Diccionario,* 3:75–76.

18. His *Nociones de historia de Cuba* was published in eight editions from 1904 to 1945.

19. *El Álbum; numero extraordinario en obsequio de Plácido,* 28 June 1904, esp. Pío D. Campuzano, "Algo sobre Plácido," n.p.

20. See, for example, the articles in *La Lucha* and *La Discusión,* 18 March 1909, and *El Figaro,* 21 March 1909.

21. On this point see Duvon C. Corbitt, "Señor Joaquín Llaverías and the Archivo Nacional de Cuba," HAHR 20 (May 1940):283–86, and Smith, "Cuban Historiography," 52.

22. Fernando Ortiz Fernández, *Hampa afro-cubana: los negros esclavos; estudio sociológico y de derecho público* (Havana, 1916), 434–35.

23. "Extracto de una comunicación de Francis Ross Cocking á Lord Palmerston . . . con fecha 24 de Enero de 1852," BAN 3, no. 5 (1904):3–9; 3, no. 6 (1940):1–9. See also "Comunicación del Secretario de Estado de España . . . sobre maquinaciones revolucionarias," BAN, 3, no. 4 (1904):17–20; 3, no. 5 (1904):1–2; "Traslado de una importante comunicación reservada del ministro español en Washington al Capitán General de Cuba," BAN, 5, no. 3 (1906):41–45.

24. "Documentos para la historia de la conspiración de 1844," *Yucayo,* [?] December 1909 to [?] January 1910. I am indebted to Enildo García for allowing me to examine his copies of these issues.

25. On Escoto, see William Belmont Parker, ed., *Cubans of To-Day* (New York, 1919), 139–41.

26. Carlos M. Trelles, *Biblioteca histórica cubana,* 3 vols. (Matanzas, 1922–1926), 1:268.

27. Enildo García is working on a catalogue of the Escoto Collection. For a preliminary sketch of its holdings, see his "Cuba en la obra de Plácido (1809–1844): análisis y bibliografía comentada" (Ph.D. diss., New York University, 1982), 212–16. Escoto left behind letters in Cuba. I cannot be sure that the letters at Harvard are the ones referred to by Trelles, although I strongly believe this to be the case.

28. Dolores María de Ximeno, "Aquellos tiempos . . . Memorias de Lola María," RBC 19 (November–December 1924), 449. The *Revista bimestre cubana* serialized the memoirs of Dolores María de Ximeno y Cruz from 1924 to 1929. For Plácido and the events of 1844, see vol. 19 (1924), 374–76, 446–54, esp. 448–49. Her memoirs were also published as *Aquellos tiempos . . . memorias de Lola María* in vols. 6 and 7 of the *Colección cubana de libros y documentos inéditos o raros . . .* ed. Fernando Ortiz, 11 vols. (Havana, 1913–1932).

29. Francisco González del Valle, *¿Es de Plácido la Plegaria a Dios? Discurso de*

recepción leído ante la Academia de la Historia el 16 de julio de 1923 (Havana, 1923).

30. Francisco González del Valle, *La Conspiración de la Escalera. I. José de la Luz y Caballero.* (Havana, 1925), 7. The discourse was first published as "José de la Luz y Caballero en la conspiración de 1844," in *La vida de la Academia de la Historia (1924–1925)* (Havana, 1925), 39–93. For biographical information on González del Valle, see Santa Cruz y Mallén, *Familias cubanas,* 5:128–29; Peraza, *Diccionario,* 2:58.

31. The *Centón epistolario de Domingo Del Monte* was eventually published by the Cuban Academy of History in seven volumes, from 1923 to 1957. Figarola-Caneda died after editing the first three. His studies of Plácido include *Milanés y Plácido. Réplica al Sr. Federico Milanés* (Havana, 1914) and *Plácido (poeta cubano). Contribución histórico-literaria* (Havana, 1922).

32. González del Valle, *Conspiración de la Escalera,* 29.

33. Ibid., 32.

34. Ibid., 34.

35. See, e.g., the letter of Elías Entralgo, Chair of Cuban History at the University of Havana, to Benjamin Frederick Carruthers, 17 April 1941, in Carruthers's "The Life, Work and Death of Plácido" (Ph.D. diss., University of Illinois, 1941), 259.

36. Ramiro Guerra y Sánchez, *Manual de historia de Cuba (económica, social y política)* (Havana, 1938), 412–24; Herminio Portell Vilá, *Historia de Cuba en sus relaciones con los Estados Unidos y España* (Havana, 1938), 336, 343–45; idem, *Narciso López y su epoca,* 3 vols. (Havana, 1930–1958), 1:151.

37. Roberto P. De Acevedo and Benito Alonso y Artigas, "Nuevas noticias y documentos acerca del poeta Plácido," *El País,* 25 January 1941, 12.

38. Entralgo to Carruthers, 17 April 1941, in Carruthers, "Plácido," 259–60.

39. José Manuel de Ximeno, "Un pobre histrión (Plácido)," in *Primer Congreso Nacional de Historia,* 2 vols. (Havana, 1943), 2:371–77. See also idem, "Apuntes para la historia constitucional de Cuba. Los complicados con Plácido," *Libertad nacional,* 4 May 1944.

40. Cited in José Manuel Pérez Cabrera, "Plácido y la Conspiración de 1844" RH 2, no. 24 (August 1944):534.

41. Duvon C. Corbitt, "Cuban Revisionist Interpretations of Cuba's Struggle for Independence," HAHR 43 (August 1963):398–99; Smith, "Cuban Historiography," 49–50; Sheldon B. Liss, *Roots of Revolution: Radical Thought in Cuba* (Lincoln, Neb., 1987), 74–83.

42. Sagua la Grande, Cuba. Instituto de Segundo Enseñanza de Sagua la Grande. *El Seminario de redacción del Instituto de segundo enseñanza de Sagua la Grande, fundado y dirigido por Ana María Arissó, rinde homenaje a Plácido en el centenario de su muerte* (Sagua la Grande, [1944]), 58–69. For a good earlier example of Placidiana, see Carlos A. Cervantes, "Bibliografía Placidiana," RC 8 (April–June 1937):155–86. The best current bibliography of works by and about Plácido can be found in Enildo A. García, *Cuba: Plácido, poeta mulato de la emancipación (1809–1844)* (New York, 1986), 189–228.

43. Jorge Casals Llorente, *Plácido como poeta cubano; ensayo biográfico crítico* (Havana, 1944).

44. Jesús Saíz de la Mora, "El poeta Plácido," RH 2, no. 22 (June 1944):86–104.

45. José Antonio Portuondo, "Plácido, 1844," GC 1 (March 1944):22–23; Elías Entralgo, "La personalidad angular de Plácido," GC 1 (July 1944):4; idem,

"Aponte y Plácido," GC 1 (June 1944):32; José A. Ramos, "Una muerte que no debe olvidarse," GC 1 (July 1944):5–7. Enildo García kindly allowed me to examine his copies of these articles.

46. Leopoldo Horrego Estuch, *Plácido, el poeta infortunado* (Havana, 1944).

47. Pérez Cabrera, "Conspiración de 1844," 530–39.

48. Congreso Nacional de Historia. Tercer. *La colonial hacia la nación* (Havana, 1946), 57–58, 75–81.

49. Ibid., 77–78.

50. Emilio Roig de Leuchsenring. "A una centuria de la conspiración de la Escalera y el fusilamiento de Plácido," *Carteles,* 23 July 1944, 38–39, and "Una revisión contemporánea de 'Plácido,'" *Carteles,* 30 July 1944, 38–39.

51. Pérez Cabrera, "Conspiración de 1844," 534–39. Neither Rafael Estenger, "Plácido," RBC 52 (July–December 1943):18–34, nor Adrián del Valle, "Esclavitud y anexionismo en Cuba," RBC 55 (January–February 1945):29–41, esp. 33–35, mention Ximeno.

52. Ángel Augier, "Silueta de Plácido," *Bohemia,* 4 July 1948, 50, 82. This article appears to have been first published in *Policía,* [Volume not known] (May 1944), 3, 25.

53. Leopoldo Horrego Estuch, "En defensa de Plácido, réplica y esclarecimiento," *Bohemia,* 8 August 1948, 30, 93. See also his "Plácido y la conspiración," *Mensuario de arte, literatura, historia y crítica* (June 1950):6, 19. For Augier's response, see "Realidad y posteridad de Plácido o una defensa sin lugar," *Bohemia,* 12 September 1948, 12, 114–15. I address the question of the authenticity of Plácido's revelation in chapter 9.

54. *Historia de la nación cubana,* ed. Ramiro Guerra y Sánchez, et al., 10 vols. (Havana, 1952). See also Corbitt, "Revisionist Interpretations," 402.

55. Cf., e.g., pp. 71–72, written by José M. Pérez Cabrera, derived from his earlier essay on the Conspiracy (see note 40), and pp. 318–19, written by Elías Entralgo.

56. Mario Hernández y Sánchez-Barba, "David Turnbull y el problema de la esclavitud en Cuba," *Anuario de estudios americanos* 14 (1957):292. His research assistants were Lydia Cabrera and María Teresa de Rojas. See Cabrera, *Reglas de Congo. Palo monte mayombe,* 2nd ed. (Miami, 1986), 45.

57. Louis A. Pérez, Jr., "In the Service of the Revolution: Two Decades of Cuban Historiography, 1959–1979," HAHR 60 (February 1980):79–89, esp. 80.

58. Nicolás Guillén, "El Faro Plácido," *Hoy,* 22 May 1962 and the following issues: May 24, 27, 29, 30, 31; June 3, 5, 9, 12, 14. See also José Luciano Franco *Plácido; una polémica que tiene cien años y otros ensayos* (Havana, 1964), 7–19.

59. Renée Méndez Capote, *Cuatro conspiraciones* (Havana, 1972), 99.

60. Leonardo Griñan Peralta, "La defensa de los esclavos," in *Ensayos y conferencias* (Santiago de Cuba, 1964), 69.

61. Humberto Castañeda, "El caso de Mr. David Turnbull, el consul inglés," RUH 168–69 (July–October 1964):127–53, esp. 150.

62. Pedro Deschamps Chapeaux, *El negro en la economía habanera del siglo XIX* (Havana, 1971), 25. See also his articles republished in Deschamps Chapeaux and Juan Pérez de la Riva, eds., *Contribución a la historia de la gente sin historia* (Havana, 1974), 5–27, 55–110. For a similar perspective on the events of 1844, see Rita Llanes Miqueli, *Victimas del año del cuero* (Havana, 1984), which is dedicated to Deschamps Chapeaux.

63. Cf. *Hoy,* 30 May 1962, with *Hoy,* 5 June 1962.

64. José Luciano Franco, "La rebeldías negras," in *Tres ensayos* (Havana, 1951), 88.

65. Ibid., 107.

66. José Luciano Franco, "Introducción al proceso de la Escalera," BAN 67 (January–December 1974):54–63, esp. 54–55. See also his "La conjura de los negreros," in *Ensayos históricos* (Havana, 1974), 193–200; "Origen y consecuencias de la sublevación de los esclavos en 1843," *Granma*, 12 September 1973; *La gesta heroica del Triunvirato* (Havana, 1978).

67. Daisy Cué Fernández, "Plácido y la conspiración de la Escalera," *Santiago*, no. 42 (June 1981):145–206, esp. 151. This essay has been substantially reprinted in *Acerca de Plácido*, ed. Salvador Bueno (Havana, 1985), 427–83.

68. Cué, "Plácido," 163.

69. Rodolfo Sarracino, "Inglaterra y las rebeliones esclavas cubanas: 1841–1851," RBNJM 28 (May–August 1986):81.

70. Ibid., 80–82. Cf. David R. Murray, *Odious Commerce: Britain, Spain and the Abolition of the Cuban Slave Trade* (Cambridge, Eng., 1980), 159–180, and Robert L. Paquette, "The Conspiracy of La Escalera: Colonial Society and Politics in Cuba in the Age of Revolution" (Ph.D. diss., University of Rochester, 1982), esp. 34–66, 184–203. Sarracino's study contains a number of factual errors. For example, David Turnbull had not worked as a member of the Mixed Commission in Havana before becoming British consul. He had not written his 1840 polemic against the Cuban slave trade, *Travels in the West*, "as a representative of the Anti-Slavery Society of London." Captain-General Tacón had not attempted to remove Turnbull from Cuba because Tacón had left the Captain-Generalcy well before Turnbull arrived as consul.

71. Walterio Carbonell, "Plácido, ¿Conspirador?" *Revolución y cultura*, no. 2 (February 1987):57. I am indebted to Rebecca Scott for bringing this essay to my attention.

72. Smith, "Cuban Historiography," 44.

73. See, e.g., [Maria Weston Chapman], "Placido," *Liberty Bell* (1845), 67–71; "Placido-Cuba-Liberty," *New York Tribune*, 18 August 1847; Amelia E. Barr, "Placido: Slave, Poet, and Martyr," *The Christian Union* 8 (July 1873): 62–63; William Wells Brown, *The Black Man, His Antecedents, His Genius, and His Achievements* (New York, 1863), 88–90; "Signs of the Times," *The Harbinger*, 1 May 1847; [William H. Hurlbert], "The Poetry of Spanish America," *North American Review* 68 (January 1849):145–53; R. R. Madden, *The Island of Cuba . . .* (London, 1849), 107–8. As Frederick S. Stimson, *Cuba's Romantic Poet: The Story of Plácido* (Chapel Hill, N.C., 1964), 92–102, has pointed out, this literature should be pursued with caution since it contains many exaggerations and errors.

74. Arthur A. Schomburg, "An Epoch in Cuba's Struggle for Liberty: Plácido," *The New Century*, 25 December 1909. See also the references to Plácido in *Calendar of the Manuscripts in the Schomburg Collection of Negro Literature* (New York, 1942), 214–15, 249–50, 300, 338.

75. Carruthers, "Plácido"; Stimson, *Cuba's Romantic Poet*.

76. Duvon C. Corbitt, "A Petition for the Continuation of O'Donnell as Captain General of Cuba," HAHR 16 (November 1936):537–43.

77. Frank Tannenbaum, *Slave & Citizen. The Negro in the Americas* (New York, 1947); Stanley Elkins, *Slavery: A Problem in American Institutional and Intellectual Life* (Chicago, 1959). See also Joseph C. Miller, *Slavery: A Worldwide Bibliography, 1900–1982* (White Plains, N.Y., 1985).

78. Philip S. Foner, *A History of Cuba and Its Relations with the United States,* 2 vols. (New York, 1962–1963), 1:214–28, esp. 217.
79. Ibid. See also Franco, "Proceso de la Escalera," 55.
80. Hugh Thomas, *Cuba: The Pursuit of Freedom* (New York, 1971), xxi.
81. Ibid., 200–6, esp. 203–6.
82. Herbert S. Klein, *Slavery in the Americas: A Comparative Study of Virginia and Cuba* (Chicago, 1967), 193–222, esp. 221.
83. Ibid., 221–22. In this and subsequent quotes Klein fails to accent some Spanish names. His reference to "the so-called Placido conspiracy" is misleading because this is not the customary term in Cuba. Klein also errs in saying that José Erice informed Captain-General O'Donnell about the Conspiracy in January and that Erice's confession could not be corroborated.
84. Herbert S. Klein, *African Slavery in Latin America and the Caribbean* (New York, 1986), 212. On p. 213 Klein presents as the total number of those executed by all the military courts the number of persons executed as conspirators in only one judgment of the Matanzas branch of the Military Commission. His generalization that "in all its aspects the Placido conspiracy had much in common with the Denmark Vesey plot in the United States in 1831 [1822]" is mistaken.
85. Cf. Corwin, *Spain and the Abolition of Slavery in Cuba, 1817–1886* (Austin, Texas, 1967), 81, n. 44, with Klein, *Slavery in the Americas,* 221, n. 52. The source to which both refer is José M. Pérez Cabrera, in *Historia de la nación cubana,* 4:71–72.
86. Corwin, *Abolition of Slavery,* 81.
87. Franklin W. Knight, *Slave Society in Cuba during the Nineteenth Century* (Madison, Wis., 1970), 81, 96.
88. Ibid., 81, n. 72.
89. On this point see Morales to Jimeno, 11 July 1882, EC, box 20, HL. Also Morales, *Iniciadores,* 150; Castañeda, "David Turnbull," 149.
90. *Cuba desde 1850 á 1873. Colección de informes, memorias, proyectos y antecedentes . . . que ha reunido por comisión del gobierno D. Carlos de Sedano y Cruzat* (Madrid, 1873), 15. Accents are as in original.
91. Knight, *Slave Society,* 95.
92. Gwendolyn Midlo Hall, *Social Control in Slave Plantation Societies: A Comparison of St. Domingue and Cuba* (Baltimore, 1971), 57–62, esp. 58, n. 19.
93. Ibid., 61.
94. Murray, *Odious Commerce,* 159–80, esp. 172, 178.
95. Ibid., 172–73.
96. Jorge Castellanos, *Plácido, poeta social y político* (Miami, 1984); García, *Poeta mulato.*
97. Franklin W. Knight, "Plácido and Cuban History during the Nineteenth Century," in García, *Poeta mulato,* 15.
98. Eugene D. Genovese, *From Rebellion to Revolution: The Afro-American Slave Revolts in the Making of the Modern World* (Baton Rouge, 1979); Michael Craton, *Testing the Chains: Resistance to Slavery in the British West Indies* (Ithaca, N.Y., 1982), esp. 14, 330–34; David Patrick Geggus, *Slave Resistance Studies and the Saint Domingue Slave Revolt: Some Preliminary Considerations* (Miami, 1983); idem, "The Enigma of Jamaica in the 1790s: New Light on the Causes of Slave Rebellions," WMQ 44 (April 1987):276, 298–99.
99. David Barry Gaspar, *Bondmen & Rebels: A Study of Master-Slave Relations*

in Antigua with Implications for Colonial British America (Baltimore, 1985): xiv.

100. E. J. Hobsbawm, *The Age of Revolution, 1789–1848* (New York, 1962), xv.

1. LAND, COLOR, AND CLASS

1. Herman Merivale, *Lectures on Colonization and Colonies, Delivered before the University of Oxford in 1839, 1840 & 1841* (London, 1861), 35.
2. I have relied on Manuel Mereno Fraginals, *El ingenio: complejo económico social cubano del azúcar*, 3 vols. (Havana, 1978) 3:43–44, for the figures on sugar production. See Susan Schroeder, *Cuba: A Handbook of Historical Statistics* (Boston, 1982), 400–1, for statistics on the value of Cuban commerce in the nineteenth century.
3. Ramón de la Sagra, *Historia económico-política y estadística de la isla de Cuba ó sea de sus progresos en la población, la agricultura, el comercio y las rentas* (Havana, 1831), 122, estimates the land in cultivation for 1827 at 38,276 *caballerías;* the *Cuadro estadístico de la siempre fiel isla de Cuba, correspondiente al año 1846 . . .* (Havana, 1847), places the land in cultivation in 1846 at 65,677 *caballerías.* One *caballería* equals about thirty-three acres. A convenient source of colonial Cuban census data with analysis is Kenneth F. Kiple, *Blacks in Colonial Cuba, 1774–1889* (Gainesville, Fla., 1976).
4. A good introduction to the study of the geography of Cuban soils is Leví Marrero, *Elementos de geografía de Cuba* (Havana, 1946), and vol. 1 of his *Cuba: economía y sociedad*, 13 vols. to date (Madrid, 1972–). See also Alexander von Humboldt, *The Island of Cuba*, trans. J. S. Thrasher (New York, 1856), 124–49.
5. Hugh Thomas, *Cuba*, 18, says Cuba has no snakes. It does have snakes but no venomous snakes. The *majá*, from the boa family, is Cuba's largest snake and happily lethargic. In fact, *majá* is a Cubanism for lethargic.
6. For my description of Cuban municipalities, I have relied on Dan Stanislawski, "Early Spanish Town Planning in the New World," *Geographical Review* 38 (January 1947):94–105; Francisco González del Valle, *La Habana en 1841* (Havana, 1952); Marrero, *Economía*, 8:241–50; José María de la Torre, *The Spanish West Indies, Cuba and Porto Rico. Geographical, Political, and Industrial*, trans. Richard Swainson Fisher (New York, 1855), 87–88; Joaquín E. Weiss, *La arquitectura colonial cubana*, 2 vols. (Havana, 1979) 1:11–28, 60–63, 86–87; 2:1–30.
7. Torre, *Spanish West Indies*, 80.
8. Alexander Hill Everett to Lucretia O. Everett, 19 December 1840, in Alexander Hill Everett, *Prose Pieces and Correspondence*, ed. Elizabeth Evans (St. Paul, 1975), 237–38.
9. For my description of Havana, I have relied on González del Valle, *Habana,* 79–140; Lolo de la Torriente, *La Habana de Cecilia Valdés* (Havana, 1946), 23–66; *Cuadro estadístico . . . 1846*, p. 53; Emilio Roig de Leuchsenring, *La Habana: apuntes históricos* (Habana, 1939), 47–48; *New York Herald,* 12 November 1842; *The Daily Picayune* (New Orleans), 23 June 1843, 13 October 1844; [?] Bienvenue to Armand Bienvenue, 17 March 1848, Bienvenue Family Papers, HML; Weiss, *Arquitectura*, 2:31–89; [John G. F. Wurdemann], *Notes on Cuba . . .* (Boston, 1844), 28–32.
10. Raymond A. Mohl, ed., "A Scotsman in Cuba, 1811–1812," *Americas* 29

(October 1972):239; Thomas, *Cuba*, 147; Journal of Sir John Maxwell Tylden, 5 March 1815, NYPL; Journal of Eulalia Keating, 28 March 1839, Papers of the Bauduy family, EMHL; N. Jarvis, "Journal of a trip from Boston to Havana . . . 1832 & 1833," 10 January 1833, HUL.

11. Frances Erskine Calderón de la Barca, *Life in Mexico: The Letters of Fanny Calderón de la Barca*, ed. Howard T. Fisher and Marion Hall Fisher (Garden City, N.Y., 1966), 21. See also Thomas, *Cuba*, 147, and José Antonio Saco, *La vagancia en Cuba*, reprint ed. (Havana, 1946), 53.

12. For the transformation of Cuba into a plantation society, see Marrero, *Economía*, vols. 1–10; Moreno, *El ingenio*, vols. 1–3; Knight, *Slave Society*, 3–24; Roland T. Ely, *Cuando reinaba su majestad el azúcar. . . . El monocultivo en Cuba, origen y evolución del proceso* (Buenos Aires, 1963), 55–115; Allan Kuethe, *Cuba, 1753–1815: Crown, Military, and Society* (Knoxville, 1986). On the size of the nineteenth-century Cuban slave trade and the role of Spanish merchants, see David Eltis, *Economic Growth and the Ending of the Transatlantic Slave Trade* (New York, 1987), 55–56, 245.

13. Herbert Klein, *The Middle Passage: Comparative Studies in the Atlantic Slave Trade* (Princeton, N.J., 1978), 209–27; Philip D. Curtin, *The Atlantic Slave Trade: A Census* (Madison, Wis., 1969), 36–43, 244–49; David Eltis, "The Direction and Fluctuation of the Transatlantic Slave Trade, 1821–1843: A Revision of the 1845 Parliamentary Paper," in *The Uncommon Market: Essays in the Economic History of the Atlantic Slave Trade*, ed. Henry A. Gemery and Jan S. Hogendorn (New York, 1979), 285–86. Klein, *Middle Passage*, 220, suggests the connection between the slave-trading voyages and the sugar harvest.

14. Martínez to Ángel Jimenez, 26 September 1838, FO 84/234, PRO. This series and FO 84/98 contain a number of such documents seized by British cruisers from Cuban slavers.

15. Joseph John Gurney, *A Winter in the West Indies, Described in Familiar Letters to Henry Clay of Kentucky* (London, 1841), 209; Pedro Diago to Juan González Cepeda, 12 June 1829, FO 84/98; Martínez to Andrés Ynsua, 16 June 1828, FO 84/98; A. Everett to L. Everett, 19 December 1840, in Everett, *Prose Pieces*, 234–35; Ortiz, *Hampa afro-cubana*, 164–68.

16. On the price of slaves in Cuba circa 1840, see Ortiz, *Hampa afro-cubana*, 174; Hubert H. S. Aimes, *A History of Slavery in Cuba, 1511 to 1868* (New York, 1907), 267–68; *Fourth Annual Report of the British and Foreign Anti-Slavery Society* (London, 1843), 146; Eltis, *Economic Growth*, 263. I have checked these numbers against the advertisements of slaves for sale in the *Diario de la Habana* for 1840 to 1845. Humboldt estimates the rate of seasoning deaths in *Ensayo político sobre la isla de Cuba*, trans. J. B. de V. Y. M., new ed., 2 vols. (Havana, 1930), 1:115–60. See also Kenneth F. Kiple, *The Caribbean Slave: A Biological History* (Cambridge, Eng., 1984), 64–65, and Richard Sheridan, *Doctors and Slaves: A Medical and Demographic History of Slavery in the British West Indies, 1680–1834* (Cambridge, Eng., 1985), 131–34.

17. Ortiz, *Hampa afro-cubana*, 25–62; Curtin, *Atlantic Slave Trade*, 245–49; Cabrera, *Reglas*, 13–27; Pedro Deschamps Chapeaux, "Cabildos solo para esclavos," *Cuba* 7 (1968):50–51.

18. Ortiz, *Hampa afro-cubana*, 25–62; Wurdemann, *Notes*, 257–58; Condesa de Merlin María de las Mercedes Santa Cruz y Montalvo, "Les esclaves dans les colonies espagnoles," *Revue des deux mondes* 36, quatrième série (1841):753,

761; Abiel Abbot, *Letters Written in the Interior of Cuba . . . 1828* (Boston, 1829), 14; Henri Dumont, *Antropología y patología comparadas de los negros esclavos* (Habana, 1922), 14–50.

19. William R. Bascom, "Yoruba Acculturation in Cuba," *Memoire de l'Institut Français de l'Afrique Noire* 27 (1953):163–67, and "The Yoruba in Cuba," *Nigeria* 37 (1937):14–20; Harold Courlander, "Musical Instruments of Cuba," *The Musical Quarterly* 28 (April 1942):227–31. Manuel Moreno Fraginals, "Africa in Cuba: A Quantitative Analysis of the African Population in the Island of Cuba," in *Comparative Perspectives on Slavery in New World Plantation Societies,* eds. Vera Rubin and Arthur Tuden (New York, 1977), 189.

20. Juan Francisco Manzano, *The Life and Poems of a Cuban Slave,* ed. Edward J. Mullen (Hamden, Conn., 1981), 80.

21. Computed from data in *Cuba, resumen del censo de población de la isla de Cuba á fin de año de 1841* (Havana, 1842). For the growth of the free colored population from 1774 to 1841, see the data in Kiple, *Blacks,* 84–91.

22. F. W. P. Greenwood, "Slavery in Cuba," *Christian Examiner,* 23 (1837):92.

23. Hiram Hastings to Daniel Webster, 8 December 1842, DC, Trinidad, Cuba, RG 59, USNA.

24. "Un interrogatorio absuelto por el Capitan General Don Francisco Dionisio Vives," in José Antonio Saco, *Historia de la esclavitud desde los tiempos mas remotos hasta nuestros días,* 2nd ed., 6 vols. (Havana, 1936–1945), 5:380–81. See also the favorable comments on free colored industriousness by the outspoken French racist A. Granier de Cassagnac, *Voyage aux antilles, françaises, anglaises, danoises, espagnoles . . . ,* 2 vols. (Paris, 1842–1844), 2:366–67.

25. "Resumen general," in *Cuadro estadístico . . . 1846,* 10; [Robert Francis Jameson], *Letters from the Havana during the Year 1820; Containing an Account of the Present State of the Island of Cuba, and Observations on the Slave Trade* (London, 1821), 10. Articles 34 and 93 of the *Bando de gobernación y policía de la isla de Cuba . . .* 2nd ed. (Havana, 1842), 14, 26, suggest the suspicions of rural peddlers in general. See also the "Modificaciones" appended to the *Bando,* p. III.

26. Verena Martínez-Alier, *Marriage, Class and Colour in Nineteenth-Century Cuba: A Study of Racial Attitudes and Sexual Values in a Slave Society* (Cambridge, Eng., 1974), 1–99.

27. Peter Boyd-Boyman, "Patterns of Spanish Emigration in the Indies until 1600," HAHR, 56 (November 1976):580–604. For the genealogies of the Cuban elite, see Santa Cruz y Mallén, *Familias cubanas,* vols. 1–8, and the more limited but frequently more careful Rafael Nieto y Cortadellas, *Dignidades nobiliarias en Cuba* (Madrid, 1954). Clarke H. Garnsey, "Early XIX Century Residences in Central Cuba: The Trinitarian Style" (Ph.D. diss., Western Reserve University, 1962), 2, comments on the Andalusian influence in Cuban architecture.

28. Jordi Maluquer de Motes, "La burguesía catalana y la esclavitud en Cuba: política y producción," RBNJM 18 (May–August 1976):11–81; Wurdemann, *Notes,* 41–43. The letters of Gaspar Betancourt Cisneros to Domingo Del Monte in *Centón,* vol. 5, contain numerous references to the attempts to use Catalan labor on the plantations.

29. "Resumen general" in *Cuadro estadístico . . . 1846,* 9; Duvon C. Corbitt, "Immigration in Cuba," HAHR, 22 (May 1942): 280–308. On the Frías, Alfonso, and Betancourt families, see Santa Cruz y Mallén, *Familias cubanas,*

2:145–46; 3:3–17; 4:60–101 and Nieto, *Dignidades nobiliarias*, 92, 337–38, 395–99.

30. For the French and British contributions, see, e.g., Gabriel Debien, "Les colons de Saint-Domingue refugies a Cuba (1793–1815)," *Revista de Indias* 14 (1954):11–36; William R. Lux, "French Colonization in Cuba, 1791–1809," *Americas,* 29 (July 1972):57–61; Thomas, *Cuba,* 129–31; David Turnbull, *The Jamaica Movement for Promoting the Enforcement of the Slave-Trade Treaties, and the Suppression of the Slave-Trade* . . . (London, 1850), 222; Torre, *Spanish West Indies,* 51; John Glanville Taylor, *The United States and Cuba: Eight Years of Change and Travel* (London, 1851), 165; and the distributions by nationality of the white population in the *Cuadro estádistico* . . . *1846.*

31. Wurdemann, *Notes,* 8, 271; Joseph Sánchez to Daniel Webster, 12 October 1843, DC, Nuevitas, Cuba, RG 59, USNA; Roland T. Ely, "The Old Cuban Trade: Highlights and Case Studies of Cuban-American Interdependence during the Nineteenth Century," *Business History Review* 37 (Winter 1964): 456–78. See also the distribution by nationality in the *Cuadro estadístico* . . . *1846.*

32. Bohumil Badura, "Sobre la immigración alemana en Cuba durante la primera mitad del siglo, XIX." *Ibero-Americana Pragensia* 10 (1976):111–36; Francisco Pérez de la Riva, *El café: historia de su cultivo y explotación en Cuba* (Havana, 1944), 70; Jean Stubbs, *Tobacco on the Periphery: A Case Study in Cuban Labour History, 1860–1958* (Cambridge, Eng., 1985), 17.

33. Wurdemann, *Notes,* 188, 85, 159–64. For a description of *monteros,* see also Condesa María Merlin de las Mercedes Santa Cruz y Montalvo, *La Havane,* 3 vols. (Paris, 1844), 2:43–84; Mohl, "Scotsman in Cuba," 245; [William H. Hurlbert], *Gan-Eden: or, Pictures of Cuba* (Boston, 1854), 146, 175; Abbot, *Letters,* 81–82, 159–65; Diary of a Plantation Manager in Cuba, 25 November 1821; 31 March 1823; 3 April 1823; 21 February 1826, NYHS; Anselmo Suárez y Romero, *Colección de artículos* (Havana, 1859), 177–93; Guerra y Sánchez, et al., *Historia de la nación cubana,* 4:311; J. Q. Suzarte, "Los Guajiros," in *Colección de artículos tipos y costumbres de la isla de Cuba* . . . , ed. Miguel de Villa (Havana, 1881), 57–64.

34. Alexander von Humboldt, *Political Essay on the Kingdom of New Spain,* ed. Mary Maples Dunn (New York, 1972), 87.

35. "Un interrogatorio" in Saco, *Historia de la esclavitud,* 5:380; idem, *Vagancia,* 93–94. See also the occupational distribution in the "Resumen General" of the *Cuadro estadístico* . . . *1846,* 10.

36. For my discussion of the titled nobility, I have relied on *Guía de forasteros en la siempre fiel isla de Cuba para el año 1840* (Havana, n.d.), 45–47; Santa Cruz y Mallén, *Familias cubanas,* vols. 1–6; Franklin Knight, "Origins of Wealth and the Sugar Revolution in Cuba, 1750–1850," HAHR 58 (May 1977):231–53; Saco, *Historia de la esclavitud,* 5:376–77; Thomas, *Cuba,* 204; Nieto, *Dignidades nobiliarias.*

37. On the preferences of the Spanish nobility, see, e.g., Raymond Carr, "Spain," in *The European Nobility in the Eighteenth Century: Studies of the Nobilities of the Major European States in the Pre-Reform Era* (London, 1953), 43–59, esp. 50, and Carlos Marichal, *Spain (1834–1844): A New Society* (London, 1977), 14.

38. Ely, *Su majestad el azúcar,* 320–27; Wurdemann, *Notes,* 158; Marrero, *Economía,* 10:210–11; Vicente Vázquez Queipo, *Informe fiscal sobre fomento*

de la población blanca en la isla de Cuba y emancipación progresiva de la esclava . . . (Madrid, 1845), 69–70.

39. Demoticus Philalethes, *Yankee Travels Through the Island of Cuba . . .* (New York, 1856), 60–63, 122. Philalethes may have been a pseudonym for the Cuban notable Ignacio Franchi Alfaro. For more on the Conde de Villanueva, see AL. Daumont, *L'île de Cuba: le Comte de Villanueva et le General Tacón* (Paris, 1837), 42.

40. Julián Zulueta receives attention from Thomas, *Cuba,* 136–37; his cousin, in the *Trial of Pedro de Zulueta, Jun., on a Charge of Slave Trading . . .* (London, 1844). See also Santa Cruz y Mallén, *Familias cubanas,* 4:448, and Campbell J. Dalrymple and James Kennedy to Lord Aberdeen, 14 January 1842, FO 84/395.

41. Jacinto de Salas y Quiroga, *Viages,* reprint ed. (Havana, 1964), 73–77. For my crude estimate of the contribution of the top ten families to Cuban sugar production, I included only those names in the statistical record for the Province of Havana in the "Estadística de la isla de Cuba. Escribiala en la Habana de orden superior D. Ventura Pascual Ferrer. Año de 1827," EC, box 4, HL, that could be matched with the genealogical data in Santa Cruz y Mallén, *Familias cubanas.* The record listed 437 sugar plantations, 46,037 slaves, and 15,584 *caballerías* of land, which produced 4,133,563 loaves of sugar. I identified members of the ten families as owning 78 sugar plantations, 11,818 slaves, and 3,546 *caballerías* of land, which produced 1,015,884 loaves of sugar. These figures suggest about a one-quarter share of the sugar production in the province of Havana for the ten families but likely underestimate the reality for three reasons: 1) The genealogical data in Santa Cruz y Mallén has shortcomings, and I did not count several sugar plantations owned by individuals with the appropriate surnames who could not be matched with the genealogical data. 2) The statistical record covers seventy-nine districts in the province of Havana, forty-nine of which had sugar plantations. Although these seventy-nine districts encompass much of the western department and the western department produced the lion's share of Cuba's sugar, undoubtedly members of the ten families owned sugar plantations not covered by the statistical record. 3) My estimate did not include owners of sugar plantations who had married into the ten families. Thus I believe a figure of between one-quarter and one-third is reasonable for the contribution of these families to the total sugar production in the western department.

42. Moreno, *El ingenio,* vols. 1–2; Knight, "Origins of Wealth," 231–53; Marrero, *Economía,* vols. 7–8; Kuethe, *Cuba.*

43. In determining the intermarriage patterns of the high nobility, I have again relied on Santa Cruz y Mallén, *Familias cubanas.*

44. "Un interrogatorio," in Saco, *Historia de la esclavitud,* 5:383. On attachment of people of color to the white elite, see also José del Castillo to Andrés de Arango, May 1838, *Centón,* 3:152–53; Juan Pérez de la Riva, ed., *Correspondencia reservada del Capitán General don Miguel Tacón con el gobierno de Madrid: 1834–1836* (Habana, 1963), 52; Lydia Cabrera, *La sociedad secreta Abakuá* (Havana, 1959), 50–51, n. 1; Calderón de la Barca, *Life in Mexico,* 45.

45. Vázquez Queipo, *Informe fiscal,* 69, refers to the abuse of the *privilegio de ingenios.* On the problem of interest charges, see Marrero, *Economía,* 10: 210–11; Ely, "Old Cuba Trade," 472–74.

46. Santa Cruz y Mallén, *Familias cubanas*, 1:33; 4:250; 5:113–14; Moreno, *El ingenio*, 1:268; Philalethes, *Yankee Travels*, 61.

47. Guerra y Sánchez, et al., *Historia de la nación cubana*, 4:306. The peninsular dominance of political office can be readily seen in the listings for government officials in the *Guía de forasteros . . . 1840*, 82–131. Following the custom of the day, I have capitalized the word "creole" when referring to American-born whites.

48. For an arresting glimpse of the life-style of Cuba's high nobility around 1840, see the writings of Fanny Calderón de la Barca: her letter of 16 February 1842 in *The Correspondence of William Hickling Prescott, 1833–1847*, ed. Roger Wolcott (Boston, 1925), 284–88, and Calderón de la Barca, *Life in Mexico*, 16–45, 625–27.

49. For my discussion of colonial government, I have relied on Clarence Haring, *The Spanish Empire in America* (New York, 1947), 122; Duvon C. Corbitt, "The Colonial Government of Cuba" (Ph.D. diss., University of North Carolina at Chapel Hill, 1938), 1–191; Richard M. Morse, "The Heritage of Latin America," in Louis Hartz, et al., *The Founding of New Societies* (New York, 1964), 151–59. See also William Whatley Pierson, "The Establishment and Early Functioning of the Intendencia of Cuba," *James Sprunt Historical Studies* 19 (1927):74–133.

50. Corbitt, "Colonial Government," 1–191.

51. Joaquín Llaverías, *La Comisión Militar ejecutiva y permanente de la isla de Cuba* (Habana, 1929), esp. 14. See also Antonio Armas to Joseph Crawford, 9 April 1844, FO 72/664.

52. Hortensia Pichardo, ed., *Documentos para la historia de Cuba*, 4 vols. (Havana, 1976–1980), 1:289–90. See also Juan Clemente Zamora, ed., *Cuba: Colección de documentos selectos para el estudio de la historia política de Cuba* (Havana, 1925), 176–80.

2. OF BLOOD AND SUGAR

1. Eltis, *Economic Growth*, 190–93; Pérez de la Riva, *Café*, 53–75; Marrero, *Economía*, 11:97–122. See Francisco Scarano, *Sugar and Slavery in Puerto Rico: The Plantation Economy of Ponce, 1800–1850* (Madison, Wis., 1984), 184, for a table comparing world sugar and coffee prices in the first half of the nineteenth century. I have used the *Censo de población . . . 1841* and the *Cuadro estadístico . . . 1846* to obtain the number of sugar and coffee plantations.

2. Calculated from data in the "Estadística . . . 1827," EC, box 4, HL.

3. Moreno, *Sugarmill*, 21; Scarano, *Sugar and Slavery*, 66–67.

4. Fernando Ortiz, *Cuban Counterpoint: Tobacco and Sugar*, trans. Harriet de Onís (New York, 1947), 33. See also Noel Deerr, *The History of Sugar*, 2 vols. (London, 1949–1950), esp. 1:115–45, and Moreno, *Sugarmill*, esp. 142–53. J. Carlyle Sitterson, *Sugar Country: The Cane Sugar Industry in the South, 1753–1950* (Lexington, Ky., 1953), 112–32, gives a good description of sugar cultivation in antebellum Louisiana.

5. Eugene D. Genovese, *Roll, Jordan, Roll: The World the Slaves Made* (New York, 1974), 285–324, esp. 286. See also Moreno, *Sugarmill*, 144, 148–49; G. F. Afolabi Ojo, *Yoruba Culture: A Geographical Analysis* (London, 1966), 51–67. For an insightful comparison, see Stuart Schwartz, "Resistance and

Accommodation in Eighteenth-Century Brazil: The Slaves' View of Slavery," HAHR 57 (February 1977):69–81.

6. See Abbot, *Letters*, 39–40; Wurdemann, *Notes*, 258; Ortiz, *Hampa afro-cubana*, 183–99; Suárez y Romero, *Artículos*, 196–200; J. A. Leon, *On Sugar Cultivation in Louisiana, Cuba, & c. and the British Possessions* (London, 1848), 75–76, for a description of the regimen on Cuban sugar plantations. See also Philip D. Morgan, "Work and Culture: The Task System and the World of Lowcountry Blacks, 1700 to 1800," WMQ 39 (October 1982): 563–99.

7. Leon, *Sugar Cultivation*, 21–22; Ward Barrett, "Caribbean Sugar-Production Standards in the Seventeenth and Eighteenth Centuries," in *Merchants & Scholars: Essays in the History of Exploration and Trade*, ed. John Parker (Minneapolis, 1965), 156–57; Manuel Moreno Fraginals, "Technology and Labor: Influence of the Development of Sugar Technology on the Slaves' Way of Life," in *Papers Presented at the 3rd Annual Conference of Caribbean Historians*, ed. Woodville K. Marshall (Guyana, 1971), 75–85, 123–25; Moreno, *El ingenio*, 2:33; Madden, *Island of Cuba*, 173–77.

8. Wurdemann, *Notes*, 258.

9. *Cuba en 1830: Diario de viaje de un hijo del Mariscal Ney*, ed. Jorge J. Beato Núñez (Miami, 1973), 56.

10. Abbot, *Letters*, 40.

11. Cirilo Villaverde, *The Quadroon or Cecilia Valdés: A Romance of Old Havana*, trans. Mariano J. Lorente (Boston, 1935), 260. For information on Villaverde's life, see Calcagno, *Diccionario*, 687–88 and *Acerca de Cirilo Villaverde*, ed. Imeldo Alvarez (Havana, 1982), esp. 42–44, 417–18.

12. Moreno, "Africa in Cuba," 200; *Cartilla práctica del manejo de ingenios ó fincas destinados á producir azúcar* (Irun, 1862), 81. The *Cuadro estadístico . . . 1846* contains data on the number of steam-powered mills.

13. Sheridan, *Doctors and Slaves*, 192.

14. David Eltis, "The Nineteenth-Century Transatlantic Slave Trade: An Annual Time Series of Imports into the Americas Broken Down by Region," HAHR 67 (February 1987):121.

15. Francisco Arango y Parreño, *Obras*, 2 vols. (Havana, 1888), 2:194–95.

16. David Turnbull, *Travels in the West. Cuba, with Notices of Porto Rico and the Slave Trade* (London, 1840), 64–65. At the time Turnbull wrote these words, he had never set foot in Louisiana or along the banks of the Mississippi. His contact with the South was limited to a brief stop in Charleston, South Carolina, in 1839. See Turnbull to Lord John Russell, 22 January 1841, FO 72/584.

17. Jack Ericson Eblen, "On the Natural Increase of Slave Populations: The Example of the Cuban Black Population, 1775–1900," in *Race and Slavery in the Western Hemisphere: Quantitative Studies*, eds. Stanley L. Engerman and Eugene D. Genovese (Princeton, N.J., 1975), 245. Eblen demonstrates the need to convert slave populations subject to substantial in- and out-migration to stable populations in order to obtain rates of natural increase or decrease that are more useful for comparative purposes. But his argument for a naturally increasing Cuban slave population suffers from the use of 1) the inflated slave enumeration in the 1841 census; 2) a probable overestimation of the rate and duration of seasoning mortality; 3) low estimates of slave imports; and 4) model life tables of problematic applicability.

18. "Tarifa de la Protectora," FO 84/664. I am indebted to David Eltis for this reference. See also Barry Higman, *Slave Population and Economy in Jamaica, 1807–1834* (Cambridge, Eng., 1976), 123.

19. [Domingo Del Monte], "In RE, Slave-Trade. Questions Addressed to Señor ———— of Havana, by R. R. Madden," in Juan Francisco Manzano, *Poems by a Slave in the Island of Cuba,* trans. R. R. Madden (London, 1840), 118.

20. Jimeno to Sanguily, 22 January 1886, SC, NYPL.

21. For information on the Cuban slave diet, see *Cartilla práctica,* 70–71; Thomas Moore Commonplace Book, 232–43, PML; Ortiz, *Hampa afro-cubana,* 220–21; Moreno, *Sugarmill,* 55, 100; *Bando de gobernación,* 60; Hurlbert, *Gan-Eden,* 146; *Fourth Annual Report of the British and Foreign Anti-Slavery Society,* 146; Bernardo de Chateausalins, *El vademecum de los hacendadoes cubanos . . .* (Havana, 1874), 13–15; Barrera y Domingo, *Reflexiones,* 239; Arango, *Obras,* 2:655.

22. Kenneth F. and Virginia H. Kiple, "Deficiency Diseases in the Caribbean," *JIH* 11 (Autumn 1980):212. See also Kiple, *Caribbean Slave,* 96–103; Ángel José Cowley y Albirle, *Ensayo estadístico-médico de la mortalidad de la diócesis de la Habana durante el año 1843* (Havana, 1845), 2.

23. My discussion of this issue derives from Kiple, *Caribbean Slave,* 23–28; B. W. Higman, "Growth in Afro-Caribbean Slave Populations," *American Journal of Physical Anthropology* 50 (March 1979):373–85; Robert Dirks, "Resource Fluctuations and Competitive Transformation in West Indian Slave Societies," in *Extinction and Survival in Human Populations,* eds. Charles D. Laughlin, Jr., and Ivan A. Brady (New York, 1978), 122–80; David Eltis, "Nutritional Trends in Africa and the Americas: Heights of Africans, 1819–1839," *JIH* 12 (Winter 1982):453–75.

24. Gabriel de la Concepción Valdés, *Poesías completas* (Havana, 1886), 536–37.

25. Turnbull, *Jamaica Movement,* 53. For information on the cholera epidemic, see Ortiz, *Hampa afro-cubana,* 271–78; Kiple, *Blacks,* 54; Jorge Le-Roy y Cassá, *Estudios sobre la mortalidad de la Habana durante el siglo XIX y los comienzos del actual* (Havana, 1913), 14–15.

26. Daniel C. Littlefield, *Rice and Slaves: Ethnicity and the Slave Trade in Colonial South Carolina* (Baton Rouge, 1981), 59–60; Abbot, *Letters,* 155.

27. Eltis, *Economic Growth,* 257; Klein, *Middle Passage,* 223.

28. Arango, *Obras,* 2:238–41.

29. Suárez y Romero, *Artículos,* 207–8, 228. See also Rebecca Scott, *Slave Emancipation in Cuba: The Transition to Free Labor, 1860–1899* (Princeton, N.J., 1985), 243; Abbot, *Letters,* 40; Moreno, *El ingenio,* 2:16.

30. Ibid.

31. Cabrera, *Reglas de Congo,* 35. Cf. *Cartilla práctica,* 82–83; Genovese, *Roll, Jordan, Roll,* 497.

32. Jorge Le-Roy y Cassá, *La mortalidad infantil en Cuba: notas demográficas* (Havana, 1914), 35.

33. On the dearth of slave women on Cuban sugar plantations, see Turnbull, *Travels in the West,* 146; Del Monte, "Questions," in Manzano, *Poems by a Slave,* 118; Madden, *Island of Cuba,* 171; Abbot, *Letters,* 155; Arango, *Obras,* 2:238–41; Leopoldo O'Donnell to Secretary of State, 15 February 1845, AHN, Ultramar, leg. 4655. Sex ratios were calculated from data in the *Cuadro estadístico . . . 1846.*

34. See Sophia Peabody to Elizabeth Peabody, 25 March 1834, Cuba Journal of

the Peabody Sisters, Berg Collection, NYPL, for revealing comments on slave infant mortality. Sophia Peabody, who eventually married Nathaniel Hawthorne, while in Cuba became friends with the noble planter Andrés Zayas, whom she called "brilliant" and who answered questions raised by her keen powers of observation. See also Higman, *Slave Populations,* 314, 317–18, for estimates on slave infant mortality in the British Caribbean. Because of a dearth of reliable data, virtually no attempts have been made to estimate white infant mortality in any of the sugar-producing slave societies in the Americas. For the southern United States in 1850, Robert William Fogel and Stanley L. Engerman, *Time on the Cross: The Economics of American Negro Slavery* (Boston, 1974), 123, have estimated a slave infant mortality rate of 183 deaths per year per thousand live births during the first year and a rate of white infant mortality of 146 deaths per thousand live births. Herbert S. Klein and Stanley L. Engerman, "Fertility Differentials between Slaves in the United States and the British West Indies: A Note on Lactation Practices," *WMQ,* 35 (April 1978):357–374, point out that prolonged breast-feeding offers "some limited contraceptive protection," and whereas slaves in the U.S. South spent about one year on the breast, infants in the British West Indies often spent from two to three years. The pattern in Cuba resembled that in the British West Indies.

35. Cited in Hall, *Slave Plantation Societies,* 45.
36. Turnbull, *Travels in the West,* 285. See also Moreno, *Sugarmill,* 51–58; José del Castillo to John Scoble, 5 October 1843, BFASP, C 15/3, RHL; Journal of Eulalia Keating, 13 January 1839, 24 February 1839, 6 March 1839, Papers of the Bauduy Family, EMHL.
37. N. Jarvis, "Journal," 22 January 1833, HUL.
38. Journal of Eulalia Keating, 28 February 1839, Papers of the Bauduy Family, EMHL.
39. "Informe de D. Pedro Hernández Morejón . . . sobre las causas que influyen el aumento de criminalidad en la raza de color de la isla de Cuba," DDMC, LC; Varela, *Escritos,* 140–45.
40. For the Catholic Church during the sugar boom, see, e.g., Knight, *Slave Society,* 111; Moreno, *Sugarmill,* 51–58; Juan Martín Leiseca, *Apuntes para la historia eclesiástica de Cuba* (Havana, 1938), 151–56; *National Intelligencer,* 6 January 1842.
41. Castillo to Scoble, 5 October 1843, BFASP, C 15/3, RHL.
42. I have computed the priest/slave ratios from data in the *Cuadro estadístico . . . 1846.* For 1861 I have used data in Kiple, *Blacks,* 96, and Ramón de la Sagra, *Cuba en 1860 . . .* (Paris, 1863), 13. On the price of burials, see Wurdemann, *Notes,* 169, and [Del Monte], "Questions," in Manzano, *Poems by a Slave,* 127.
43. Ibid., 130–31.
44. "Diary of a Plantation Manager in Cuba," 14 April 1821, NYHS.
45. Hubert H. S. Aimes, "Coartación: A Spanish Institution for the Advancement of Slaves into Freedmen," *Yale Review* 17 (February 1909):412–31; Marrero, *Economía,* 13:163–68.
46. Turnbull, *Travels in the West,* 147–48. See Madden, *Island of Cuba,* 127–31 and José María Zamora y Coronado, *Biblioteca de legislación ultramarina en forma de diccionario alfabético,* 7 vols. (Madrid, 1844–1849), 5:462–63, for a description of the *síndico's* several functions.

47. J. I. Rodríguez, "La coartación y sus efectos," RJ 1 (1856):355. See also the responses of N. Azcarate, Antonio Bachiller y Morales, Ramón de Armas, and José Cintra in RJ 1 (1856):362–64; 426–34, 474–81.

48. Rodríguez, "Coartación y sus efectos," 360.

49. Calculated from data in Kiple, *Blacks*, 55; B. W. Higman, *Slave Populations of the British Caribbean, 1807–1834* (Baltimore, 1984), 381; José Luciano Franco, *Afroamérica* (Havana, 1961), 129.

50. Robert William Fogel and Stanley L. Engerman, *Time on the Cross: The Economics of American Negro Slavery* (Boston, 1974), p. 150, give the manumission rate for the South in 1850.

51. Manzano, *Life and Poems*, 80–106.

52. Ibid., 83–84.

53. Ibid., 84.

54. Manzano to Del Monte, 25 June 1835, in *Autobiografía, Cartas y versos de Juan Fco. Manzano*, ed. José L. Franco (Havana, 1937), 83–84.

55. José Montalvo y Castillo, *Tratado general de escuela teórico-práctica para el gobierno de los ingenios de la isla de Cuba en todos sus ramos* (Matanzas, 1856), 9.

56. Félix Varela and Tomás Gener to Del Monte, 15 September 1834, *Centón*, 2:93.

57. Fernando Ortiz, *Un cátauro de cubanismos: apuntes lexicográficos* (Havana, 1923), 56. On whipping practices, see idem, *Hampa afro-cubana*, 246–48; Zoila Danger Roll, *Los cimarrones de El Frijol* (Santiago, 1977), 10–11; *Bando de gobernación*, 66–67; Chateausalins, *Vademecum*, 17.

58. Diary of a Plantation Manager in Cuba, 20 January 1823, NYHS.

59. Peter S. Townsend Diaries, vol. 2, 1830, 59–60, New York Academy of Medicine.

60. See the comments of Cabrera, *Reglas*, 40–43.

61. "Sentencia contrados negros alzados en el cafetal de la Esperanza, 1817," EC, box 10, HL; José Luciano Franco, ed., *La conspiraciones de 1810 y 1812* (Havana, 1977), 86; Juan Iduate, "Noticias sobre sublevaciones y conspiraciones de esclavos: Cafetal Salvador. 1833," RBNJM 24 (January-August 1982):122. See also the discussion of slave drivers in Genovese, *Roll, Jordan, Roll*, 365–88.

62. Francisco Diago to Henry A. Coit, 1 February 1841, Moses Taylor Paper, NYPL.

63. Nicolo Machiavelli, *The Prince*, trans. Daniel Donno (New York, 1966), 16.

64. Andrés Zayas, "Observaciones sobre los ingenios de esta isla," *Memorias de la Sociedad Económica de Amigos del País*, 1, third series (1836):264.

65. George Fitzhugh, *Cannibals All! or Slaves Without Masters*, ed. C. Vann Woodward (Cambridge, Mass., 1960), p. 79.

66. Turnbull, *Travels in the West*, 288.

67. For the anonymous report of March 1839, see EC, box 11, HL. See also the comments of planters in the "Diligencias practicadas á consequencia de la queja producidos por Mr. Phiney ó Llamese D. Teodoro Finis, al Sr. Consul de S. M. Britanica en esta Isla," FO 97/382.

68. Sidney Mintz, "Toward an Afro-American History," *Journal of World History* 13 (1971):321. See also Eugene D. Genovese, "Rebelliousness and Docility in the Negro Slave: A Critique of the Elkins Thesis," in Ann J. Lane, ed., *The Debate Over Slavery: Stanley Elkins and His Critics* (Urbana, University of Illinois Press, 1971), 43–74, and Genovese, *Rebellion to Revolution*, esp. xiii–50.

69. Journal of Eulalia Keating, 15 March 1839, Papers of the Bauduy Family, EMHL. *See also* Santa Cruz, *La Havane*, 2:156–62; Carlos Ghersi to Governor of Matanzas, 15 March 1839, EC, box 11, HL. Box 11 of the Escoto Collection has numerous documents on this and other uprisings.

70. Diary of a Plantation Manager in Cuba, 28 September 1821, NYHS. See also Marrero, *Economía*, 9:182, and William Piersen, "White Cannibals, Black Martyrs: Fear, Depression, and Religious Faith as Causes of Suicide Among New Slaves," *Journal of Negro History*, 62 (April 1977):147–59.

71. Report to the Secretary of State, 19 August 1852, AHN, Ultramar, leg. 3550. See also Germán Carrera Damas, "Huida y enfrentamiento," in *Africa en America Latina*, ed. Manuel Moreno Fraginals (Paris, 1977), 43, and Marrero, *Economía*, 9:182.

72. Knight, *Slave Society*, 95.

73. I cannot be precise on the numbers of slaves involved in these uprisings without having seen the records in Cuban archives. Since what data I have point out that entire estates rose up, I can be sure that at least dozens of slaves were involved. For information on these slave revolts, I have relied on Jimeno to Sanguily, 22 January 1886, SC, NYPL; Ortiz, *Hampa afro-cubana*, 432–33; Deschamps Chapeaux, *Negro en la economía habanera*, 21–23; *Catalogo de los fondos de la Comisión militar ejecutiva y permanente de la isla de Cuba* (Havana, 1945), 1–2, 8, 13–14, 17–18, 20; Zaragoza, *Insurreciones*, 1:494–96; Iduate, "Noticias sobre sublevaciones," 117–53; *Diario de la Habana*, 15 September, 24 October, 1 December 1840; 12 March 1841; *Fourth Annual Report of the British and Foreign Anti-Slavery Society*, 148–49; Juan Sánchez, "Los oscuros gladiadores," *Bohemia*, 19 July 1974, 64–67; José Luciano Franco, "Africanos y sus descendientes criollos en las luchas liberadora, 1533–1895," *Casa de las Américas* 16 (November–December 1975), 15. Box 11 of the Escoto Collection has much documentation on slave uprisings in Cuba from 1818 to 1839. That for the uprisings in 1835 and 1839 is particularly abundant. Recently, David Geggus, "Causes of Slave Rebellions," 274–99, has argued that Cuba was "free from internal strife" from 1799 to 1804 and that "Cuban society went through a period of intense slave resistance with a curious lull (scarcely noticed by historians) from 1813 to 1824" (pp. 296–97), which he correlates with fluctuations in troop levels. If slave resistance counts as internal strife he is wrong, because slave uprisings occurred in 1798 and 1799 (see the references in *Bibliografía sobre estudios afro-americanos*, ed. Tomás F. Robaina [Havana, 1968], 84). The period from 1813 to 1824 might well be a lull, although it is far too early to tell based on the limited research done on this subject in Cuban archives. Institution of the Military Commission in 1825 led to far more systematic record-keeping on slave uprisings. For uprisings in 1817 and 1818, see "Sentencia contra los negros alzados en el Cafetal de la Esperanza—1817," EC, box 10, HL. Ignacio González to Sr. Comandante de las Armas, 17 March 1818, EC, box 11, HL.

74. Saúl Vento, *Las rebeldías de esclavos en Matanzas* (Havana, 1976), 23.

75. Carlos Franqui, *Family Portrait with Fidel: A Memoir*, trans. Alfred MacAdam (New York, 1985), 163.

76. Moreno, *Sugarmill*, 100.

77. Buenaventura Rodríguez to Governor of Matanzas, 29 December 1830, EC, box 11, HL.

78. Kennedy and Dalrymple to Aberdeen, 1 January 1844, FO 84/508. I have relied on the following for my discussion of Cuba's maroons: Richard Price, "Maroons and their Communities," in *Maroon Societies: Rebel Slave Com-*

munities in the Americas, ed. Richard Price (Garden City, N.Y., 1973), 1–30; Franco, *Afroamérica,* 120–30; Franco, *Plácido,* 27–41; Franco, *Tres ensayos,* 87–108; Franco, "Cuatro siglos de lucha por la libertad: Los palenques," *RBNJM,* 9 (January–March 1967):5–44; Francisco Pérez de la Riva, "La habitación rural en Cuba," *Revista de arqueología y etnología* 7 (January–December 1952):316–20; Pérez de la Riva, "El negro y la tierra, el conuco y el palenque," RBC 58 (September–December 1946):97–139; Pedro Deschamps Chapeaux, "Cimarrones urbanos," RBNJM 11 (May–August 1969): 145–64; Gabino La Rosa, "El Apalencamiento," *Bohemia,* 10 August 1984, 82–89; and idem, "Los Palenques," *Bohemia,* 17 August 1984, 84–89.

79. Prince of Anglona to Minister of Foreign Affairs, 20 August 1840, in BAN 10 (September–October 1911):289–90.
80. Juan Sánchez, "Cimarrones y palenques en la lucha secular por la libertad," *Bohemia,* 11 October 1974, 7–8; La Rosa, "Los Palenques," 86–87. See also J. A. Cosculluela, *Cuatro años en la Ciénaga de Zapata* (Havana, 1965), 247–60; Ramon García de [?] to Governor of Western Department, 10 May 1828, EC, box 9, HL.
81. Cirilo Villaverde, *Diario del rancheador* (Havana, 1982), 57.
82. Ibid., 115.
83. Gaspar, *Bondmen & Rebels,* esp. 171–84.
84. Moreno, "Africa in Cuba," 192.
85. For these and other reasons, I believe that Geggus, "Causes of Slave Rebellions," 274–99, esp. 289, 298, has reduced Genovese's thesis in *Rebellion to Revolution* beyond recognition in his criticism.
86. Craton, *Testing the Chains,* devalues external ideological factors in shaping slave resistance. The book is richly documented and deserves an extended critique. Suffice it to say here that most writers on slave resistance would agree with his assertion (p. 13) that "above all, the ideology of resistance to slavery in the Americas was not simply an extension of an external ideology." But Craton's work, I believe, accords too much weight to the motives of class and too little weight to the vision of its leadership. Nor does he properly distinguish between the ideas of state and nation or revolution and Age of Revolution. To say, as he does (p. 158), that "all [*sic*] that changed, or varied, were the forms of defiance and the occasions" is in reality to concede the essential point, since substance does not exist without form, since ideology, unlike some mask to be donned or discarded at will, is inseparable from reality. To the extent that an individual's ideology changes so does his reality. For a splendid analysis of the Antigua conspiracy of 1736 as well as a judicious discussion of Genovese's thesis, see Gaspar, *Bondmen & Rebels,* 255–58. On the question of external ideological influences, see also Monica Schuler, "Akan Slave Rebellions in the British Caribbean," *Savacou* 1 (June 1970):8–31; idem, "Ethnic Slave Rebellions in the Caribbean and the Guianas," *Journal of Social History* 3 (Summer 1970):374–85; Mary Record, "The Jamaica Slave Rebellion of 1831," *Past & Present* no. 40 (July 1968):108–25; Stuart B. Schwartz, *Sugar Plantations in the Formation of Brazilian Society: Bahia, 1550–1853* (Cambridge, Eng., 1985), 472–88.
87. C. L. R. James, *The Black Jacobins: Toussaint L'Ouverture and the San Domingo Revolution,* 2nd ed. (New York, 1963).
88. Knight, *Slave Society,* 131–32. For Valdés's thinking behind the slave code of 1842 and *coartación* in particular, see the letter of Ramón de Armas, 26 November 1856, in RJ 1 (1856):430–34. For the slave code of 1789, see

Richard Konetzke, ed., *Colección de documentos para la historia de la formación social Hispanoamérica, 1493–1810*, 3 vols. (Madrid, 1953–1962), 3: 643–51.

89. Betancourt to Del Monte, 11 December 1842, *Centón*, 5:86.
90. Castillo to Scoble, 14 February 1844, BFASP, C 15/10, RHL.
91. Arango, *Obras*, 1:49.
92. Castillo to Scoble, 14 February 1844, BFASP, C 15/10, RHL.
93. Castillo to Scoble, 4 February 1844, BFASP, C 15/8, RHL.
94. Moreno, *Sugarmill*, 100; Marrero, *Economía*, 13:199.
95. Betancourt to Del Monte, 11 December 1842, *Centón*, 5:86.
96. Valdés's circular of 14 November 1842 is translated in FO 84/396. See also Wurdemann, *Notes*, 260.
97. V. S. Naipaul, *The Middle Passage* (New York, 1963), 53.

3. CUBAN WHITES AND THE
PROBLEM OF SLAVERY

1. Cornelius P. Van Ness to John Forsyth, 10 December 1836, in *Diplomatic Correspondence of the United States: Inter-American Affairs, 1831–1860*, ed. William R. Manning, 12 vols. (Washington, 1936–1939), 11:303.
2. Lorenzo Allo, *Domestic Slavery in Its Relations with Wealth, an Oration Pronounced in the Cuban Democratic Athenaeum of New York* (New York, 1855), 13. On Allo, see Calcagno, *Diccionario*, 35, and Elías Entralgo, *La liberación étnica cubana* (Habana, 1953), 48–51.
3. For further information on liberal influences in these movements, see Franco, ed., *Conspiraciones de 1810 y 1812;* Morales, *Iniciadores*, 11–118; José Manuel de Ximeno, "Genealogía de las ideas separatistas en Cuba," *Anales de la Academia de la Historia de Cuba*, 16 (January–December 1934):55–107; E. Roque Garrigo, *Historia documentada de la conspiración de la Gran Legión del Aguila Negra* (Havana, 1930); and Francisco Morales Padrón, "Conspiraciones y masonería en Cuba (1810–1826)," *Anuario de estudios americanos* 29 (1972):343–77.
4. Wurdemann, *Notes*, 72. On the influence of French political thought, see also Antonio Bachiller y Morales, *Los negros* (Barcelona, [188?]), 63–64; Castillo to Scoble, 5 October 1843, BFASP C 15/3, RHL.
5. John Lynch has demonstrated unusual sensitivity to the social dimensions of *The Spanish American Revolutions, 1808–1826* (New York, 1973), although his assertion (p. 294) that Cuba "neither wanted nor received [an external stimulus to independence]" needs qualification in light of the work of Cuban scholars such as Vidal Morales, *Iniciadores*.
6. Allan J. Kuethe, "The Development of the Cuban Military as a Socio-political Elite, 1763–83," HAHR 61 (November 1981):695–704; idem and Lowell Blaisdell, "The Esquilache Government and the Reforms of Charles III in Cuba," JGSWGL 19 (1982):117–36; Kuethe and G. Douglas Inglis, "Absolutism and Enlightened Reform: Charles III, the Establishment of the Alcabala, and Commercial Reorganization in Cuba," *Past & Present* no. 109 (November 1985):118–43.
7. Castillo to J. H. Hinton, 13 December 1843, BFASP, C 15/4, RHL.
8. Allan Kuethe, *Cuba, 1753–1815: Crown, Military, and Society* (Knoxville, 1986), 176.
9. For Arango and his work in the *consulado*, see William Whatley Pierson,

"Francisco de Arango y Parreño," HAHR 16 (November 1936):451–78; Ramiro Guerra y Sánchez, "Introducción" to Arango, *Obras*, 1:11–23; Francisco Ponte Domínguez, "Don Francisco de Arango y Parreño," RC, 24 (1949):284–328; Felipe Pazos y Roque, "La economía cubana en el siglo XIX," RBC 47 (January–February 1941):96–98; Peter James Lampros, "Merchant-Planter Cooperation and Conflict: The Havana Consulado, 1794–1832," (Ph.D. diss., Tulane University, 1980), 1–56.

10. Moreno, *Sugarmill*, 47–51, esp. 50.

11. Robert J. Shafer, *The Economic Societies in the Spanish World, 1763–1821* (New York, 1958), 178–98; Rafael Montoro, *Historia de la Sociedad Económica* (Havana, 1930), esp. 4–32.

12. The *Discurso* can be found in Arango, *Obras*, 1:53–161.

13. Cited in Corbitt, "Immigration in Cuba," 284. See also Arango, *Obras*, 2: 333–40.

14. Guerra y Sánchez, *Manual*, 218–20; Pierson, "Arango," 469–71; Arango, *Obras*, 2:175–227, 271–82.

15. Saco, *Historia*, 5:25.

16. Arango, *Obras*, 2:340.

17. Cited in Pierson, "Arango," 463–64. See also Francisco J. Ponte Domínguez, "Arango Parreño y la idea de la independencia de Cuba," RC 7 (January–March 1937):199–209.

18. Calculated from data in the *Guía de forasteros . . . 1840*, 45–46.

19. Cited in Edward D. Fitchen, "Primary Education in Colonial Cuba: Spanish Tool for Retaining 'La Isla Siempre Leal?' " *Caribbean Studies* 14 (April 1974):107.

20. Ibid., 107–9; "Sobre la prohibición del gobierno a los jovenes cubanos de estudiar en los Estados Unidos," BAN 33 (January–December 1934):20–25.

21. "Informe sobre el estado actual de la ensenanza primaria en la Isla de Cuba en 1836, su costo y mejoras de que es susceptible," in Domingo Del Monte y Aponte, *Escritos*, José A. Fernández de Castro, 2 vols. (Havana, 1929), 1: 267–86.

22. Ibid., 1:288.

23. [Alexander H. Everett], "State of Education and Learning in Cuba," *Southern Quarterly Review* 1 (April 1842), 378.

24. Ibid., 378–79. See also Larry Russel Jensen, "The Mania to Write and Read: Culture and Repression in Colonial Cuba, 1790–1840," (Ph.D. diss., Stanford University, 1981), esp. 266–308.

25. Moreno, *Sugarmill*, 61–62.

26. Del Monte to Gener, 27 March 1830, EC, box 4, HL. See also Gener's reply, 30 April 1830, *Centón*, 1:92–93.

27. "Address of the Young Creoles to the London Anti-Slavery Society," FO 84/ 359.

28. Valdés to Secretary of State, 18 September 1843, AHN, Ultramar, leg. 4616.

29. Secretary of State to O'Donnell (copy), 18 October 1844, FSPC carton 2, file #0063, BL.

30. Calculated from data in "Resumen General," *Cuadro estadístico . . . 1846*, 10 and *Noticias estadísticas de la isla de Cuba, en 1862* (Havana, 1864), n.p. The figure for white students in the census of 1861 is adjusted for error in enumeration.

31. "Un Interrogatorio," in Saco, *Historia de la esclavitud*, 5:380. On the problem of vagrancy in Spain, see Bartolomé Bennassar, *The Spanish Character:*

Attitudes and Mentalities from the Sixteenth to the Nineteenth Century, trans. Benjamin Keen (Berkeley, 1979), 103–77.

32. Charles Augustus Murray, *Travels in North America during the Years 1834, 1835, & 1836* . . . , 2 vols. (London, 1839), 2:210–34.

33. [Robert Francis Jameson], *Letters from Havana during the Year 1820* . . . (London, 1821), 11.

34. Ibid., 12.

35. Kuethe, *Cuba,* 56.

36. Based on data in the "Resumen General," of the *Cuadro estadístico . . . 1846,* 10.

37. Joseph B. Loring to his wife, 7 April 1844, Joseph B. Loring Papers, NYPL. See also Philalethes, *Yankee Travels.* Anton L. Allahar, "The Cuban Sugar Planters (1790–1820) 'The Most Solid and Brilliant Bourgeois Class in All of Latin America,' " *Americas,* 41 (July 1984):37–58, offers little original research to support his thesis, which largely derives, I believe, from an inadequate reading of Moreno Fraginal's *El ingenio.* Moreno Fraginals himself refers to the planters of Cuba's sugar boom as the "sugar bourgeoisie" and "bourgeois slaveholders" in attempting to reconcile Cuba's dramatic economic growth, planter acquisitiveness, and the progressive rhetoric that flowed from the Havana Economic Society and *consulado* with the operation of the slave labor system. For a concise statement of his position, see "Azúcar, esclavos y revolución (1790–1868)" *Casa de las Américas* 5 (September–October 1968): 35–45. Unlike Allahar, the Russian scholar Adelaida Zorina, "On the Genesis of Capitalism in Nineteenth-Century Cuba," *Latin American Perspectives* 2 (Supplement 1975):7–20, understands the difference between a high level of commercialization, the penetration of merchant capital, and capitalism. My interpretation of Cuban political economy has benefited from Jay R. Mandle, "The Plantation Economy: An Essay in Definition," *Science & Society* 26 (Spring 1972):49–62; Eugene D. Genovese and Elizabeth Fox-Genovese, "The Slave Economies in Political Perspective," *Journal of American History* 66 (June 1979):7–23, and their *Fruits of Merchant Capital: Slavery and Bourgeois Property in the Rise and Expansion of Capitalism* (New York, 1983), esp. 3–25.

38. Gordon K. Lewis, *Main Currents in Caribbean Thought: The Historical Evolution of Caribbean Society in Its Ideological Aspects, 1492–1900* (Baltimore, 1983), 109.

39. Turnbull, *Travels in the West,* 171. See also "Address of the Young Creoles," FO 84/359. An indispensable source for the reaction of the Creole intelligentsia to the contraband slave trade and related issues is the correspondence to Del Monte in *Centón,* vols. 1–7.

40. José de la Luz y Caballero, *Aforismos y apuntaciones* (Havana, 1945), 13.

41. For the study of Tacón's rule, *Correspondencia reservada del Capitán General Don Miguel Tacón, 1834–1836,* ed. Juan Pérez de la Riva (Havana, 1963), is indispensable as is Pérez de la Riva's introduction (pp. 13–96). See also James Kennedy to Palmerston, 15 September 1841, FO 84/347; Thomas, *Cuba,* 194–98; Corwin, *Abolition of Slavery,* 55–59; and especially Larry R. Jensen, *The Children of Colonial Despotism: Press, Politics, and Culture in Cuba, 1790–1840* (Tampa, 1987), which has a particularly good discussion of the reasons for Saco's expulsion.

42. Calderón de la Barca, *Life in Mexico,* 45; Pérez de la Riva, "Introducción," in *Correspondencia,* 13–96.

43. Whereas the census of 1827 enumerated 286,942 slaves and 311,051 whites, 40.7 percent and 44.2 percent of the total population respectively, the census of 1841 enumerated 436,495 slaves and 418,291 whites, 43.3 percent and 41.5 percent of the total population respectively. Questions about the accuracy of the slave enumeration in the 1841 census were raised soon after its publication and more recently. José Antonio Saco, *La supresión del tráfico de esclavos africanos en la isla de Cuba* (Paris, 1845), 47–48, and *Carta de un cubano . . .* (Seville, 1847), 19–25, on behalf of the anti-slave-trade Creoles, argued that the slave enumeration, if anything, understated the number of Africans because slaveholders, chronically fearful that a census presaged a tax increase and, particularly in 1841, fearful that a census presaged some British-imposed program of emancipation, concealed the true number of their slaves from census-takers. As evidence, Saco cited the statements of officials in charge of the census in the western and eastern departments that obtaining the true number of slaves proved difficult because of the "propensity" of the inhabitants to conceal their possessions. Vázquez Queipo, *Informe fiscal,* 6–7, argued the opposite, that the slave enumeration was "clearly overstated," perhaps by as much as 50,000, "because far from suspecting concealments . . . exactly the opposite occurs in this country by the proverbial propensity that everyone has of boasting about their wealth, especially the administrators and overseers of the estates who give importance to themselves by increasing the true number of their slaves." The debate between Saco and Vázquez Queipo preceded the publication of the census of 1846, which showed the number of slaves to have dropped by more than 100,000 to 323,759, or 36.0 percent of the total population. Students of colonial Cuban history have tended to accept the 1841 enumeration and doubt the 1846. Kenneth Kiple, *Blacks,* 47–58, has marshaled quantitative and qualitative evidence to argue for acceptance of the 1846 enumeration but not the 1841. Even though Kiple's projection of the demographic experience of Cuba's slaves between 1827 and 1846, in light of work by David Eltis, probably underestimates slave imports, revised projections still cast doubt on the 1841 enumeration.

44. Tanco to Del Monte, *Centón,* 7:113.

45. Pedro José Morillas, "Medios de fomentar y generalizar la industria," *Memorias de la Sociedad Económica de Amigos del País,* 5 (April 1838):449–85. The comment of the editor is on p. 475. Alvaro Flórez Estrada's *Curso de económica política* (London, 1828) had at least six editions and became a basic text throughout Latin America. Robert Sidney Smith, "Wealth of Nations," 120, notes that the *Curso* has been regarded as the "first systematic treatise on economics written by a Spaniard." See also H. E. Friedlaender, *Historia económica de Cuba* (Havana, 1944), 279–318.

46. Pedro Diago to Henry Coit, 29 March 1841, Moses Taylor Papers, NYPL.

47. Stanley L. Engerman, "The Southern Slave Economy," in *Perspectives and Irony in American Slavery,* ed. Harry P. Owens (Jackson, Miss., 1976), 87.

48. Francisco de Armas y Cespedes, *De la esclavitud en Cuba* (Madrid, 1866), 164.

49. Eltis, *Economic Growth,* 148–52, esp. 152; Francis Ross Cocking to Turnbull, 1 August 1841, FO 84/358.

50. Anastasio Orozco to Del Monte, 16 June 1834, *Centón,* 2:74.

51. "Relación conceptuada de los individuos que deben embarcarse para la Peninsula por prejudiciales a la tranquilidad y seguridad de la Isla," AHN, Ultramar, leg. 4618.

52. Ibid. For a description of a Cuban coffeehouse, see N. Jarvis, "Journal," 22 January 1833, HUL.
53. José Luis Alfonso to Del Monte, 27 February 1841, *Centón,* 5:10. Marrero, *Economía,* 9:139–69, has a succinct and well-documented discussion of the problem of white immigration into colonial Cuba. The racial fear behind the Creole promotion of white immigration comes through in the writings of most of the prominent liberal Creoles. See, for example, the various essays by physician Tomás Romay, *Obras completas,* 2 vols. (Havana, 1965), 2:139–80; Félix Varela, *Escritos políticos,* (Havana, 1977), 260–67; and the appendix in Saco, *Historia,* 5:111–394. See also Francisco de Frías, *Colección de escritos sobre agricultura, industria, ciencias y otros ramos de interés para la isla de Cuba* (Paris, 1860), 348–59.
54. Vázquez Queipo, *Informe fiscal,* 29–30.
55. Miguel de Aldama to Del Monte, 9 August 1845, *Centón,* 5:230–31.
56. Santiago (James) Drake to Henry A. Coit, 17 April 1841, Moses Taylor Papers, NYPL.
57. For an extension of this argument, see my "The Political Economy of Slavery and Freedom in Cuba," *Slavery & Abolition,* 9 (September 1987), 226–33.
58. Knight, *Slave Society,* 111; Murray, *Odious Commerce,* 148.
59. The report of the Junta de Fomento can be found in Saco, *Historia de la esclavitud,* 5:211–31 and FO 84/359.
60. "Informe del Conde de Santovenia," FO 84/359.
61. "Informe de Wenceslao de Villa-Urrutia," FO 84/359.
62. The report of the majority faction follows the Calvo-Chacón report in FO 84/359. Turnbull to Palmerston, 30 October 1841, FO 84/358, and 25 November 1841, FO 84/359, mention the factional dispute in the Economic Society. The report of the Calvo-Chacón faction is in FO 84/359. I established the kinship of Calvo and Chacón by using Santa Cruz y Mallén, *Familias cubanas,* 3:143–44; 4:107.
63. "Actas de las sesiones de la Real Sociedad Económica de Amigos del País de la Habana, referentes a la expulsión de Mr. David Turnbull de dicha corporación," in Saco, *Historia de la esclavitud,* 5:266–68.
64. For Luz y Caballero's role, see ibid., 5:268–75; José Ignacio Rodríguez, *Vida de Don José de la Luz y Caballero* (New York, 1874), 120–48; Sanguily, *José de la Luz y Caballero,* 142–62; Cocking to J. H. Tredgold, [?] November 1841, BFASP, G77, RHL; "Real Orden disponiendo reformas en los estatutos de la Sociedad Económica de Amigos del País . . . ," BAN 26 (January–(December 1927):52–53; "Expediente sobre la investigación . . . en virtud de la moción hecha en la Real Sociedad Económica de la Habana para la incorporación en ella de Mr. David Turnbull," BAN 26 (January–December 1927):54–55. For Valdés's response, see his letter to Secretary of State, 18 September 1843, AHN, Ultramar, leg. 4616.
65. Cited in González del Valle, *Conspiración de la Escalera,* 25–26.
66. Ivan Schulman, "The Portrait of the Slave: Ideology and Aesthetics in the Cuban Antislavery Novel," in *Comparative Perspectives,* 357.
67. Tanco to Del Monte, 20 August 1838, *Centón,* 7:113. Tanco's *Petrona y Rosalía* did not appear in print until 1925 in *Cuba contemporánea* 39 (December 1925):261–87. Pedro Barreda has a good discussion of Tanco and other Cuban antislavery writers in *The Black Protagonist in the Cuban Novel,* trans. Page Bancroft (Amherst, Mass., 1979), 37–82. See also Manuel Moreno Fraginals, "Anselmo Suárez y Romero," RBNJM 1 (February 1950):59–72;

José Antonio Fernández de Castro, *Tema negro en las letras de Cuba* (*1608–1935*) (Havana, 1943), 38–43; idem, *Esquema histórico de las letras en Cuba* (*1548–1902*) (Havana, 1949), 67–102; Schulman, "Portrait of the Slave," 356–67; Jean Franco, *An Introduction to Spanish-American Literature* (Cambridge, Eng., 1971), 59–61. Edith Kelly, "La Avellaneda's Sab and the Political Situation in Cuba," *Americas*, 1 (January 1945):303, 309, and the *Autobiografía y cartas de la ilustre poetisa Gertrudis Gómez de Avellaneda,* ed. Lorenzo Cruz de Fuentes (Madrid, 1914), 41, suggest how the problem of slavery influenced the life of one of Cuba's first prominent women writers.

68. On this point see the remarkable letter of Suárez y Romero to José Jacinto Milanés, 11 April 1839, EC, box 6, HL. See also Del Monte, *Escritos,* 1:195, and Del Monte to Everett, 28 June 1844, AEP, MHS.

69. Allo, *Domestic Slavery,* 11.

70. Arango, *Obras,* 2:375–76.

71. "Address of the Young Creoles," FO 84/359. See C. Vann Woodward's essay "The Northern Crusade Against Slavery" in *American Counterpoint: Slavery and Racism in the North-South Dialogue* (Boston, 1964), 140–62, for racial attitudes within the party of Lincoln.

72. [Francisco de Frías], *Isla de Cuba. Refutación de varios artículos concernientes á ese país* . . . (Paris, 1859), 12.

73. Justo Reyes, *Memoria sobre la vagancia* (Havana, 1831), 57.

74. Tomás Gener to Agustín de Argüelles, 3 December 1834, EC, box 4, HL.

75. Cited in Jorge Ibarra, *Ideología mambisa* (Havana, 1967), 13–14.

76. Betancourt to Del Monte, 30 April 1843, *Centón,* 5:94–95. See also Betancourt to Del Monte, 20 June 1841, *Centón,* 5:32.

77. Cited in Francisco Pacheco, "Aspectos del pensamiento esclavista en el siglo XIX," *Unión* 11 (December 1972):175.

4. THE FREE PEOPLE OF COLOR

1. For Vives's accomplishments, see Guerra, *Manual de historia,* 286–344.

2. "Un interrogatorio," in Saco, *Historia de la esclavitud,* 5:383.

3. Ibid.

4. Computed from data in David W. Cohen and Jack P. Greene, eds., *Neither Slave Nor Free: The Freedman of African Descent in the Slave Societies of the New World* (Baltimore, 1972):335–39.

5. Calculated from data in the *Censo de población* . . . *1841* and the *Cuadro estadístico* . . . *1846.*

6. Martínez-Alier, *Marriage, Class and Colour,* 168–69, presents a "Distribution of crafts and trades by colour in Cuba, 1846," but her distribution is drawn from the *Noticias estadísticas* . . . *en 1862,* not the *Cuadro estádistico* . . . *1846* as she claims.

7. For a discussion of the free colored militia, see Herbert Klein, "The Colored Militia of Cuba: 1568–1868," *Caribbean Studies* 6 (July 1966):17–27; Pedro Deschamps Chapeaux, *Los batallones de pardos y morenos* (Havana, 1976); Allan J. Kuethe, "The Status of the Free Pardo in the Disciplined Militia of New Granada," *Journal of Negro History* 56 (April 1971):105–17; "Reglamento para las milicias de infantería y caballería de la isla de Cuba . . . 1769," EC, box 1, HL; Kuethe, *Cuba,* 48–49, 74–76. See also Lyle N. McAlister, *The "Fuero Militar" in New Spain, 1764–1800* (Gaines-

ville, Fla., 1957); Deschamps Chapeaux, "El negro en la economía habanera del siglo XIX: Augustín Ceballos, capataz de muelle," RBNJM 10 (January–April 1968):53–59, and his *Negro en la economía habanera,* 87–102.

8. José Benites and José Policeto Gómez to Captain-General Vives, 6 April 1828, EC, box 20, HL.

9. For my discussion of the cabildos, I have relied on Fernando Ortiz, *Los cabildos afrocubanos* (Havana, 1921); Deschamps Chapeaux, *Negro en la economía habanera,* 31–46; José Luciano Franco, *La conspiración de Aponte* (Havana, 1963), 23–26; Roger Bastide, *African Civilizations in the New World,* trans. Peter Green (London, 1971), esp. 89–99; Marrero, *Economía,* 8:157–61. For comparisons with Brazil, see Patricia A. Mulvey, "Slave Confraternities in Brazil: Their Role in Colonial Society," *Americas* 39 (July 1982):39–68, and the "Commentary" by Mary Karasch in *Roots and Branches: Current Directions in Slave Studies,* ed. Michael Craton (Toronto, 1979), 138–41.

10. Pedro Deschamps Chapeaux, "Cabildos solo para esclavos," 50–51; Ortiz, *Cabildos,* 1–19; Lydia Cabrera, *Reglas,* 14–15.

11. Fernando Ortiz, "La fiesta afrocubano del día de reyes," RBC 15 (January–June 1920):5–26; Wurdemann, *Notes,* 83–84, 113–14; X. Marmier, *Cartas sobre la América,* 2 vols. (Mexico City, 1851), 2:39–46.

12. Deschamps Chapeaux, *Negro en la economía habanera;* Rita Llanes Miqueli, "La familia Pimienta-Dodge," RBNJM 15 (1973):111–23. See also the articles by Deschamps Chapeaux in *Gente sin historia,* 5–110.

13. On this point see Richard L. Jackson, *Black Writers in Latin America* (Albuquerque, 1979), 25–35, esp. 28–29. See also Franco's excellent introduction to *Autobiografía,* 9–32.

14. Manzano, *Poems by a Slave,* 3.

15. Francisco Calcagno, *Poetas de color* (Havana, 1878), 49–83; Jackson, *Black Writers,* 28–29. On Manzano's reputation in Cuba, which made him a target for white authorities, see O'Donnell to Antonio García Oña, 22 March 1844, EC, box 17, HL.

16. Cited in Pedro Deschamps Chapeaux, "Autenticidad de algunos negros y mulatos de *Cecilia Valdés,* in *Acerca de Cirilo Villaverde,* ed. Imeldo Alvarez (Havana, 1982), 228.

17. For a good discussion of Plácido and his poetry, see García, *Poeta mulato,* 19–46; Castellanos, *Plácido,* 11–97; Leopoldo Horrego Estuch, *Plácido, el poeta infortunado,* 2nd ed. (Havana, 1960), 5–146; Stimson, *Plácido,* 44–75.

18. See, e.g., Antonio Domínguez Ortiz, *Las clases privilegiadas en la España del antiguo régimen* (Madrid, 1973), 19–197; J. H. Elliott, *Imperial Spain, 1469–1716* (New York, 1966); H. B. Johnson, Jr., ed., *From Reconquest to Empire: The Iberian Background to Latin American History* (New York, 1970); Morse, "The Heritage of Latin America," 123–69; Bennassar, *Spanish Character,* 103–45; Magnus Morner, *Race Mixture in the History of Latin America* (Boston, 1967); Martínez-Alier, *Marriage, Class and Colour,* 11–41. See also John Tate Lanning, "Legitimacy and *Limpieza de Sangre* in the Practice of Medicine in the Spanish Empire," JGSWGL 4 (1967): 37–60.

19. On the debate about the Tannenbaum thesis, see the excellent collection of articles in *Slavery in the New World: A Reader in Comparative History,* eds. Laura Foner and Eugene D. Genovese (Englewood Cliffs, N.J., 1969).

20. J. G. F. Wurdemann to William Gilmore Simms, 6 January 1845, Miscellaneous Papers, Wurdemann Folder, NYPL; Wurdemann to Lewis R. Gibbes,

3 January 1845, Lewis R. Gibbes Papers, LC. See also the observation of N. Jarvis, "Journal," 9 January 1833, HUL.

21. Morner, *Race Mixture,* 59; Esteban Pichardo, *Diccionario provincial casi razonado de vozes y frases cubanas,* reprint ed. (Havana, 1985), 541.

22. Martínez-Alier, *Marriage, Class and Colour,* 11–119. Villaverde finished part 1 of *Cecilia Valdés* in 1838 and, largely because of the unhealthy political climate, the final part in 1878. Some scholars have referred to it, I believe misleadingly, as Cuba's *Uncle Tom's Cabin.* After publication in 1879, it went through many editions, including an abridged version in English entitled *The Quadroon.* As perhaps the most outstanding example of Cuban *costumbrista* literature, it offers valuable information on Cuban slavery and race relations. See William Luis, "La novela antiesclavista: texto, contexto y escritura," *Cuadernos americanos* 40 (May–June 1981), 103–16, and Marshall Nunn, "Some Notes on the Cuban Novel, *Cecilia Valdés,*" *Bulletin of Spanish Studies* 24 (July 1947):184–86.

23. Manzano to Del Monte, 3 April 1834 and 25 February 1835, in *Autobiografía,* 81–83.

24. J. B. Rosemond de Beauvallon, *L'île de Cuba* (Paris, 1844), 119.

25. Lewis, *Main Currents,* 118. On the wedding of racism with slavery in the New World, see especially David Brion Davis, *The Problem of Slavery in Western Culture* (Ithaca, N.Y., 1966), 391–421; Kenneth F. and Virginia H. Kiple, "The African Connection: Slavery, Disease and Racism," *Phylon,* 41 (Fall 1980):211–22; William Stanton, *The Leopard's Spots: Scientific Attitudes Toward Race in America, 1815–59* (Chicago, 1960); and Ortiz, *Engaño de las razas.* The profound shift from environmental and religious explanations to racial explanations in Cuba is reflected in the difference between physician Francisco Barrera y Domingo, *Reflexiones: histórico físico naturales, médico, quirúrgicas* . . . reprint ed. (Havana, 1953), 36–55, who wrote in 1798, and physician Henri Dumont, *Antropología y patología,* 11–55, who wrote in the 1860s.

26. Castillo to Scoble, 14 February 1844, BFASP, C 15/10, RHL.

27. Betancourt to Del Monte, 11 December 1842, *Centón,* 5:85; Manuel de Castro Palomino to Del Monte, 9 September 1841, *Centón,* 5:39; *Diario de la Marina,* 31 January 1856, trans. in *House Executive Documents,* 36th Cong., 2d sess. no. 14; Charles Minguet, "Liberalismo y conservadurismo en Cuba en la primera mitad del siglo XIX. Contradicción entre 'lo específico y lo general,'" *Historiografía y Bibliografía Americanista* 16 (March 1972):59–67. Antonio Bachiller y Morales, *Los negros,* 83–84, remembered how he and Felipe Poey at the lyceum in Guanabacoa in 1859 gave lectures on the fundamental equality of the races to combat the widespread secular racism in Cuba.

28. Del Monte, *Escritos,* 2:43–44.

29. Mariano Torrente, "Appendix," in *Memoria sobre la esclavitud en la isla de Cuba* . . . (London, 1853), 3.

30. Alexis de Tocqueville, *Democracy in America,* reprint ed., 2 vols. (New York, 1945), 1:9; 2:xii. See also Robert Roswell Palmer, *The Age of the Democratic Revolution: A Political History of Europe and America, 1760–1800* (Princeton, N.J., 1959–1964), and Hobsbawn, *Age of Revolution.*

31. O'Donnell to Secretary of State, 28 February 1844, AHN, Ultramar, Leg. 4618.

32. Jameson, *Letters,* 37.

33. Reyes, *Consideraciones,* 11.

34. John Owen to Louis McLane, 20 October 1833, DC, Porto (Puerto) Príncipe and Xibara, Cuba, RG 59, NA.

35. "Décima" and "El Juramento" can be found in Gabriel de la Concepción Valdés, *Poesías escogidas,* ed. Salvador Arias (Havana, 1977), 124–25. For "A Grecia" and "A Polonia," see idem, *Poesías completas,* 34–35.

36. Villaverde, *The Quadroon,* 67.

37. Cited in Morales, *Iniciadores,* 130–31. The date of Castillo's letter is erroneously given as 1836.

38. Salvador García Agüero, "Lorenzo Menéndez (ó Meléndez).—El negro en la educación cubana," RBC 39 (1937):347–65. Deschamps, *Negro en la economía habanera,* 119–32; Del Monte, *Escritos,* 1:307; Justo Reyes, *Consideraciones,* 3, 11, 26–27.

39. Reyes, *Consideraciones,* 83–84; García Agüero, "Lorenzo Menéndez," 355–60.

40. Francisco Cartas, *Efemérides cubanas: calendario, histórico, con los hechos más notables sucedidos en cada día* (Havana, 1921), 93. The percentages are computed from data in García Agüero, "Lorenzo Menéndez," 360.

41. "Resumen General," *Cuadro estadístico . . . 1846,* 10.

42. Ibid.

43. Saco, *Vagancia,* 92–95.

44. Turnbull to Palmerston, 1 May 1841, FO 84/357. The *Bando de gobernación,* 11, article 23, restates the 1837 law.

45. *Reglamento interior del ferro-carril de Matanzas a la Sabanilla del Encomendador* (Matanzas, 1845), 12.

46. See articles 17, pp. 8–9; 87, p. 25; and 88, p. 25, in the section on "Public Order" and articles 143, p. 36, and 159, p. 40, in the section on "Public Security" in the *Bando de gobernación.*

47. O'Donnell to Fulgencio Salas, 7 March 1844, EC, box 10, HL. The *Diario de la Habana,* 22 October 1840, put the number of lashes at two hundred and of years in prison at eight.

48. [Richard Burleigh Kimball], "Letters from Cuba," *Knickerbocker* 26 (December 1845): 545–47.

49. See, e.g., Klein, *Slavery in the Americas,* 194–96.

50. Both the *Censo de población . . . 1841* and the *Cuadro estadístico . . . 1846* have crude distributions by color, age, and sex.

51. Calculated from data in the *Noticias estadísticas de la isla de Cuba en 1862* (Havana, 1864), n.p.

52. The percentages for *pardo* slaves were calculated from data in the *Cuadro estadístico . . . 1846* and the *Noticias estadísticas . . . 1862.* See Edward L. Cox, *Free Coloreds in the Slave Societies of St. Kitts and Grenada, 1763–1833* (Knoxville, 1984), 33–58; B. W. Higman, *Slave Populations,* 379–86, 689–95; and Jerome S. Handler, *The Unappropriated People: Freedmen in the Slave Society of Barbados* (Baltimore, 1974), 48–52, for manumission patterns in the British Caribbean.

53. Cited in Franco, *Afroamérica,* 129. See also *Bando de gobernación,* 17.

54. Betancourt to Del Monte, 29 January 1843, *Centón,* 5:90. See also Cocking to British and Foreign Anti-Slavery Society, 8 March 1843, BFASP, G77, RHL; Betancourt to Del Monte, 2 April 1843, *Centón,* 5:92–93, and 15 May 1843, *Centón,* 5:100.

55. Frías, *Refutación,* 14. See Kiple, *Blacks,* 55, for the estimate of manumissions.

56. Kuethe, *Cuba,* 166–72; Klein, "Colored Militia," 22–23.

57. On Aponte's conspiracy, see Franco, *Conspiración de Aponte,* esp. 23–55;

José de J. Márquez, "Conspiración de Aponte," RC 19 (1894): 441–54; Elías Entralgo, *Liberación étnica*, 23–28. Franco, ed., *Conspiraciones de 1810 y 1812*, introduces an indispensable collection of documents.

58. Cited in the "Manifiesto" of the Marqués de Someruelos in Márquez, "Conspiración de Aponte," 450.

59. José Luciano Franco, "La conspiración de Morales," *Revista de la Universidad de Oriente* 6 (March 1972):128–33. See also James F. King, "The Case of José Ponciano de Ayarza, a Document on Gracias al Sacar," HAHR 31 (August 1951):640–47, and Kuethe, *Cuba*, 155. Geggus, "Causes of Slave Rebellions," says that the Conspiracy of Morales was apparently not "influenced by the example of St. Domingue," using as his source Thomas, *Cuba*, 81. But Thomas clearly allows for that possibility by calling Morales "a would-be Cuban Toussaint." At any rate, the superior source is Franco, who establishes a connection.

60. On this point, see *Catalogo de los fondos de la Comisión militar ejecutiva y permanente de la isla de Cuba* (Havana, 1945), 1–23.

61. *Diario de la Habana*, 15 July 1840. See also Llaverías, *Comisión militar*, 84–85.

62. Cited in Deschamps Chapeaux, *Negro en la economía habanera*, 22–23. See also *Catalogo de los fondos*, 2, 3, 10.

63. The reasons for Lorenzo's *pronunciamiento* are well discussed in Jensen, *Children of Colonial Depotism*.

64. William Jones to Vice-Admiral Peter Hackett, 7 December 1836, William Jones Papers, LC. See also Pérez de la Riva, ed., *Correspondencia*, 60–64.

65. Cited in Morales, *Iniciadores*, 130–31. Martínez-Alier, *Marriage, Class and Colour*, 99, incorrectly attributes this quote to Juan Francisco Manzano. On the social habits of the free people of color, see also Antonio de las Barras y Prado, *La Habana a mediados del siglo XIX* (Madrid, 1925), 124, and Ximeno, *Aquellos tiempos*, 55.

66. *Fourth Annual Report of the British and Foreign Anti-Slavery Society*, 149.

5. DAVID TURNBULL AND THE CRUSADE AGAINST SLAVERY

1. The reasons for this shift have been explored with brilliance and erudition by David Brion Davis, *The Problem of Slavery in the Age of Revolution, 1770–1823* (Ithaca, N.Y., 1975). See also his *Slavery and Human Progress* (New York, 1984), esp. pp. 107–226; Roger T. Anstey, *The Atlantic Slave Trade and British Abolition, 1760–1810* (London, 1975); and Seymour Drescher, *Capitalism and Antislavery: British Mobilization in Comparative Perspective* (New York, 1987).

2. The best source of estimates for the nineteenth-century trans-Atlantic slave trade is Eltis, *Economic Growth;* see p. 245 for annual estimates of Cuban imports. North America appears to have imported about 516,000 slaves between 1620 and 1810. Those interested in the measurement of the Atlantic slave trade to North America, Cuba, and elsewhere should start with Curtin, *Atlantic Slave Trade*. Paul Lovejoy, "The Volume of the Atlantic Slave Trade: A Synthesis," *Journal of African History* (1982), 473–501, ably discusses revisions of Curtin's figures for certain branches of the trade, including the North American. Corwin, *Abolition of Slavery*, 17–34, and Murray, *Odious Commerce*, 50–71, are the best sources for the diplomacy of the 1817 Anglo-Spanish anti-slave-trade agreement.

3. Howard Temperley, *British Antislavery, 1833–1870* (Columbia, S.C., 1971), 62–92; Henry Richards, *Memoirs of Joseph Sturge* (London, 1864), 203–19.

4. John Bowen Colthurst, *The Colthurst Journal: Journal of a Special Magistrate in the Islands of Barbados and St. Vincent, July 1835–September 1838,* ed. Woodville K. Marshall (Millwood, N.Y., 1977), 199. My sources for Turnbull's early life include W. Innes Addison, *The Matriculation Albums of the University of Glasgow from 1728 to 1858* (Glasgow, 1913), 216; Turnbull to Lord John Russell, 22 January 1841, FO 72/584; Robert Campbell to Abel P. Upshur, 14 January 1843, in Manning, *Diplomatic Correspondence,* 11:28; David Turnbull, *The French Revolution of 1830, the Events Which Produced It, and the Scenes by Which It Was Accompanied* (London, 1830), esp. preface; idem, *Travels in the West;* idem, *An Address by the Chief Judge of the Court of Mixed Commission for the Suppression of the Slave Trade* . . . (London, 1851); "Minute Books of the British and Foreign Anti-Slavery Society," BFASP, vol. I, 216, 218, RHL. Turnbull's correspondents attest to his stature in the antislavery international. See, for example, Turnbull to David Lee Child, 16 October 18[?], David Lee Child Papers, BPL; Turnbull to James Gillespie Birney, undated, James Gillespie Birney Papers, William L. Clements Library, University of Michigan. See also Lewis Tappan to John Scoble, 25 June 1851, in *A Side-light on Anglo-American Relations, 1830–1858. Furnished by the Correspondence of Lewis Tappan and Others with the British and Foreign Anti-Slavery Society,* eds. Annie Heloise Abel and Frank J. Klingberg (Lancaster, Pa., 1927), 264–65, and Thomas Fowell Buxton to Turnbull, 18 July 1840 and 29 July 1840, Buxton Papers, RHL.

5. Turnbull, *Travels in the West,* iii–vi; Turnbull to Lord Leveson, 9 March 1840, FO 84/342; American Anti-Slavery Society, Executive Committee Minutes, 21 March 1839, BPL.

6. Turnbull to Lord Palmerston, 13 March 1840, FO 84/342.

7. For a copy of the 1817 Treaty of Madrid, see Great Britain, Foreign Office, *British and Foreign State Papers, 1816–1817,* 4:33–62.

8. William Howell Reed, *Reminiscences of Elisha Atkins* (Cambridge, Eng., 1890), 68. On the problem of corruption, see also Corwin, *Abolition of Slavery,* 59–60; Thomas, *Cuba,* 193–99; Ortiz, *Hampa afro-cubana,* 162–64; Manzano, *Poems by a Slave,* 121–22.

9. Pedro Diago to Juan González Cepeda, 12 June 1828, FO 84/98.

10. Ines Roldan de Montaud, "Origen, evolución y supresión del grupo de negros 'emancipados' en Cuba (1817–1870)," *Revista de Indias* 42 (July–December 1982):559–64, esp. 568.

11. Ibid. 563.

12. Calculated from this table in ibid., p. 584. See also Manzano, *Poems by a Slave,* 122–24; Turnbull, *Jamaica Movement,* 129–32; Moreno, *Sugarmill,* 140.

13. On the diplomacy behind the Treaty of 1835, see Corwin, *Abolition of Slavery,* 47–67, and Murray, *Odious Commerce,* 72–113. A copy of the treaty can be found in Great Britain, Foreign Office, *British and Foreign State Papers, 1834–1835,* 23:343–74.

14. On the abuse of the United States flag and the use of U.S. ships in the illicit Cuban slave trade, see Warren S. Howard, *American Slavers and the Federal Law, 1837–1862* (Berkeley, 1963), 32; Turnbull, *Travels in the West,* 435–64; Murray, *Odious Commerce,* 104–5; and Wurdemann, *Notes,* 65.

15. Cuba imported more slaves in the 1830s than in any other decade. Only in

the five years prior to the legal end of the slave trade in 1820 did Cuba import more slaves than in 1836–1840. See Eltis, *Economic Growth,* 245. The distribution of the slave traders' bribes comes from Ortiz, *Hampa afro-cubana,* 162.

16. Turnbull to Palmerston, 13 March 1840, FO 84/342.
17. Memorandum of Lord Palmerston, 15 March 1840, FO 84/342. See also Turnbull to Palmerston, 28 February 1840; Turnbull to Leveson, 9 March 1840; and Leveson to Turnbull, 10 March 1840, FO 84/342. Turnbull explained his plan to Palmerston in 13 March 1840, FO 84/342. A concise statement of Palmerston's anti-slave-trade policy can be found in his letter to John Murray of the Glasgow Emancipation Society, 3 April 1844, Miscellaneous Papers, National Library of Scotland, Edinburgh.
18. Turnbull to Leveson, 1 April 1840, FO 84/342. See also London *Times,* 17 March 1840; Tredgold to Turnbull, 18 March 1840, BFASP, C 10/132, RHL; Turnbull to Leveson, 19 March 1840, FO 84/342.
19. *The Monthly Review* 1 (April 1840):449–64, esp. 453.
20. Turnbull to Leveson, 14 April 1840, FO 84/342. On Turnbull's role at the World Anti-Slavery Convention, see Lucretia Mott, *Slavery and "The Woman Question": Lucretia Mott's Diary of Her Visit to Great Britain to Attend the World's Anti-Slavery Convention of 1840,* ed. Frederick B. Tolles (Haverford, Pa., 1952), 34; *Proceedings of the General Anti-Slavery Convention Called by the Committee of the British and Foreign Anti-Slavery Society* (London, 1841); Turnbull to Palmerston, 25 June 1840, FO 84/342.
21. Turnbull to Leveson, 11 April 1840; Turnbull to Leveson, 14 April 1840; Turnbull to Palmerston, 4 July 1840; Leveson to Turnbull, 20 July 1840; Turnbull to Leveson, 21 July 1840; Turnbull to Tredgold, 25 July 1840, FO 84/342.
22. Howard Jones, *Mutiny on the Amistad: The Saga of a Slave Revolt and Its Impact on American Abolition, Law, and Diplomacy* (New York, 1987), esp. chapter 10.
23. Kenneth Bourne, *Palmerston: The Early Years, 1784–1841* (New York, 1982), 622–24.
24. See the Minute Books of the British and Foreign Anti-Slavery Society, 1839–1868, 31 July 1840, BFASP, RHL.
25. Turnbull to Tredgold, 25 June 1840, BFASP, C 10/135, RHL.
26. Tanco to Del Monte, 13 November 1840, *Centón,* 7:151–52; 25 November 1840, *Centón,* 7:153; Castañeda, "Caso de Mr. David Turnbull," 131–32; Turnbull to Palmerston, 30 December 1840, FO 84/319.
27. Prince of Anglona to Secretary of State, 19 November 1840, BAN 10 (September–October 1911):292–94; Junta de Fomento to Queen Isabel, 28 November 1840, in Marrero, *Economía,* 9:291–92. For a description of the prince, see Gurney, *Winter in the West Indies,* 203. Corwin, *Abolition of Slavery,* 75, n. 21, confuses the Prince of Anglona with his successor, Gerónimo Valdés.
28. For the hostile response to Turnbull and the *Romney,* see Torrente, "Appendix," in *Memoria sobre la esclavitud,* esp. 15–18. Numerous documents in AHN, Estado, leg. 8025, and Turnbull to Palmerston, 6 April 1841, FO 84/356, concern the free black soldiers from the *Romney.*
29. Government concern with the spread of abolitionism from Jamaica shows in various letters in AHN, Estado, leg. 8038: for example, Antonio Brosa to Secretary of State, 20 September 1839, and Captain-General Ezpeleta to Secre-

tary of State, 24 October 1839, and various entries in the "Record Book of the Spanish Consulate in Jamaica, 1837–1843," HTML, esp. entry no. 16, Carlos Duquesnay, Spanish vice-consul in Jamaica to Juan Tello, Governor of Santiago de Cuba.

30. See W. E. F. Ward, *The Royal Navy and the Slavers: The Suppression of the Atlantic Slave Trade* (London, 1969), 167–74, and *The Daily Picayune* (New Orleans), 6 February 1841, on Captain Denman's activities. Before the House of Commons, Turnbull, *Sessional Papers,* vol. 9, 1850, 655–75, remembered how they "paralysed" Cuba's slave traders.

31. Two articles by David R. Murray, "Richard Robert Madden: His Career as a Slavery Abolitionist," *Studies: An Irish Quarterly,* 61 (1972):41–53, and "British Abolitionists in Cuba, 1833–1845," *Historical Papers* (1976):105–13, shed light on both Madden and the controversy that surrounded him in Cuba. Madden's role in the *Amistad* proceedings is discussed in Jones, *Mutiny on the Amistad,* 99–110.

32. Betancourt to Del Monte, 22 May 1841, *Centón,* 5:24; Turnbull to Del Monte, 5 June 1841, *Centón,* 5:26–27; Betancourt to Del Monte, 6 June 1841, *Centón,* 5:30.

33. Wurdemann, *Notes,* 97.

34. Betancourt to Del Monte, 30 March 1841, *Centón,* 5:14.

35. Castillo to Hinton, 13 December 1843, BFASP, C 15/4, RHL.

36. Turnbull to Palmerston, 2 December 1840, FO 72/559. On the rescued British subjects, see Turnbull to Palmerston, 2 January 1841, FO 84/356.

37. Turnbull, Jamaica Movement, 135. See also Turnbull to Kennedy and Dalrymple, 4 January 1841, FO 313/18.

38. Turnbull to Palmerston, 30 December 1840; Turnbull to Palmerston, 31 December 1840; Turnbull to Prince of Anglona, 21 December 1840; Turnbull to Prince of Anglona, 28 December 1840, FO 84/319. See also Turnbull to Palmerston, 29 December 1840, FO 72/559.

39. Prince of Anglona to Turnbull, 22 December 1840, FO 84/319.

40. Ibid.

41. Turnbull to Prince of Anglona, 28 December 1840, FO 84/319.

42. Correspondence on the Shirley affair fills FO 84/356. Of the more important letters, see Turnbull to Governor Metcalfe, 4 January 1841; Turnbull to Palmerston, 2 January 1841; Turnbull to Palmerston, 24 January 1841; Turnbull to Metcalfe, 23 January 1841. See also Francis Ross Cocking to Tredgold, 28 June 1841, BFASP, G77, RHL.

43. Jimeno to Sanguily, [?] April 1886, SC, NYPL.

44. Torrente, "Appendix," in *Memoria sobre la esclavitud,* 16.

45. For the many complaints of Spanish officials, see AHN, Estado, leg. 8054. See also Joaquín M. de Ferrer to Arthur Aston, 16 February 1841, FO 84/353; Antonio González to Aston, 3 November 1841, FO 84/355; Hernández y Sánchez-Barba, "David Turnbull," 38–39.

46. Fernando Armario Sánchez, "La esclavitud en Cuba durante la regencia de Espartero, 1840–1843," *Hispania; revista española de historia* 43 (1983), 134–36, 149–50.

47. Turnbull to Palmerston, 30 December 1840, FO 84/319. For one of Palmerston's reprimands, see his memorandum, 8 May 1841, FO 84/357.

48. Turnbull to Lord Aberdeen, 30 October 1841, FO 84/358. See also Turnbull to Palmerston, 26 May 1841, FO 84/357.

49. Alexander Everett to John Forsyth, 21 July 1840, U.S., 26th Congress, 2nd Session, *Senate Executive Documents,* no. 115.
50. Cocking to the British and Foreign Anti-Slavery Society, 8 March 1843; Cocking to Tredgold, 28 June 1841, BFASP, G77, RHL.
51. On Tolmé see the letter of Nicholas Trist, 6 November 1841, in the Charleston *Mercury,* 7 January 1842; Turnbull to Palmerston, 1 December 1840, FO 84/319; Murray, *Odious Commerce,* 139–41; and Everett to Forsyth, 10 November 1840, MLDS, RG 59, USNA.
52. Turnbull to Palmerston, 1 December 1840, FO 84/319; R. B. Jackson to Palmerston, 18 August 1841, FO 84/347. On the commissioners' view of the Gabino case, see their letter to Palmerston, 3 June 1841, FO 313/18. The following letters reveal the stormy relations between the commissioners and Turnbull: Turnbull to Kennedy and Dalrymple, 12 January 1841, FO 84/356; Cocking to Tredgold, 10 March 1841, BFASP, G77, RHL; Turnbull to Palmerston, 12 March 1841, FO 84/356; Turnbull to Palmerston, [?] May 1841, FO 84/357; Cocking to Tredgold, 1 May 1841, BFASP, G 77, RHL; Turnbull to Kennedy and Dalrymple, 18 May 1841, FO 84/357; Palmerston to Kennedy and Dalrymple, 22 July 1841, FO 313/7; Cocking to Tredgold, 20 March 1841, 1 September 1841, BFASP, G77, RHL.
53. On the rise of Espartero, see Raymond Carr, *Spain, 1808–1939,* (Oxford, 1966), 169–84, and E. Christiansen, *The Origins of Military Power in Spain, 1800–1854* (London, 1967), 47–98. Marichal, *Spain,* 156–57; Murray, *Odious Commerce,* 146; and Casteñeda, "Caso de Mr. David Turnbull," 132, say a few words about Valdés's background. On the early optimism in the British consulate, see Cocking to Tredgold, 20 March 1841, BFASP, G77, RHL; Cocking to Tredgold, 1 May 1841, BFASP, G77, RHL; Turnbull to Metcalfe, 23 January 1841, FO 84/356.
54. Turnbull to Kennedy and Dalrymple, 26 April 1841, 18 May 1841, FO 84/357; Kennedy and Dalrymple to Palmerston, 22 May 1841, FO 84/358.
55. Turnbull to Palmerston, 28 June 1841, FO 84/358.
56. Valdés to Turnbull, 12 October 1841, FO 84/359. See also Valdés to Turnbull, 23 May 1841 and 25 May 1841, and Turnbull to Valdés, 24 May 1841, FO 84/357.
57. George Villiers to Edward Villiers, 6 March 1836, in *Life and Letters of the Fourth Earl of Clarendon,* ed. Herbert Maxwell, 2 vols. (London, 1913), 1:94. MacGregor Laird's review of *Travels in the West* in *Westminster Review* 24 (June 1840):64–65 predicted some of the obstacles to the implementation of Turnbull's plan. See also González to Aston, 28 August 1841, FO 84/355.
58. On the question of the *Romney,* see Valdés's letter to Madrid of 28 July 1841 in BAN 67 (January–December 1974):86. Mariano Torrente, Appendix, in *Memoria sobre la esclavitud,* 17–18, indicates Spain's desire to remove the *Romney* as well as its unwillingness to offend Britain in the process.
59. Valdés to Secretary of State, 3 November 1841, AHN, Estado, leg. 8053.
60. Ibid.
61. Ibid.
62. Valdés to Minister of Foreign Affairs, 13 September 1842, AHN, Estado, leg. 8038.
63. Parts of the Santander petition were published, no doubt to Valdés's cost, in the *Diario de la Habana,* 10 September 1842. An English translation of the entire petition is in FO 313/19. José Luciano Franco has reproduced the

original in *BAN*, 67 (January–December 1974):106–10. See also Morales, *Iniciadores*, 120.

64. Ortiz, *Hampa afro-cubana*, 94; Pérez de la Riva, ed., *Correspondencia*, 40.

65. Turnbull to Thomas Clarkson, 31 May 1841, BFASP, G77, RHL. For Turnbull's mounting difficulties, see Valdés to Turnbull, 24 May 1841; Turnbull to Palmerston, [?] May 1841; Turnbull to Kennedy and Dalrymple, 18 May 1841, FO 84/357. See also Turnbull to Palmerston, 13 April 1841, FO 84/356 and Cocking to Tredgold, 8 April 1841, BFASP, G77, RHL.

66. Palmerston to Turnbull, 5 August 1841, FO 84/358.

67. Cocking to Tredgold, 1 May 1841, BFASP, G77, RHL.

68. Valdés to First Secretary of State, 9 October 1841, AHN, Estado, leg. 8015. Turnbull gives his version of what happened at the Aldama palace in his letter of 30 October 1841, FO 84/358.

69. Betancourt to Del Monte, 5 December 1841, *Centón*, 5:50.

70. Turnbull to Aberdeen, 25 November 1841, FO 84/359. An anonymous letter of 15 November 1841, FO 84/359, warned Turnbull that an assassin had been paid to kill him.

71. Tanco to Del Monte, 20 November 1841, *Centón*, 7:163–64. See also "Diligencias formadas en Matanzas . . . ," AHN, Estado, leg. 8054.

72. Turnbull to Joseph Crawford, 24 July 1842, FO 84/401; Robert Goff to Turnbull, 15 November 1841, FO 72/586; Turnbull to Aberdeen, 27 December 1841, FO 72/586. On García Oña see Crawford to Aberdeen, 21 May 1843, FO 84/463.

73. On the Thompson affair, see Turnbull to Aberdeen, 31 January 1842, FO 84/401; *Slave Testimony: Two Centuries of Letters, Speeches, Interviews, and Autobiographies,* ed. John W. Blassingame (Baton Rouge, 1977), 239–45; Turnbull, *Jamaica Movement*, 219–20.

74. Aberdeen to Aston, 19 February 1842, FO 84/400, and Aberdeen to General Sancho, 12 February 1842, in *The Fourth Annual Report of the British and Foreign Anti-Slavery Society,* 143, tell of Aberdeen's relaxation of pressure in regard to the implementation of the so-called Turnbull convention. Thomas Lloyd, *A Letter to Lord Viscount Palmerston* (London, [1850]), expresses his anger over Turnbull's sweeping charges against British merchants allegedly tied to the Cuban slave trade. See also Sturge to Charles Gilpin, 15 June 1850, Charles Gilpin Papers, PML. Joseph Crawford, Turnbull's successor as consul, investigated the merchants and found no convincing evidence of their involvement. See Crawford to Aberdeen, 14 October 1842, FO 84/401.

75. Turnbull to Sturge, 12 April 1842, BFASP, C 110/56, RHL. See also Aberdeen to Turnbull, 10 February 1842, FO 72/608.

76. Sancho to First Secretary of State, 4 January 1842, AHN, Estado, leg. 8054. See also Armario Sánchez, "Esclavitud en Cuba," 140–41.

77. See Cocking to the British and Foreign Anti-Slavery Society, 1 July 1842, BFASP, G77, RHL; Turnbull to Aberdeen, 26 March 1842, FO 72/608; Turnbull to Lt. Burton, 9 June 1842, FO 313/33; Crawford to Aberdeen, 13 June 1842, FO 84/401; Crawford to Aberdeen, 15 June 1842, FO 72/609, on Turnbull's decision to seek asylum on the *Romney.*

78. Turnbull to Sturge, 12 April 1842, BFASP, C 110/56, RHL. See also Turnbull to Sturge, 14 June 1842, BFASP, C 110/57, RHL.

79. On the Forbes matters, see Turnbull to Crawford, 21 June 1842; Turnbull to Crawford, 24 July 1842; Turnbull to Crawford, 26 July 1842; Valdés to

Crawford, 27 July 1842; Crawford to Aberdeen, 1 August 1842, FO 84/401. On Crawford's antislavery feelings, see Crawford to Scoble, 6 May 1843, BFASP, C 15/87, RHL.

80. Betancourt to Del Monte, 1 April 1842, *Centón* 5:73. Turnbull to Crawford, 15 August 1842, FO 84/401, tells of his wife's illness.

81. Crawford to Bidwell, 1 October 1842, FO 72/609. See also Crawford to Bidwell, 15 June 1842; Crawford to Bidwell, 1 August 1842, FO 72/609.

82. Luis Payne to Valdés, 3 November 1842, BAN 67 (January–December 1974):118. I have pieced together the rousing story of Turnbull's departure, return, and expulsion from the *British and Foreign Anti-Slavery Reporter,* 19 October and 14 December 1842, and the following letters: Cocking to John Beaumont, 7 December 1842, BFASP, G77, RHL; Jimeno to Sanguily, [?] April 1886, SC, NYPL; Turnbull to Crawford, 17 September 1842, FO 313/33; Crawford to Bidwell, 5 November 1842, FO 84/401; Crawford to Bidwell, 6 February 1843, Crawford to Aberdeen, 4 May 1843, Crawford to Bidwell, 7 May 1843, Crawford to Aberdeen, 20 May 1843, FO 72/634; Turnbull to Lt.-Gov. Nesbitt, 22 October 1842, CO 23/113; Valdés to First Secretary of State, 5 November 1842, AHN, Ultramar, leg. 4617; and finally, the documents in BAN, 67 (January–December 1974):115–23. See also *The Daily Picayune* (New Orleans), 13 November 1842. Thomas Catto did not learn. He returned to Cuba in 1845 and was jailed again. See Crawford to Aberdeen, 10 September 1845, FO 84/578.

83. The judgment of a government legal advisor (*asesor*), signed by Valdés on 5 November 1842, is in BAN 67 (January–December 1974):123–25.

84. Ibid.

85. *The Daily Picayune* (New Orleans), 13 November 1842.

86. Crawford to Bidwell, 7 May 1843, FO 72/634.

87. Aberdeen to Turnbull, 15 November 1842, London, Aberdeen Papers, BM. Word of Turnbull's presence in Jamaica reached Cuba quickly. See the letter, Betancourt to Del Monte, 2 April 1843, *Centón,* 5:93. Duquesnay to First Secretary of State, 21 March 1843, AHN, Estado, leg. 8054, tells of Turnbull's arrival in Jamaica.

6. FRANCIS ROSS COCKING AND INTERNATIONAL CONSPIRACY

1. On Cocking, see Cocking to Turnbull, 26 January 1841, Turnbull to Palmerston, 18 March 1841, Cocking to Turnbull, 22 March 1841, Turnbull to Palmerston, 2 April 1841, FO 72/584; Valdés to First Secretary of State, 3 April 1841, AHN, Estado, leg. 8053; Cocking to Turnbull, 1 August 1841, FO 84/358; Cocking to Scoble, 30 May 1843, BFASP, G77, RHL. On the Drakes, see Ely, *Su majestad el azúcar.*

2. Tanco to Del Monte, 8 April 1841, *Centón,* 7:161.

3. Scoble to Cocking, 14 August 1841, 10 July 1841, BFASP, G77, RHL. See also Tredgold to Cocking, 10 July 1841, BFASP, G77, RHL.

4. Cocking to Scoble, 6 November 1841, BFASP, G77, RHL. See also Cocking to Turnbull, 26 January 1842, FO 72/608.

5. Crawford to Turnbull, 27 June 1842, FO 84/401.

6. Monica Schuler, *"Alas, Alas, Kongo": A Social History of Indentured African Immigration into Jamaica, 1841–1865* (Baltimore, 1980), 2–6, 11–18, discusses Barclay and his plans to attract labor to Jamaica. Turnbull to Craw-

ford, 9 June and 14 June 1842, FO 313/33, and Turnbull to Richard Hill, 1 July 1842, FO 72/709, tell of Turnbull's plan to use Cocking to stimulate emigration from Cuba.

7. Turnbull to Crawford, 13 June, 14 June, 27 July 1842, FO 313/33.

8. Cocking to Beaumont, 14 October 1842, BFASP, G77, RHL.

9. Cocking to British & Foreign Anti-Slavery Society, 6 March 1842 [1843], BFASP, G77, RHL.

10. Cocking to Beaumont, 14 October 1842, BFASP, G77, RHL.

11. Cocking to Scoble, 30 May 1843, BFASP, G77, RHL. See also Cocking to the British & Foreign Anti-Slavery Society, 29 June 1843, BFASP, G77, RHL; Crawford to Scoble, 27 March 1843, BFASP, C 15/88, RHL; Crawford to Scoble, 6 May 1843, BFASP, C 15/87, RHL.

12. *Proceedings of the General Anti-Slavery Convention, Called by the Committee of the British and Anti-Slavery Society and Held in London, from Tuesday, June 13th to Tuesday, June 20th, 1843* (London, [1843]), 144, 180; *Anti-Slavery Reporter,* 21 June 1843, 106–7.

13. Cocking to the British and Foreign Anti-Slavery Society, 29 June 1843, BFASP, G77, RHL. On Cocking's plight and the Society's response, see also Scoble to Cocking, 1 July 1843 and Cocking to Scoble, 3 July 1843, BFASP, G77, RHL.

14. Cocking to Palmerston, 1 October 1846, FO 72/709.

15. The confession is in ibid.

16. Ramón Lozano to First Secretary of State, 9 November 1852, AMAE, Venezuela, leg. 1800. Among the enclosures with Cocking's confession are translations of a letter of introduction, Crawford to Richard Hill, 1 July 1842; a note of thanks from R. Bruce, secretary of Lord Elgin, to Cocking, 2 September 1842, for delivery of a work by Turnbull; and Cocking's confession to Lord Palmerston, 1 October 1846. They have been published in BAN 3 (September–October 1904): 3–9 and (November–December 1904): 1–9. The original confession to Palmerston of 1 October 1846 in FO 72/709 reveals the Spanish translations to be incomplete and occasionally inaccurate. Names of individuals involved with Cocking are lacking in the Spanish translations. My recapitulation of Cocking's confession relies on the first confession. Cocking to J. Stanley, 31 December 1846, FO 72/709, expresses his disappointment after learning that Palmerston not only refused to reward his past conduct in Cuba with an appointment but disapproved of his past conduct entirely. Cocking to Bedford Wilson, 10 April 1844, 18 April 1844, 6 May 1844, and 10 July 1846, FO 199/20, record Cocking's chronic financial woes.

17. For Mariño I have consulted Salvador Villalba Gutiérrez, *Biografía compendiada del General Santiago Mariño* (Puerto La Cruz, Venezuela, 1955), esp. 85–89. See also Carraciolo Parra-Pérez, *Mariño y la independencia de Venezuela,* 5 vols. (Madrid, 1954–1957), and idem, *Mariño y las guerras civiles,* 3 vols. (Madrid, 1958–1960), although neither provides information on his exile in Jamaica.

18. Cocking to Palmerston, 1 October 1846, FO 72/709.

19. Ibid.

20. On López, see Herminio Portell Vilá, *Narciso López y su época, 1848–1850,* 3 vols. (Havana, 1930–1952), 1:143–66; [Anon.], "General Lopez, the Cuban Patriot," USMDR, 26 (February 1850): 97–112.

21. Cocking to Palmerston, 1 October, 1846, FO 72/709.

22. *Proceedings at the First Public Meeting of the Society for the Extinction of*

the Slave Trade, and for the Civilization of Africa (London, 1840), 6, identifies Trew as the secretary of the Society.

23. Murray, *Odious Commerce,* 162.
24. Nothing in FO 72/634, FO 313/33, or FO 84/401 suggests Crawford's support of Cocking's plotting.
25. Crawford to Aberdeen, 12 August 1842, FO 72/609.
26. The words of the Charleston *Courier* were reprinted in the *National Intelligencer,* 29 September 1841. A translation of the anonymous letter to the Conde de Villanueva, dated 3 October 1841, is in FO 72/609.
27. Crawford to Aberdeen, 12 August 1842, FO 72/609. Anyone interested in the evolution of liberal thought in Cuba must read Varela's *Escritos políticos.* Among the few treatments of Varela in English are Luis Leal, "Félix Varela and Liberal Thought," in *The Ibero-American Enlightenment,* ed. A. Owen Aldridge (Urbana, Ill., 1971), 234–42; Joseph J. McCadden, "The New York-to-Cuba Axis of Father Varela," *Americas* 20 (April 1964), 376–92; and Joseph J. and Helen McCadden, *Father Varela: Torchbearer from Cuba* (New York, 1969).
28. Crawford to Aberdeen, 12 August 1842, FO 72/609.
29. See fragment of letter, Manuel Márquez Sterling to Manuel Mestre Ghigliazza, 16 April 1926, in *Documentos y datos para la historia de Tabasco* ed. Mestre Ghigliazza, 4 vols. (Mexico City, 1916–1940), 4:621–24; Diógenes López Reyes, *Historia de Tabasco* (Mexico City, 1980), 272–73, for biographical information on Sentmanat.
30. *L'Abeille de la Nouvelle Orleans,* 11 July 1844; Mestre, *Documentos* 4:621–25; Morales, *Iniciadores,* 85, 106; Llaverías, *Comisión Militar,* 79; López Reyes, *Historia de Tabasco,* 244–61.
31. *El Revisor político y literario,* 14 April 1823.
32. Crawford to Bidwell, 1 October 1842, FO 72/609.
33. Crawford to Aberdeen, 8 November 1842, FO 84/401. See also Crawford to Aberdeen, 20 November 1842, FO 84/401.
34. Crawford to Aberdeen, 8 November 1842, FO 84/401.
35. Ibid.
36. Spain obtained the intelligence from G. W. Courtenay, the British consul in Port-au-Prince. See Courtenay to Palmerston, 1 May 1837, FO 35/19; Ussher to Palmerston, 9 June 1837, FO 35/19; Minister of Foreign Affairs to Miguel Tacón, 14 July 1837, leg. 39, signatura 17, CIH. For Boyer's interest in Cuba, see José Luciano Franco, *Relaciones de Cuba y Mexico durante el periodo colonial* (Havana, 1961), 89–91.
37. Minister of Foreign Affairs to Tacón, 14 July 1837, leg. 39, signatura 17, 21 July 1837, leg. 39, signatura 21, CIH.
38. See Crawford to Aberdeen, 6 December 1842, 7 December 1842, 21 December 1842, FO 72/609; Sánchez, "Esclavitud en Cuba," 149–50 on Cooke. Pérez, *Guide to the Materials for American History,* 40–41, shows that Cooke was the subject of at least three letters from Valdés to the Department of State, dated 30 November 1842, 12 April 1843, and 30 June 1843. The last can be found in its entirety in BAN, 67 (January–December 1974): 151–53, and in AHN, Estado, leg. 8039.
39. Even to prominent Virginians in 1842, John Cooke was something of a mystery. Daniel Webster refers to "John R. Cooke of Virginia" as his appointment for consul in Gibara in a letter to Washington Irving, 8 September 1842, ACC, ARC. Valdés referred to him as John K. Cooke. I suspected

that the Cooke in question was the father of the well-known Southern writer John Esten Cooke, but Philip Pendleton Cooke to John Rogers Cooke, 3 September 1842, John Esten Cooke Papers, PML, asks, "What 'John R. Cooke of Virginia' is it that has been made consul at a port of Cuba? I thought you were the only person of the name in the state."

40. Crawford to Aberdeen, 7 December 1842, FO 72/609.

41. Crawford to Aberdeen, 21 December 1842, FO 72/609. I have used Santa Cruz y Mallén, *Familias cubanas,* and the *Guía de forasteros . . . 1840* to decipher Crawford's rendering of the names.

42. Crawford to Bidwell, 6 January 1843, FO 72/634.

43. Ibid. See also the many documents on the Mitchell case in AHN, Estado, leg. 8057, exp. 3.

44. Juan Rodríguez to Crawford, 22 March 1843, FO 72/634.

45. Ibid.

46. Crawford to Aberdeen, 18 April 1843, FO 72/634.

47. Crawford to Aberdeen, 22 May 1843, FO 72/634.

48. Turnbull to Aberdeen, 29 June 1843, FO 84/459, responds to Aberdeen to Turnbull, 31 March 1843, FO 84/459.

49. Trew to Cocking, 5 December 1842, FO 72/709.

50. Murray, *Odious Commerce,* 171. See *Proceedings . . . of the Society,* 7, for reference to Turnbull.

51. "Address of the Young Creoles of the Havana to the London Anti-Slavery Society," FO 84/359; "Address of the Young Creoles of the Havana to the London Anti-Slavery Society," *Sessional Papers,* vol. 53, 1842, 402–9.

52. See Max Henriquez Urena's preface to José María Morillas, *Siete biografías dominicanas* (Ciudad Trujillo, 1946), 1–6, and Calcagno, *Diccionario,* 441, for biographical information. Calcagno drops the *s* in José María Morillas; Urena does not, although he confesses doubt (p. 1) as to whether the spelling is Morilla or Morillas. Joaquín Llaverías confuses José María Morilla with Pedro José Morillas in his note to the letter of José Mayol to Del Monte, 19 November 1843, *Centón,* 5:155.

53. United States consul in Havana William Robertson took Morillas's sworn testimony on 12 October 1853 and affixed it to a letter of Cristobal Madan to President Franklin Pierce, 4 October 1853, to be found in DC, Havana, RG 59, USNA.

54. See, e.g., Turnbull to Palmerston, [?] May 1841, FO 84/357.

55. The list of Turnbull's admitted contacts can be found in ibid. I have used Calcagno, *Diccionario,* and Santa Cruz y Mallén, *Familias cubanas,* to decipher Turnbull's rendering of the names and to obtain biographical data. On the San Carlos Seminary, see Jensen, "Mania to Write and Read," 130, 207; McCadden and McCadden, *Félix Varela,* 13–48.

56. Del Monte to Turnbull, 18 December 1841, FO 84/359.

57. Turnbull to Aberdeen, 7 October 1843, FO 84/460. See also Mariño to Turnbull, 25 September 1843, Turnbull to Mariño, 26 September 1843, "Memorandum" of Antonio Falques, 30 September 1843, and R. Bruce to Turnbull, 1 October 1843, FO 84/460.

58. J. M. Morales to Henry Coit, 1 April 1843, Moses Taylor Papers, NYPL.

59. *British and Foreign Anti-Slavery Reporter,* 31 May 1843. See also Crawford to Aberdeen, 18 April 1843, FO 72/634; José Luciano Franco, *Revoluciones y conflictos internacionales en el Caribe, 1789–1854,* vol. 2 of *La batalla por el dominio del Caribe y el Golfo de México* (Havana, 1965), 201; Wurde-

mann, *Notes* 272–73; [Domingo Del Monte], "Memorial on the Present State of Cuba . . ." USMDR, 15 (November 1844):478.

60. *Diario de la Habana,* 29 March and 31 March 1843.

61. Wurdemann, *Notes,* 271–72.

62. Franco, *Triunvirato,* 23–25.

63. Juan Sánchez, "José Dolores, capitán de cimarrones," *Bohemia,* 15 November 1974, 50–53; Vento, *Rebeldías de esclavos,* 25–30; *The Times* (London), 24 April 1844; Antonio Pirala, *Anales de la guerra de Cuba,* 3 vols. (Madrid, 1895–1898) 1:55.

64. Crawford to Aberdeen, 12 August 1842, FO 72/609.

65. Numerous letters in AHN, Estado, leg. 8038 and 8039, relay intelligence gathered by Carlos Duquesnay, Spain's vice-consul in Kingston. See, for example, Valdés to Secretary of State, 31 March 1842 and 31 October 1842, in leg. 8038. See also Franco, *Revoluciones,* 186–99; Charles Clarke to Aberdeen, 2 June 1843, FO 72/634; and "Record Book of the Spanish Consulate in Jamaica," esp. the entries for 1842, HTML. Crawford to Aberdeen, 12 April 1843, FO 84/463, transmits the results of a long candid conversation that a frustrated Valdés had with Crawford on the subject of the slave trade. Valdés's circular of July 1843 on estate security has been reproduced in Vento, *Rebeldías de esclavos,* 54. Crawford to Aberdeen, 22 May 1843, FO 72/634, is one of several letters that noted Spanish troop movements. Valdés to García Oña, 22 December 1842, EC, box 12, HL, tells of the restrictions on passports. For other measures, see Valdés to Secretary of State, 28 February 1843 and 21 May 1843, AHN, Ultramar, leg. 4617.

66. Crawford to Aberdeen, 27 September 1842, FO 84/401, and 12 April 1843, FO 84/463.

67. Betancourt to Del Monte, [?] December 1842, *Centón,* 5:58–59.

68. Betancourt to Del Monte, 11 December 1842, *Centón,* 5:85.

69. Betancourt to Del Monte, 29 January 1843, *Centón,* 5:90.

70. Valdés to Secretary of State, 1 December and 6 December 1842, AHN, Ultramar, leg. 4617. The sentence of the Military Commission can also be found in leg. 4617.

71. Valdés to [?], 14 March 1842, in BAN 67 (January–December 1974):99–100; "Record Book of the Spanish Consulate in Jamaica," entry of 6 May 1842.

72. Valdés to Secretary of State, 5 May 1843, AHN, Ultramar, leg. 4617.

73. *Fondos de la Comisión Militar,* 21–23; Acevedo and Alonso, "Nuevas noticias," 12.

74. Pérez de la Riva, "Negro y la tierra," 130.

75. Charles Clarke to Aberdeen, 2 June 1843, FO 72/634; Crawford to Aberdeen, 6 June 1843, FO 72/634.

76. "Instrucciones pa. el Sr. Dn. Eduardo Fesser," in BAN 67 (January–December 1974):145–47; Fesser to Valdés, 22 June 1843, ibid., 148–50; Valdés to Secretary of State, 19 June 1843 and 6 July 1843, AHN, Ultramar, leg. 4617. See also Franco, *Revoluciones,* 187–88, 193–95.

77. Fesser to Valdés, 22 June 1843, BAN 67 (January–December 1974):149.

7. AFRICANIZATION OR ANNEXATION
TO THE UNITED STATES?

1. For the Cuban policy of the United States, see Foner, *A History of Cuba,* 1:124–69; Portell Vilá, *Historia de Cuba,* 1:141–291; James Morton Callahan, *Cuba and International Relations: A Historical Study in American Diplomacy* (Baltimore, 1899), 83–164.

2. During its anti-slave-trade discussions with the United States, Britain tried to argue for a distinction between the right to search and the right to visit. Whereas both rights involved the verification of a ship's nationality, the second involved only the examination of the ship's papers; the first went further to an actual examination of cargo. The distinction was strained at best and had no sanction in international law. Furthermore, the right to search was considered a war or belligerent right, that is, it could not be exercised in peacetime except against pirates or in cases covered by treaty. A ship's papers could be fabricated with only a little more work than a ship's flag, as even Prime Minister Robert Peel conceded, such that a visitation would be ineffective for the purpose intended, a "mere ceremony" in the words of one English jurist. And if a visitation went beyond the papers, it would constitute a search. See H. G. Soulsby, *The Right of Search and the Slave Trade in Anglo-American Relations, 1814–1862* (Baltimore, 1933), 58–77; Howard Jones, *To the Webster-Ashburton Treaty: A Study in Anglo-American Relations, 1783–1843* (Chapel Hill, N.C., 1977), 69–86; Richard W. Van Alstyne, "The British Right of Search and the African Slave Trade," *Journal of Modern History,* 2 (March 1930):37–47; Alan R. Booth, "The United States African Squadron, 1843–1861," *Boston University Papers on Africa* (1964): 79–86.

3. Calhoun to King, 12 August 1844, in *Reports and Public Letters of John C. Calhoun,* ed. Richard K. Crallé (New York, 1856), 385.

4. Nicholas Trist to Daniel Webster, 23 March 1841, DC, Havana, Cuba, RG 59, USNA. See also Lester D. Langley, "Slavery, Reform, and American Policy in Cuba, 1823–1878," *Revista de historia de América,* nos. 65/66 (1968), 71–73; C. Stanley Urban, "The Africanization of Cuba Scare, 1853–1855," HAHR 37 (February 1957), 30–31; Basil Rauch, *American Interest in Cuba: 1848–1855* (New York, 1948), 11–38; John McCardell, *The Idea of a Southern Nation: Southern Nationalists and Southern Nationalism 1830–1860* (New York, 1979), 239.

5. William W. Freehling, *Prelude to Civil War: The Nullification Controversy in South Carolina, 1816–1836* (New York, 1965), 89. See also Rollin G. Osterweis, *Romanticism and Nationalism in the Old South* (Baton Rouge, 1972), 132–54; Fletcher M. Green, *Constitutional Development in the South Atlantic States, 1776–1860: A Study in the Evolution of Democracy* (New York, 1966), 60–62, 248–51, 261–64; Charles M. Wiltse, *John C. Calhoun: Sectionalist, 1840–1850* (New York, 1951).

6. Simms to Hammond, 20 May 1848, in *Letters of William Gilmore Simms,* ed. Mary C. Simms Oliphant, et al. 5 vols. (Columbia, S.C., 1952), 2:411–12.

7. On Calhoun's long-standing interest in Cuba, see the entry for 27 September 1822 in *The Diary of John Quincy Adams, 1794–1845,* ed. Allan Nevins (New York, 1929), p. 289. See also James Henry Hammond, *Selections from the Letters and Speeches of the Hon. James H. Hammond of South Carolina* (New York, 1866), 77.

8. As quoted in J. Fred Rippy, *Joel R. Poinsett, Versatile American* (New York, 1968), 230. See also "Report of J. R. Poinsett to the President of the United States Concerning Cuba—Importance of Cuba to the Southern States [1823]," in *Publications of the Southern History Association* 10 (July 1906):206–14; Joel Roberts Poinsett, *Notes on Mexico, Made in the Autumn of 1822 . . .* , reprint ed. (New York, 1969), 219–20.

9. "Statement Showing the Condition of Cuba in Reference to United States Residents Therein," 25 June 1840, vol. 19, folder 16, pp. 157–58, Poinsett Papers, HSP. See also Poinsett to Charles Ingersoll, 29 April 1824, Chas J. Ingersoll Correspondence, box 4, folder 13, HSP and Rippy, *Joel R. Poinsett,* 112–13, 118 n. 19.

10. Thomas Worthington King to Sarah King, 10 February 1844, Rufus King Papers, PML.

11. [Daniel Whitaker], review of *Notes on Cuba . . .* by J. G. F. Wurdemann, in *Southern Quarterly Review* 7 (January 1845), 251. See also William Gilmore Simms to William Cullen Bryan, 5 May 1849, in *Letters of William Gilmore Simms,* 2:509.

12. William Gilmore Simms, *Slavery in America, being a Brief Review of Miss Martineau on that Subject* (Richmond, 1838); James Henry Hammond, *Letters on Southern Slavery Addressed to Thomas Clarkson* (Charleston, 1845).

13. On Moses Taylor, see Ely, *Su majestad el azúcar,* and Daniel Hodas, *The Business Career of Moses Taylor: Merchant, Finance Capitalist, and Industrialist* (New York, 1976). Ely, "Old Cuban Trade," 458, presents U.S. Department of Treasury figures on the combined value of United States–Cuban trade for 1835. See also Sidney Mintz, "Time, Sugar & Sweetness," *Marxist Perspectives,* 2 (Winter 1979/80):56–73.

14. *New York Herald,* 25 November 1842.

15. *The Daily Picayune* (New Orleans), 17 June 1843.

16. *Hunt's Merchant Magazine,* 11 (December 1844):550–51.

17. On the U.S. presence in Cuba, see "Resumen," *Cuadro estadístico . . . 1846,* 9; Moreno, *Sugarmill,* 152; John Hartmann to Daniel Webster, 2 September 1843, DC, Baracoa, Cuba, RG 59, USNA; Joseph Sánchez to Webster, 12 October 1843, DC, Nuevitas, Cuba, RG 59, USNA; Wurdemann, *Notes,* 177, 243, 271.

18. Adams to Hugh Nelson, 28 April 1823, in *Writings of John Quincy Adams,* ed. Worthington Chauncey Ford, 7 vols. (New York, 1913–17), 7:372–73.

19. Jones, *Mutiny on the Amistad,* 138–40, 163–65.

20. Aaron Vail to John Forsyth, 15 January 1841, in Manning, *Diplomatic Correspondence,* 11:315. For background, see the following letters in ibid., vol. 11: Van Ness to Forsyth, 10 December 1836, 300–4; John Eaton to Forsyth, 29 April 1837, 305–6; Eaton to Forsyth 10 August 1837, 307; the Count de Ofalia to Eaton, 22 February 1838; 307–9; Eaton to the Count de Ofalia, 10 March 1838, 310–13; Eaton to Forsyth, 25 March 1838, 313–14. See also Brison D. Gooch, "Belgium and the Prospective Sale of Cuba in 1837," HAHR 39 (August 1959):413–27, and G. Colmache, "How Cuba Might Have Belonged to France," *Fortnightly Review,* 347 (November 1895):747–52.

21. See Howard, *American Slavers,* 30–36; Forsyth to Alexander Everett, 1 February 1840, 4 March 1840, DISM, RG 59, USNA; U.S. 26th Congress, 2nd Session, *House Executive Documents,* no. 115, for the background to the in-

vestigation of Trist. John Marland to Trist, 10 August 1836, and "Disbursements of Sugar Estate, Flor de Cuba, April 30, 1836–July 12, 1836," Trist Papers, LC, prove Trist's involvement in Cuban slavery. *A letter to Wm. E. Channing, D.D. in Reply to One Addressed to Him by R. R. Madden on the Abuse of the Flag of the United States in the Island of Cuba . . .* (Boston, 1840) defends Trist.

22. *The National Cyclopaedia of American Biography,* 9:256; [Anon.], "Alexander H. Everett," USMDR 10 (May 1842): 460–78; Stanley T. Williams, *The Spanish Background of American Literature,* 2 vols. (New Haven, 1955), 2:3–121; Forsyth to Everett, 1 February 1840, DISM, RG 59, USNA.

23. Everett to Adams, 30 November 1825, in "Cuba Without War," *Scribner's Monthly,* 11 (April 1876):876–79. The letter was reprinted in *The Everett Letters on Cuba,* ed. Edward E. Hale (Boston, 1897), 5–14. See also Everett to Albert Gallatin, 19 October 1827, Gallatin Papers, NYHS. Everett speaks of his close relationship with O'Sullivan in his letter to Del Monte, 14 December 1843, *Centón,* 5:178–79.

24. Everett to Adams, 30 November 1825, in "Cuba Without War," 877.

25. Ibid., 878.

26. Alexander H. Everett, "The Texas Question," USMDR 15 (September 1844): 251–52.

27. Frederick Merk, "A Safety Valve Thesis and Texan Annexation," *Mississippi Valley Historical Review* 49 (December 1962):432–33. See also Everett to Del Monte, 12 September 1844, *Centón,* 6:106–7; Alexander Everett, *New Ideas on Population: With Remarks on the Theories of Malthus and Goodwin* (Boston, 1823).

28. Everett to Forsyth, 10 November 1840, MLDS, RG 59, USNA. Everett believed that Trist had been lax in his duties but that proof of his direct involvement with Cuba's slave-trading interests could not be established. See draft, Everett to Webster, 15 July 1841, HML. See also Everett to Kennedy, 5 June 1840, and Everett to John Quincy Adams, 21 July 1841, Papers of the Hale Family, LOC; *House Executive Documents,* no. 115, 471–95. See Everett's Cuban Diary for 1840, ENP, MHS, for references to his many contacts with leading Cuban whites.

29. Turnbull, *Jamaica Movement,* 33.

30. Turnbull to Commodore Douglas, 11 January 1841, FO 72/584. See also Turnbull to Palmerston, 25 November 1840, FO 72/559, and Turnbull to Palmerston, 27 January 1841, FO 72/584.

31. Alexander Everett to Lucretia O. Everett, 19 December 1840, AEP, MHS. See also Alexander Everett to Lucretia O. Everett, 13 January and 24 January 1841, AEP; Turnbull to Palmerston, 10 November 1840, and Turnbull to Everett, 9 December 1840, FO 72/559.

32. See the letters of Everett to Del Monte in *Centón,* vol. 5, and Everett's Cuban Diaries for 1840 and 1841, ENP, MHS.

33. See the entries for 24 November 1840 and 2 December 1840 in Everett's Cuban Diaries for 1840, ENP, MHS.

34. Turnbull to Palmerston, 23 February 1841, FO 72/584. See also Turnbull to Minister Fox, 23 February 1841 and Turnbull to Commodore Douglas, 11 January 1841, FO 72/584.

35. Everett to Del Monte, 10 August 1841, *Centón,* 5:38.

36. Everett, "State of Education and Learning in Cuba," 377–97, esp. 389–97.

37. Ibid., 389.

38. Ibid., 395–96.

39. *The Daily Picayune* (New Orleans), 10 April 1842.

40. Vail to Webster, 30 November 1841, in Manning, *Diplomatic Correspondence,* 11:326–28.

41. *New York Herald,* 1 October 1841. See also *National Intelligencer* (Washington, D.C.), 29 September 1841.

42. Enclosure Argaiz to Valdés, 12 October 1841, in Valdés to First Secretary of State, 4 November 1841, leg. 8053, Estado, AHN.

43. See Minister Argaiz's confidential memorandum of June 1844 in Carlos Seco Serrano, "Espartero y Cuba: Entre Inglaterra y Norteamerica," *Revista de Indias* 39, nos. 115–18 (1969):592–604. See also Argaiz to First Secretary of State, 22 November 1841, in BAN 5 (May–June 1906):41–45; Ahumada, *Memoria,* 218–19.

44. Seco Serrano, "Espartero y Cuba," 594–95.

45. Vail to Webster, 28 December 1841, in Manning, *Diplomatic Correspondence,* 11:329–30.

46. James Calhoun to Webster, 14 February, 1842, DC, Havana, Cuba, RG 59, USNA.

47. *New York Herald,* 11 December and 16 December 1842. See also Charleston *Mercury,* 7 January and 7 November 1842; *The Daily Picayune* (New Orleans), 17 May 1842.

48. Everett to Del Monte, 16 September 1842, *Centón,* 5:82.

49. Del Monte to Everett, 20 November 1842, AEP, MHS. David Murray, *Odious Commerce,* 167, errs in saying this was Del Monte's first letter to Everett.

50. Everett to Del Monte, 6 January 1843, *Centón,* 5:86–87.

51. Everett to Del Monte, 20 May 1843, *Centón,* 5:101–2.

52. Ibid.

53. See, for example, Calhoun to Everett, 24 September 1844, Everett-Peabody Papers, MHS; Everett to Calhoun, 17 June 1844, in *Annual Report of the American Historical Association for the Year 1929* (Washington, 1930), 240; Everett to Calhoun, 13 April 1844, MLDS, RG 59, USNA.

54. Waddy Thompson to William Butler, 24 November 1841, in *The Papers of Daniel Webster. Diplomatic Papers, Volume I, 1841–1843,* ed. Kenneth E. Shewmaker (Hanover, N.H., 1983), 367–69.

55. Tyler to Webster, 16 December 1841, in ibid., 367; Trist to Tyler, 4 September 1841, ACC, ARC.

56. Webster to Campbell, 14 January 1843; Webster to Cookendorfer, 14 January 1843, DISM, RG 59, USNA.

57. Webster to Irving, 17 January 1843, in Manning *Diplomatic Correspondence,* 11:28.

58. Seco Serrano, "Espartero y Cuba," 596–97; Jerónimo Becker, *Historia de las relaciones exteriores de España durante el siglo XIX,* 3 vols. (Madrid, 1924–1926), 2:56–57.

59. Carr, *Spain,* 158–227, describes the social composition and political views of both factions. Argaiz's memorandum, in Seco Serrano, "Espartero y Cuba," 593–604, describes his courtship of the United States. See also Becker, *Historia,* 2:56–63.

60. On Argaiz's role, see Becker, *Historia,* 2:58–59; Valdés to Secretary of State, 8 February 1843, Valdés to Secretary of State, 30 June 1843, Department of State to Valdés, 15 July 1843, in BAN 67 (January–December 1974):143–

45, 151–55; Secretary of State to Valdés, 5 May 1843, in BAN 3 (July–August 1904):17–20; (September–October 1904):1–2. See also the correspondence in AHN, Estado, leg. 8039.

61. Irving to Webster, 10 March 1843, in Manning, *Diplomatic Correspondence*, 11:331–32.

62. Webster to Irving, 14 March 1843, in ibid., 11:30–31. See also Adams, *Memoirs*, 354.

63. Quoted in Alexander Everett to Del Monte, 20 May 1843, *Centón*, 5:102. The quote also appears in an extract of Edward Everett to Alexander Everett, 29 April 1843, *Centón*, 6:78.

64. Del Monte to Everett, 12 July 1843, AEP, MHS. *Centón*, 5:97–99, reproduces Whitaker's letters of introduction. On the affinity of prominent colonial Cuban exiles for Philadelphia, see Rafael Heliodero Valle, "Conspiradores, hispano-americanos en Filadelfía," in *Miscelánea de estudios dedicados á Fernando Ortiz*, 3 vols. (Havana, 1955), 3:1469–85.

65. Del Monte to Everett, 12 July 1843, AEP, MHS.

66. Del Monte to Everett, 10 August, 1843, AEP, MHS. Pufendorf's name is misspelled in the letter.

67. Everett to Del Monte, 15 August 1843, *Centón*, 5:120–22.

68. Everett to Del Monte, 24 September 1843, *Centón*, 5:136.

69. On Tyler's politics, see Frederick Merk, *Slavery and the Annexation of Texas* (New York, 1972), and his *Fruits of Propaganda in the Tyler Administration* (Cambridge, Mass., 1971). Claude H. Hall, *Abel Parker Upshur: Conservative Virginian, 1790–1844* (Madison, Wis., 1963), is a good biography. Abel Upshur, "Domestic Slavery," *Southern Literary Messenger* 5 (October 1839): 677–87, shows Upshur in the forefront of Southern thinking on slavery. After Webster resigned in May, Hugh S. Legaré was appointed secretary of state *ad interim*. He died in office in June. Upshur took over the duties *ad interim* until July when his appointment was made permanent.

70. Upshur to Irving, 9 January 1844, in Manning, *Diplomatic Correspondence*, 11:32.

71. Seco Serrano, "Espartero y Cuba," 588; Becker, *Historia*, 2:59, Carr, *Spain*, 218–27; A. Calderón de la Barca to Everett, 21 June 1843, AEP, MHS; Charleston *Mercury*, 11 August 1843.

72. Harrison to Legaré, 11 June 1843, Harrison to Upshur, 14 July 1843 and 3 October 1843, DC, Jamaica, RG 59, USNA. Joe Bassette Wilkins, Jr., "Window on Freedom: The South's Response to the Emancipation of the Slaves in the British West Indies, 1833–1861" (Ph.D. diss., University of South Carolina, 1977), 107–65, devotes a chapter to the influential Harrison, showing how he pumped ruling-class Southerners full of negative information on the results of slave emancipation in the British West Indies.

73. Campbell to Upshur, 5 October 1843, in Manning, *Diplomatic Correspondence*, 11:332.

74. Merk, *Fruits of Propaganda*, 17–23; St. George L. Sioussat, "Duff Green's 'England and the United States': With an Introductory Study of American Opposition to the Quintuple Treaty of 1841," *Proceedings of the American Antiquarian Society* 40 (October 1930):175–77, 204–18.

75. Upshur to Calhoun, 14 August 1843, WMQ 16 (January 1936):554–57. See also Upshur to Edward Everett, 28 September 1843, Edward Everett Papers, MHS.

76. Upshur to Calhoun, 14 August 1843, in WMQ 16 (January 1936):555.

77. Calhoun to Upshur, 27 August 1843, MLDS, RG 59, USNA.
78. A. Everett to Del Monte, 8 February 1845, *Centón,* 6:158; David Henshaw to Upshur, 14 November 1843, MLDS, RG 59, USNA.
79. Seco Serrano, "Espartero y Cuba," 590; Campbell to Upshur, 9 November 1843, in Manning, *Diplomatic Correspondence,* 11:334–35.

8. THE YEAR OF THE LASH

1. A good biography of O'Donnell has yet to be written. I have used Rafael Del Castillo, *Historia de la vida militar y política del Excmo. Sr. Capitán Leopoldo O'Donnell* . . . (Cádiz, 1860), 7–338; Manuel Ibo Alfaro y Lafuente, *Apuntes para la historia de d. Leopoldo O'Donnell* (Madrid, 1868), 7–176; and Francisco Melgar, *O'Donnell* (Madrid, 1946), 7–60, for information on O'Donnell's early life.
2. Aldama to Del Monte, 9 November 1843, *Centón,* 5:147–49. The revolt on Triunvirato is also described in O'Donnell to Secretary of State, 8 November 1843, AHN, Estado, leg. 8038; *Diario de la Habana,* 8 November 1843; Franco, *Triunvirato,* 27–33.
3. "Exposición al excelentismo Sr. Gobernador y Capitán General de la Isla de Cuba," in Saco, *Historia,* 5:283. See also Franco, "Sublevación de los esclavos en Matanzas en 1843," 2; Saco, *Supresión del trafico,* 50; Del Monte, "Present State of Cuba," 478–80.
4. Ibid., 478.
5. Ibid., 480.
6. Alfonso to Del Monte, 10 December 1843, *Centón,* 5:181.
7. "Importante exposición de los hacendados de Matanzas al Gobernador Capitán General, pidiendo la supresión de la trata," in Saco, *Historia,* 5:279–85. See also Betancourt to Del Monte, 7 December 1843, *Centón,* 5:177.
8. Dalrymple and Kennedy to Aberdeen, 1 January 1844, FO 84/508.
9. Philalethes, *Yankee Travels,* 107–11.
10. O'Donnell to García Oña, 7 January 1844, EC, box 19, HL.
11. Campbell to Upshur, 9 November 1843, in Manning, *Diplomatic Correspondence,* 11:334–35.
12. Irving to Upshur, 2 March 1844, in Manning, *Diplomatic Correspondence,* 11:335–36. See also Seco Serrano, "Espartero y Cuba," 591–92.
13. Alfonso to Del Monte, 10 December 1843, *Centón,* 5:181–82.
14. Ibid. See also Castillo to Hinton, 13 December 1843, C 15/4, RHASP; Castillo to Scoble, 14 February 1844, C 15/10, RHASP.
15. Alfonso to Del Monte, 22 December 1843, *Centón,* 5:185.
16. Ibid., 5: 184.
17. Ibid., 5:183; Aldama to Del Monte, 29 December 1843, *Centón,* 5:186–87; *Colección de los fallos pronunciados por una seccion de la Comisión Militar establecida en la ciudad de Matanzas para conocer de la causa de conspiración de la gente de color* (Matanzas, 1844), case 38a.
18. Moreno, *El ingenio,* 2:48, 50. Justo Cantero, *Los ingenios. Colección de vistas de los principales ingenios de azúcar de la isla de Cuba* (Havana, 1857), n.p., has a lithograph of Santísima Trinidad with commentary.
19. Morales, *Iniciadores,* 158.
20. Aldama to Del Monte, 9 November 1843, *Centón,* 5:148–49.
21. Aldama to Del Monte, 29 December 1843, *Centón,* 5:186–87. See also Crawford to Aberdeen, 27 December 1843, FO 84/463.

22. Aldama to Del Monte, 29 December 1843, *Centón*, 5:186.
23. Crawford to Aberdeen, 27 December 1843, FO 84/463.
24. Castillo to Scoble, 4 February 1844, BFASP, C 15/7, 9 February 1844, BFASP C 15/8, RHL.
25. "Exposición al Excmo. Sr. Gobernador y Capitán General," in Saco, *Historia de la esclavitud*, 5:283–85.
26. Ibid.
27. For O'Donnell's response to the events in Sabanilla, see Ahumada y Centurión, *Memoria*, 238; *Colección de los fallos*, case 38a. On the response to Santa Cruz de Oviedo and his relationship to Hernández Morejón, see Hernández Morejón to García Oña, 16 January 1844, and Santa Cruz de Oviedo to Hernández Morejón, 8 February 1844, ECS, box 2, HL. The latter has been reproduced in its entirety in García, *Poeta mulato*, 230. According to documentation in EC, box 11, HL, Hernández Morejón participated in the suppression of the slave uprisings in Sumidero in 1825 and Aguacate in 1839. See also Castillo's letter to Morales in *Iniciadores*, 158, for further biographical information.
28. *Colección de los fallos*, case 38a.
29. Ibid.; Hernández Morejón to García Oña, 19 January 1844, ECS, box 2, HL.
30. Alfonso to Del Monte, 11 January 1844, *Centón*, 6:2. See also Castillo to Scoble, 3 January 1843 [1844], BFSAP, C 15/5 RHL.
31. *The Republic* (New York) 9 March 1844. On Martí, see also José Luciano Franco, *Comercio clandestino de esclavos* (Havana, 1980), 225–33; Pérez de la Riva, ed., *Correspondencia*, 37, 146; *The Daily Picayune* (New Orleans), 25 June 1843.
32. *New York Herald*, 15 November 1841.
33. O'Donnell to Secretary of State, 28 February 1844, with enclosures, AHN, Ultramar, leg. 4618. See also Philalethes, *Yankee Travels*, 335–40; Zaragoza, *Insurreciones*, 1:538–41; Alvaro de la Iglesia, *Tradiciones cubanas* (Madrid, 1974), 38–42.
34. *The Daily Picayune* (New Orleans), 27 February 1844.
35. Mestre, ed., *Documentos*, 4:621–23.
36. E. Porter to John Calhoun, 20 July 1844, DC, Tabasco, Mexico, RG 59, USNA; *The Daily Picayune* (New Orleans), 2 June, 12 June, 4 July, 20 September 1844.
37. O'Donnell to Salas, 22 February 1844, EC, box 10, HL; Hall, *Slave Plantation Societies*, 59. See García Oña to O'Donnell, 10 February 1844, ECS, box 2, for the reason for Salas's elevation to interim governor. By March 19 García Oña had resumed his duties.
38. O'Donnell to Salas, 6 March 1844, EC, box 10, HL.
39. See Llaverías, *Comisión Militar*, 16–17, for a description of how that tribunal operated. References to people of color who were unable to attend their trials because of sickness or death can be found in the majority of the case summaries in *Colección de los fallos*.
40. Richard Burleigh Kimball, "Letters from Cuba," 26 (July 1845), 43.
41. Ibid.
42. Ibid., 43–47.
43. Jimeno to Sanguily, 22 January 1886, SC, NYPL.
44. Kennedy and Dalrymple to Aberdeen, 8 June 1844, FO 84/508. See also Kennedy and Dalrymple to Aberdeen, 15 March 1844, FO 84/508.
45. Kennedy and Dalrymple to Aberdeen, 8 June 1844, FO 84/508.

46. On the maroon problem, see O'Donnell to García Oña, 3 January 1844, ECS, box 2, HL, and its enclosures; London *Times,* 24 April 1844; La Rosa, "Palenques," 86; Sánchez, 'Cimarrones y palenques," 8–9. On the suicides, see report to the Secretary of State, 19 August 1852, AHN, Ultramar, leg. 3550; Marrero, *Economía,* 9:182. The general unrest in one plantation district is mentioned in O'Donnell to Salas, 12 February 1844, EC, box 10, HL.

47. William Norwood Diary, 18 April 1844, MsslN8394al, VHS; J. M. Morales to Henry A. Coit, 20 April 1844, Moses Taylor Papers, NYPL; *New York Herald,* 7 June 1844.

48. Kennedy and Dalrymple to Aberdeen, 8 June 1844, FO 84/508.

49. George Bell to Crawford, 29 July 1844, FO 84/520.

50. Ximeno, *Aquellos tiempos,* 52.

51. T. M. Rodney to John Calhoun, 13 April 1844, DC, Matanzas, Cuba, RG 59, USNA.

52. William Norwood Diary, 18 February, 26 February, 8–10 March 1844, VHS.

53. Ibid., 9–14 April 1844, VHS.

54. Ortiz, *Hampa afro-cubana,* 434.

55. *The Republic* (New York), 13 July 1844.

56. William Norwood Diary, 8–10 March 1844, VHS.

57. Ramón Flores de Apodaca to Salas, 26 February 1844, ECS, box 2, HL.

58. George W. Brinkerhoff to Henry A. Coit, 26 February 1844, Moses Taylor Papers, NYPL. See also Joaquín Morill to Miguel Buch, 28 April 1844, Papers of Miguel and Emilio Buch, NYHS.

59. "The Banning of Sab in Cuba," *Americas* 1 (January 1945):350. See also González del Valle, *Conspiración de la Escalera,* 34–40.

60. Rodney to John Calhoun, 13 April 1844, DC, Matanzas, Cuba, RG 59, USNA.

61. O'Donnell to Secretary of State, 15 March 1844, AHN, Ultramar, leg. 4618.

62. *The Daily Picayune* (New Orleans), 27 February 1844.

63. William Norwood Diary, 9–14 April 1844, VHS.

64. Downing's undated statement is in FO 72/664.

65. William Sim to Crawford, 31 May, 1 July 1844, FO 72/664.

66. "Sumaria información para aberiguar . . . el fallecimiento de Mr. Patricio O'Rorke [sic] y Mr. Jose Lemnig [sic] subditos Ingleses," FO 97/382.

67. Theodore Phinney to Crawford, 29 June 1844, FO 72/664.

68. Ibid.

69. Ibid.

70. "Diligencias practicadas á consequencia de la queja producidos por Mr. Phiney . . ." FO 97/382.

71. Thomas Savage to Campbell, 18 September 1844, DC, Havana, Cuba, RG 59, USNA. See also Phinney to Rodney, 5 July 1844, DC, Matanzas, Cuba, RG 59, USNA.

72. Wurdemann, *Notes,* 355–59.

73. Rodney to John Calhoun, 10 April 1844, DC, Matanzas, Cuba, RG 59, USNA.

74. Rodney to Susan Rodney, 13 March 1844, RC, HSD.

75. Rodney to Susan Rodney, 22 March, 15 April 1844, RC, HSD.

76. For the government's response to the free colored class, see Deschamps Chapeaux, *Negro en la economía habanera,* 25–26; Rodney to John Calhoun, 10 April 1844, DC, Matanzas, Cuba, RG 59, USNA; Crawford to Aberdeen, 8 May, 9 May 1844, FO 72/664; O'Donnell to García Oña, 26

March 1844, EC, box 10, HL; Zamora y Coronado, *Biblioteca de legislación,* 4:285; Klein, "Colored Militia of Cuba," 24; Pedro Pascual de Oliver to Marqués de Viluma, 24 August 1844, in *Relaciones diplomáticas hispano-mexicanas (1839–1898),* 4 vols. (Mexico City, 1949–1966), 3:85–86; José Luciano Franco, *Esclavitud, comercio y tráfico negreros* (Havana, 1972), 39.

77. Rodney to Susan Rodney, 28 June 1844, RC, HSD.
78. Deschamps Chapeaux, *Negro en la economía habanera,* 77, 101, 108, 147; *Colección de los fallos,* case 12a.
79. Computed from data in ibid.
80. *Times* (London), 24 April 1844.
81. *The British and Foreign Anti-Slavery Reporter,* 21 August 1844, 165.
82. Reprinted in *Niles National Register* (Baltimore), 6 July 1844.
83. Aldama to Del Monte, 9 November 1843, *Centón,* 5:149.
84. Kennedy and Dalrymple to Aberdeen, 1 January 1844, FO 84/508; Murray, *Odious Commerce,* 196. For the estimates of the slave trade, see Eltis, *Economic Growth,* 245.
85. Cited in Murray, *Odious Commerce,* 196.
86. Corwin, *Abolition of Slavery,* 86–87.
87. Kennedy and Dalrymple to Aberdeen, 1 January 1844, FO 84/508.
88. *Diario de la Habana,* 15 September 1844; *Diario de la Marina,* 15 September 1844.
89. The document is reproduced in Corbitt, "Petition for the Continuation of O'Donnell," 539–40.
90. Cited in Franco, ed., *Autobiografía,* 13.
91. *British and Foreign Anti-Slavery Reporter,* 21 August 1844, 165.
92. See *Diario de la Habana,* 8 October to 16 October 1844, for detailed reports on the damage caused by the hurricane. See also *The Daily Picayune* (New Orleans), 11 October 1844; Aldama to Del Monte, [?] October 1844, *Centón,* 6:113.
93. Wurdemann to Simms, 6 January 1845, Wurdemann folder, Miscellaneous Papers, NYPL. Saint Placid was indeed martryred on 5 October. See *Butler's Lives of the Saints,* 4 vols. (Westminster, Md., 1981), 4:34–36.

9. LA ESCALERA REEXAMINED

1. *Cuba desde 1850 á 1873,* 15.
2. On Manzano, see O'Donnell to García Oña, 22 March 1844, EC, box 10, HL; Manzano to Rosa Alfonso de Aldama, 5 October 1844, DDC, LC; and the documents in Robert Friol, *Suite para Juan Francisco Manzano* (Havana, 1977), 188–212.
3. *Colección de los fallos,* cases 7a, 11a, 14a, 19a, and 25a.
4. Crawford to Aberdeen, 31 December 1844, FO 84/520. Pedro Deschamps Chapeaux, "El Negro en la economía habanera del siglo XIX: flebotomianos y dentistas," RBNJM 13 (January–April 1971):79–85, provides evidence of the hostility of white tradesmen toward free colored competitors. On Del Monte, see O'Donnell to Foreign Minister, 22 March 1847, BAN 17 (March–June 1918):232, and Aldama to Del Monte, 9 April 1844, *Centón,* 6:30.
5. Kennedy and Dalrymple to Aberdeen, 8 June 1844, FO 84/508. See also Kennedy and Dalrymple to Aberdeen, 8 May 1844, FO 84/508.
6. For the trial records and sentence see AGI, Causas Militares, leg. 1049-A, esp. the fifth *pieza.*

7. "Diligencias practicadas á consequencia de la queja producidos por Mr. Phiney," FO 97/382.

8. See García, "Cuba en la obra de Plácido," 212–16, for a preliminary sketch of its holdings.

9. O'Donnell to García Oña, 20 January 1844, EC, box 10, HL.

10. See especially the documentation in EC, boxes 10, 21, and ECS, box 2, HL.

11. O'Donnell to García Oña, 26 March 1844, EC, box 10, HL.

12. Francisco Ruiz to Salas, 11 March 1844, ECS, box 2, HL. See also O'Donnell to Salas, EC, box 10, HL.

13. O'Donnell to García Oña, 5 February 1844, EC, box 10, HL.

14. This discussion is based on the following: O'Donnell to García Oña, 25 January 1844, O'Donnell to Salas, 7, 12, 13, 14 February 1844, 3, 4 March 1844, EC, box 10, HL; Francisco Marcotegui to García Oña, 3 February 1844, Juan Francisco [?] to García Oña, 3 February 1844, [?] Olives to García Oña, 7 February 1844, ECS, box 2, HL.

15. Pedro Cruces to García Oña, 23 March 1844, ECS, box 2, HL. See also Rafael Mariscal del Hoyo to García Oña, 24 March 1844, and Ramón Flores de Apodaca to García Oña, 25 March 1844, ECS, box 2, HL.

16. O'Donnell to García Oña, 25 January 1844, EC, box 10, HL; Hernández Morejón to García Oña 19, 23 January 1844, 2, 9 February 1844, ECS, box 2, HL.

17. "Declaraciones privadas tomadas por el Tente Coronel Dn Franco Hernández Morejón á algunos esclavos de Don José Jáuregui . . ." ECS, box 2, HL.

18. O'Donnell to García Oña, 26 January 1844, ECS, box 2, HL.

19. Casimiro Custardoy to García Oña, 5 February 1844, ECS, box 2, HL.

20. O'Donnell to Salas, 24 February 1844, 10, 13 March 1844, EC, box 10, HL; Mariscal del Hoyo to García Oña, 8, 9 February 1844, ECS, box 2, HL. See also *Colección de los fallos,* case 22a.

21. Cruces to Salas, 26 February 1844, ECS, box 10, HL; Cruces to Salas, 29 February 1844, EC, box 14, HL; O'Donnell to Salas, 6 March 1844, EC, box 10, HL; Cruces to García Oña, 23 March 1844, ECS, box 2, HL.

22. Cruces to Salas 29 February 1844, EC, box 14, HL.

23. Flores de Apodaca to Salas, 26 February 1844, ECS, box 2, HL.

24. Carlos Ghersi to García Oña, 30 March 1844, ECS, box 2, HL. See also Flores de Apodaca to García Oña, 25 March 1844, ECS, box 2, HL.

25. Pedro Linares to Javier Quintairo, 29 March 1844, EC, box 14, HL; "Diligencias practicadas á consequencia de la queja producidos por Mr. Phiney," FO 97/382; *Colección de los fallos,* case 27a. See also, Morales, *Iniciadores,* 152, n.3.

26. José María Velasco to García Oña, 26 March 1844, ECS, box 2, HL.

27. O'Donnell to Salas, 20, 29 February 1844, EC, box 10, HL.

28. O'Donnell to Salas, 6 March 1844, EC, box 20, HL.

29. Salas to O'Donnell, 13 March 1844, EC, box 14, HL. Antonio Ceulino [?] to Salas, 13 March 1844, EC, box 14, tells of Erice's jailing. See *The Republic* (New York), 13 July 1844, for a report on how the suicide was performed.

30. Mariano Fortun to García Oña, 29 March 1844, EC, box 10, HL. On the arrest of Flores, see O'Donnell to García Oña, 22 March 1844, EC, box 10, HL.

31. O'Donnell to Salas, 14 March 1844, EC, box 10, HL.

32. O'Donnell to Salas, 15 March 1844, EC, box 14, HL.

33. Antonio Lara to García Oña, 22, 23 March 1844, EC, box 21, HL.
34. Ramón González to García Oña, 23 March 1844, EC, box 14, HL; González to García Oña, 26 March 1844, EC, box 21, HL.
35. Anonymous letter to Mrs. William Chapman, May 1844, HML. See O'Donnell to García Oña, 26 March 1844, EC, box 10, HL, for the disarming of the free colored militia and "Relación de los presos que ecsisten a cargo de la espesada pertenecientes a la causa de conspiración," 30 March 1844, EC, box 21, HL, for the numbers in the royal prison.
36. O'Donnell to Pascual de Oliver, 8 July 1844, in *Relaciones diplomáticas,* 3:71. See also O'Donnell to Secretary of State, 30, 31 March 1844, 20 April 1844, AHN, Ultramar, leg. 4620; O'Donnell to Salas, 15 March 1844, EC, box 10, HL; O'Donnell to First Secretary of State, 30 April 1844, AMAE, Cuba, leg. 2911.
37. *Colección de los fallos,* case 3a. See also Mariscal del Hoyo to García Oña, 3 September 1844, EC, box 14, HL.
38. *Colección de los fallos,* case 12a.
39. Ibid.
40. Ibid., case 29a. See also ibid., case 27a.
41. Ibid., cases 4a, 15a, 22a, 27a, 31a, 38a, 42a, 65a.
42. Ibid., case 29a. See also ibid., case 12a and Cruces to Salas, 26 February 1844, ECS, box 10, HL.
43. Ibid., case 46a.
44. Ibid., case 10a.
45. Ibid., case 11a.
46. Ibid., case 24a.
47. Ibid., case 29a.
48. Ibid., cases 17a, 23a.
49. Ibid., case 17a.
50. Ibid., case 23a.
51. Most of the documents ended in AHN, Estado, leg. 8057. The certified copies that went to the Foreign Office exceed what is in leg. 8057 and can be found in FO 84/576.
52. See chapter 1. The most complete set of records are in the Archivo Nacional de Cuba, Havana, in the holdings of the Comisión Militar.
53. Turnbull to Sturge, 12 April 1842, BFASP, C 110/56, RHL.
54. Rodríguez to Crawford, 22 March 1843, FO 72/634.
55. Valdés to First Secretary of State, 1 February 1842 (copy), FSPC, carton 1, file 0025, BL.
56. Turnbull to Palmerston, 30 December 1840, FO 84/319.
57. Duque de Sotomayor to Aberdeen, 25 June 1845, FO 84/576.
58. "Amplicación del pardo libre Gabriel de la Concepción Valdés," AHN, Estado, leg. 8057, exp. 1.
59. Jimeno to Sanguily, [?] April and 22 January 1886, SC, NYPL.
60. "Segundo acto declaratorio del pardo Antonio Bernoqui," AHN, Estado, leg. 8057, exp. 1.
61. Crawford to Aberdeen, 7 December 1842, FO 72/609.
62. Castro Palomino to Del Monte, 16 September 1844, *Centón,* 6:111.
63. Manuel Federico D'Aure to Escoto, 7 February 1901, EC, box 17, HL.
64. "Quarterly Abstracts of Passenger Lists of Vessels Arriving at New Orleans," microcopy 272, roll no. 1, frame 183, New Orleans Public Library.
65. "Declaración de Miguel Flores," AGI, Causas Militares, leg. 1048-A, pieza 1.

Cf. "Testimonio de la instructiva ministrada por el moreno Miguel Flores . . ." AMAE, Cuba, leg. 2911, in which Flores says he knew Gigaut well and of his involvement in a "revolutionary conspiracy."

66. González del Valle, *Conspiración de la Escalera,* 22.

67. O'Donnell to García Oña, 22 March 1844, EC, box 10, HL.

68. Turnbull to Aberdeen, 7 January 1846, Aberdeen Papers, BM. See also Turnbull to Aberdeen, 7 February 1846, Aberdeen Papers, BM.

69. "Declaración del pardo libre Jorge López," AHN, Estado, leg. 8057, exp. 1; O'Donnell to García Oña, 22 March 1844, EC, box 10, HL.

70. González del Valle, *Conspiración de la Escalera,* 37–39. See also the record of Flores's testimony in the proceedings against Pedro Salazar, AGI, Causas Militares, leg. 1048-A, piezas 1–5.

71. Calculated from data in *Colección de los fallos.*

72. Del Monte to A. Everett, 12 July 1843, AEP, MHS.

73. Del Monte to A. Everett, 28 June 1844, AEP, MHS.

74. Castro Palomino to Del Monte, 16 September 1844, *Centón,* 6:111.

75. Crawford to Hinton, 11 December 1843, BFASP, C 154/216, RHL.

76. Tanco to Del Monte, 13 May 1836, *Centón,* 7:59. Volume 7 of the *Centón* contains 194 letters from Tanco to Del Monte.

77. Cocking to Palmerston, 1 October 1846, FO 72/709.

78. On this point see, for example, Ximeno, *Aquellos tiempos,* 55; Deschamps Chapeaux, *Batallones de pardos y morenos,* 21, 41–46; Walterio Carbonell, "Plácido, ¿Conspirador?" 53.

79. Franco, *Conspiración de Aponte,* 19–20; Adrián del Valle, *Historia documentada de la conspiración de la Gran Legión del Aguila Negra* (Havana, 1930), 41.

80. Crawford to Aberdeen, 21 December 1842, FO 72/609.

81. Friol, *Suite,* 196–97.

82. Acevedo and Alonso, "Nuevas noticias," 12. See also *Colección de los fallos,* case 12a.

83. "Instructiva del pardo libre Antonio Bernoqui," AHN, Estado, leg. 8057, exp. 1. See also Castellanos, *Plácido,* 129–36.

84. "Segundo acto declaratorio del pardo Antonio Bernoqui," AHN, Estado, leg. 8057, exp. 1.

85. Ibid.

86. Ibid.

87. On this point see Schuler, "Ethnic Slave Rebellions," 382; Genovese, *Roll, Jordan, Roll.* 381–88.

88. "Declaración de Valentín Espinosa," Estado, AHN, Estado, leg. 8057, exp. 1.

89. "Declaración de Félix Ponce," AHN, Estado, leg. 8057, exp. 1. On Santiago Pimienta, see also Llanes Miqueli, "Familia Pimienta-Dodge," 11–18. D'Aure to Escoto, 7 February 1901, EC, box 17, HL, recalls Pimienta's contact with Gigaut.

90. "Compulsa se varios lugares de la causa que sigue el fiscal Don Fernando Perchet," AHN, Estado, leg. 8057, exp. 1.

91. Ximeno, "Un pobre histrión," 375.

92. On this point see the suggestive remarks of Craton, *Testing the Chains,* 27–28. The *Colección de los fallos* contains numerous references to the use of *brujería* in raising support for the conspiracy.

93. On the notion of reconstituted peasantries, see Mintz, "Slavery and the Rise of Peasantries," *Historical Reflections* 6 (Summer 1979):213–42.

94. Roig de Leuchsenring, "Fusilamiento de Plácido," 39.

95. Ximeno, "Un pobre histrión," 75; Acevedo and Alonso, "Nuevas noticias," 12; Jimeno to Sanguily, [?] April 1886, SC, NYPL.

96. Ibid. See also Jimeno to Morales, 16 July 1882, EC, box 6, HL.

97. Rafael Padro y Oliva to Escoto, 16 June 1904, and Ignacio María de Acosta y Garrido, [?] June 1904, in El Álbum, n.p.

98. Campuzano, "Algo sobre Plácido," in ibid., n.p.

99. For this poem, see Valdés, Poesías completas, 237.

100. See Valdés, Poesías escogidas, 125–27, for "Al general mejicano (hijo de Cuba) D. A. de la Flor." Castellanos analyzes these and other of Plácido's poems for political content in Plácido, esp. chapter 2. Zaragoza, Insurreciones, 1:424, places de la Flor with Sentmanat.

101. Ibid., 1:493–94; Stimson, Story of Plácido, 109; Alberto Gutiérrez de la Solana, "En torno al siboneyismo y la poesía cubana alusiva á la emancipación," in Literatura de la emancipación hispanoamericana y otros ensayos (Lima, 1972), 66–74.

102. Guerra, et al., Historia de la nación cubana, 4:353.

103. "Ampliación del pardo libre Gabriel de la Concepción Valdés (a) Plácido," AHN, Estado, leg. 8057, exp. 1.

104. "Careo entre Antonio Bernoqui y Gabriel de la Concepción Valdés," AHN, Estado, leg. 8057, exp. 1.

105. On this point see the discussion of Castellanos, Plácido, 67–80.

106. Ximeno, "Un pobre histrión," 374.

107. "Ampliación del pardo libre Gabriel de la Concepción Valdes (a) Plácido." AHN, Estado, leg. 8057, exp. 1. Plácido also declared that he had "never associated with the vile black canaille." See Carbonell, "Plácido, ¿Conspirador?" 54.

108. O'Donnell to García Oña, 1 February 1844, EC, box 21, HL. See also García Oña to Salas, 9 July 1844, EC, box 21, HL; Llanes Miqueli, Victimas del año del cuero, 53. On the reputation of Plácido among Cuba's people of color, see Roque Betancourt y Hernández to Escoto, 22 June 1904, in El Álbum, n.p., and assorted testimony in AHN, Estado, leg. 8057, exp. 1.

109. Jimeno to Sanguily, [?] April 1886, SC, NYPL.

110. On this point, see also the discussion in Cué, "Plácido," 162, 176–87.

111. "Ampliación del pardo libre Gabriel de la Concepción Valdés (a) Plácido," AHN, Estado, leg. 8057, exp. 1.

112. Cited in Ximeno, "Un pobre histrión," 376.

113. T. Rodney to S. Rodney, 28 June 1844, RC, HSD. Cf. "Ultimas horas de Poeta Cubano Gabriel de la C. Valdés = (Plácido)," EC, box 19, HL.

114. For my discussion and translation of Plácido's revelation, I have used the version published as the "Anexo" in Cué, "Plácido," 192–206. Cué derived her version from a transcription of the original, apparently in its entirety, by Manuel Sanguily. Morales, Iniciadores, 175–77, contains a misleading abridgment of Plácido's revelation.

115. Alfonso to Del Monte, 11 May 1844, Centón, 6:31.

116. Del Monte, Escritos, 1:199.

117. Ibid., 1:195.

118. Del Monte to Everett, 28 June 1844, AEP, MHS.

119. Memorandum of Bidwell, 11 November 1846, FO 72/709.

120. Eltis, Economic Growth, 245, 263. On the recruitment of Chinese labor,

see Juan Jimenez Pastrana, *Los chinos en las luchas por la liberación cubana, 1847–1930* (Havana, 1963), 7–24.

121. Letter of Bernardo Costales y Sotolongo, [?] 1882, in *El Álbum,* n.p. See also "Oficio del Capitán-General, D. Joaquín Manzano," 28 June 1867, DDC, LC.

122. The best study of the process of emancipation after La Escalera and the role of the slaves in attaining their own freedom is Scott, *Slave Emancipation in Cuba.* Note particularly her epigraph p. 255.

123. On their arrest, see Jimeno's letter in Morales, *Iniciadores,* 158. On Cuba and the annexation of Texas, see Everett, "Texas Question," 250–70, and Robert L. Paquette, "The Everett–Del Monte Connection: A Study in the International Politics of Slavery," *Diplomatic History* 11 (Winter 1987): 20–21.

124. David Turnbull, *An Address by the Chief Judge of the Court of Mixed Commission for the Suppression of the Slave Trade* . . . (London, 1851). See also David King, *The State and Prospects of Jamaica* (London, 1850), 175–76.

125. Martin R. Delany, *Blake or the Huts of America* (Boston, 1970).

Index

ABOUT THE AUTHOR

As a graduate student at the University of Rochester, Robert L. Paquette uncovered, in the Massachusetts Historical Society, letters from Domingo Del Monte to Alexander Everett, pieces of the La Escalera puzzle long sought by Cuban scholars. He searched archives on several continents. Although he was denied access to state archives in Cuba, he found the José Escoto Collection at Harvard University, one of the richest sources for colonial Cuban history, virtually unused since its purchase in the early 1900s.

Paquette is an assistant professor of history at Hamilton College. He was graduated from Bowling Green State University (B.A. 1973) and received his Ph.D. from the University of Rochester (1982). In 1987 he won an Albert J. Beveridge grant of the American Historical Association for research in history of the Western Hemisphere. He lives in Clinton, New York.

ABOUT THE BOOK

Sugar Is Made with Blood is composed in Linotype Garamond No. 3. Garamond was introduced in America by American Type Foundry in 1919, when their cutting, based on the *caractères de l'Université* of the Imprimerie Nationale, appeared. Many other versions were made for Linotype, Monotype, Intertype, Ludlow, and the Stempel foundry. The face has since been adapted for phototypesetting, CRT typesetting, and laser typesetting.

The book was composed by Yankee Typesetters of Concord, New Hampshire, and designed by Kachergis Book Design, Pittsboro, North Carolina.

WESLEYAN UNIVERSITY PRESS, 1988